ISLAMIC CIVILIZATION AND MUSLIM NETWORKS

Carl W. Ernst and Bruce B. Lawrence, editors

A complete list of titles published in this series appears at the end of the book.

Sufi Narratives of Intimacy

Ibn ʿArabī, Gender, and Sexuality

Saʿdiyya Shaikh

THE UNIVERSITY OF NORTH CAROLINA PRESS Chapel Hill

Manufactured in the United States of America

Designed and set in Gentium Plus with Biographer display by Rebecca Evans.

The paper in this book meets the guidelines for permanence and durability of the Committee on Production Guidelines for Book Longevity of the Council on Library Resources.

The University of North Carolina Press has been a member of the Green Press Initiative since 2003.

Library of Congress Cataloging-in-Publication Data

Shaikh, Saʿdiyya.
Sufi narratives of intimacy : Ibn ʿArabī, gender, and sexuality / Saʿdiyya Shaikh.
p. cm.—(Islamic civilization and Muslim networks)
Includes bibliographical references and index.
ISBN 978-0-8078-3533-3 (cloth : alk. paper)
ISBN 978-1-4696-1890-6 (pbk. : alk. paper)
1. Ibn al-ʿArabī, 1165–1240—Criticism and interpretation.
2. Anthropology of religion—Islamic Empire. 3. Women in Islam. I. Title.
PJ7755.I175Z92 2012
297.4092—dc23 2011030429

cloth 16 15 14 13 12 5 4 3 2 1
paper 18 17 16 15 14 5 4 3 2 1

THIS BOOK WAS DIGITALLY PRINTED.

To Ashraf,

for generosity and love,

. . . and much laughter!

Contents

Acknowledgments ix

Introduction: Tales of Contention 1
Muslim Gender Imaginaries

CHAPTER 1 Craving Completion 35
Sufism, Subjectivity, and Gender before Ibn ʿArabī

CHAPTER 2 Charting Ibn ʿArabī's Religious Anthropology 61

CHAPTER 3 Mysticism and Gender 95
A Hermeneutic of Experience

CHAPTER 4 Reading Gender and Metaphor in Ibn ʿArabī's Cosmos 113

CHAPTER 5 The Poetics and Politics of Adam and Eve 141

CHAPTER 6 Witnessing God in Women 173
A Different Story of Creation

CHAPTER 7 Ibn ʿArabī and Islamic Feminism 203

Appendix: Selected Poems from the *Dīwān Ibn ʿArabī* 229

Notes 233

Bibliography 255

Index of Qurʾānic Verses 267

Index of Traditions (*Aḥadīth*) 269

General Index 271

Acknowledgments

This book has been a long and full journey. My traveling companions along the way have been invaluable. First and foremost, this book would not have been possible without the love, support, and perseverance of my husband, Ashraf Kagee. He has balanced his academic career with a genuine commitment to sharing household responsibilities and caring for our young children, allowing me to complete this book. Our children, Nuriyya and Ismael, have provided much joy, inspiration, deep learning, and more than occasional exhaustion! My parents, Zohra and Ahmed Suleman, are a source of unceasing love, generosity, and graciousness in my life. I am deeply grateful to them for always being there, for their unwavering support, and for their gentle inspiration in my life in so many different ways. I am especially grateful to our caring family in Cape Town—Fawzia Pansari and her family in particular—for showering our children with an abundance of love and attention, as well as (too) many treats. All of my siblings have gifted my life: Laila with her zany sense of humor and compassionate heart, Nazia with her sparkle and strong resilient spirit, Ismail with his beautiful character. My other set of siblings, Zakir and Hassina, in different ways embody aspects of the remarkable legacy of our late father, Sulayman Shaikh. I pay tribute to him for inspiring my childhood imagination with wondrous stories of great Sufis and igniting my heart with a hunger for "seeing with two eyes." I also have been graced by the presence of Shaykh Muhammad Raheem Bawa Muhaiyaddeen, a teacher of unparalleled beauty, alive in the hearts and lives of the Fellowship community in Philadelphia. In particular, Dr. Abdul Gafoor and Siti Fatima Ganeshan, Raghavan Moorthy, Shams and Ahmed Hahn, Zoharah Simmons, and Myra Diaz carry Bawa's fragrance and have made the Fellowship a place of shimmering plenitude, restoration, learning, and sheer delight for me.

A number of colleagues and friends have inspired me in many ways. Scott Kugle's various readings and contributions to this book have been invaluable at so many different levels. Most significantly, his poetic soul made our collaborations over translating Ibn ʿArabī's texts illuminating, productive, and deeply joyful. Ebrahim Moosa and Abdulkader Tayob were my first graduate teachers and have transitioned into being peerless peers, wonderful friends, and inspiring scholars. I am profoundly indebted to Ebrahim, whose large spirit, erudition, and passion first drew me to the study of religion. His mentorship and feedback during the process of writing this book in particular were genuinely transformative for my writing. Abdulkader is one of the most generous and astute intellectuals I have the fortune to work closely with. I truly appreciate the support and patience of department chairs David Chidester and Chuck Wanamaker, who made space and time for me to write. Nina Hoel is a brilliant colleague and a dear friend whose insight and energy contribute to making our joint research forays dynamic, intellectually challenging, and fun. Each one of the rest of my colleagues in the Department of Religious Studies at the University of Cape Town makes it an exceptional place to work in, and for this I am deeply appreciative. I duly recognize the National Research Foundation and the Thuthuka Program as well as the Andrew Mellon Foundation for funding my research.

Important influences on my scholarship have been and are Denise Ackerman, Kecia Ali, and Mahmoud Ayoub. Amina Wadud is an enduring inspiration—her foundational scholarship, spiritual largesse, and personal courage have inspired a generation of Islamic feminist scholars. Omid Safi is a brother of the spirit and a gifted scholar who has lent his support to my work and my life in so many ways. I am indebted to the works of William Chittick and Sachiko Murata, whom I have never met but whose erudite scholarship first introduced me to the world of Ibn ʿArabī.

A number of friends and colleagues have contributed in various ways to the final preparation of this manuscript. I am especially thankful to Roshila Nair, whose feminist eye and editorial skill have added clarity and nuance to this manuscript. Ebrahim Moosa, Ali Mabrook, and Sarra Tlili provided invaluable translation assistance. Elaine Maisner and the talented editorial team at the University of North Carolina Press were genuinely supportive. I am particularly grateful for the skilled, insightful, and transformative editorial guidance provided by Ellen D. Goldlust-Gingrich. Carl Ernst as well as my anonymous reviewers at the University of North Carolina Press gave me invaluable and rich feedback. I am indebted to my dear friend Abdul Aleem Somers for his meticulous eye and bountiful heart in the final and most trying period of corrections. I thank Annie Leatt, Laury Silvers, and

Andrea Brigaglia for rich, fruitful, and provocative conversations on mysticism and gender; Muḥammad Khalid Sayyid, who generously made himself available for all kinds of administrative and technical help; and Trish Kratz for her graceful welcoming presence as I worked for many inspired hours at her quaint coffee shop, Starlings. Friends who enrich my life and work include Gabeba Baderoon, Shabbir Banoobhai, Jacquie Bouille, Estelle Cloete, Shirlaine Douglas, Carola Eyber, Yumnaa Firfirey and Rashid Toefy, Razia and Mohammad Jeebhay, Trusha Khatri, the Manjras (Ayesha and Shuaib, Saeeda and Zaid), Sarra Tlili, and Tahija Vikalo. I am deeply indebted to all my family, friends, colleagues, and students, who contribute to making my life work a journey of enduring grace and renewal.

Sufi Narratives of Intimacy

Introduction

Tales of Contention

Muslim Gender Imaginaries

Once upon a time, a wise and generous story unfolded. This is how it might be imagined.[1] It is Cairo on a sweltering afternoon, and the faithful are streaming into a beautiful, simple mosque. The Friday (*jumuʿa*) prayers are about to begin. In the courtyard, people take their ablutions in the cool fountain water that provides welcome relief from the heat of the Cairene afternoon. A group of women sitting close together is silently reciting the Qurʾān. An old man, his face kissed gently by time, is sitting easily upright with eyes closed, meditating on the beautiful names of God. Two old friends, both returning to the city after years of travel, trade, and learning, are greeting each other with a tender embrace. A young man, hands raised in supplication, is softly murmuring his deepest yearnings into the hearing of the omniscient One. As the call to prayer is given, a hush falls over the crowd, with each person repairing to his or her private supplications before the sermon begins.

The preacher ascends the stairs to the pulpit. She is the accomplished spiritual savant Umm Zaynab Fāṭima bint ʿAbbās al-Baghdādiyya, not only the spiritual leader (*shaykha*) of the Ribāṭ al-Baghdādiyya but renowned among the religious divines of Cairo as a jurist (*faqīha*) who provides practical legal responses to people's questions (*muftiyya*).[2] And yes, it is the fourteenth century. And no, there is no outrage or shock among the congregants that Shaykha Fāṭima is preaching to a mixed gathering of males and females in a mosque. In fact, Shaykha Fāṭima's reputation as a scholar has traveled with her to Cairo. While living in Damascus, she had trained as a jurisconsult among an elite group of Hanbalī scholars known as the Maqādisa, having studied with one of the great teachers of the city, Shaykh Ibn Abī ʿUmar.[3] Among the women of Damascus and more recently Cairo, she has come to be loved and revered as the wise one who provides refuge and guidance in their spiritual strivings.

She has studied with no less than one of the leading male intellectuals of her time, the protean Taqī al-Dīn ibn Taymiyya. In public circles, he has on occasion praised Shaykha Fāṭima, not only for her intelligence and knowledge but also for her personal qualities of enthusiasm and excellence. Yet on this hot day in the Cairene mosque, he sits among the congregants unable to quell his state of discomfort. To his great chagrin, Shakhya Fāṭima easily, even presumptuously, ascends and descends from the pulpit as if unaware of the fact that she is, after all, only a woman. This woman appears to be oblivious to any limitations of her sex. As he leaves the mosque after the service, Ibn Taymiyya realizes that his unease and acute irritation with Shaykha Fāṭima's presence on the pulpit had so overwhelmed him that he had not even heard a word of her sermon. He goes home and falls into a restless afternoon sleep.

Ibn Taymiyya later recalled this incident: "It unsettled me that she mounted the pulpit to deliver sermons and I wished to forbid her."[4] In Ibn Taymiyya's inner struggle to stop this self-assured woman from public preaching, he saw the Prophet of Islam in a dream. The Prophet put an end to his anxieties and, according to Ibn Taymiyya, rebuked him, saying, "This is a pious woman."[5] The prophetic instruction quelled Ibn Taymiyya's agitation, reconciling him with Shaykha Fāṭima's role as public preacher.[6]

Who would have thought that one of the most renowned *mujtahids* of the premodern Muslim world, Taqī al-Dīn ibn Taymiyya, an individual whom many present-day chauvinists claim as their religious luminary, would have been subdued into accepting a woman's authority by a dream? Indeed, it was no less than the prophetic command that had castigated the Hanbali jurisconsult. This dream not only challenged his fourteenth-century gender lenses but continues to do so for others today, providing a stark contrast with the visions of women that are promoted by the contemporary votaries of Ibn Taymiyya. Very few of Ibn Taymiyya's followers will energetically recover this view of their intellectual exemplar, either in terms of its gender implications or of the Sufilike recognition of a prophetic dream. But many Muslims have not had the good fortune of an emancipatory prophetic dream foretelling that women's spiritual equality does in fact have social and ritual implications.

In the contemporary period, a worldwide Muslim debate was sparked in 2005 when Professor Amina Wadud led Friday ritual prayers in full view of the international media in New York City. A number of Muslim leaders around the globe issued fatwas (legal decrees) regarding women's leadership, and have taken a variety of positions on the subject. Sohaib BenCheikh, the former grand *muftī*[7] of Marseilles, belonging to an older generation of male graduates of Egypt's Al-Azhar University, publicly participated in a congregational prayer led by another woman in solidarity with the event in New York. Conversely, Dr. Soad Saleh, a female Islamic law professor at Al-Azhar, declared that women-led prayers with mixed congregations constitute apostasy in Islam, an offense punishable by death under classical interpretations of Islamic law. Among her reasons for rejecting female imams, Saleh declared that "the woman's body, even if veiled, stirs desire." Ironically, a few years earlier, Saleh had applied to become Egypt's first female *muftī*, an application that was still officially pending at the time of the New York incident but might well be considered de facto unsuccessful. Saleh's positioning in the debates on women's leadership in the mosque and in public rituals demonstrates current contestations over embodiment and gender, spirituality and leadership, sexuality and power within the Muslim world.

Our perspectives on this fraught contemporary debate might be enriched by turning to the counsel provided by an eminent thirteenth-century Muslim scholar, Muḥyī al-Dīn ibn al-ʿArabī. In a striking contrast to the present-day focus on women's bodies as the inappropriate provocateur of male desire, the premodern Ibn ʿArabī has a very different entry point for the understanding of gendered ritual leadership. He unperturbedly claims ungendered and equal access to the position of imam on the basis that men and women have identical spiritual potential in the Islamic tradition. Without much fanfare, Ibn ʿArabī informs us that spiritual equality between men and women has very clear social and ritual consequences. It is not simply centuries that divide Saleh from this premodern personality; it is also radically different assumptions on the nature of gendered human beings in light of an ontological, spiritual, and religious telos. Ibn ʿArabī thus categorically asserts that women may lead mixed congregations of men and women in ritual prayers.

The story of women's contemporary ritual leadership began in South Africa, my birthplace, in events that shaped me and planted the seeds for deeper study and clarity on issues of gender and spirituality in Islam. The year 1994 was particularly memorable for Muslim South Africans because of two significant events. First, the first nonracial democratic elections took place, signaling the official death of apartheid. Second, Professor Amina Wadud, a visiting scholar and author of a pioneering Islamic feminist work, *Qur'an and Woman*, delivered the Friday sermon (*khuṭba*) at the Claremont Main Road Mosque, which I attended. The mosque had invited Wadud to share her insights on Islam with its members, who also decided to use the occasion to transform the gendered nature of their prayer space. Not only was a woman going to give the all-important Friday sermon, but the female congregants would move from the balcony into the central space of the *masjid*, on par with, albeit separate from, the men. For me, a young committed Muslim woman, entering the newly open and receptive *masjid* felt like stepping into the warmth of the sunshine after a lifetime of being concealed in the shadows, a feeling somewhat akin to voting in my country of birth for the first time. In my experiential framework, this minority congregation was boldly embodying a fundamental social justice imperative that was intrinsic to Islam. However, even as this act of liberation unfolded, many broader community contestations of this event were pervaded by assumptions that women are somehow peculiarly and inferiorly defined by their bodies and that these female bodies, in the proximity of men, somehow diminish and threaten the sacredness of the mosque. Integrating justice and harmony into both personal and communal religious spaces constitutes a serious religious challenge for a number of contemporary Muslims, which is why women's free access to central spaces of worship and women's ritual leadership remain controversial topics.[8]

Wadud's *khuṭba* at the Claremont Main Road mosque was inspirational. Her words were like a glorious, warm summer rain, drenching us in mercy and radiating all kinds of existential possibilities. This was a spiritually ripe sermon, inspired and inspiring, beautiful and beautifying, luminous and illuminating. She went to the very heart of the matter, to the understanding of Islam as a state of engaged surrender in all of our most intimate and immediate relationships as human beings—marriage, pregnancy, childbirth—and sites of intimate relationship to the divine One. For the first time in my adult life in a public religious space, I felt myself sincerely validated as a Muslim *woman*. While some sectors of the South African Muslim community enthusiastically hailed the event, other segments of that community became incensed. The resulting conflict reflected fierce struggles regarding Muslim understandings of sexuality, sacrality, and human embodiment.[9]

Contemporary gender politics relating to Islam is not restricted to the issue of women imams or internal differences within the Muslim world.

Wide-ranging geopolitical dynamics and ideological contestations are played out on the bodies of Muslim women. Representations of Muslim women vacillate between dominant Western images of Muslim women as oppressed and apologist Islamist images of Muslim women as the only truly liberated women.[10] The debates on both sides are often simplistic, rigidly formulated, authoritarian, ideologically loaded, and contingent on the political forces of the day. Examples abound. French public schools prohibit Muslim women from wearing head scarves (*ḥijāb*), ostensibly as a marker of a secular society; conversely, postrevolutionary Iran imposes the *ḥijāb* as a symbol of authentic Islamic identity.[11] U.S. politicians strategically invoked the plight of Afghani women as a way to build public support for the American-led invasion of Afghanistan in 2001 yet are notably silent about the Saudi regime's appalling women's rights record as a result of the two countries' intimate political-economic relationship. In many parts of the Muslim world, notions of gender equality are often interwoven with larger postcolonial identity struggles about indigenous values, cultural allegiances, and loyalties and disloyalties.[12] The global context for discussions of gender justice and Islam is, therefore, ideologically fraught with contestations of the nature of religion, law, and secularism; citizenship, identity, and empire; freedom, equality, and self-expression.

Many antagonists in these debates share the assumption that Islam is a monolithic religion with a singular all-embracing gender paradigm. Such generalizations not only belie the complex varying realities of contemporary Muslim women but also ignore the rich diversity of the Islamic tradition that is informed by the mélange of Arab, Turkic, Persian, Andalusian, African, and South Asian histories and cultures.[13] Gender dynamics among Muslims are as complex and polymorphous as the realities of women (and even men, for that matter) in other religious, social, and political contexts. While there are undoubtedly universal aspects within Islam that fall within a cohesive religious category, this unity is mostly accompanied by myriad diversities.

Among contemporary Muslims, gender contestations occur within a tradition characterized by diverse gender epistemes. Contenders in gender debates often cull the primary Islamic sources of the Qurʾān and *ḥadīth* and their traditional legacy of interpretation, especially jurisprudence, to find positions that, for example, either support or reject women's ritual leadership. Many of the arguments are of an epistemological nature—that is, contestation over which among these various legal positions count as authoritative Islamic knowledge. Such arguments often are limited in scope, primarily addressing the outer symptoms of gender injustice, such as women's imamate or the politics of *ḥijāb*. These types of debates fail to address the ways in which the underlying theological category of the "human being" is gendered.

While such gender contestations are necessary and important, a richer understanding of gender debates in Islam requires more than simple epistemological disputations about which traditional sources to prioritize and authorize in relation to a specific issue. Debates on women's role as imam or the religious necessity of *ḥijāb*, for example, demand exploration and interrogation of the foundational premises and constructs of gender. Contesting positions on gender are, after all, underpinned by specific assumptions regarding human nature and existence—in fact, by specific anthropological, cosmological, and ontological constructs. A thorough investigation of gender thus demands an analysis of these related philosophical constructs in Islam.

Islam, Gender Politics, and the "Deeper Questions"

I use the term "religious anthropology" to indicate a focus on the fundamental concern of what it means to be human within the Muslim tradition.[14] This focus addresses questions of the nature and vision of human beings as depicted within an Islamic worldview. For the believer, it addresses the age-old ontological questions "Who am I?" and "What is the nature of existence?" within the context of Islam.

The question of what it means to be a human being immediately beckons the inquirer to the next level of inquiry: What does it mean to be a *gendered* human being? Does Islam provide notions of a universal human essence that transcends gender? Does Islam teach that men and women have essentially different natures? And if so, do all women and all men share some universal female or male essence, respectively? Or, rather, is there a combination of sameness and differences between men and women—that is, do men and women share certain attributes while differing in terms of other attributes? Definitions of being human invariably provide meanings of being gendered.

A final related question in addressing religious anthropology focuses on the relationship between gender and moral capacity. Does the religion set out different moral and existential goals for men and women? Or does Islam posit a single, ungendered map for human moral agency? Are the ultimate goals of human morality within an Islamic framework the same for men and for women? In sum, how do gender differences relate to a person's moral capacity?

Definitions and understandings of religious anthropology are closely linked either implicitly or explicitly to an ontological framework. "Ontology" refers to a theory about the nature of reality or the nature of being. Its most basic questions and concerns are the following: What actually exists? What is the nature of being? What *is*? An ontological level of inquiry in terms of human nature asks the question "Who am I?" in relation to the entire universe of existence, to all that is. Ontology focuses on "the most fundamental categories of being and . . . the relations among them."[15] Ontological questions thus place our understandings of gendered human beings and a religious anthropology within a broader framework of understanding the nature of reality.

While ontology deals with existence in general, its intimate companion, cosmology, provides a map for understanding the universe in its totality—its origin, purpose, and destiny, including the human being's place within it.[16] Cosmology concerns an understanding of the order and relationships between the various parts of the created universe. Questions that arise in relation to cosmology might include the following: What is the nature of the universe? How was it created? For what purpose and toward what destiny was it created? What are a human being's origin, place, and purpose in this universe? Thus, a cosmological level of inquiry in Islam enables the inquirer to situate notions of human nature and existence within a broader framework of understanding the nature of all creation. In a study of Islamic cosmology, one also finds macrocosmic mappings of gender that resonate in varying ways with understandings of human genderedness.

A strong relationship exists between these seemingly abstract constructs of religious anthropology, ontology, and cosmology on the one hand and the realpolitik of gender on the other. Underlying many of the gender inequalities in traditional Islamic legal and ethical formulations are problematic assumptions about the nature of men and women. Many opponents of women's imamate, for example, argue that a woman in a central sacred space stirs sexual desire in male congregants, distracting them from their religious devotion. How might these individuals respond to the challenge of men being stirred sexually by the presence of other *men* in the mosque? Their stated argument against women's imamate is premised on a rather convoluted gendered view of humanity in which a carefully constructed and highly problematic religious universe is created for the moral benefit of men at the expense of women.

On the one hand, men are assumed to be the natural leaders and spiritual authorities in sacred spaces. The prevailing status quo naturalizes male control of the public religious space so that women's mere presence in a mosque often needs to be explicated, explained, justified, or vilified. The dominant order of things is such that women are inherently positioned as impostors in the public sacred space. Women's Otherness is defined in this view as primarily in relation to a powerful sexualized body that ultimately desacralizes the mosque for male worshippers, particularly if the woman occupies center stage as the leader of the ritual congregational prayer.

These constructs reflect a patriarchal religious anthropology that is at once binary and hierarchical. Women and femaleness are constructed as sexual, carnal, and often by extension emotional and irrational, engendering chaos. This sexualized feminine realm is seen as oppositional to spirituality, intellect, and rationality, which are associated with maleness and men. Thus, men are superior and are inevitably leaders and authorities over the lesser human being, who is the female. This gendered split between the principles of body and the mind presents us with Cartesian dualism in Muslim garb.

On the other hand, this argument attributes enormous power to female sexuality and paradoxically reduces men to hapless victims of their own libidos. While women possess an overwhelming sexual allure, heterosexual men have little capacity for resistance. Because of men's inability to focus on God in the presence of the female body, women need to be outside men's field of vision. Male subjectivity in this guise is defined by and caught in conflict between the realm of the transcendent divine that men are seeking and the presence of the immanent female body that they simultaneously desire.

Ironically, even perhaps humorously, such an argument significantly diminishes male humanity. From this perspective, a man is effectively a perpetual moral adolescent subject to uncontainable heterosexual instincts, and his locus of self-control has escaped into the shadows, just outside of his personal command. His ineffectiveness in monitoring his own body and behavior necessitates vigilant policing of the outer environment. Woman, whose essence is characterized by a chaos-creating sexuality, needs to be removed, rendered invisible, dispatched into liminal spaces, and deprived of voice. Thus, with such effort toward and effect on women, the spiritual sanctity of the mosque (for men) is retained—a dubious notion of moral agency, indeed.

These types of arguments are based on a religious anthropology that defines men and women as *essentially* different and more especially gives gender differences distinct hierarchal values. Ontologically, women are lesser than men and are hence accountable to divergent moral and ethical standards. Men and women are anointed with varying types and levels of moral capacity in the world. This asymmetrical moral compass generates a normative framework where men dominate and lead in the public world and women are ideally relegated to the invisible spheres of the private and the domestic. As such, the contemporary Muslim politics of the imamate is essentially underpinned by questions about human nature that are based on specific understandings of genderedness. These understandings must be rendered fully and on an individual basis if gender contestations are to move forward in terms of changing social mind-sets rather than merely tackling issues or "symptoms."

These debates on the imamate also illustrate that anthropological and ontological assumptions prefigure ethical and legal norms. Thus, genuinely challenging the widest possible forms of sexism in society requires delving into questions about the constituent nature of humanity, male and female, from a religious perspective. How is the primary God-human relationship gendered? As well, how are these perspectives understood to mediate relationships between the sexes? Framing questions in this way might intimately link ontology to understandings of religious anthropology while simultaneously addressing gender as an intrinsic part of a broader Islamic cosmology.

The Islamic tradition in fact possesses some rich, multitextured, and deeply grounded approaches to gender with regard to politico-legal issues. The thirteenth-century Muslim polymath Muḥyī al-Dīn ibn al-ʿArabī offers precisely such an approach when addressing the issue of women's imamate. Within an Islamic cosmology, Ibn ʿArabī the contemplative mystic asserts, men and women have equal capacity to attain the divinely ordained vision of spiritual completeness. Indeed, for Ibn ʿArabī, the equal ontological capacity for spiritual completeness shared by men and women defines an Islamic view of human nature. On the basis of his assumptions regarding a universal and ungendered human capacity promoted in Islam, the incisive jurist[17] asserts that a women's leadership in ritual prayer is licit before men and women, adding somewhat dismissively that "one should not pay heed to anyone who opposes it without proof."[18] In his arguments on the subject, Ibn ʿArabī skillfully unmasks the pervasive problematic or limited web of ontology and religious anthropology underlying gendered political issues in Muslim thought.

Understanding Sufism, Understanding Gender

Ibn ʿArabī's deep-rooted response to the issue of women's imamate is also suggestive of his primary discursive tradition, Sufism. In addressing the nature of human beings, society, and God, Sufi scholars often reveal a specific preoccupation with ontology, or the nature of reality. Drawing both on contemplative interpretations of the primary Islamic sources, the Qurʾān and *ḥadīth*, and mystical experiences, Sufi thinkers address most questions, including understandings of gender, in relation to the ultimate nature of reality.

Within the Islamic tradition, Sufism is often described as the inner path (*ṭarīqa*) that allows a person to attain the goals of ethical and spiritual cultivation. When relating Sufism to other dimensions of the Islamic tradition, a popular *ḥadīth* tradition suggests a tripartite structure of moral obligation—that is, *islām* (outward conformity), *īmān* (inward faith), and *iḥsān* (virtuous excellence).[19] Some Muslim thinkers suggest using the metaphor of the embodied human being to understand these different elements of moral obligation for the seeker.[20] Jurists, they suggest, focus on assessing outward conformity with religious precepts that might be associated with the limbs of the body. Theologians and philosophers are concerned with notions of faith and belief, which in turn correspond to the mind. Sufis focus on the inner processes of spiritual cultivation and experiential knowledge, both of which culminate in virtue and may be seen to be located in the heart. As such, Sufism seeks deeper and more complete knowledge of the inner dimensions of reality (or realities) that will facilitate a more intimate relationship with God and greater submission to the divine will. *Islām*, *īmān*, and *iḥsān* are all considered integral to the optimal moral functioning of each human being. To make full sense within this schema, inner understandings take as given the outer forms of religion. Historically, Sufism has for the most part operated within the norms of Islamic tradition while concurrently pointing to realities beyond them.[21]

My focus on gender in Ibn ʿArabī's works is largely framed by the potential of Sufi discourse to address gender questions at a deeply rooted level of religious meaning. I examine the dynamic interplay among sacred texts, mystical cosmologies, and social reality, engaging at the nexus of these three critical junctures the religious constructions of gender. Assisted by a feminist lens, I explore in particular, how love, sexuality, marriage, and related gender dynamics are conceived, imagined, and created in the works of a major Sufi thinker in a formative period of the Islamic legacy. I probe questions about the elements that constitute humanity, male and female, from a religious perspective; the processes by which the primary God-human relationship is gendered; and the understanding of these perspectives to mediate intimate relationships between the sexes. I hence unpack various narratives of "masculinity" and "femininity" within these texts.

My investigations into the relationship between gender and ontology are vested in the possible implications for core ethical values in Islam. Focusing on intimate relationships and the realm of sexuality as well as public gender dynamics, the framework of Ibn ʿArabī's mystical cosmology is rich ground for an examination of seemingly abstract philosophical concepts such as ontology and religious anthropology on the one hand and the concrete daily relationships between men and women on the other.

Islamic narratives about personal, intimate relationships and public gender imaginaries often share central gendered assumptions. In particular, patriarchal epistemologies have often configured the intimate realms of love, marriage, and sexuality as domestic, private, and outside of the political sphere, thereby rendering them invisible and inviolable. Feminists have rendered transparent the insidious reach of ideology and patriarchal politics into the sphere of the private.[22] Deconstructing the binary between the private and the political has revealed the systemic nature of gendered power dynamics that pervade intimate and family relationships.[23] Whether sexual, marital, emotional, or familial, all intimate relationships are entwined in dominant narratives of gender that are imminently political in nature.

Drawing on these feminist insights, I examine the interconnections between the personal and the political in my sources, focusing specifically on the way in which marriage, sexuality, and intimate relationships are configured. I keep these personal/political narratives of gender in conversation with Sufi ontology and anthropology to contribute to the contemporary search for a relevant Islamic ethics of gender justice.

I claim neither that Sufis hold a monolithic position on gender nor that

Sufism is an ahistorical panacea of all things good and wonderful for women. To be sure, Ghazālī, a central Sufi thinker who exposed the limitations of a law not based on ethical praxis, concurrently conceptualized an ethics of justice that is comfortable and even often complicit with male domination. Thus, Sufism does not automatically cure people of sexism. In its historical development and its multiple contexts, Sufism, like all other areas of Islamic thought, has been characterized by tensions between patriarchal inclinations and gender-egalitarian impulses.

While negative understandings of women have been evident in some strands of Sufi thought and practices from its inception, particularly during its earlier ascetic variety, Sufism in other instances has also provided gender-egalitarian spaces. As discussed in more detail in chapter 1, significant evidence indicates the multitudinous approaches to piety adopted by early Sufi women.[24] While varying levels of asceticism and spiritual discipline formed an integral part of the religious life of these women, their lifestyles varied from traditional gender roles as mothers and wives to nontraditional roles as independent individuals, travelers, teachers, disciples, and solitary mystics. The departures of early Sufi women from traditional gender norms may have been rendered acceptable to other Sufis, male and female, largely by the greater priority most Sufis accord to the individual's inner state and by the concomitantly diminished significance of gender identity on the spiritual path. In some cases, Sufi practices have subverted traditional patriarchal religious anthropology in ways that might provide contemporary Muslims with creative resources for expanding the paradigm for gender justice in their societies.

In other instances, however, some Sufis have accepted the traditional sexist understanding of the gendered human person, thereby excusing the normative injustice characterizing patriarchal society. For example, some Sufi anthropologies have reinforced the associations of women with the baser, material spheres of existence, thereby positing women as a threat to male spiritual seekers.[25] While such an underlying anthropology shares much with popular and highly visible patriarchal Islamic discourses, the anthropology characterizing the more positive Sufi constructions of women is largely hidden. I elaborate on both types of anthropological constructs and engage them in dialogue with one another. Instead of avoiding contradictions, this dialectical criticism embraces competing rationalities as an instrument for engaging conflict that may offer new alternatives.

In the pages that follow, I illustrate that despite competing gender narratives, core Sufi assumptions are inherently critical of power configurations that assert the superiority of particular human beings on any basis other than spiritual stature.[26] In fact, some Sufi stories reflect a critique of prevalent notions of intrinsic male superiority. I choose to focus on this area precisely because of the rich complexity of Sufi thought that addresses the core vision of reality within Islam as well as its intrinsically egalitarian spiritual impetus. From the polyphony of Sufi gender narratives, Ibn ʿArabī's ideas in particular exemplify a superb articulation of these interrelated discursive possibilities concerning cosmology and gender. His hermeneutics reflects a rich mélange of scholarly and scriptural tradition, Sufi unveilings, and, like all other interpreters, his sociohistorical positioning. While Ibn ʿArabī and Sufi discourse in general offer some exciting possibilities for creatively and critically engaging questions of gender ethics, neither the individual nor the discipline are monolithic.

Situating Ibn ʿArabī

Abū ʿAbd Allāh Muḥammad ibn ʿAlī ibn al-ʿArabī al-Ḥaṭimī al-Ṭaʾī, more commonly known as Ibn ʿArabī, was born in Murcia, in southern Spain, in 1165.[27] Muslim political rule over Spain lasted approximately eight centuries (711–1492 C.E.). Andalusia, as Muslim Spain was called, reflected a fusion of its various legacies: the Roman Empire, the Christianized Visigoths, and elements of Arab civilization brought by immigrants from the Islamic heartlands of Syria, Arabia, and Yemen.[28] It was also an intellectual and cultural center characterized by rich interactions among Jewish, Christian, and Muslim thinkers as well a site where the intellectual legacies of ancient Greece and Rome were translated and studied. The Muslims of Spain, together with their other religious and intellectual cohorts in Andalusia, served as a conduit by which many of the lost scientific and philosophical texts of the ancient Greco-Roman civilization were reintroduced to the Western world. The collective intellectual corpus was to leave an indelible mark on European civilization.[29]

Rom Landau, a modern scholar, argues that at its peak, the intellectual zest and material splendor of Cordova and Seville surpassed those of Paris and possibly even of Constantinople.[30] In this diverse sociointellectual milieu, Ibn ʿArabī received his early education. He was exposed to Zoroastrian and Manichaean lore, Jewish and Christian theology, Greek philosophy and mathematics, and every variety of Muslim intellectual achievement.[31]

Ibn ʿArabī was of Arab lineage, born to a family that was relatively well-off. He was an only son and had close relationships with both of his sisters. Details regarding his mother are sparse. His father served in the military retinue of the Almohad sultan and became fairly well acquainted with some of the intelligentsia of the day, including Ibn Rushd. Ibn ʿArabī's family members appear to have been religious, with inclinations toward Sufism. At a young age, Ibn ʿArabī experienced mystical visions of God and subsequently traveled to various cities of learning in Andalusia, seeking out the learned and the wise. In the formative period of his life, Ibn ʿArabī studied with two women saints, Fāṭima of Cordova and Yasmīna of Mashena, both of whom influenced him significantly and contributed to his spiritual development.[32]

Until 1198, Ibn ʿArabī traveled around Spain and North Africa, meeting with scholars and Sufis. During this time, he continued to have mystical visions, which became the basis of his numerous writings. He began to write his magnum opus, *Al-Futūḥāt al-makkiyya* (The Meccan Openings) in 1201, during his first visit to Mecca. Here, he met a Persian Sufi woman, Nizām, who came to represent for him the embodiment of divine love and beauty.[33] In fact, Ibn ʿArabī appears to have had pervasive and rich interactions with women, not only among his spiritual teachers but also within his family and among his disciples.

From Mecca, Ibn ʿArabī traveled to various cities, encountering the spiritual figure of Khidr, the prophet who initiates people directly into spiritual life from the unseen realms without the regular initiation into a traditional Sufi *ṭarīqa* (path).[34] Ibn ʿArabī finally settled in Damascus, where he completed the *Futūḥāt*, which is considered an encyclopedia of esoteric knowledge and spiritual insight. This work took him close to thirty years to finish. He died in Damascus in 1240 at the age of seventy-five.

His Works

There is no exact record of the number of books Ibn ʿArabī wrote. He mentions three hundred, a significant number of which are extant, with copies in various libraries in the Muslim world and in Europe.[35] The *Futūḥāt* is the largest of his works, comprising 560 chapters dealing with a great variety of topics, among them highly abstract principles of metaphysics and Ibn ʿArabī's personal spiritual experiences. One contemporary scholar of Sufism, Seyyed Hossein Nasr, remarks that this compendium of esoteric sciences in Islam surpasses in scope and depth anything of its kind composed previously or since.[36] Ibn ʿArabī states that the *Futūḥāt* was the product of unveilings given to him by God rather than a product of personal reflection.[37] This work has been studied and commented on by generations of Sufi and other scholars of Islam.

Perhaps the most popular of Ibn ʿArabī's works is the *Fuṣūṣ al-ḥikam* (The Bezels of Wisdom), which was written in 1229. Ibn ʿArabī reported that this work was inspired by a vision of the Prophet Muḥammad, who commanded Ibn ʿArabī to take a book from the Prophet's hand and transmit it to the world for the benefit of humankind.[38] In this text, each "bezel" symbolizes a facet of divine wisdom respectively revealed to each of the prophets recognized in Islam. The human and spiritual nature of each prophet was a vehicle for communicating and manifesting particular facets of the divine. The *Fuṣūṣ* and the *Futūḥāt* are considered Ibn ʿArabī's two most significant works.

Ibn ʿArabī's corpus also includes numerous works on cosmology, such as *Inshaʾ al-dawāʾir* (The Description of the Encompassing Spheres) and *ʿUqlat al-mustawfiz* (The Spell of the Obedient Servant); meditations on the Qurʾān, such as *Ishārāt al-qurʾān fi ʿālam al-insān* (Allusions of the Qurʾān in the Human World); practical advice to spiritual aspirants, such as *Risāla al-khalwa* (A Treatise on Spiritual Retreat); and poetry, such as the *Tarjumān al-ashwāq* (The Interpreter of Desires).

Ibn ʿArabī moved among discursive expressions ranging from theology, mysticism, philosophy, and Qurʾānic exegesis to poetry, biography, and mythology. He constantly challenged normative boundaries in his substantive teachings. His style of presentation often involved antinomies, paradoxes, and unusual allegories to convey spiritual insights or esoteric exegeses of the Qurʾān—methods that were commonly employed in works of mystical expression. Ibn ʿArabī's utilization of this vast, varying range of expressions and discursive windows makes for a hermeneutically rich body of spiritual insights.

Alexander Knysh marvels at Ibn ʿArabī's adept and extraordinary style, wherein even the recurring motifs he used escape being mundane or repetitive. According to Knysh, the variety of different discursive expressions flowing from Ibn ʿArabī's expert hand "colours the very visions and experiences he endeavors to convey, making it difficult to neatly separate content from form. . . . [T]he new verbal shells transform the very meaning of these motifs."[39] The diversity of disciplinary and linguistic expressions that Ibn ʿArabī employs to present his ideas adds a textured fluidity to his thought.

Ibn ʿArabī was heralded as one of the earliest and most sophisticated theoreticians of Sufi metaphysics and as a distinguished practical master in his time, and contemporary scholars have illustrated the pervasive impact of his legacy in both popular and intellectual Sufi discourses.[40]

Contesting Ibn ʿArabī

Ibn ʿArabī is also perhaps one of the most contested figures in Muslim intellectual history. In a detailed study on polemical literature surrounding Ibn ʿArabī, Knysh notes that from the thirteenth century onward, practically every significant Muslim thinker found it necessary to comment on the "controversial Sufi master."[41] In Muslim literature, refutations of his work are interlaced with accusations of dangerous heresy—a heresy that many of his accusers saw as the combination of a riotous mystical imagination with a pantheistic philosophy that threatened to destroy the foundations of Islam. Opponents of Ibn ʿArabī included those antagonistic to Sufism as well as reformist Sufis, who accused him of deviating from "true Sufism" or "*Sharīʿa* Sufism," a Sufism keenly observant of the law.

However, some of his supporters revere him as one of the most erudite intellectuals and spiritual savants within the Islamic tradition. The extraordinary stature and iconic position that he enjoys among his disciples and admirers is reflected in the epithet accorded him, Shaykh al-Akbar (the Greatest Master). According to Qūrī, a fifteenth-century jurist, among religious scholars, opinions of Ibn ʿArabī ranged from claims that he was an infidel to arguments that he was an axial saint.[42] Qūrī judiciously reserved judgment on Ibn ʿArabī's status.

One of the most strident and consequential critics of Ibn ʿArabī was the fourteenth-century Ibn Taymiyya.[43] Incensed by what followers of Ibn ʿArabī described as the doctrine of "*waḥdat al-wujūd* [unity of being],"[44] Ibn Taymiyya launched a frontal attack on the monistic tendencies of Akbarian metaphysics.[45] In Ibn Taymiyya's somber view, such a metaphysical system disturbingly ruptured the clear boundaries between God and humanity, between human freedom and predestination, between good and evil. The intractable jurist argued that the goal of true Sufism was to serve God more perfectly, not to delve into the impregnable mysteries of God's being or desire intimacy with the divine.

Underlying much of the controversies about Ibn ʿArabī's metaphysical system were contestations of God's relationship to humanity. Particularly threatening to Ibn Taymiyya and his ilk was the fact that Ibn ʿArabī's metaphysics blurred the clear hierarchy between God and humanity, leading to particular types of immanentist inclinations that were not regarded as properly observant of God's transcendence. For Ibn Taymiyya, the view that human beings, through love, might know an existential intimacy with God was heretical, bordering on Christian doctrines of incarnation (*ḥulūl*) and union (*ittiḥād*).[46]

Patriarchal theologies, as reflected in some of the objections to women's imamate, often hold an excessive focus on elements of God's distance and transcendence. Proponents of such approaches may also often denigrate materiality and the body and, by extension, women, who are identified primarily with the bodily principle. It is not therefore surprising that Ibn ʿArabī's worldview, which integrates notions of humanity's intimacy with God and views creation as a sphere of divine manifestation, were also accompanied by positive evaluations of materiality, of embodiment, and of women. Ibn ʿArabī's particular assimilation of the notion of God's immanence into a theological schema was found too bold in its assertions on human nature and too dangerous in terms of its social consequences. At the same time, Ibn ʿArabī's insistence on both the transcendence and immanence of God pointed to the paradox of the divine nature that could never be contained by the fetters of human reason.[47]

Yet other Muslim thinkers were known personally to have admired Ibn ʿArabī's ideas while denouncing him publicly. Some religious scholars believed that Ibn ʿArabī's teachings should be restricted to an elite group of qualified adept Sufis able to understand the complexities and intricacies of his metaphysics. In this view, the deep esoteric nature of his insights, with their nuanced constellation of ideas, would not be accessible to the general Muslim population, which would invariably misunderstand and distort them. Adherents of this perspective saw Ibn ʿArabī's ideas as perilous only when they were exposed to the limitations of spiritually unrefined human beings.

Conversely, other advocates of Ibn ʿArabī reject depictions of him as an anarchist unconcerned with social order and as a metaphysician tearing away the shield of divine transcendence. On the contrary, they argue, he was one of the greatest living saints, and his ideas reflect profound and startling insights into the heart of the Qurʾān and sunna. Based on these primary sources and inspired by mystical unveilings, proponents of this view assert that Ibn ʿArabī's cosmological panoply superbly integrated both divine immanence and transcendence into his theological schema. They astutely point to the glaring absence of peer opposition to Ibn ʿArabī during his lifetime, indicating that his contemporaries recognized his personal piety and impeccable adherence to Islamic rites.[48]

Debates regarding Ibn ʿArabī have not been limited to religious scholars. Rulers and politicians have also instrumentalized the enduring Ibn ʿArabī controversy. The Ottoman rulers were particularly enamored of the Shaykh al-Akbar. Kemal Pashazade, a sixteenth-century Ottoman statesman and scholar, issued an official ban on public defamations of Ibn ʿArabī, while Sultan Selim I commissioned an official defense for Ibn ʿArabī's ideas.[49] Conversely, as recently as 1979, some members of the People's Assembly, the lower house of the Egyptian bicameral parliament, unsuccessfully attempted to enact an official ban on Ibn ʿArabī's teachings.[50] Th. Emil Homerin points out how the Egyptian government attempted to use this religious controversy to gain political leverage.[51] Conflicting images of Ibn ʿArabī have thus for centuries also been utilized to enable and disable varying ideological agendas.

The history and depth of engagement with Ibn ʿArabī's ideas, even when mired in controversy, reflect the importance of this thinker in Muslim tradition. The profound nature of his ideas and their possible and actual ramifications have persistently intervened in Muslim intellectual life from the thirteenth century onward. In part, the earlier controversies regarding Ibn ʿArabī's ideas also prefigure some of the more intense debates on the place and nature of Sufism in the modern world.

Contesting Sufism

Despite the ideals of a complementary relationship between Sufi concerns with virtue and juristic concerns with practical conformity, Islamic history attests to varying modes of engagement between those inclined to esoteric and exoteric knowledge respectively. In premodern Islam, there was "no historically uniform pattern of hostility between Sufism and the lawyers."[52] Indeed, some of the most brilliant Muslim scholars who authored erudite legal treatises were also dedicated practitioners of Sufism. Other Sufis dismissed disproportionate attention to legal hairsplitting without attention to the spiritual realities that the laws attempt to embody. Still others were simultaneously legal scholar and Sufi, condemning other Sufis for insufficient attention to the law. In yet other contexts, Sufis were persecuted when they became too powerful, with large numbers of followers, and were thus perceived as constituting a threat to the political authorities rather than because of opposition to Sufism per se. And finally, there were the less frequent though sensational cases of Sufis executed at the gallows for heresy, perceived in these instances as imminently threatening the dominant articulations of Islam. These sociological trajectories reflect the multiple interpretive possibilities as well as varying historical and political configurations within which Sufism was embodied.[53]

Modern contestations of the relationship of Sufism to Islam have a complex and textured history. Current conceptions of Sufism are colored by the influence of the Wahhabi movement, born in the eighteenth century in what is today Saudi Arabia, as well as the wider Salafi movements that developed in the nineteenth and twentieth centuries in different parts of the Muslim world. Wahhabism and many Salafi movements have at different times provided powerful opposition to Sufism.

Islamist movements based on a reformist orientation advocate a return to ways of the pious predecessors (*al-salaf al-ṣāliḥ*) of the early Muslim community. Salafis maintain that Muslims have over time deviated and drifted from the norms of the devout early communities. Proponents of Salafism have approached much of the Muslim intellectual tradition critically, condemning large segments of Islam's theological, legal, and mystical corpus. Salafism, with its literalist tendencies, deals selectively with the primary sources and exhibits a particular suspicion toward the imaginative and creative dimensions of Muslim thought and culture. Many Salafis have been particularly critical of Sufi practices, targeting them as foreign innovations (*bidʿa*) responsible for derailing Islamic practice from its original purity.

Wahhabism, a revivalist movement based on the ideas of Muḥammad ibn ʿAbd al-Wahhāb (d. 1792), has been particularly intolerant of Sufi practices, persecuting Sufis and destroying Sufi tombs, graveyards, and books. Historically, Wahhabi rejection of Sufism was also imbricated in the political antagonisms against the Ottomans, the non-Arab Ḥanafīs, who were sympathetic to Sufism as well as major patrons of the works of Ibn ʿArabī in particular. The Wahhabis not only attacked popular Sufi practices and folk piety but also launched a strong doctrinal and theological attack on Sufi thought. In fact, ʿAbd al-Wahhāb himself unleashed a scathing assault on Ibn ʿArabī's ideas in many of his writings, explicitly declaring him an unbeliever.[54]

On the one hand, the impact of certain Salafi and Wahhabi influences has resulted in outright rejection of Sufism by a small but significant Muslim minority. As a result of the Saudi oil wealth that buttresses Wahhabism, its ideology has been actively transported to many parts of the Muslim world, with an insidious impact on more mainstream Muslim societies. A related wariness of Sufism has trickled into segments of the global Muslim community, where it coexists somewhat paradoxically with the reality that elements of Sufism, such as veneration of the Prophet and the saints, pervade the religious practices of vast expanses of the Muslim world.[55]

On the other hand, Salafi trends have also influenced specific groups of Sufis, who attempted to return Sufism to a more sober *Sharīʿa*-oriented focus. These reformist Sufis have become particularly vigilant toward practices like saint veneration and popular visits to saints' tombs, Sufi music, and dance. They also adopt a greater skepticism and wariness regarding more speculative and creative elements in Sufi thought, including the ideas of Ibn ʿArabī and his ilk. Like the Wahhabis and other Salafis, such reformist Sufis also draw strongly on Ibn Taymiyya's works.

In addition, as illustrated by Carl Ernst, Western rationalism, colonialism, and European Orientalist writing have also affected Muslim debates on the value of Sufism.[56] Accordingly, some Muslim modernists also condemned the mystical, irrational, popular elements of Sufism for contributing to the demise of Islamic civilization vis-à-vis the modern, rational, and triumphant West. Some Muslims have internalized European Orientalist depictions of Sufi leaders ranging from the bizarre, howling dervish to the wandering rogue and charlatan to the fanatic charismatic leader.[57] Ernst points to the uncanny alliance between Muslim fundamentalists and European Orientalists in this regard.[58] He illustrates that both these groups have been complicit in straitjacketing Islam as a narrowly legal and ideological system, thereby bringing into question the legitimacy of Sufism.

The contemporary period has also seen a flowering of Sufi movements and literature both in the West and in the Muslim world.[59] All types of Sufi orders have emerged in Europe and the United States, from very traditional forms to New Age types. An increase has occurred in the number of globalized Sufi orders with transnational networks and highly mobile Sufi *shaykhs* supervising communities internationally. Shaykh Fadlallah Haeri, an Iraqi-born Sufi leader, and Shaykh Abdalqadir as-Sufi al-Murabit, the Scottish leader of the Murabitun, are two contemporary Sufi *shaykhs* who have established international communities headquartered in South Africa. Disciples and teachers traverse the globe to consult, advise, guide, and be guided.

Even in Muslim countries where the state is resistant to Sufism, the movement continues to grow in visible ways. In Islamist Iran, violent confrontations occurred between the Iranian authorities and the Sufi community in a Sufi lodge (Husseinieh) in Qom in 2006. In secular Turkey, the reemergence of the Naqshbandiyya Sufi order had the surprising consequence of being credited with founding the first Islamist party.[60] For many other contemporary Muslims, the events of September 11 confirmed that Islamism is not a viable alternative. The search for more appealing, humane forms of Islamic tradition and more enriching ways of being Muslim has led some to Sufism.

In the contemporary period, both popular and scholarly publications of Sufism have grown exponentially. Anthologies of works of a thirteenth-century Sufi poet, Jalāl al-Dīn Rūmī, top American best-seller booklists. Academic and popular publishing houses including Curzon, Fons Vitae, Pir Press, and Hurst publish a plethora of books and journals dedicated to Sufism. Ibn ʿArabī in particular has received enormous attention from scholars and spiritual aspirants. The Beshara School, a study and retreat center founded in Scotland in 1973 by Bulent Rauf (d. 1987), a Turkish aristocrat inspired by Sufism, teaches about self-knowledge and the realization of esoteric truth without alignment with specific religious traditions. The study curriculum draws heavily on Ibn ʿArabī's and Rūmī's writings as sources of inspiration.

The year 1977 saw the founding of the Muhyiddin Ibn ʿArabī Society, a multinational network of devotees of Ibn ʿArabī. This group holds annual conferences with international speakers and publishes a biannual journal to promote greater understanding of Ibn ʿArabī's works and ideas. The society has circulated and publicized Ibn ʿArabī's ideas among a group of scholars with more esoteric and philosophical orientations. Drawing on the sophisticated and erudite works of many of these scholars, I direct the scope and audience of my study somewhat differently, focusing on the political potential of Ibn ʿArabī's philosophical, intellectual, and spiritual teachings, especially with regard to the possibilities it might offer Islamic feminism.

Feminism and Islamic Feminism

My definition of the term "feminism" includes the three critical components of awareness, activism, and vision.[61] "Feminism" refers to a critical awareness of the structural marginalization of women in society; it engages in activities directed at transforming gender power relations to strive, according to its vision, for a society that facilitates the development of human wholeness based on principles of gender justice, equality, and freedom from structures of oppression.[62]

"Islamic feminism," in particular, addresses questions of human wholeness from the perspective of a foundational God-human relationship that roots the process and goals of individual, societal, and political life in the attainment of a right relationship with God. Questions of justice, freedom, and equality, therefore, are always situated and valued vis-à-vis a larger framework for understanding the nature of reality.

Current debates on feminism in Islam are ideologically charged, embedded as they are in a history of larger civilizational polemics between the Islamic world and the West.[63] For many Muslims, Western feminist approaches have historically collaborated with colonial and Orientalist depictions of Islam as fundamentally oppressive to women and continue to reiterate reductionist views of Muslim women. In the past four decades, Western feminists have also been subject to criticism from a whole spectrum of other women outside of the centers of white, Euro-American privilege on the basis of the biased and culturally imperialist assumptions that characterized the dominant strands of Western feminist literature at the time.[64]

Western feminists, particularly from the 1980s onward, have subsequently attempted to respond to issues of pluralism, representation, and hegemony.[65] These attempts have succeeded to varying and debatable degrees; however, in the case of Islam and Muslim women, Western feminists still easily discard judicious analyses offered by their Muslim sisters and reiterate negative stereotypes. More particularly, some Western feminists who claim to be generally cognizant of questions of diversity persist in making sweeping claims about Muslim women or Islam without engaging the necessary levels of complexity and specificity. This type of reductionism is not unrelated to an increasing presence of Islamophobia globally. Such Western discourses on Muslim women are also often predicated on unquestioned cultural, social, and political assumptions that do not allow for the engagement of specific Muslim societies on their own terms.

Yet over the past two decades, postmodernism, Third World feminism, and critiques from other women on the margins have resulted in the development of varying understandings and different articulations of feminism. Thus, the contours of feminism have been reconfigured to be more attuned to the specificities attending different groups of women and to acknowledge the diverse forms of feminist praxis. Within this type of fluid and dynamic understanding of *feminisms*, it is possible to detect a range of Muslim women's gender activism, or *Islamic feminisms*.[66]

While some Muslims eschew the term "feminist," increasing numbers have begun to utilize it to describe themselves. Retaining the term "feminism" enables Muslim women to situate their praxis in a global political landscape, thereby creating greater possibilities for alliances, exchanges, and mutually enriching interaction among different groups of women.

The usage of feminist language is helpful in that it creates a finely tuned vocabulary for a constellation of ideas that are linked to a critical consciousness surrounding gender politics. Muslim women and men with feminist commitments engage in "multiple critique": they are critical of sexist interpretations of Islam and patriarchy in their religious communities while condemning neocolonial feminist discourses on Islam.[67] Muslims nonetheless come from heterogeneous groups that sometimes have very different understandings of gender justice.[68] The point of convergence is, however, a general view that gender justice is a priority in the understanding and embodiment of Islam, and these varying approaches consequently fall under the broader rubric of "Islamic feminisms."

Among the most revolutionary elements of Islamic feminisms is the view that feminist commitments are responsive to the broader Qurʾānic call to justice and to the advancement of just Muslim communities. Muslim feminist scholars adopt varied approaches to the texts and traditions in their struggles for gender justice. The primary incentive for some feminist Muslim scholars is the dissonance between the ideals of Islam that they believe to be premised on an ontology of radical human equality, and the varying social contexts in which Muslim women experience injustice in the name of religion.[69] Some feminist scholars analyze the way in which Islamic teachings are subject to social contexts and argue that patriarchal interpretations result from the exclusively male constitution of much of institutional Islam.[70] Others acknowledge the tension between patriarchy and egalitarianism in the Islamic legacy, including within the Qurʾān itself, but argue for the primacy of egalitarianism as representative of the spiritual and ethical ideals of Islam, ideals toward which Muslims must constantly strive.[71]

Some of the most cutting-edge Islamic feminist scholars have argued compellingly for recognizing the complexity implicit in invoking wide-ranging notions such as justice and equality that may mean very different things in different contexts.[72] Such scholars have persuasively illustrated that when engaging Islamic texts and traditions, it is imperative to recognize the centrality of interpretive choices and human agency without arrogantly claiming absolute supremacy of particular contemporary understandings. Muslim feminist scholars increasingly are foregrounding the importance of human vicegerency, or moral agency, a fundamental Islamic teaching, as part of the unfolding dynamic of gender justice in contemporary Muslim communities.

I analyze the varying and even ambivalent discourses of sexuality and gender found in Sufi thought. In particular, I explore this crucial tension between what I consider clear Islamic ethical ideals of justice and the simultaneous heritage of patriarchy within the Islamic legacy and the current practices of some Muslims. In particular, I engage these Sufi discourses in ways that illuminate contemporary challenges of gender justice in Muslim communities. Traditional discourses have not applied the Islamic ethics of justice to gender issues in the revolutionary ways that Islamic feminists are currently doing. This sharpening of gender-just perspectives is a natural and necessary development that both engages the tradition creatively and responds to the evolving sensibilities on gender within some present-day Muslim communities. My reading of Sufi texts is invariably informed by my particular historical positioning, including my interlocking commitments to Islam and feminism. It is by now a truism that all readers bring their assumptions, ideologies, and worldviews to their interpretations of texts, as debates in the field of hermeneutics and cultural criticism have indicated. Seemingly objective, neutral, and disinterested interpretations of texts are also always in fact the products of the multiple positioning of its readers.

I find significant and relevant overlaps between Islamic and certain feminist discourses. Despite the dominance of the patriarchy in Muslims' civilizational and textual heritage, the spiritual core of Islam is nonetheless characterized by a fundamental belief in the equal capacity and potentiality of all human beings, a core to which Sufism inherently addresses itself. At this level, a profound confluence exists between the pervasive Islamic ethos of social justice and feminism's appeal for human equality. Despite the complexities associated with the connection between Islam and feminism, this vision is worth pursuing.

One of the conundrums of doing feminist research in both secular and religious contexts is the male-dominated nature of the textual tradition and the pervasiveness of male subjectivity articulated in such texts. Most often, the subject, the audience, and the authors of these texts are male. One thus encounters only the voice and lifeworlds of men on all issues, even when women's realities are recorded. One way to get around this problem is to seek out female subjectivity outside of official religious canons, a venture that many feminist theologians in Christianity, Judaism, and more recently Islam have creatively and successfully undertaken.[73] Nonetheless, the traditional textual canon continues to be profoundly influential and meaningful for both women and men within Islam, as in other religious traditions. Therefore, it is imperative for committed Muslim feminist scholars to examine traditional and canonical texts, to read from gender-sensitive lenses, and to engage with the variety of gender discourses within these teachings. Even the male voices in the canon are not homogenous. In some instances, male scholars dissent from the reigning patriarchal order. At other times, these same scholars reinforce such norms.

A feminist reading of the past always raises the methodological specter of anachronism. Is it really illuminating to discuss the past in terms of contemporary frames of reference, such as "patriarchy," "feminism" or "gender equality"? In response to this legitimate question, I borrow some related theoretical insights culled by feminist Buddhist scholar Rita Gross regarding an "accurate" and "usable" past.[74] Accuracy, as Gross defines it, has to do with redressing the androcentric silence and trivialization of women in much of the inherited historical canon. Therefore, critically addressing the questions of women and gender redresses a historically inaccurate bias that focuses primarily on the male half of humanity while largely ignoring women. She illuminates how historical records are always selective and partial, reinforcing particular values and perspectives. For feminists, this perspective encourages the uncovering of marginalized and potentially liberating gender models that empower contemporary struggles for justice.

Reflecting on Gross's perspicacious insights in relation to my engagement with premodern Muslim texts, I suggest that there is an additional facet of engaging with silences around women. When reading many androcentric texts, one is not simply gazing into a void regarding women—often, through the process of absenting the feminine, glimpses of Otherness and traces of female subjectivity glimmer elusively at the borders of discourse. It is especially important to note that the exercise of interrogating male subjectivities within the text involves a dialogical process that concurrently creates space for female subjectivities in relation to that text.

Gross notes that history is profoundly important in the present because "a religious community constitutes itself by means of its collective memory, the past that it recalls and emulates."[75] A politics of recovering feminist histories thus is invaluable to those living religious communities that want to create new, bountiful, future visions for their own humanity within their traditions.

I have no desire to engage in a politics of blame or apology that simply foregrounds empowering gender narratives while ignoring the systematic history of male domination that has constantly rendered women the objects of male subjectivities in so much of the Islamic tradition, including Sufism. There is a vital need for a solid critique of this history, which I have attempted in other works as well as here. However, as Gross helpfully points out, the assessment of history as "androcentric in its thought-forms and patriarchal in its institutions is an *analysis*, an *accurate description*, not an *accusation*. . . . We would be guilty of an inappropriate projection of feminist values onto the past only if we did not stop with an analysis of its thought-forms and institutions, but also railed against the humans who participated in those modes of thinking and living."[76]

Heeding this observation, I avoid unthinkingly projecting contemporary feminist ambitions onto the past. Earlier scholars and writers were clearly subject to their own set of codes, assumptions, and historical imperatives. My critical analysis of their work is not prompted by an ahistorical desire to lambaste these individuals or their ideas. Rather, my feminist critique is particularly focused on unearthing the problematic ways in which patriarchal assumptions from the past still find currency in the social present.

I also remain sensitive to the ways in which past works might reflect patriarchal constructs while simultaneously and somewhat ambivalently gesturing toward alternative and more expansive ways of understanding human nature. I endeavor to delicately hold together the subtlety and potential carried by a mixed tradition that embodies both androcentric and egalitarian gender narratives.

This volume attempts to recoup a usable past for Islamic feminists, dislodging some of the dominant readings of the tradition by using critical feminist tools that open up an alternative horizon of possibilities for future readings of Sufi texts. My approach highlights and expands on voices of dissent to patriarchy that exist in the plethora that is Islamic tradition.

In this study, I draw on an established tradition of feminist hermeneutics that begins with a "hermeneutic of suspicion" that critically analyzes patriarchal biases in the texts and destabilizes accepted interpretations of "truth."[77] This approach exposes discriminatory structures and values embedded within texts emerging from an exclusively male experiential reality. Such an approach enables us to understand how androcentric historical formations compromised and sometimes even sabotaged the egalitarian ethical call of Islam.

Second, I use a "hermeneutics of reconstruction" that uncovers alternative egalitarian gender narratives within texts. I unearth underlying images of women from predominantly male-centered records, with the goal of both redressing the broader silences and marginalization of women's lives and retrieving powerful and empowering images of women. A reconstructive approach also demands vigilance in detecting inconsistencies and moments of disruptions within the texts. Hence, I creatively engage moments of resistance to patriarchy in its varying forms.[78]

For an audience unfamiliar with feminist method, I emphasize the creative excavation of women represented at the borders of texts. Such a feminist approach to the past does not always accord with the demand for historically verifiable data that might characterize traditional scholarship. Here feminist literary scholar Gayatri Spivak provides some astute insights in relation to linguistic theory: she encourages reading symptomatically beyond a text to explore its gaps, absences, and contradictions, which reveal the text's "unnaturalness" and thus uncover "another logic haunting its surface."[79] This is not for Spivak a purely literary experiment, since attending to these "marginal moments" in the text enables the reader to reflect critically on the ways in which a text might participate in a given ideology. This approach prompts the reader to explore the political and ethical implications of marginal traces residing on the borders of the dominant ideology.

So, for example, when I foreground and creatively elaborate on women referred to in Ibn ʿArabī's writings, I am holding an alternative mirror to the past that is suggestive about possibilities for understanding events that can neither be proved or disproved empirically. In using this type of feminist reading, I explore untrodden paths for analyzing the life and works of Ibn ʿArabī. This literary approach reflects the earlier feminist epistemological impetus for retrieving images and traces of women in texts that are largely male-dominated. The other critical point is that we encounter representations of women as they are mediated through male subjectivities in androcentric contexts—they are not in fact self-representations of women. Moreover, Ibn ʿArabī's depictions of women are in dialogue with and influenced by dominant representations of women by other scholars in his intellectual milieu, what French feminist and literary scholar Julia Kristeva would describe as the component of "intertextuality."[80] As such, we must remain cognizant of the ways in which Ibn ʿArabī's depictions of women and gender are filtered through prevailing "codes" of representation, where "every text is from the outset under the jurisdiction of other discourses which impose a universe on it."[81]

Additional considerations also arise when examining the varying depictions and images of women within the works of Ibn ʿArabī. He moves between more descriptive depictions of particular women as historical subjects in his life and representations of such women in ways that communicate his own ideas. In such instances, I engage with how his representations of women might serve as literary tropes or narrative constructs to communicate particular mystical concepts of Ibn ʿArabī. Yet I am in no way denying that such women might simultaneously have been actual women who might well have said and did whatever Ibn ʿArabī attributes to them.

These critical approaches within feminist hermeneutics inform my examination of gender in the Sufi Islamic legacy. I focus especially on Ibn ʿArabī's works because some of his radically egalitarian gender narratives challenge more traditional hegemonic Islamic discourses on gender. At the same time, I subject other gendered elements of his work to rigorous ideological examination and critique. In particular, I keep his complex gender narratives in constant conversation with his ontological, cosmological, and anthropological mappings of human possibilities. Ibn ʿArabī's work reflects some of the diversity, complexity, and sophistication that characterize the Islamic intellectual tradition. To sustain this vitality within the tradition, it is religiously, ethically, intellectually, and politically imperative to concentrate on emancipatory gender discourses indigenous to the Islamic legacy. This project is particularly urgent in light of the dogmatic, absolutist, repressive, and misogynist positions that are part of certain contemporary Islamic political trends.

My approach is one of a number of ways to read the legacy, neither more nor less "authentic" than other approaches. However, I consciously mobilize resources from the past for a different future. In accordance with the articulate reflections of Jewish feminist scholar Daniel Boyarin, I freely acknowledge that my selection of particular Sufi narratives reflects my identifications and my desire to foreground, highlight, and amplify one set of compelling possibilities within the tradition.[82] In tracing these feminist narratives, I do not claim dominance or exclusivity for these possibilities; I am merely pointing out that they exist and that I would like to hold them forth as beacons for the contemporary Muslim community.

Broadly, my project contributes toward a rethinking of Islamic tradition to invigorate contemporary Muslim approaches to gender issues. Some Christian scholars who have similarly explored different imaginings of God and humanity to imbue more egalitarian modes of relationality between men and women and between human beings in general have described their work as "constructive theology."[83] While my goals are comparable, simply using the language of "theology" or a "theological" project does not resonate in the same way within Muslim tradition, since theology is simply one aspect of how Muslims have dealt with the divine-human relationship. In addition to theology (*ʿilm al-kalām*), Muslims have historically developed the disciplines of jurisprudence, philosophy, and Sufism that cumulatively reflect their vision and understandings of God, humanity, ethics, and salvation. Islamic mysticism is replete with theological understandings that have profound implications for understanding human relationships and ethics. Given that language and its nuances invariably convey an entire intellectual genealogy and more subtly the relationship between knowledge and power, I have chosen not to describe my work as feminist "theology" but rather to cast it as a feminist rethinking of tradition that crucially involves theological reflections, among other things.

On questions of feminism, theology, and language, it is also necessary to reflect on my usage of gendered God language in this book. Muslim theology has historically been radically iconoclastic—God is not simply beyond gender but also beyond all anthropocentric imagery and similitudes. The Qurʾān introduces instead the concept of divine attributes as a way for humanity to relate to the One God. Despite the clear theological rejection of any form of gendered anthropomorphism, Arabic, the language of the Qurʾān and earliest Muslim theology, is a deeply gendered language. All Arabic nouns, whether animate or inanimate, are grammatically gendered and are rendered in the pronoun "he" or "she" since there is no gender-neutral term equivalent to the English "it." Such gendered linguistic conventions in Arabic are completely arbitrary and have no resonance whatsoever with supposedly human gendered qualities.[84] As such, *Allāh*, the Arabic name for God, is conventionally rendered into the pronoun *huwa* ("He"), which in Muslim theology is not conflated with any human understanding of masculinity since the singular deity is understood to transcend all duality.

Contemporary scholars of Sufism Michael Sells and Scott Kugle address the theological, poetic, and hermeneutical failure of rendering God in the masculine "He" or "Him."[85] Kugle also explicitly reflects on the contemporary Islamic ethics of gender justice compromised by using masculine pronouns for God. Thus, in his superb English translation of an important premodern Sufi treatise, Kugle refrains from using gendered pronouns for the divine, instead consistently using the ungendered term "God" and when necessary using the term "One" to stand in for the name of God.[86] A scholar focusing on the works of Ibn ʿArabī in particular must take into account some additional considerations.

Ibn ʿArabī uniquely uses traditionally "feminine" and "masculine" metaphors for God, invoking images of "fathers," "mothers," pregnancy, and birthing to describe aspects of divine creativity and relationality. Simultaneously, Ibn ʿArabī destabilizes and unsays all his theological constructs by using an apophatic mode of "unsaying or speaking-away" all fixed or reifying human conceptions of the divine.[87] Informed by Ibn ʿArabī's subtle and dialectical theological language of gender as well as the incisive positions on gendered God language discussed by both Sells and Kugle, I have chosen to use only "Allah" or "God" in my reflections on and discussions of the texts. This was not a simple decision for me since a compelling alternative would have been to use *both* pronouns "He" and "She" for God. Such an approach might well have drawn attention to the fluid and layered gendered metaphors Ibn ʿArabī employs in depicting aspects of the divine despite the fact that he rarely uses the pronoun "She."[88] Such a gender-inclusive approach to Muslim God language might also cause some Muslims to reflect on the deeper underlying reasons that they unquestioningly accept the male pronoun "He" for God yet instinctively express deep aversion to the usage of the feminine pronoun "She" despite everyone's sincere declarations that God is beyond gender. One could certainly make the case that using paradoxical (or inclusive) gendered language where God is referred to with both pronouns "He" and "She" mimics and exemplifies a mystical mode of saying and "unsaying" any human gender constructs in relation to God. If the Muslim view is that God is truly beyond gender, perhaps using both "She" and "He" demands that Muslims break all their fixed gendered conceptual idols.

Despite all of these compelling arguments for using both "He" and "She" for God, I decided to stay faithful to the direct literal translation of the divine *Huwa* as "He" for God in Ibn ʿArabī's texts. Thus, I use "Allah" or "God" in all my references to the divine and use "He" when translating Ibn ʿArabī's references to God as *Huwa*. I do so for the primary reason that I want the reader to access in an unadulterated manner the multiple and nuanced ways that Ibn ʿArabī more broadly troubles normative gender categories in his God talk. Ibn ʿArabī presents complex and nuanced formulations of feminine and masculine aspects of the divine One. My presentation of Ibn ʿArabī's theological language in its original gendered formulations attempts to adhere as faithfully as possible to Ibn ʿArabī's intricate, fluid, and sometimes paradoxical articulations of gender.

Chapter 1, "Craving Completion: Sufism, Subjectivity, and Gender before Ibn ʿArabī," provides a historical and thematic map of Sufism as it relates to the interconnected mappings of self and of gender. As such, it provides an overview of the various ways in which Sufi men and women have historically addressed issues of marriage, sexuality, embodiment, and the spirit.

Chapter 2, "Charting Ibn ʿArabī's Religious Anthropology," begins with some central epistemological reflections on the nature of mystical knowledge. I then examine some core formulations resulting from Ibn ʿArabī's mystical experiences—his cosmology and related understandings of human nature and purpose. Finally, I explore how his formulations on human nature translate into issues of law, gender, and society.

In chapter 3, "Mysticism and Gender: A Hermeneutic of Experience," I examine the epistemological intersections between feminist and mystical methodologies as they relate to the category of "experience." By providing some in-depth reflections on Ibn ʿArabī's life and relationships to women in particular, I examine how mystical and mundane experiences interweave to produce his views on gender and male and female subjectivities. I suggest that Ibn ʿArabī's textured relationships with women were integral to the formulation of the worldview presented in his scholarly and other writings.

Chapter 4, "Reading Gender and Metaphor in Ibn ʿArabī's Cosmos," consists of two parts. The first part outlines a hermeneutical and theoretical map with which to approach Ibn ʿArabī's nuanced and at times paradoxical writings on gender. The second part outlines some of his core constructions of gender in relation to his cosmic principles of activity and receptivity and especially how such principles pervade all existence.

Having mapped his gender principles macrocosmically in chapter 4, I proceed in the next two chapters to explore his views regarding the more intimate relationships that may occur between men and women—love, desire, sex, and marriage. Chapters 5 and 6 thus form a conceptual unit in that both center on multiple readings of the Abrahamic creation narratives, involving Adam and Eve, which form the mythic heart of varying understandings of relationships of love, sexuality, and marriage between men and women.

Chapter 5, "The Poetics and Politics of Adam and Eve," begins by adumbrating the figures of Adam and Eve in the Qurʾān and within Muslim exegeses of different periods. My concise survey of the related premodern commentaries provides readers with a broad overview of the dominant gendered religious imagination informing Ibn ʿArabī and his ideas. The rest of the chapter presents an in-depth analysis of his fluid interpretations and refashioning of the creation narratives and related texts.

Chapter 6, "Witnessing God in Women: A Different Story of Creation," focuses on the manner by which Ibn ʿArabī brings to bear antinomian perspectives on the feminine, sexuality, and women. Here, I explore his notions of the divine feminine; the view that God is most perfectly witnessed in women; and the linkages Ibn ʿArabī makes between sexual intimacy and knowledge of God. I also examine how he transforms the dominant gender model of creation by reflecting on another creation story—that involving Jesus' birth from the Virgin Mary.

The final chapter, "Ibn ʿArabī and Islamic Feminism," outlines some of the central differences between my reading of Ibn ʿArabī and other contemporary interpreters of his work. I do so to reflect on the creative and enriching ways in which Sufism and Ibn ʿArabī's teachings in particular might enhance contemporary Islamic feminism and indeed general feminist debates more broadly.

Drawing on some of the lucid theoretical categories outlined by Ebrahim Moosa in his study of Ghazālī, I suggest that Ibn ʿArabī is one of those "frontier thinkers" within the Islamic tradition, an intellectual luminary working on the threshold of multiple narratives and creatively weaving together a variety of genres.[89] The corpus of Ibn ʿArabī's work reflects not only an assimilation of the past but also innovative and creative contributions addressing the concerns of his time, an approach that often subverted and realigned the parameters of the dominant religious imagination in fundamental ways. I illustrate in the course of this book how his intellectual legacy provides us with vibrant "conditions of possibility" when addressing questions of gender, ontology, and feminism in the twenty-first century.

Moosa's discussion of "future friendships" as originally outlined by Jacques Derrida is instructive.[90] Innovative thinkers of the past might have been marginalized or even exiled in their own time, but through their creativity and intellectual precociousness, they can speak to future generations in nontotalitarian ways, resulting in an unpredictable and indeterminate impact of their ideas in the future. Such thinkers would not have been in a position to determine the future impact of their work or the ways in which their ideas might wedge open the future horizons of human imagination. It could be said that such great thinkers of the past wrote courageously and daringly right into the future.

These past scholars thus serve as heralds and precursors to intellectual communities of the future, who expand and develop their ideas in novel and relevant ways. A critical engagement with Sufism and Ibn ʿArabī in particular offers contemporary Muslims a visionary way to configure and interlock the prophetic visions of Islam and of feminism, holding out possibilities for developing and creating a more just world. I think of my Islamic feminist project as a spirited response to the hand of an "*Uwaysī*" friendship extended by Ibn ʿArabī some seven hundred years ago.[91]

Chapter One

Craving Completion

Sufism, Subjectivity, and Gender before Ibn ʿArabī

> The heavens and earth contain Me not, but the heart of my faithful servant contains Me.—*Ḥadīth qudsī*

> I love nothing that draws my servant near to Me more than I love what I have made obligatory for him. My servant never ceases drawing near to Me through superogatory works until I love him. And when I love him I am his hearing through which he hears, his sight through which he sees, his hand through which he grasps, and his foot through which he walks.—*Ḥadīth qudsī*

Springing from the heart of Islam's spiritual reservoir, *Taṣawwuf*, or Sufism, can be described as the process by which a believer embraces the full spiritual consequences of God's oneness (*tawḥīd*).[1] The goal of the Sufi path is to enable a human being, through the cultivation of virtuous excellence (*iḥsān*), to commune directly and experientially with her Creator. In the historical development of Sufism, one encounters varied and increasingly sophisticated notions of the mystical path, or *ṭarīqa.* Such a path generally entails that the Sufi aspirant, under the guidance of a spiritual master, follows a practical method of purification and refinement of the self, undergoing many states (*aḥwāl*) and stages (*maqāmāt*) that lead to progressive unveilings of the divine reality (*ḥaqīqa*).[2]

Notions of the self and its refinement, the rigors of the mystical path, and the nature of the God-human relationship are core concerns in Sufism. All of these concerns inform Sufi approaches to issues of gender, sexuality, and marriage. Historically, both male and female Sufis have reflected a continuum of positions on sexuality and marriage: some have strongly rejected marriage and sexuality; others have accepted the normative status of marriage and sex in Islam without fuss; while still others have heartily extolled the spiritual virtues of marital and sexual relationships.

This chapter commences by exploring some of the preliminary constructs of personality, psychology,[3] and purification in Sufism. These perspectives on human nature and spiritual endeavor provide a foundation from which to analyze varying Sufi approaches to questions of gender. Exploring Sufi understandings of human nature and psychology nudges open some of the ways in which an Islamic anthropology and its gendered dimensions are configured. I examine the ways that these underlying religious anthropologies serve varying Sufi views on asceticism, celibacy, sexuality, and marriage. I also analyze the manners in which gender ideologies permeated the lives and relations between Sufi women and men as gleaned from biographical writings. In particular, I devote careful and critical attention to the complex ways in which Sufis used gendered language to navigate discussions of spirituality, gender, and social power differentials.

Core Sufi concepts of self and the spiritual path as well as the real-life interactions between Sufi men and women covered in this chapter allow for a social contextualization of Ibn ʿArabī's ideas within a whole history of Sufi anthropologies and gender ideologies. This review chapter provides readers with a mapping on issues of self, gender, and some of the related developments in Sufism. While this chapter is less analytical than other chapters in this book, it provides background on some of the historical and conceptual terrain of Sufism and gender.

Personality and Sufi Psychology

Since the goal of the Sufi path is to deepen the God-human relationship, meticulous attention is given to removing spiritual obstacles within the individual that may impede progress along that path. This focus on purifying and disciplining the self has resulted in an elaborate and detailed inquiry into the mechanics of personality. Some of the organically genderless assumptions within Sufism include the priority given to an individual's inner state in relation to behavior and thought, the view that the same spiritual imperatives apply to all humanity, and the accompanying notion that the inner is not determined by one's biology. Exploring notions of personality and psychology within Sufism provides a necessary starting point for the exploration of its gender ideology.

The components and dynamics of personality in Sufism may be conceptualized in relation to the tripartite relationship between the soul (*nafs*), the heart (*qalb*), and the spirit (*rūḥ*) as identified in the Qurʾān.[4] The *nafs*, which can be identified as one's self-awareness, is a dynamic entity determined by the spiritual state of the individual.[5] It can range from being dominated by base instincts and cravings to being characterized by a state of peace and submission to God, with varying intermediate possibilities. Its most unrefined state is what the Qurʾān calls *al-nafs al-ammāra*, the commanding soul, or "the soul that incites to evil" (Q. 12:53). In this sense, it is defined by self-centered, egoistic, and compulsive tendencies. Drawing a person to the realm of selfhood and transient desires, the *nafs al-ammāra* is responsible for the separation and dispersion from the original unitive state between God and humanity. In its blindness to the true nature of reality, the *nafs al-ammāra* perceives worldly attractions such as power, fame, wealth, and physical gratification as meaningful in themselves. Thus, it has an inordinate love for the ephemeral attractions of the world.

On the Sufi path, the greater *jihād* (struggle) against the inclinations of the *nafs al-ammāra* is reflected in the statement of an early Sufi woman, Umm Talq, that "the *nafs* is king if you indulge it, but is a slave if you torment it."[6] One well-known Sufi, Ḥujwīrī, compares the *nafs* to an animal such as a wild horse or dog that needs to be trained or even enslaved to change its nature and teach it its place on the spiritual path.[7] Subduing the instinctual elements of self is seen as essential to spiritual purification, which in turn facilitates a deeper knowledge of God. Another early Sufi, Umm ʿAlī, reflects this insight in the view that "one who is confirmed in the knowledge of true servitude will soon attain the knowledge of lordship."[8] Thus, the first step in spiritual practice relates to the subjugation of the commanding self. Only then is it possible to attain knowledge of lordship—that is, the realization of the complete divine imperative of vicegerency that exists latently within all humanity.

The entity that represents the opposite of the lower soul is the spirit (*rūḥ*), which is a subtle life-giving entity blown into every human being from God's self (Q. 15:29). While the *nafs* is associated with the self-centeredness and blindness of the devil, the *rūḥ* has been associated with the angelic qualities of luminosity and discernment.[9] The Qurʾān states that "the spirit is from the command of my Lord and you [humanity] have been granted but a little knowledge of it" (Q. 17:85). Human beings are unable to understand the real nature of the *rūḥ*; suffice it to say that it reflects on that which pulls one toward God and the higher echelons of spiritual awareness.

The opposing spiritual forces activated by the respective inclinations of the *nafs al-ammāra* and the *rūḥ* struggle for supremacy within the individual's heart (*qalb*) and give rise to various thoughts, ideas, and impulses known as *khawāṭir*. Moral choice for the early masters depended on a careful analysis and discernment of these forces, the resultant *khawāṭir*, and the aspirants' responses.[10]

The third constituent, the *qalb*, is the center of human spiritual receptivity in the Sufi scheme. In a *ḥadīth qudsī*, God calls the human heart God's own abode, which is not to be confused with the physical heart, the emotions, or the rational mind. The heart is the spiritual center of the human being. However, the level of receptivity of the heart is contingent on the spiritual state of the individual. Through succumbing to evil *khawāṭir* and the torpor of earthly desires, most hearts become rusted or opaque.

This rust or veil on the heart can only be removed by persistent remembrance and invocation of God, abstinence from incorrect behavior, performance of good actions, including service to other human beings, and other rigorous spiritual practices.[11] As the aspirant pursues such spiritual disciplines, the commanding soul is weakened, abandoning evil commands and transforming into a different state of being known as the *nafs al-lawwāma*, "the blaming soul" (Q. 75:2). This transformation marks the emergence of the conscience, where the striving for good has been integrated and internalized. Thus the soul, aware of its own imperfections, reprimands the person if he or she inclines toward anything that constitutes spiritual negligence.

With consistent striving and purification, the heart is cleansed and illuminated by the divine light of the spirit, and the soul of the seeker is satisfied. It is then that the *nafs al-muṭmaʾinna*, "the soul at peace" (Q. 89:27), dominates the individual. This state is described in the *ḥadīth qudsī*, where God says, "The heavens and earth contain me not, but the heart of my faithful servant contains me."[12] For the mystic to fully realize the presence of God in the heart, it is necessary to entirely subdue and surrender those individualistic instincts that battle to remain sovereign. For Sufis, it is through the complete submission of the self to the Creator, through a pervasive state of *islām*, that real human potentiality can be attained.[13]

Gender Imbrications on the Sufi Path

Some Sufis have used gendered language to understand the different modes of spiritual engagement on the path. For example, some Sufis have described active spiritual striving, as reflected in the process of struggling against the instincts of the commanding self, as a "masculine" mode. At the same time, the soul, when it assumes the correct relationship of receptivity to the luminous impact of the spirit, can be cultivated, thereby facilitating the spiritual refinement of the human being. Some Sufis have described this receptive spiritual state as "feminine." Both "activity" described as "masculine" and "receptivity" depicted as feminine are necessary and complementary modes of being that are determined by the needs of a particular situation and relationship. Thus, all human beings, male or female, must assume a posture of receptivity to the divine while being active in subduing the commanding self. Only by successfully balancing these modes of spiritual refinement can human beings genuinely attain their inherent primordial capacity as God's vicegerent in the world. Despite the gendered use of these spiritual postures, they apply in equal measure to men and women on the spiritual path who generally share the assumptions, framework, and goals of Sufi psychology.

The *rūḥ*, *qalb*, and *nafs* constitute some of the central coordinates of human personality and psychology as reflected in Sufi thought. The primary focus on the spiritual dimensions of the human being, who, irrespective of gender, needs to traverse the spiritual path, provides Sufism with the resources to counter patriarchal constructs that emphasize gender hierarchy on the basis of biology. In particular, Sufism's essential critique of egotism presents an opportunity to challenge notions of male superiority. As such, an awareness of God's absolute sovereignty counters the human instinct to claim power, including men's claims to authority and lordship over women. Such human claims of supremacy demand interrogation and may be suspected as a potential trap of the lower self (*al-nafs al-ammāra*). The introductory anecdote concerning Ibn Taymiyya and Shaykha Fāṭima of Baghdad illustrates the possibilities for reproaching and disciplining the *nafs al-ammāra* as the provocateur of male chauvinism. No less than a vision of the Prophet himself allayed Ibn Taymiyya's prejudice and annoyance at a woman's assumption of public ritual leadership.[14]

Despite these resources for an internal critique of a patriarchal consciousness within Sufism, male Sufis have often not been immune to misogynist and sexist tendencies. Misogyny is mirrored in Sufi literature, where, for example, womankind is associated with the destructive attractions of the commanding soul.[15] Among some Sufi men, trepidation about the sexual drive as the malleable conduit of the *nafs al-ammāra* was translated into a more generalized trepidation regarding women.[16] This wariness toward women may have represented an outward projection of these men's inner struggle with their desires and desiring selves. Yet other male Sufis used more nuanced analogies. Abū Ṭālib al-Makkī (d. 996) equates the different states of the soul with different kinds of women: the licentious woman is associated with the soul that commands to evil, *al-nafs al-ammāra*; the blaming soul, *al-nafs al-lawwāma*, is mirrored by the righteous woman; while the virtuous woman whose being is characterized by a state of peace reflects the contented soul, *al-nafs al-muṭma'inna*.[17] Irrespective of the diverse images of women in these Sufi discourses, they all reflect the partiality and limitations of particular types of male subjectivity.

Notwithstanding the dominance of male subjectivities in these images, Sufis have also presented emancipatory possibilities for understanding and enacting gender. In a number of noteworthy cases, Sufism counts independent women among its most accomplished spiritual authorities. There are also examples of male Sufis who held gender-egalitarian views in their lives and their relationships with women. Many other Sufis effectively dismissed gender as irrelevant to spiritual station. Gender-emancipatory possibilities manifested in societies that were otherwise very patriarchal partly and perhaps significantly because of a central defining principle of Sufism—the primary value of a human being seems to lie in the state of the soul and not in biology or any other external marker.

Sufi psychology, with its approach to human drives and spiritual purification, has had varied implications for understandings of marriage and sexuality. On the one hand, one finds ascetic tendencies that in their most extreme manifestation have resulted in celibacy. Some Sufi men and women rejected marriage and sexual expression as an obstruction on the spiritual path. The general wariness toward the *nafs al-ammāra* resulted in sexual instincts also being viewed with suspicion. Some practitioners of asceticism, particularly among earlier Sufis, imposed arduous discipline on the body, such as abstinence from food, sleep, and physical comforts, as well as celibacy.

On the other hand, most Sufis have firmly advocated marriage on the basis of the *Sharīʿa*, have focused on the spiritual benefits accrued through marital relationships, and have married and had large families. Proponents of this approach have reflected the broader Islamic perspective that the legitimate satisfaction of the libido is natural and unproblematic for spiritual practice. Yet others suggested that sexual union allowed possibilities for spiritual epiphanies.

The coexistence of these different approaches to marriage and sexuality has been manifested throughout the history of Sufism. Some of the early strands in Islamic mysticism were defined by more strongly ascetic and celibate impulses. However, these impulses soon gave way to a more fully fledged mysticism that generally viewed marriage and sexuality in positive ways. The prevalence of this perspective among Sufis also reflected the dominant Islamic attitude that held marriage and sexuality as normative.

Asceticism, Celibacy, and Sexuality: Historical Developments

Origins

Muslim discourses on celibacy and marriage began during the Prophet Muḥammad's lifetime. Despite the reality that the Prophet Muḥammad, the preeminent Muslim role model, was fully immersed in the world as a spiritual, social, and political leader; as a husband and father; and as a prophet and reformer, some segments within the earliest Muslim community expressed world-renouncing tendencies. This phenomenon is reflected in various *ḥadīth* that record the Prophet's critique of rigid asceticism.

In one tradition, a group of exceedingly zealous companions reported to the Prophet that they prayed without sleeping, continually fasted, and remained celibate. He responded by encouraging moderation, stating, "I fast and I break fast, I pray and I sleep, I also marry women. This is my example. Those who are averse to my example are also averse to me."[18] Another tradition reports that when the Prophet heard that one of his followers had taken a vow of celibacy, he stated, "If you want to be a Christian monk, join them openly. If you are one of us you must follow our example and our example is married life."[19] That a significant number of such traditions exist where the Prophet rejected extreme asceticism suggests that he was speaking within a context where this tendency was already present and reaffirms the normative Muslim position that countered such tendencies.[20]

The Culture of Empire

After the Prophet's death, the flowering of an ascetic movement in Islam was part of a reaction to the sociopolitical ethos of the developing Muslim empire of the Umayyads and early ʿAbbāsids. The extensive corruption, hedonism, and materialism in the behavior of many Muslim rulers followed the accrual of vast wealth and earthly power by the expanding empire. With conquest came large numbers of female slaves and a growing imperial harem. Concubines were bought and sold, valued for beauty and providing sexual pleasure and other entertainment, including singing, dancing, poetry, and literary skills.[21]

Many Muslims became increasingly dissatisfied with the overall ethos of indulgence and hedonism that accompanied conquest. They rejected the way in which Islam was becoming merely a framework for political acquisition, material consumption, and physical gratification in ways that deflected from its fundamental ideals. Within this broader context of discontent with the status quo, a movement emerged whose proponents preached against the prevailing obsession with worldliness and sensual pleasure and were mostly practitioners of ascetic renunciation (*zuhd*). One famous early Sufi, Ḥasan al-Baṣrī (d. 728), personified this early asceticism, describing the world as a venomous snake, smooth to the touch but deadly.[22]

Many ascetics focused on forms of self-discipline. Many fasted continuously; when they ate, they were scrupulous about the permissibility of the food, not only in terms of its content but also in how it had been acquired. Furthermore, overeating was thought to provoke excessive sexual libido. Sufis believed that the endurance of hunger and discipline of the sexual instincts were integral parts of ascetic spiritual exercise.[23] Their mistrust toward sexual instincts constituted a part of the broader stringency toward all the senses and against the incitement of the *nafs al-ammāra*.[24]

Early Sufi wariness toward sexuality partly constituted a response to contextual realities of sexual excess and sensual satiety. Many ascetics were aware that they were living in a time of heightened moral decay, requiring aspirants to be supervigilant. That the degenerate nature of the times, different from the prophetic period, required the pious to adopt atypical coping mechanisms is reflected in a purported prophetic tradition: "After two hundred years, celibacy shall be permitted in my community."[25] For some of these ascetics, the translation of political power into sexual excess was cause for an anxiety that had implications for their constructions of gender relations and women.

In keeping with this point of view, Abū Sulaymān al-Dārānī (d. 830) held that as soon as his disciples married, they regressed a few steps on the spiritual ladder,[26] while the celibate Ibrāhīm ibn Adham (d. 776 or 790) warned that excessive preoccupation with marriage and family might result in spiritual destruction.[27] However, when a married Sufi admiringly commented on Ibn Adham's solitude and freedom to worship unburdened by family responsibilities, Ibn Adham circumspectly responded, "Your concern for your dependents is preferable to all which I now enjoy."[28] Ibn Adham thus presented a nuanced view of marriage that included an appreciation of the spiritual merit of marriage and family.

In contrast, an early married ascetic, Sufyān al-Thawrī, cautioned his disciples, "It will never go well for one who accustoms himself to the thighs of women."[29] What Thawrī meant by this comment is unclear. It is open to several interpretations. One obvious meaning is that he was cautioning about the incompatibility between excessive sex or carnal indulgence and spiritual growth. Excessive sexual desire stokes the baser instincts and no longer performs the role of pleasure, comfort, and relief. The views echoed by both Ibn Adham and Thawrī regarding sexual desire as potentially precarious for spiritual aspirations suggest understandings of embodiment characterized by the ancient split between body and spirit.

In addition, Thawrī appeared to harbor a rather negative view of women and wives. In his advice to novices, he cast the bachelor as holding an advantageous position over the married man: if the novice had the misfortune of a foolish or talkative wife, he would be saddled by her nagging and distracted by her disruptive behavior.[30] If Thawrī had a wicked sense of humor, his statement could be redeemed. If he truly held such denigrating views of women, then he would be consistent with other male Sufis who, despite their reverence for women who achieved spiritual excellence, could not unshackle themselves from broader prevailing negative gender stereotypes.

Some later Sufis retained negative images of wives with disagreeable personalities but nonetheless saw value in marriage. They suggested that a man who patiently endured a difficult wife was experiencing a substitute for the punishment of hellfire, so the experience was spiritually valuable.[31] In these cases, irrespective of whether marriage was viewed as spiritually beneficial, women's nature was stereotyped in rather negative ways.

Abū Ṭālib al-Makkī (d. 996), Ghazālī's forerunner, provided a more positive framing of the spiritual education that marriage might provide. He noted that "women require a large measure of gentle consideration, noble wisdom, goodness, generosity, a friendly manner and kind words."[32] For Makkī, marriage provides the spiritual aspirant with an opportunity for internal cultivation—a good Sufi is a caring, considerate, and compassionate husband. Indeed, the personal qualities that Makkī advises his disciples to foster in marriage reflect the broader demands of the Sufi path that call for character refinement through exemplary behavior. Makkī's particular description of desirable conduct in a husband fosters an ideal of marriage that promotes nurturing relationships rather than harsh, controlling interaction between spouses. Despite the fact that Makkī does not use negative stereotypes of women, he, like the other Sufis discussed, implicitly assumes that the spiritual aspirant is male.

These varying early Sufi narratives on marriage can be interpreted in a number of ways. One might read the pervasive male subjectivity reflected in all these positions as simply reflecting particular male voices that warn other men of the possible spiritual dangers of marriage and of meeting the needs of a spouse. In this case, the dominant female stereotypes embedded in such statements may simply reflect contextual understandings of women. One might thus read their cautionary approach to be less related to the nature of women than to the nature of marriage. If so, then the female spiritual aspirant could theoretically learn from these warnings in relation to the potential hazards of marriage and the difficulties of dealing with the needs of a male spouse. When read with sensitive gender lenses, these positions can be culled for a contemporary audience in ways that remain valuable to spiritual cultivation.

Conversely, the pervasive male subjectivity embedded in these narratives that speak unquestioningly to an implicitly male subject mirror an androcentric worldview. Women, when they do appear, are often objectified and constructed primarily in ways instrumental to their husband's spiritual progress. The assumption of a male Sufi norm implies a conceptualization of spiritual striving and progress as the prerogative of men. Such a reading also foregrounds the greater social visibility enjoyed by Sufi men as well as the dominance of male voices in knowledge production and dissemination. Within patriarchal societies, men certainly enjoyed more freedom than women to make unusual and nonnormative lifestyle choices such as asceticism.

Yet despite social obstacles, a significant number of women pursued the Sufi path. A marginalization of Sufi women in most official records reflects broader sociocultural factors and the more explicit gender biases of some male Sufis. Such marginalization may also be explained by the prevalence of a culture that placed (and quite often continues to place) women within the sanctified domestic realm, their honor implicitly respected through privacy.[33] Collectively, this approach has contributed to the general anonymity surrounding the lives of many of the earliest Sufi women. In spite of these impediments, some extant primary sources depict the lives of female Sufis. Like their male counterparts, these women have engaged with the realities of asceticism, spiritual discipline, celibacy, and marriage. Foregrounding the lives of some of these women by focusing on particular Sufi biographical or *ṭabaqāt* literature enables the construction of a more gender-balanced view of early Sufi approaches to questions in this area.

Sufi Women

Reading the Sufi biographical literature brings up some significant methodological issues. As with most other premodern literatures, the creators and authors of the *ṭabaqāt* genre are men. With few if any exceptions, early Sufi women appear only in images painted by male biographers.[34] Feminist historians have alerted us to the fact that male subjectivities dominate premodern texts across various religious and cultural contexts. The challenges of trying to arrive at understandings of women's realities in literary, historical, and religious canons authored by men are thus not limited to Islam or Sufism.

The importance of carefully studying all available sources is part of a feminist hermeneutics of recovery. A critical feminist reading of the canon not only exposes patriarchal biases and contests accepted interpretations but also excavates and creatively retrieves images of women positioned on the margins of the canon. Rita Gross's epistemological lead in retrieving images of women's historical and religious legacies is followed to redress the historical imbalance of depicting just half the human race as its religious ancestors.

So while the *ṭabaqāt* sources authored by men might or might not provide the most technically "accurate" representations of Sufi women's lives, the inclusion of women as Sufi practitioners in these sources creates a conceptual space for "accuracy" according to Gross's definition—that is, more accurately engaging the complete human condition by including women as part of its discourse.[35]

Given that Sufi *ṭabaqāt* literature has tended to focus largely on male Sufis, Abū ʿAbd al-Raḥmān al-Sulamī's (d. 1021) recently discovered manuscript on early Sufi women is a veritable treasure trove. This exceptional biographical text, *Dhikr al-niswa al-muta ʿabiddāt al-ṣūfiyyāt* (Memorial of Female Sufi Devotees), is devoted solely to the lives of Sufi women. In her illuminating translation of Sulamī's text, Rkia Cornell points out that even male biographers offered differing constructions of gender and varying depictions of female Sufis. She draws our attention to the way in which, for example, the earlier Sulamī tends to present Sufi women as equal to Sufi men in intellectual and religious capacities, whereas the later Abū al-Faraj ibn al-Jawzī (d. 1201) depicts the same Sufi women as more emotional and "woman-like."[36] Nonetheless, in a manner that would make any Islamic feminist proud, Ibn al-Jawzī firmly castigates another earlier biographer, Abū Nuʿaym al-Iṣfahānī (d. 1039), for generally ignoring pious women in his collection and thus continuing the stereotyping of women.[37] Similarly, as Cornell points out, Sulamī effectively counters popular notions of female deficiency in religion and intellect in a number of his biographies. He describes the sisters of Sulaymān al-Dārānī as having "attained an exalted level of intellect and religious observance"; he depicts Lubāba al-Mutaʿabbida as an expert in *fiqh al-ʿibāda* (the jurisprudence of worship); he states that Ḥukayma was a spiritual master of Damascus (and her name, as Cornell notes, also means "Dear Sage" or "Dear Philosopher").[38]

These assertions of women's religious and intellectual excellence by premodern Sufis are particularly meaningful in a context characterized by a pervasive discourse of female incapacity. A purported *ḥadīth* tradition that "women were deficient in intellect and religion" permeated the premodern gender landscape. In fact, this tradition seems to infuse the topography within which most premodern conversations on gender were articulated. The tradition links this female deficiency in intellect to the legal ruling that two women's legal testimony is equal to that of one man's in case of contracts of debt; further, the deficiency in religion is derived from the fact that women traditionally do not perform ritual prayer and fasting during menstruation. Notions of female legal incapacities are interwoven in the *ḥadīth* tradition with vivid depictions of hell as dominated by female inhabitants, who have been sent there as a result of their cursing and the ingratitude shown to their spouses.

Such female images within the canonical traditions fortified an entrenched discourse of female shortcomings vis-à-vis men within the broader religious imagination. The notion of "female deficiency" was embedded in the cultural backdrop inherited by all the Sufi premoderns, including Ibn ʿArabī. Echoes, affirmations, and refutations of this insidious trope of female deficiency flit through many Sufi engagements with gender. Despite their differing constructions of women, both Sulamī and Ibn al-Jawzī foreground the religious, intellectual, and spiritual accomplishments of Sufi women; these articulations contain unmistakable instances of defiance and resistance to patriarchal discourses of female deficiency. Unpacking these moments of resistance in the texts allows for the development of a "hermeneutics of reconstruction."

However, an intersecting methodological complication relates to the genre of *ṭabaqāt* literature. As Mojaddedi points out, the Sufi *ṭabaqāt* genre has a hagiographical flavor rather than presenting accurate biographical details.[39] The genre of sacred biographies shapes the representation of Sufis, both female and male, in ways that might be more connected to Muslim imaginations of piety and holiness than to historical accuracy.[40] The Sufi *ṭabaqāt* literature thus reflects a canvas of dominant Muslim images of pious personalities with possibly some level of insight into the lives of these individuals.

With these methodological caveats in mind, some of the early biographical collections do offer some significant insights into the images and at least some aspects of the lives of Sufi women. The earliest extant text is Sulamī's *Dhikr al-niswa al-muta ʿabiddāt al-ṣūfiyyāt*, discovered in 1991 and translated into English by Rkia Cornell in 2000. The manuscript has eighty-two entries, all of them about women. Abū Nuʿaym al-Iṣfahānī entered twenty-eight biographies of women in his collection, *Ḥilyat al-awliyāʾ wa ṭabaqāt al-aṣfiyāʾ* (The Ornaments of God's Friends and the Generations of the Pure Ones). Ibn al-Jawzī included 240 women in his *Ṣifāt al-ṣafwa* (The Description of the Elect).[41] Between the eighth and tenth centuries, many of the female mystics were located in Egypt, Khurasan, and Syria, especially in the major cities of Nishapur, Baghdad, and Basra.[42]

Some of these primary sources document the diverse ways in which early Sufi women pursued the path of piety. On the one hand, recent research suggests that many early women who pursued varying degrees of asceticism and spiritual discipline were also in fact subject to the normative social constraints—they lived typical lives, married, and bore children.[43] On the other hand, some independent female mystics apparently lived relatively free from much of the androcentric gender role expectations otherwise evident in their broader sociohistorical milieu. Some of these Sufi women, like their male contemporaries, lived independently, traveled on their own in search of knowledge, and had teachers and disciples of both sexes.[44] Yet others chose reclusive lives of solitude.

In the early period, ascetic female mystics appear to have provided an alternative to the dominant constructs of women as sexual objects associated with the realm of the senses. The early period saw two prominent schools of female mysticism led by female Sufi masters. One in Basra flourished between the eighth and ninth centuries C.E.; the other, in Syria, was most active in the ninth century C.E.[45]

Muʿādha al-ʿAdawiyya, who was both a wife and a mother, was the founder of the Basran school of female asceticism. She focused on prayer, extensive night vigils, and fasting and was extremely vigilant about eating permissible food.[46] When observing all-night prayer vigils and threatened with being overtaken by sleep, Muʿādha reportedly would wander around the house reprimanding herself, "Oh, soul! Eternal sleep is ahead of you. If I were to die, your repose in the grave would be a long one, whether it be sorrowful or happy."[47] Muʿādha's female disciples were known for their equally rigorous discipline. This Basran milieu of female asceticism provided the context for the emergence of Islam's most famous female mystic in Islam, Rābiʿa al-ʿAdawiyya (d. 801).

Ḥukayma of Damascus was one of the leading spiritual masters of the Syrian group of female ascetics. According to Sulamī, Syrian women's Sufism was defined by love for God (*maḥabba*), intimacy with God (*uns*), and fear of God (*khawf*).[48] While many of the Basran women Sufis were of foreign descent and tied to the Arab families as clients (*mawlayāt*), the Syrian women were generally of free Arab origin. Some of the Syrian women were independently wealthy and made philanthropy a significant part of their ascetic practice.[49] That early Muslim women practiced philanthropy is powerful and suggestive; at the very minimum, it suggests a level of socioeconomic clout that allowed them to engage powerfully with the public sphere.

Some Sufi women also appear to have bent normative gender expectations of place and space for women. Ibn al-Jawzī relates that some Syrian women, such as Umm Hārūn, undertook retreats into the countryside, and others, including ʿAthāma, took up peripatetic wandering and traveling for the sake of religion.[50] The fearless Umm Hārūn reportedly walked once a month from Damascus to Jerusalem, undaunted by any potential physical dangers.[51] While ordinary women might have generally been limited to the domestic sphere, obliged to undertake particular types of family responsibilities, and to embody traditional gender roles, these female Sufis embarked on solitary retreats or journeyed in search of knowledge.

Sufi recluses or travelers who had families would have been unavailable to them at least some of the time. In these instances, it appears that Sufi women's spiritual vocation allowed them an independence and mobility that contravened normative spatial boundaries of gender. Such Sufi women effectively reconstituted the dominant sexual geography that limited and contained the spaces that women inhabited and redefined the nature of their social and familial relationships with men.

While some early Sufi women married, others did not and remained celibate. Celibate Sufi women were generally excluded from the traditional female roles of wife and mother as well as the domestic responsibilities these roles generally entailed in that era. Moreover, some Sufis, apparently influenced by Christian asceticism, entered into "spiritual marriages," in which a Sufi woman and man married and lived together as "sister and brother," without engaging in sexual relations.[52]

Rābiᶜa bint Ismāᶜīl proposed a nonsexual marriage to the Sufi Aḥmad ibn al-Ḥawārī (d. 851). She candidly informed him that she had no desire for sexual relations with him but felt a spiritual kinship with him. Her proposal, she explained, was motivated by a longing to serve him and his Sufi brethren by putting at their disposal her considerable finances. Once married, she rebuffed his sexual advances because of her desire to maintain her fast during the day and her exclusive devotion to God at night. Rābiᶜa actively encouraged Aḥmad to take other wives to satisfy his sexual needs and even provided him with the money for their dowries.[53] Indeed, as he prepared to visit his other wives, she would perfume him and present him with sweetmeats to take to them. This early Sufi woman thus was not only the financial guardian in her marriage but also a powerful inscriber of conjugal boundaries, dictating the sexual dynamics of her relationship.

On hearing that Aḥmad had taken another wife, Rābiᶜa's female spiritual teacher, Ḥukayma, commented somewhat acerbically, "Given what I have been told about his good judgment, how could his heart be distracted from God by two women?"[54] More than mere female solidarity, such a comment represents hard-hitting criticism of the spiritual station of a man with multiple spouses. Aḥmad is implicated as the less evolved spiritual seeker, self-indulgent, and preoccupied with relations other than with God. By contrast, Rābiᶜa occupies a superior rank in this particular discursive space. These Sufi women seem to view celibacy as a superior spiritual choice made by more valiant seekers of God.

Some Sufi women entered into more conventional marriages that did not appear to obstruct their progress on the mystical path. On the contrary, some married Sufi women shared their spiritual vocations with their husbands and appear to have had relationships marked by tenderness and great affection. Muʿādha and her husband spent entire nights together in ascetic devotion. When he died, she revealed her enduring love for him by expressing her deep desire to be reunited with him in heaven. On her own deathbed, she laughed joyfully at a vision of her late husband heralding her transition to the next world.[55]

Evidence also suggests that the marriages of some Sufi women were characterized by unusual power dynamics. These married Sufi women did not assume submissive gender roles and behaved rather assertively and autonomously. Umm ʿAlī Fāṭima (d. 849) proposed marriage to her future husband, a Sufi aspirant, Aḥmad Khiḍrūya; when he failed immediately to accept her offer, she persisted until he acquiesced.[56] Umm ʿAlī Fāṭima is also known to have consulted with some of the most prominent mystics of the time, including Bāyazīd al-Bisṭāmī. On one such occasion, she lifted her veil in the presence of Bāyazīd al-Bisṭāmī, causing her husband consternation and jealousy. She responded, "You are intimate with my physical self. Abū Yazīd is intimate with my spiritual way. You rouse my passion. He brings me to God. The proof of this is that he can dispense with my company, whereas you need me."[57]

According to Ḥujwīrī, Fāṭima continued to treat Bāyazīd with the same boldness until the day he commented on her henna-stained hands, when she terminated their relationship, informing him, "Oh Bāyazīd so long as you did not see my hand and henna, I was at ease with you, but now that your eye has fallen on me, our companionship is unlawful."[58] Fāṭima's comment is revealing and compelling: Sufi friendships between men and women had to navigate the complex and at times contradictory and fraught realm of materiality and sexuality. When Fāṭima perceived a shift in awareness in Bāyazīd—a preoccupation with the realm of the body—she reinstated socially appropriate boundaries.

Annemarie Schimmel notes that the authenticity of this story is uncertain given that it expresses a deeper motif of "spiritual friendship destroyed by a worldly glance" that characterizes Sufi hagiography.[59] Other stories concerning Fāṭima and her husband suggest that they were fellow travelers on the mystical path and that her husband acquiesced to her in decisions on various matters.[60] The narratives surrounding Fāṭima present us with images not only of a self-assured and spiritually developed individual but also of a powerful woman who singularly determines the contours and parameters of her interactions with men.

Female Virtuosity, Power, and Language

While some Sufi women were also disciples of male teachers, some Sufi women taught male Sufis. Rābiʿa al-ʿAdawiyya is known to have been a teacher to Sufyān al-Thawrī;[61] Fāṭima of Nishapur instructed famous male Sufis such as Bāyazīd al-Bisṭamī and Dhūʿn-Nūn al-Miṣrī; and the public lectures of Wahaṭiyya Umm al-Faḍl in Nishapur were attended by most of the city's Sufi masters.[62]

Fāṭima of Nishapur was recognized as a spiritual authority by her male cohorts and students. Asked by an older male Sufi to reveal the identity of the most excellent person he knew, Dhūʿn-Nūn singled out Fāṭima, whom he described as "a saint from among the friends of God, the Glorious and Mighty. She is also my teacher [*ustādhī*]."[63] Similarly, Bāyazīd al-Bisṭāmī said of Fāṭima, "In all my life I have only seen one true man and one true woman. The woman was Fāṭima of Nishapur. There was no station about which I had told her that she had not already undergone."[64] Bāyazīd's construction of gender is ripe and suggestive—the "one true woman" preceded him in the attainment of all spiritual stations. The true woman embarks and attains the same spiritual stations as does the true man—the path of spiritual cultivation does not heed gender differences.

Elsewhere, Bāyazīd uses somewhat more ambivalent gendered language to describe Fāṭima's exalted spiritual state: "If any man desires to see a true man hidden in women's clothes, let him look at Fāṭima."[65] This ideologically loaded manner of describing spiritually accomplished women as male is not uncommon in Sufism. As with Sulamī's description of Ḥukayma of Damascus, Dhūʿn-Nūn's description of Fāṭima employs the masculine form of the word *ustādh*.

Cornell points out that the use of the masculine term *ustādh* is intended to signify these women's spiritual mastery.[66] This technique parallels a use of gendered language also found in *ḥadīth* literature, where all authoritative transmitters are described as *rijāl* (men), irrespective of their physical identities. According to Cornell, the practice is intended to convey that these women were considered as knowledgeable as and equal to the male Sufi masters of the time.[67] Similarly, Ibn ʿArabī uses the term *rujūliyya* (manliness) in a gender-inclusive way to signify the state of spiritual realization characterizing the friends of God. He explicitly informs us that this realization of *rujūliyya* lies in embodying the virtues of such a state, irrespective of whether a person is male or female.[68]

Another masculine term that is applied in a gender-inclusive manner in the Sufi tradition is *futuwwa*, which literally translates as "young manliness," signifying the concept of spiritual chivalry. Sulamī states that "*futuwwa* means following the ordinances of perfect devotion, leaving all evil and attaining in action and in thought the best of visible and hidden good conduct."[69] In the Sufi tradition, the *fatā* (spiritual warrior) wages a war against her lower self (*jihād al-nafs*) and consistently prioritizes the needs of others. Once again, we find that active struggle and spiritual exertion are described as a "masculine" mode of being.

In Sufism, the defining qualities of nobility, generosity, and altruism of a true spiritual warrior were epitomized in the Prophet Muḥammad, as reflected in a statement by Abū ʿAlī al-Daqqāq (d. 1015): "This characteristic [*futuwwa*] only reached its perfection in the Messenger of God. At the resurrection, everyone will be saying 'Myself, myself!' but he will be saying 'My people, my people!'"[70] According to Sulamī, spiritual refinement aims to foster a state of being in the practitioner so that he or she responds in precisely the appropriate manner with the correct etiquette demanded in each and every situation and relationship.[71]

The virtue encompassed by the concept of *futuwwa* appears to capture some of the central goals of the Sufi path, which is why a Sufi such as Kāshānī (d.1335) suggests that *futuwwa* is the penultimate stage of the spiritual path, just prior to reaching the *walāya*, or status as friend of God.[72] Thus, it is not surprising that despite its masculine form, Sufis, including Ibn ʿArabī and Sulamī, have also used the term *fityān* or *futuwwa* to describe a number of exemplary Sufi female practitioners.[73] In addition, a complementary if underdeveloped term, *niswān*, is used to describe the collective identity of female practitioners of spiritual chivalry. Derived from the term *nisāʾ*, which refers to ordinary women, *niswān* in this context denotes an expression of enhancement—that is, a special group of women of the spirit.[74] As Cornell points out, insufficient early source material is currently available to determine the exact meaning and significance of *niswān*.

Farīd al-Dīn ʿAṭṭār's entry on Rābiʿa al-ʿAdawiyya in his *Tadkhirat al-awliyāʾ* is accompanied by a revealing comment.[75] He states that if he were asked why he included Rābiʿa in the "ranks of men," he would answer that God does not look at the outward form but at the intention of the heart.[76] This statement is noteworthy on two counts. First, ʿAṭṭār begins with a defense of his inclusion of Rābiʿa in his biographical collection, thereby suggesting that he anticipated resistance from his readers. Perhaps his male audience was still reluctant to accept women as Sufi masters. Second, despite his declaration that God does not look at the outward form, Rābiʿa is the only woman included in this biographical collection.

ʿAṭṭār is reported to have said, "When a woman becomes a man in the path of God she is a man and one can no longer call her a woman."[77] He added that the first *man* to enter paradise would be Mary, the mother of Jesus.[78] The Indian Sufi Farīd al-Dīn Ganji Shakar (d. 1265) called the female Sufi master Fāṭima "a man sent in the form of a woman."[79] Some Sufis have used this type of gender discourse in descriptions of spiritually advanced women as either being quintessentially "male"—that is, men sent in female form—or as women whose unusual progress has gained them the status of "male."[80]

Such views and gendered language about accomplished Sufi women are double-edged. On the one hand, these men attempted to describe women as spiritual savants in societies that were becoming increasingly patriarchal. Being enmeshed in the mores and gendered language of their time, they attempted to articulate a reality that transcended biology. The fact that the ninth-century Dhūʾn-Nūn describes Fāṭima as the most excellent Sufi he knew or that the thirteenth-century ʿAṭṭār placed Mary at the apex of spiritual attainment, even preceding men into paradise, implies recognition of women's full spiritual capacities. On the other hand, that spiritual mastery is fundamentally connected to maleness and that these female Sufis can be fully celebrated only when they are depicted as taking on a male persona reflects the deeply patriarchal nature of the discursive field. The metaphor of "becoming male" used for spiritually enlightened women is premised on a religious anthropology that does not assimilate the category of femaleness into a notion of human spiritual completion. In these instances, "maleness" almost assumes the status of an ontological category and is understood as the de facto norm and point of departure for complete spiritual attainment.

Within the Sufi paradigm, real "maleness" symbolized more than gender. It signified the state of spiritual activity that was seldom accorded even to biological men, as Bisṭāmī indicated with his comment that he had seen only one "true man." The language and consciousness are fully steeped in androcentric norms. Yet the fact that women attained the most exalted spiritual stations and were recognized as having done so simultaneously negated the patriarchal dominance in Sufism. In fact, Bisṭāmī's recognition that Fāṭima, the "one true woman," had full access to all spiritual stations presents a linguistic counternarrative to the prevalent Sufi language on gender. In addition, in that context, there are "gender-rich" anecdotes regarding the lives of Sufis that counter some of the androcentricism of the prevalent language.

These rich, ambivalent, and contesting uses of gendered language suggest the complexities of ways in which gender, power, and spirituality were negotiated within the early Islamic tradition. In fact, such usage exemplifies an observation by Grace Jantzen, a scholar of Christian mysticism, who notes that there were various ways in which "women and men of spirit forced reconsideration of the categories by which they were defined and thereby in turn effected changes in the structures of power and gender which delimited them."[81]

Counternarratives on Gender

Stories and anecdotes about the lives of Sufis present a number of narratives of women that disrupt masculinist assumptions. According to one such tale, Dhūʿn-Nūn al-Miṣrī rejected a present from Fāṭima of Nishapur early in their acquaintance because she was a woman. She neatly responded that a true Sufi does not focus on the secondary cause—in this case, the fact that the giver was a woman—but rather on the Original Cause and the Eternal Giver.[82] Instead of disputing the relative merits of women and men, she incisively transcends superficial ego-based discussions, invoking instead questions of ultimate reality.

In another narrative, Rābiʿa al-ʿAdawiyya was visited by a group of religious men who tried to goad her into responding inappropriately. They declared, "All the virtues have been scattered on the heads of men. The crown of prophethood has been placed on men's heads. The belt of nobility has been fastened around men's waists. No woman has ever been a prophet." Rābiʿa calmly replied, "All that is true, but egoism and self-worship and 'I am your Lord' have never sprung from a woman's breast. . . . All these things have been the specialty of men."[83] She thus points out how the *nafs al-ammāra* has conquered men through their chauvinism and male ego, blinding them to the real nature of power and truth. More especially, Rābiʿa articulates the quintessential Sufi principle that the ultimate concerns are the state of one's soul and correct orientation to God. Everything that detracts from this orientation, such as social prestige and gender hierarchy, may be spiritually detrimental.

Other Sufi narratives reflect unconventional relationships between men and women in contexts that otherwise appear to be fairly restrictive. These accounts often describe egalitarian and intense relationships between unrelated Sufi men and women who share a spiritual vocation. Sufi literature also recognizes women as accomplished spiritual savants who were teachers to men and women alike in stories that are rather evocative and suggestive.

One of the most well known of such stories reflects the superior spiritual attainment of a woman Sufi vis-à-vis her male counterpart. Ḥasan saw Rābiʿa near a lake and sought to impress her by throwing his prayer rug onto the surface of the water and calling to her to join him in prayer. She responded, "Ḥasan, when you are showing off your spiritual goods in the worldly market, it should be things that your fellow people are incapable of displaying." She then threw her prayer mat into the air, flew up to it, and asked Ḥasan to join her. Since Ḥasan's spiritual powers did not extend to this station, he was silenced. Rābiʿa used this as a teaching moment: "Ḥasan, what you did, fish also do, and what I did, flies also do. The real work transcends both these tricks. One must apply oneself to the real work."[84]

This anecdote ironically illustrates that Rābiʿa's "spiritual goods" are in fact of a superior nature and capacity to those of Ḥasan, one of the foremost male Sufis of the time. However, far more significant is the fact that Rābiʿa unmasks the fruitless nature of spiritual conceit and sensationalist miracles. She teaches that spiritual progress is about stripping the self of delusions of superiority; that ego-based desire for social recognition can insidiously penetrate spiritual pursuits; and that the focus on God is never to be compromised by such inclinations. By clearly depicting Rābiʿa's greater wisdom, the story illustrates that spiritual attainment is not determined by gender. In some of these stories, men exhibit the baser spiritual vices of arrogance, vanity, and self-importance, and women emerge as witty, wise, and spiritually advanced, displaying superior insights into mystical realities.

All these narratives present woman savants who have truly internalized the essential dimensions of Islam and who are thus singularly concerned with purifying the God-human relationship through diminishing the *nafs al-ammāra* so that the heart can reflect the realities of the divine. The men in these stories are depicted as conceited and chauvinistic, creating gender hierarchies that veil them from perceiving the true nature of reality. Men's assumptions of superiority are depicted as reflections of their spiritual inadequacies and are confronted as such. The women in these stories appear to be free from delusions of self-importance and thus appear to have attained more profound insights into the real power that animates all beings. In these tales, women articulate central Sufi principles, compelling challenges to the basis of gender discrimination. The stories of Rābiʿa and Fāṭima teach us to challenge patriarchy insomuch as it reflects humanity's baser inclinations of the *nafs al-ammāra*. If interpreted in this manner, progress on the spiritual path can imply direct challenges to patriarchal impulses as they arise.

Love Mysticism

Rābiʿa al-ʿAdawiyya exemplifies women's capacity to represent the heights of spiritual progress in Sufism. She may have been among the first Sufis to advocate the doctrine of pure, disinterested love of God for God's own sake, unattached and disinterested in its outcome, combining this idea with a doctrine of *kashf*, or unveiling of the divine Beloved.[85] Prioritizing the element of sincere and selfless love for God as the focus of her existence, she was skeptical of those for whom asceticism became the goal, clouding the ultimate objective of attaining intimacy with the Beloved.[86] Rābiʿa lived a thoroughly ascetic life, but only as a means to this end. Unmoved by the fear of hellfire or the desire for paradise, her love for God was so absolute that there was no room left for anyone else, including the Prophet.[87] Because of her complete devotion to God, she rejected marriage proposals from a number of suitors, telling one, "The marriage knot can only tie one who exists. Where is existence here? I am not my own—I am His and under His command."[88]

In this story, too, mystical experiences implicitly imbibed a gender politics: Rābiʿa rejected marriage and the accompanying authority of a husband that was normative in her context. Mysticism freed her from traditional gender role expectations, which in turn provided her with social independence and autonomy. Moreover, the mysticism of the celibate Rābiʿa was defined by a consuming and passionate love of God that had profound implications for the subsequent development of Sufism.

Following Rābiʿa's trajectory, Dhūʿn-Nūn (d. 859) focused intently on sincerity of love and intimacy with God. Meditating on the coexistence of opposing divine qualities of beauty (*jamāl*) and majesty (*jalāl*), he focused on the manifestations of these names in creation.[89] Contrary to many earlier ascetics who despised the world as a veil distracting one from God, Dhūʿn-Nūn stated that because all of creation worshipped God, the whole world was imbued with religious meaning, waiting to be unveiled.[90] Within the development of Sufism, Dhūʿn-Nūn's approach represents some of the shift from the world-transcending approach of the earlier ascetics to a more world-affirming approach, later echoed strongly in the works of Ibn ʿArabī. Dhūʿn-Nūn's love for nature as a reflection of God's beauty marked the way in which Sufis increasingly focused on the spiritual possibilities of physical form. This shift facilitated more positive approaches to materiality and the human body, which ultimately had implications for Sufi views on sexuality.

The growth of Sufism into "love mysticism" transformed the language and understandings of the mystical quest. Asceticism was increasingly understood as a means to an end rather than as an end in itself, and approaches to celibacy became more diverse. Sahl al-Tustarī (d. 896), an advocate of severe ascetic practices such as extensive fasting, refused to practice celibacy, stating that the "lord of the ascetics," the Prophet Muḥammad, loved women.[91] However, Sufis continued to debate questions of celibacy for a significant period of time.

One eleventh-century Sufi, Ḥujwīrī, favored celibacy, advocating fasting as a means to contain sexual desire. He believed that marriage was unnecessary since lust could be extinguished by self-restraint and exertion.[92] Memorable and mordant, his views on women are reflected in the statement that from creation to the present, all mischief, both worldly and religious, was caused by women.[93] Ḥujwīrī saw sexuality as a vice and a distraction from the spiritual path. This sexuality/spirituality dualism locates women in the sexual realm as the antithesis of spirituality, which is, by definition, male. As such, women pose a threat and danger to male spiritual seekers, a view that reverberates through a range of religious positions that exclude or marginalize women in sacred spaces.

Junayd (d. 910) of Baghdad articulated a more moderate position on sexuality. He advised that only beginners along the Sufi path needed to practice celibacy and then only temporarily. Thereafter, he deemed marriage and sexuality appropriate and necessary. He decried rigid asceticism and instead advocated a balanced if somewhat functionalist approach to physical appetites, stating, "I need sex like I need food."[94] Junayd's approach reflected a view that saw the sexual appetite as a natural phenomenon needing to be legitimately satisfied. Doing so would remove distractions from the soul and allow the aspirant to focus on the spiritual path.

More optimistically yet, other Sufis did not simply view sexuality, marriage, and family in a utilitarian manner but focused on the spiritual value of human love relationships. Sahl al-Tustarī stated that while love for money and food might reflect a failure to heed God, "The love of parents and children does not drive out the love of God from [a man's] heart. God himself has planted it in a man's heart as his natural disposition. Neither is love for God excluded by the love for your wife in so far as it signifies goodness and tenderness towards her."[95]

This same ethos is reflected in the words of a much later Indian Sufi, Khwāja Mīr Dard of Delhi (d. 1785), who stated simply, "I love my wife and my children dearly."[96] The ideas of both Sahl al-Tustarī and Khwāja Mīr Dard reflect a Sufi view that human and spousal love share a divine origin, a view that formed part of the broader Islamic ethos, given its Qurʾānic basis. In the development of Sufism, an affirming view of love and marriage competed with a more celibate tendency that sought to avoid conventional expectations regarding sex, marriage, and family.[97]

Given that the love for God grew into the driving force of Islamic mysticism, Sufis such as Aḥmad al-Ghazālī (d. 1126), ʿAyn al-Quḍāt al-Hamadhānī (d. 1132), and Rūzbihān Baqlī (d. 1209) deliberated on the spiritual and pedagogic value of human love as the means through which to purify the love for God.[98] ʿAbd al-Raḥmān Jāmī (d. 1492) states that through human love, "the lover ascends on to the highest beauty, to the love and knowledge of the Divinity, by steps of this ladder of created souls."[99] Bahāʾ al-Dīn Walad (d. 1230) found female beauty and the joys of legitimate pleasure and lovemaking to be a means of reflecting on the vision of God and God's creative power.[100] These ideas echo Ibn ʿArabī's (d. 1240) approach to marriage and sexuality.

For the later Jalāl al-Dīn Rūmī (d. 1273), love can completely transform the human substance because love is an attribute of God through which humans are freed from the limitations that define their state in the world.[101] Love for God is the aim of every thought, behavior, and feeling fully consuming the seeker. For some Sufis, this love found its object in a human being who reflected divine beauty, a view that in some cases led to accusations of incarnationist (*ḥulūlī*) beliefs.[102] These developments contrast with the love mysticism of early Sufis, among them, Rābiʿa al-ʿAdawiyya, whose love for God was so absolute that it did not allow space for the love of any human being. The early mystics were much warier of directing love toward another human because of the potential for corruption.

Significant male homoerotic elements appear in some Persian and Turkish love mysticism, where the handsome adolescent boy, "radiant like the full moon," is seen as the ideal of human beauty.[103] The austere Ḥujwīrī strongly denounced associations with boys and condemned the concept of *naẓar ilā al-aḥdāth*, "looking at young men," which was prevalent among some Sufis.[104] A statement by one early Sufi, Sufyān al-Thawrī, "If a man played with the toes of a boy desiring sensual pleasure, that would be sodomy," suggests an awareness of homoerotic elements that began in the earliest period.[105] In the ninth century, Abū Saʿīd al-Kharrāz reported a dream in which Iblīs (Satan) boasted that one of the ways he beguiled Sufis was through their love for sitting with unbearded boys.[106]

Some male Sufis also saw women as repositories of divine beauty who inspired intense love, desire, and longing, as reflected in an epic romance, *Layla and Majnūn*. A Sufi woman, Niẓām, who was noted for her beauty and wisdom, inspired Ibn ʿArabī's *Tarjumān al-ashwāq* (The Interpreter of Desires). According to Ibn ʿArabī, the mystic is enraptured by the human beloved, who is a *shāhid*, or a true witness to divine beauty. This notion of the concealment of preeternal beauty in created form became known as *iltibās*.[107] Since "God is beautiful and loves beauty," beauty in creation is revealed to evoke love in the heart. This appreciation and deification of human beauty provides a remarkable contrast to the views of the early Sufi Abū Sulaymān al-Dārānī, who advised his disciples that if they needed to marry, it would be closer to ascetic practice to marry an old, poor, ugly woman instead of a rich, young, beautiful one.

Conclusion

Sufi history contains a range of competing approaches to gender, sexuality, and marriage. Stringent asceticism with proclivities toward celibacy appears most starkly apparent within the first two centuries of Islam. However, the success of the early ascetic movement must be understood within the context of the perceived spiritual depravity and sensual excesses characterizing the court culture of the Umayyad and early ʿAbbāsid empires. While asceticism was an integral part of the debates on sexuality and marriage in subsequent Sufi discourse, asceticism did not necessarily and always imply celibacy.

The proponents of marriage had varying understandings of its functions and importance. For the most part, marriage was simply part of the prophetic example and thus needed to be emulated. Some saw marriage as a means to assuage the sexual appetite in a healthy manner, thereby allowing the Sufi aspirant more easily to pursue the rigors of spiritual discipline. With the development of love mysticism, however, there was a growth in the tendency to view love and sexual desire as emotions connected to love for God and God's manifestations in the world. These varying perspectives on sexuality and marriage formed some of the spiritual currents within Islam.

Despite the diversity of approaches to marriage and sexuality, some central Sufi principles are relevant to questions of gender:

- an intrinsic prioritization of the spiritual state of the individual over external markers of identity, whether configured through gender or other social stratifications;
- the varying dynamics of personality and spiritual psychology, the *jihād* against the *nafs al-ammāra*, and the discipline necessary in the purification of the heart are all ungendered and equally applicable to men and women;
- an inherent wariness of egotism and personal claims of superiority, including those based in gender difference, which may be traps of the *nafs al-ammāra* set to lead one to spiritual destruction; and
- a fundamental assumption that the spiritual path makes equal demands on all human beings, men and women, and that all can realize the totality of its ultimate goals.

These quintessential Sufi principles embedded within the foundations of the discourse provide powerful resources for imagining a more egalitarian approach to gender. Moreover, these assumptions historically have contributed to allowing Sufi women to pursue nonnormative lifestyles and attain the heights of spiritual development. The largely accepted nature of these spiritual tenets has enabled some Sufi men to invoke, recognize, and celebrate the spiritual mastery of female adepts and to defend such stances within a Sufi discursive framework. These central principles of Sufism serve as one foundation from which to develop an organically emancipatory gender imaginary for Muslims. These primary spiritual and psychological constructs also provide generative spaces for Islamic feminists to interrogate sexist understandings of Sufism itself. These central Sufi assumptions also provide a context in which to approach the life and ideas of Ibn ʿArabī.

Chapter Two

Charting Ibn ʿArabī's Religious Anthropology

It is a beautiful starlit night. Ibn ʿArabī, a Sufi teacher revered throughout Muslim lands, is within the sacred precincts of the Kaʾba, the cubelike focal point of Muslim prayers in Mecca.[1] This evening, the house of worship is characterized by a feeling of almost intense quiet despite the large number of devotees. Savoring the gentle breeze caressing his face, Ibn ʿArabī experiences a profound state of tranquility. Circling the outer perimeter of the holy sanctuary, he becomes increasingly oblivious of his surroundings, his state of contemplation simultaneously expanding and intensifying. Suddenly, a few lines of poetry leap to his lips from within the hidden recesses of his being, reflecting an unexpectedly deep inner perplexity.

> If only I were aware whether they knew what heart they possessed!
> How my heart would like to know what mountain paths they have taken!
> Do you deem them safe and sound, or do you suppose that they have perished?
> Lovers remain perplexed in love, exposed to every peril![2]

Hardly have the words left his lips when a hand softer than silk touches his shoulder. He turns. A young woman of breathtaking beauty gazes intently at him. As if omniscient, she responds to his poetic rumination with a depth of spiritual discernment, subjecting each line of his poem to careful scrutiny, culminating in a reprimand: How can "the great mystic of the time" possibly question God's knowledge of his state? A true lover is content with the desires of the Beloved even when they entail absence and separation. Tenderly, she informs him that a sincere devotee cannot preserve even "a residue of perplexity and hesitation, since the very condition of adoration is that it fills the soul entirely"; a real love "puts the senses to sleep, ravishes the intelligences, does away with thoughts, and carries away its slave in the stream of those who vanish." "Where then is there room for perplexity?" demands the young maiden, Niẓām, again admonishing the older male sage with a final, "It is unworthy of you to say such things!"[3]

In castigating Ibn ʿArabī for his ratiocentric ruminations about God's knowledge of his spiritual state, Niẓām invokes a central teaching that lies at the heart of the mystical tradition—true knowledge and its attendant, sincere love, necessitate that one resist the intrusive anxieties of the mind. Knowledge and love are inextricably entwined and should leave no room for uncertainty in one's devotion. In this encounter, Niẓām represents divine wisdom, illuminating the ways of love and the momentary doubts that may arise in its pursuit.[4] Instructing Ibn ʿArabī about the subtleties of the inner path, Niẓām epitomizes the spiritual master who alerts the disciple to his failings and directs him to the correct path.

This encounter, reported by Ibn ʿArabī, embodies an important Sufi principle—depth of mystical insight is not contingent on outer markers of identity, be they social status and reputation, age and life experience, or gender. The narrative represents a young, relatively inexperienced woman who confidently instructs the older, well-known male sage about the appropriate existential mode for a seeker in the quest for the divine. In addition to the essential mystical teaching that Niẓām elucidates for Ibn ʿArabī, this story presents a unique depiction of female subjectivity and gender dynamics within normative structures of patriarchy.

Listening to such a compelling narrative, contemporary readers might legitimately wonder whether the woman at the center of Ibn ʿArabī's narrative is an actual historical figure or merely reflects a deeply entrenched literary trope of men representing women as purveyors and teachers of wisdom. Elizabeth Clark, a feminist historian of Christianity, notes that representations of women as teachers of wisdom can be found in a variety of male-authored works, among them Diotima in Plato's *Symposium* and a number of early Christian female ascetics, such as Macrina in Gregory of Nyssa's *Vita Macrinae*.[5] Such images of women, Clark writes, are less (if at all) concerned with the subjectivity of actual women than with creating narrative tropes of women that enable men to communicate a particular set of ideas.[6] According to Clark feminist readers examining these enduring motifs of women as teachers of wisdom will find value in the ways in which the text reflects a particular "social logic"—that is, how specific constructions of women and gender mirror social forces at work in particular texts. By attending to and expanding this social logic, Clarke suggests possibilities for uncovering the related "theological logic" articulated by male authors.[7] Drawing on Kathleen Wider's study on Diotima and other ancient Greek female philosophers, it seems that even when women are part of a larger tropological construct, one cannot infer that they were fictitious or even that they are being inaccurately depicted.[8] However, the lack of corroborating source texts often means that it is not possible to make judgments about the historical accuracy of such depictions of women.

Niẓām in particular traverses multiple registers within Ibn ʿArabī's works: she articulates core and central Sufi insights; she appears as a narrative construction of female wisdom reflecting the gendered religious and social logic at play in a male-authored text; at other times, she appears as a young woman with whom Ibn ʿArabī shared a deep relationship;[9] and she simultaneously serves as a signifier of ways in which images of women glimmer at the borders of canonical discourse. The figure of Niẓām and the varying ways in which she is depicted by Ibn ʿArabī have implications for his religious anthropology and how it is gendered.

In this chapter, I focus on the mystical hermeneutic embodied by the exchange between Ibn ʿArabī and Niẓām at the Kaʾba. Her criticism of Ibn ʿArabī's moment of rational, philosophical doubt echoes one of the major epistemological discussions in Islamic intellectual life: the relationship between cognitive, rational forms of knowledge as reflected primarily in philosophical approaches and mystical modes of knowing as embodied by the Sufis. I explore the substantive intellectual result of Ibn ʿArabī's mystical experiences—that is, his cosmology and view of human nature and purpose. I then turn to some of the ways in which Ibn ʿArabī presents an understanding of humanity in relation to the sociopolitical and legal realms.

Epistemological Contentions: Philosophy and Sufism

During Ibn ʿArabī's lifetime, the task of bringing Sufi teachings into the mainstream of Islamic intellectual life had already been initiated by his predecessor, Abū Ḥāmid al-Ghazālī. The pioneering Ghazālī nudged Sufism, which hitherto had been the preserve of smaller groups of mystical practitioners and thinkers, into the mainstream of intellectual discussions in the twelfth century. Following in the footsteps of the protean *Ḥujjat al-Islām*,

Ibn ʿArabī further expanded the boundaries of public intellectual discourse, drawing on all the major intellectual modes of expression current and using jurisprudential, poetic, theological, philosophical, and mystical languages. William C. Chittick points out that the harmonization of various intellectual perspectives within Islam occurred from the thirteenth century onward through the contributions of other major thinkers, including Shihāb al-Dīn Suhrawardī (d. 1191), founder of the Ishrāqi (Illuminationist) school of philosophy, and Naṣīr al-Dīn Ṭūsī (d. 1274), the first systematic Shiʿī theologian and reviver of the Avicennian philosophical tradition.[10] Given the ascendancy of particular philosophical debates in that intellectual milieu, Ibn ʿArabī's ability comfortably to employ philosophical language and schema while simultaneously transcending the constraints of philosophy enabled him to appeal to the intellectual ethos of his time.

One of the enduring problems that confronted not only Muslim philosophers but also their Greek predecessors was how to reconcile a God of absolute unity and perfection with the bewildering multiplicity and imperfections of creation. How does one tailor a divine originator swathed in eternity with creatures cut from the cloth of materiality and mortality? Given the fundamental Islamic belief in the oneness of God (*tawḥīd*), the philosophers struggled with the question of the emergence of multiplicity from that one reality. Muslim philosophers faced the challenge of formulating a solution that addressed the demands of logic without contradicting Qurʾānic doctrines. They were often not entirely successful in meeting this requirement.[11]

In his *Tahāfut al-falāsifa*, Ghazālī rejected precisely those ratiocentric philosophical arguments that appeared to contradict Qurʾānic teachings.[12] References to philosophy at the time primarily signified Aristotelianism, the dominant philosophical school in that intellectual landscape. Ghazālī argued that the Qurʾānic truths belonged to the realm of spiritual realities with an internal logic not always accessible through a philosophical approach but, rather, accessible through a more spiritually attuned method. To this end, mysticism provided a more appropriate epistemological framework: a direct experiential apprehension of reality unfettered by intellectual preoccupations.

A central point in these debates therefore concerned the relationship between philosophy and mysticism. While both address the connection of human beings to ultimate reality, they often prioritized different epistemological assumptions and tools. Philosophy, in the prevailing form of

Aristotelianism, had a propensity to foreground reason and logic as a means of understanding the nature and place of human beings in reality, while mystics endeavored to apprehend these truths through spiritual, experiential means. In the case of the former, knowledge was primarily cognitive, whereas the latter saw knowledge as gnostic.[13]

The nature of these epistemological contentions is mirrored in some of Ibn ʿArabī's biographical accounts, particularly his reported encounters with the famous Aristotelian philosopher Ibn Rushd (d. 1198), also known as Averroes. Ibn ʿArabī narrates that as a "beardless youth," he had been summoned by Ibn Rushd, an older and accomplished philosopher who had heard about Ibn ʿArabī's insights during his spiritual retreats:

> When I entered, he stood up, showing me affection and respect. He embraced me and said, "Yes." And I in turn said, "Yes." His joy intensified because I had understood him. Then, becoming aware of what had caused his joy, I added, "No." His joy dissipated, and his face lost its color, and he doubted that which he knew. He asked me, "What have you come upon through unveiling and divine inspiration? Is it what rational consideration gives to us?" I replied, "Yes and no. Between the 'yes' and the 'no,' spirits take flight from their matter and necks become detached from their bodies." Averroes turned pale. I saw him trembling. He recited the ritual phrase, "There is no power and no strength but in God" because he had understood my allusion.[14]

This exchange captures some of Ibn ʿArabī's reservations about the prevailing philosophical method of acquiring knowledge. For him, while the rational intellect might be able to perceive some aspects of reality, it could not fully comprehend the nature of reality in its totality; in other words, it is only capable of explaining the one part of a bigger, more comprehensive reality that holds both rational and spiritual elements. While the rational intellect might be limited to the logical categories of a yes-and-no mode of inquiry, mystical illumination transcends these binaries and thus allows for a more complete level of apprehension. Ibn Rushd's ashen physical reaction to Ibn ʿArabī's statement reflects what Peter Coates neatly describes as an "existential wobble": Ibn Rushd has been assailed by uncertainty regarding the reliability of human reason in attaining true knowledge.[15] That Ibn Rushd immediately invokes the ritual phrase humbly acknowledging human limitations in the face of divine power suggests an acquiescence to and acceptance of Ibn ʿArabī's allusion.[16]

Ibn ʿArabī is certainly not making blanket statements against rationality and speculative reasoning. In fact, he states clearly that the intellect and rationality are divine gifts bestowed uniquely on human beings and should be used for moral purposes. However, like other Sufis, he maintains that justice and wisdom entail giving each thing its proper place and function, its *ḥaqq*. Reason, therefore, is an invaluable aid to humanity, but only in its rightful place and performing its designated role in human life.[17] It is only when reason roams outside its specific domain that it runs counter to the nature of its reality. At best, reason can lead the thinker to the knowledge that God is not knowable through rational faculties. It can point the thinker in the direction of a negative theology—the knowledge of what God is not—but it does not have the ability to render positive knowledge of God or the nature of spiritual realities. When reason attempts to stray into the contemplation of spiritual realities for which it is unequipped, the results include distorted perceptions subject to all the limitations of a rational epistemological apparatus—that is, about its object of contemplation, in this case, spiritual reality, as well as about itself, its nature, and its purpose.[18]

In this exchange, Ibn ʿArabī posits the epistemological priority of mystical insight over rational deductive logic. Mystical apprehension is an experiential mode that unveils complete and direct knowledge unlimited by purely cognitive categories. Ibn ʿArabī conveys this view more explicitly in another anecdote: while in a mystical state, he visits an older Ibn Rushd, who is absorbed in intellectual meditations and entirely unaware of the younger man's "presence." Ibn ʿArabī observed the eminent philosopher across a veil of light and concluded, "His deliberation does not lead him where I am myself."[19] Emerging from these reports is an abiding sense of the more fully encompassing nature of mystical insights vis-à-vis philosophical ruminations: Ibn ʿArabī's capacity to engage the whole intellect, including its more creative and contemplative capacities, as opposed to Ibn Rushd's method, which is generally limited to the rational and logical. Ibn ʿArabī's reports regarding Ibn Rushd also resonate with some of the elements that characterize the exchange between Niẓām and Ibn ʿArabī. In both cases, the older, well-known, socially distinguished individual, engaged in some form of cerebration or intellection, is instructed by the younger, socially less significant individual, who nonetheless emerges as spiritually superior, with access to deeper knowledge based on mystical experience. Elsewhere, however Ibn ʿArabī includes Ibn Rushd in the rare category of exceptional philosophers, "one of the great ones" among the "few truly intelligent men" who recognized Ibn ʿArabī's gift of divinely transmitted knowledge "outside ordinary learning . . . and rational consideration."[20]

Prioritizing the mystical method, Ibn ʿArabī presented his insights in a way that appealed to the philosophical and broader intellectual sensibilities of his time. In fact, when in another instance Ibn ʿArabī describes philosophy in its most comprehensive sense as the "love of wisdom," he declares the ancient philosopher Plato to be a rare sage with insights paralleling those of the people of revelation.[21] Here, he clearly acknowledges the potential for a more encompassing reach of philosophical inquiry despite the reality that most philosophers did not live up to the ideal in this regard. From this perspective Ibn ʿArabī claims that even Aristotle, an important founding figure in Western philosophy, would not have found problems with his views since they simply rectify and augment some of the same arguments Aristotle made.[22] Ibn ʿArabī illustrates that in thirteenth-century Muslim societies, the categories of Sufi, philosopher, poet, jurist, and theologian were not mutually exclusive. Given that Ibn ʿArabī was concerned with the major philosophical and mystical questions concerning truth, knowledge, and being and that he provided a comprehensive map for addressing such questions, it is not unusual that contemporary scholars have described him as "both a philosopher and a mystic."[23] However, Ibn ʿArabī consistently prioritized the mystical method of experiential access to knowledge, an approach identified strongly with Sufism.[24] He informs us that his knowledge was acquired through mystical "openings"—that is, theophanic visions.

The term "openings" is central to understanding Ibn ʿArabī's epistemology. Chittick states that in Ibn ʿArabī's technical vocabulary, "opening" is synonymous with a number of other terms associated with Sufism, including "unveiling," "tasting," "witnessing," "divine self-disclosure," and "insight."[25] The term "theophanic" also describes a vision of the divine through this process of inner receptivity, suggesting an immediate apprehension of the divine without the mediation of the intellect. While reason may be regarded as the ability that elevates humanity in creation, simultaneously and paradoxically, that faculty might diminish human ability to apprehend the divine. Philosopher Toshihiko Izutsu points out that in Ibn ʿArabī's framework, reason can weave an "opaque veil" that reinforces the idolatrous ego and thereby hinders progress on the path of knowing the One.[26] In Ibn ʿArabī's paradigm, the heart rather than the mind is the center of the "opening" to knowledge of the divine.

An "opening" can also be understood as inspired knowledge, an unveiling that comes to the persevering and patient seeker. As Chittick informs us, this experience is not given through self-exertion or even through proactively seeking that type of experience. Rather, aspirants can only prepare themselves by keeping to the discipline of the *Sharīʿa* (divine law) and the *ṭarīqa* (spiritual path) under the guidance of an accomplished spiritual master.[27] Ibn ʿArabī suggests that those who undertake spiritual retreats (*khalwa*), remembrance or invocation (*dhikr*), and other types of spiritual discipline prepare their hearts for receptivity to the divine.[28]

Furthermore, Ibn ʿArabī consistently reiterates the idea that his mystical knowledge and spiritual insights were unveilings of the meanings from the "storehouse"—that is, the Qurʾān.[29] His emphasis on faithfulness to the Qurʾān's literal meanings as well as on the importance of the *Sharīʿa* as a means of preparation for attaining deeper mystical receptivity provides evidence for the orthodox Islamic underpinnings of his methodology.[30]

Ibn ʿArabī's Cosmology and Metaphysics

Ibn ʿArabī's writings are packed with marvelous insights and rich discourses on the nature of God, creation, and humanity. His writings on these topics are by no means straightforward or easy to comprehend and interpret. In these complex narratives that encapsulate his distinct contribution to Muslim thought lie some of the secrets to the meaning of human existence and purpose.

In Ibn ʿArabī's metaphysics, theological conceptions are not disconnected from ethical praxis. Indeed, there is an intimate if not unbreakable link between the two. Understanding Ibn ʿArabī's insights on an ethics of gender requires unpacking the manifold aspects of his cosmological and theological vision. For Ibn ʿArabī and most other Sufis, understandings of God and the universe are significant primarily insofar as they may facilitate spiritual transformation. Reflections on the nature of God, the cosmos, and humanity's place therein present us with rich forms of religious anthropology with profound gender implications.

Part of the challenge of Ibn ʿArabī's metaphysics is to discern the place of divine unity and creation's multiplicity; to fathom the intimate liaison between divine essence and attributes; to grasp the intricate weaving together of God's transcendence and God's immanence. Muslim thinkers have long grappled with the conundrum of the emergence of plurality and finitude from a source that is the singular, infinite One. For Ibn ʿArabī, apprehending the correct theological vision opens up expansive ethical vistas. The goal of the spiritual journey and its attendant theological insights is not escaping the world but "the transformative task of returning by and with God."[31]

A central piece in this captivating cosmological puzzle is the relationship between God and creation. Ibn ʿArabī's point of departure, in the tradition of many Sufis, is the prophetic report of a divine utterance: "I was a Hidden treasure and I loved to be known so I created the world in order that I might be known."[32] Among Muslim mystics, this *ḥadīth qudsī* is often treated as the sine qua non of all engagement between humans and the divine. The link between God and humans emanates from divine desire to be known. Divine desire is expressed as love. Hence, the raison d'être for creation is divine love or divine desire. The means for fulfilling desire is knowledge, but it must be knowledge that reflects an intimate, direct encounter between God and creation.

If the self-revealing divine sounds almost like a needy God who expands and reaches out to nongods, then it is only half the story. The other half is a narrative of the radical otherness of God as that being beyond all existence. So while God is known and knowable, especially through divine names and attributes, a portion of that treasure remains veiled. Ibn ʿArabī explains that the divine essence (*al-dhāt*) is beyond human conception. Casting the divine essence as unknowable, inconceivable, and not subject to human experience, Ibn ʿArabī retains the notion of God's transcendence.[33] The divine essence is beyond the grasp of humanity and remains an eternal mystery.

For Ibn ʿArabī, this veiled and mysterious divine essence signifies the absolute nature of the divine. In trying to explain the absolute qua absolute, he invokes the notion of divine independence (*istighnāʾ*).[34] Divine independence is absolute, meaning that the One does not require any creative act to bring itself into being; it just *is*. Because it just is, the divine essence is pure ipseity, or pure being. Ibn ʿArabī further associates this divine essence with the Qurʾānic description of God as *bāṭin*—that is, as inward or nonmanifest.[35]

So God possesses two opposite dimensions: God is the essence who remains the eternally hidden treasure, eluding human knowledge and abjuring self-disclosure; simultaneously, God is defined through the beautiful names, divine, desiring, attributes that yearn to reveal themselves and ache to merge with forms that manifest them. Creation is the outpouring response to nothing less than the intimate decree of God's desire. The cosmos comprises a theater that bridges the chasm between the hidden mystery of the divine and God's self-revelation.[36]

For Ibn ʿArabī, the divine names are pivotal; both the divine essence and creation can be understood only in relation to them. Chittick, one of the pioneering mediators of Ibn ʿArabī to Western audiences, alerts the reader to this intimacy between the divine essence and the names: "It is precisely the Essence that is named by the Names. . . . By knowing any name of God we know God, but not necessarily in respect of another name, nor in respect of His very Self or Essence."[37]

Human beings—and, indeed, all of creation—are manifestations of the divine through relationships with God's attributes. The being of existent things is simultaneously relative and an expression of absolute existence. Indeed, God alone possesses true being, while all that is nongod receives its being on loan from the Source.[38] The universe discloses the secret of the absolute, the invisible depths of existence, the "hidden treasure" of God reflected in the mirror of the world.[39]

Invoking a *ḥadīth,* Ibn ʿArabī concurrently describes the divine names as veils surrounding God. This *ḥadīth* describes God as possessing veils of light and darkness; if they were lifted, the glories of the divine visage would annihilate all things perceived by the eyes of the creatures gazing upon it.[40] According to Ibn ʿArabī, "If the divine names were to be taken away, the veils would be lifted, and if the veils—which are the names—were to be lifted the unity [*aḥadiyya*] of the Essence would become manifest. Because of its unity, no entity would remain qualified by existence . . . since they only become qualified by existence through the names."[41]

The divine names provide the crucial isthmus to God's essence, thereby facilitating the coming into existence of creation. Comprising the vital conduit for humankind's existence in relation to the essence, the divine names simultaneously veil us from It. The divine essence is at once a profound and unknowable mystery and that from which all else derives its being. It is entirely transcendent, yet nothing in creation is separate from its qualities. It is the pervasive center in which all contradictions are transcended. Reason cannot grasp how these very opposite characteristics coalesce into a single being and act at the same time. Philosophers call this riddle the *coincidenta oppositorum.*

The point at which the conventions of logic and philosophy fail is also where mysticism comes to the rescue, gently prodding the inquirer to encounter this unfathomable relationship of the absolute to creation through the medium of metaphor. Expanding on the vivid Qurʾānic metaphors depicting God as light, Ibn ʿArabī describes the unfolding relationship between

God and creation.[42] God's being is symbolized by light, and creation constitutes the rays emanating from this iridescent center. To the extent that the rays reflect the light, they are at one with it, and inasmuch as they are not the light itself, they are in darkness. And so a creature is constituted both by its reflection of being and by a lack thereof—what Ibn ʿArabī calls the reality of "He/Not He."[43] In this ontological mosaic, darkness or nonbeing can claim no positive or independent reality; dethroned, they simply represent lack—a lack of light, a lack of being.

Ibn ʿArabī uses these varying concepts and metaphors to depict the relationship between the absolute One and the multitude of creation. Within this vast expanse that comprises creation, there are shifting relationships and shimmering configurations of the divine names, assuming varying forms and manifestations.

The Created: Macrocosm and Microcosm

Within this labyrinthine cosmic orchestra, divine attributes are scattered, dispersed, and concentrated in all created things. They change in intensity and gradation—here diffuse, there clustered. In shifting combinations and with abundant possibility, the divine names collectively form a hierarchy that is the cosmos. Every divine attribute finds loci of manifestation in the cosmos. In its totality, the cosmos reflects all of the divine names in existence. Ibn ʿArabī beckons us to reflect on two fundamental and intertwined components of the cosmos—the universe or the macrocosm, and the human being or the microcosm.[44]

As a consequence of the expansive nature of the macrocosmic universe, Ibn ʿArabī refers to it as *al-Insān al-Kabīr* (the Big Human). While possessing a number of divine attributes, the macrocosm reflects these attributes only diffusely and opaquely. It seeks out a unifying principle to connect the diverse elements into a coherent and conscious whole. Without such integration, Ibn ʿArabī laments, the universe is like an opaque mirror of the divine, lacking clarity and in need of polishing to manifest divine unity.[45]

Indeed, only the human being is constitutionally able to fulfill this cosmic need for integration and concentration. This, of course, is humanity in its archetypal capacity, what Ibn ʿArabī calls *al-Insān al-Kāmil* (the Complete Human), the ideal prototype for being human, and the essence of Ibn ʿArabī's theological anthropology. The term *al-Insān al-Kāmil* does not signify all actual individuals but rather the potential that all human beings possess, realized in some beings and not in others. It beckons to the human being to aspire to the ideal ethical self, bidding each person to strive to attain this delicate balance of divine attributes, a balance attained through vigilance with the inner self and the practice of impeccable conduct and behavior toward others. Those individuals who embody this sublime human archetype within history are the prophets and the friends of God, or *awliyāʾ*, as Sufi adepts are called.

In Ibn ʿArabī's theology, human beings are unique for two reasons. On the one hand, they have the potential comprehensively to reflect all the divine attributes. As an independent entity, *al-Insān al-Kāmil* is a polished mirror of the divine. Human beings constitute a mirror to the divine treasure seeking to be known. Coates describes this archetypal role of the human being as that of a bridge or an isthmus that connects the inner and outward dimensions of the one unitary reality.[46] This all-embracing capacity makes the human being a potential microcosm of the attributes.[47] In addition, the complete human unifies and concentrates all attributes present in a more differentiated manner than occurs in the rest of the universe, which is why Ibn ʿArabī also refers to the human as the small universe (*al-ʿālam al-ṣaghīr*).[48]

On the other hand, the human as the all-encompassing microcosm imbues consciousness into the larger universe. Ibn ʿArabī states that the cosmos without the human being is like a well-proportioned body awaiting life and spirit.[49] In this mode, the cosmos is unconscious and passive and gains spirit only when the human being, who is conscious and active, enters into it.[50] Using an evocative analogy of human creation, Ibn ʿArabī depicts humanity as the spirit blown into the pregnant universe to ensoul it. Thus, the goal of the cosmos, which exists prior to humanity, is the human being. In its archetypal form of *al-Insān al-Kāmil*, humanity is the ultimate link in the great chain of being, drawing together all the previous links of the entire cosmos into manifest existence. Through this synergy, the human being transforms the entire universe into a polished mirror of the divine attributes.

For Ibn ʿArabī, the cosmos is sustained by the existence of complete human beings and would die without them. In Ibn ʿArabī's eschatology, the end of the world as we know it will be signaled by the departure of the last complete human being, who constitutes the final living embodiment of complete spiritual cohesion.[51] Chittick suggests that in these cosmological terms, the increasing corrosion of natural and social environments in the current era is indicative of a diminishing number of complete humans in the world.[52]

The Reality of Muḥammad

A crucial figure in Ibn ʿArabī's cosmology and his discussions on *al-Insān al-Kāmil* is the Prophet Muḥammad. While all prophets reflect the archetype of the spiritually complete human, Muḥammad is unique because, according to Ibn ʿArabī, the Prophet Muḥammad was created as a cosmic being prior to his historical existence. He took on an embodied form as the historical prophet only after his original creation. Based on a *ḥadīth* where the Prophet states, "I was a prophet even while Adam was between water and clay," Ibn ʿArabī avers that since Muḥammad was the most perfect being among the human race, the entire creation began and ended with him.[53] This final seal of the prophets was given "the totality of the divine words, [all] the things named by Adam."[54]

Muḥammad thus ontologically functions as the active, unifying principle that brings together all the archetypes of creation. The cosmic Muḥammad reflects the original creative activity of the absolute, the first "self-revealing principle of the universe."[55] This level is also called the "reality of realities," referring not to the absolute in its primordial essence but to the first form of its self-manifestation.

Izutsu observes that the depiction of the cosmic Muḥammad corresponds almost exactly to the Plotinian first intellect (*Nous*), which is the "first emanation" from the absolute One.[56] He notes that the Plotinian first intellect is passive in relation to its source and active in relation to that which proceeds from it. Ibn ʿArabī refers to this dimension of the Prophet as the Muḥammadan spirit (*al-rūḥ al-muḥammadī*). As such, the "passivity" or "receptivity" of the *al-rūḥ al-muḥammadī* is reflected in its stance of servanthood (*ʿubūdiyya*) in relation to the Creator, while its "activity" is reflected in assuming lordship (*rubūbiyya*) in acting as the first principle of creation.[57] In this regard, Ibn ʿArabī proclaims that since Muḥammad was essentially created as a servant, he did not overstep the boundaries of his state to seek mastery. Rather, prostrate with humility, he received all that God directed to him. Because of Muḥammad's state of receptivity, God produced from him all that God produced, thus conferring on Muḥammad "the rank of activity over the world of Breaths."[58]

The breath referred to signifies the divine "breath of the Merciful [*nafas al-raḥmān*]" that actively imbues creation with existence through the inbreathing of spirit. The Prophet's complete receptivity and servanthood to God is the fountainhead of his subsequent creative activity and vicegerency in relation to creation. This preempts for the reader a pervasive principle in Ibn ʿArabī's spiritual psychology regarding the imperative of receptivity and servanthood in the quest for human spiritual completion. The notion that receptivity and activity are interwoven spiritual modes is also a central construct in Ibn ʿArabī's gender formulations.

The theophanic comprehensiveness of the Prophet Muḥammad is also reflected in another relevant *ḥadīth* that Sufis regularly evoke. In it, the Prophet describes his nature as "*anā Aḥmad bi lā mīm* [I am Aḥmad without the m]."[59] The Prophet in his human form is also called Aḥmad; here the *mīm* (or m) in his name symbolizes creatureliness as defined by death or the aspect of human mortality. In the Arabic language, *mawt* (death) begins with *mīm*. Without the *mīm*, the name becomes *Aḥad* (the One), a name of God, signifying Muḥammad's cosmic dimension as the first self-manifestation of the One.

Ibn ʿArabī also calls this dimension of Muḥammad the "Light of Muḥammad [*al-nūr al-muḥammadī*]" based on the prophetic *ḥadīth* that states, "The first thing that God created was my light."[60] Accordingly, the Prophet Muḥammad is depicted as preexisting any creature and is the means through which all prophets were successively manifested, culminating in the final historical manifestation of the embodied Muḥammad. The primordial light is understood as that strata in which God was first manifest to himself in the state of unity, with the personal dimension of this light called the "Reality of Muḥammad."[61]

Muḥammad is thus sealing Abrahamic prophecy, first in terms of his archetypal cosmic being and last in terms of culminating prophecy as the final historical prophet. In this view, the Prophet Muḥammad is both the cause and the goal of creation, and all prophecy and revelation originates with him. Ibn ʿArabī states, "Muḥammad was given the all-comprehensive words. Hence his Law comprises all revealed religions. He was a prophet when Adam had not yet been created. Hence from him branch out the Laws to all the prophets. They were sent by him to be deputies in the earth and in the absence of his body."[62]

Muḥammad in these multiple registers represents a circular, encompassing, and complete means for divine creativity, manifestation, and guidance. While the primal Muḥammad is distinct and more encompassing than the historical Prophet Muḥammad, Ibn ʿArabī invokes iridescent resonances and intimate connections between them. In the *Fuṣūṣ*, the characteristic wisdom of the Prophet Muḥammad is described as *farḍiyya* (singularity), demonstrating the synthesizing and encompassing nature of his reality. For Ibn ʿArabī as for other Sufis, the nature and role of the Prophet Muḥammad represents a foundational construct for understanding the cosmos, God, and humanity.

Given that the Prophet Muḥammad symbolizes such crucial dimensions of Ibn ʿArabī's worldview, it is enormously significant that some of Ibn ʿArabī's central teachings on the nature of gender, men, and women are found in the chapter on Muḥammad in the *Fuṣūṣ*. This dimension of singularity characterizes the ontological relationship between men and women, thereby providing each of them with a sign to apprehend their oneness with God.

In shifting the lens from Muḥammad to humanity in general, Ibn ʿArabī's worldview holds that humanity's spiritual realization is critical to all of existence. This position is linked to the pervasive Islamic view that the cosmos is not an end unto itself; rather, it was created so that human beings could come into existence. While all other creatures in the cosmos glorify God in terms of their station or capacity, Ibn ʿArabī asserts that only the human being as a comprehensive being is able to fully glorify God. The anthropocentric and theocentric dimensions in Ibn ʿArabī's cosmological narrative are virtually two sides of the same coin; pointing to one side prefigures the other.

The Religious Anthropology of Divine Names: A Hermeneutics of Mercy

In this Sufi account, humanity is linked to God through attributes called the divine names. These names constitute reality. The intensity of the relationship between a human subject and the names of the divine makes each relationship unique. To the extent that human beings embody these divine names in their character, they aspire, in Ibn ʿArabī's vocabulary, toward the archetype of human spiritual completion, *al-Insān al-Kāmil.*

Human beings encounter names or attributes relationally; names link and relate the created with the Creator.[63] Yet names are not fixed entities. Ibn ʿArabī construes divine names as both connectors and mediators between the divine and humans. "The divine names," notes Ibn ʿArabī, "are the mediators or isthmus [*barzakh*] between us and the One named."[64] By invoking the trope of prosopopeia and personification, he explains that the divine names behold the divine: the names "look to him in as much as they name him." When gazing upon humans, the divine names perform a different function. At that moment, the names unload the effects of the divine predicates on the human subject: "They make the One named known, and they make us known."[65]

Ibn ʿArabī further advises the seeker that in reality there is nothing but names. "He who truly wants to become aware of the names of God," Ibn ʿArabī counsels, should meditate on a particular Qurʾānic verse: "O people, you are needy [*fuqarāʾ*] of God!" (Q. 35:15). In Ibn ʿArabī's view, that state of privation (*faqr*) is alleviated only by the plenitude of the divine names. Both the primordial poverty of the human condition and the abundance of the divine names drive Ibn ʿArabī to claim triumphantly, "In reality, there is nothing in existence but his names."[66]

In Ibn ʿArabī's discourse, the names are traces of the divine desire to be known. Therefore, they return us to the primordial cosmogonic myth in which God, portrayed as a hidden treasure, aches to be known. In an ecstatic surge of self-display, the names of the One fan into creative multiplicity. While all of creation constitutes this multiplicity, human beings may uniquely integrate the complete panoply of divine names and in so doing become a mirror of the real. The divine names define the nature and purpose of human existence; they are the source of human identity (being) and the means of realizing that identity (becoming).

Via a process of embodying the divine names in increasingly refined ways, the human being begins the journey of return from multiplicity to the One, a goal only fully realized when the state of perfect balance is attained, as epitomized in *al-Insān al-Kāmil*. To arrive safely at this destination, the seeker needs to chart a course, navigating deftly amid the divine attributes. In this endeavor, the critical issue relates to the nature and qualities of the names, their interrelationships, and, more significantly, how to embody them in the appropriate manner. The Sufi tradition elucidates on these concerns in great depth.

For Ibn ʿArabī as well as for many other Muslim thinkers, the divine names can be divided into two related types, names or attributes of beauty (*jamāl*) and attributes of majesty (*jalāl*). These two types of attributes correspond to the two polar ways in which Muslim theologians have characterized the divine, some evoking notions of similarity (*tashbīḥ*) of the divine with the human, others stressing that the divine is not comparable (*tanzīḥ*) to anything humanly conceivable. Attributes of love, mercy, beneficence, gentleness, and forgiveness are more closely connected to the concept of God's similarity, while attributes of majesty, such as God's singularity, independence, inaccessibility, wrathfulness, avenging nature, overwhelming presence, exaltation, and sovereignty, are all connected to God's incomparability.[67]

How do these divine names relate to human beings? Ibn ʿArabī believes that humanity reflects all shades of the divine names, supporting his argument from the teachings of the Qurʾān and the sunna: the *ḥadīth* that "God created Adam in God's own form" and the verse that God "taught Adam all of the names" (Q. 2:30).[68] In this context, Adam represents the archetypal human being; he is neither merely a prophet nor just a male human being.

The divine names are equal in God but coalesce in varying configurations in human beings, who are a constellation of attributes. Ibn ʿArabī furnishes seekers with a map that shows them how to refine and balance these cascading attributes. At various points in a person's life, these names manifest in varying intensities and complex relationships to one another. During their life journeys, humans may experience radical changes in the manifestation of the names. Ibn ʿArabī, like other Muslim thinkers, recognizes the dynamism of the human condition and how it differs from the relatively fixed nature of the remainder of creation.[69] Humans continuously morph until mortality sets in.

Balancing the attributes within the human self is the critical task. According to Ibn ʿArabī's spiritual map, attributes come with specific limits and proportions. Transgressing the limit of an attribute implies that the servant is in opposition to the real, and Ibn ʿArabī warns that doing so may cause a person to become "alienated and expelled from blissful intimacy [with God]."[70]

How, then, might such a balance of attributes be configured in the human subject? Ibn ʿArabī reminds us that many of the majestic (*jalālī*) qualities belong to the realm of incomparability.[71] Epistemologically, human beings should refrain from actively claiming majestic qualities. To God's *jalālī* qualities, the human being should adopt the receptive posture of servitude and dependency. A contrary positioning—that is, responding to God's *jalālī* names with the individual's own unfettered *jalālī* qualities—will only distance humans from the Source, resulting in misguidance. Satan exemplified this misplaced *jalāl* when he refused God's command to prostrate himself before Adam, pompously claiming, "I am better than he." Satan's arrogance, born from a misplaced sense of power and majesty, resulted in a lack of receptivity to God. In fact, Satan's blindness to his state of servitude to God is a consequence of unaligned *jalālī* qualities. Iblīs thus is plunged into a state of distance, expelled from the realm of divine intimacy.

Human beings face a similar and grave spiritual danger in assuming *jalālī* qualities in relation to other human beings. Doing so, Ibn ʿArabī cautions, might result in heedlessness of the human being's true state of servanthood. Addressing in particular those in authority, he warns that an individual in such a position might see "himself as superior to others, failing to recognize that such superiority belongs to the position that he has been established in." Such a person, unable to differentiate between himself and his position, "is an ignorant fellow characterized by repugnant negligence."[72]

Spiritual aspirants holding positions with high social status and privilege should be particularly cautious about identifying with God's masterly *jalālī* qualities. Such a grievous error could blind people to the real nature of their relationship with God and thereby diminish their spiritual stature. While Ibn ʿArabī's warning to those occupying powerful positions in society gives contemporary readers pause, it might open up yet another insight in the critique of patriarchal social structures that attribute gender power imbalances to the "natural" superiority of men. In fact, drawing on Ibn ʿArabī's understanding, it is problematic to conflate men's social privilege in patriarchal societies with an assumption of an intrinsic male authority. Male power and authority are a product of social power relations rather than a given tenet of human nature. Although this idea has now become an obvious sociological observation, it might also serve as an important spiritual insight that averts misapprehension and inner peril for the seeker.

According to Ibn ʿArabī, submission and receptivity to God's *jalāl* enable the servant to progress along the path of spiritual refinement. On such a journey of enhancement and purification, the seeker will experience increasing states of nearness to God as well as the reality of God's beauty (*jamāl*). Ibn ʿArabī advises that love and servanthood are the key ingredients for the alchemical elixir in which "sincerity of love makes the lover take on the qualities of the Beloved . . . and the quality of his names."[73] This sincere love for God allows the seeker properly to embrace divine attributes. Thus, the devotion of the sincere lover, the recognition of the individual's own poverty and servanthood toward God, and the work of self-purification and adherence to divine commandments create a deep receptivity to God. In this process, the seeker grows increasingly closer to the Beloved, and the *jamālī* attributes begin to flower.

Classifying the *jamālī* attributes primarily as attributes of similarity between God and humanity, Ibn ʿArabī lends them an epistemological priority for the seeker that evokes the larger ontological priority of the divine *jamāl*. God invokes this abundance of *jamāl* in a *ḥadīth qudsī*, stating, "My mercy precedes my wrath." According to Ibn ʿArabī, life itself is a reflection of God's all-embracing compassion.[74] All of existence is but the breath of the All-Merciful (*nafas al-raḥmān*). Regularly quoting the Qurʾānic verse in which God states, "My mercy embraces everything" (Q. 7:156), Ibn ʿArabī asserts that nothing in the cosmos exists outside of divine mercy.[75] Reflecting on the notion that life is a sphere of essential compassion that includes all the divine names, he notes that the "attribution of life to the divine essence is the premise of every other relationship attributed to God."[76] For Ibn ʿArabī, only through these relationships, all of which are grounded in the sphere of divine compassion, can one begin to have any understanding of divinity.[77]

A hermeneutic of mercy pervades Ibn ʿArabī's cosmology, saturating his understanding of the nature of existence and all relationships and in particular his theological anthropology. When human interactions are characterized by the quality of mercy, they become exchanges of mercy between God and God's creatures. Mercy travels between God and human beings through the realm of human interactions in which the primacy of realizing God's *jamālī* qualities is foregrounded. Reflecting on the magnitude of such *jamālī* qualities, Ibn ʿArabī observes that God chooses his merciful servants as particular recipients of God's grace, since "He knows that the compassion that they actualize by bestowing grace on someone [else] is the property of His Names. And the Most High alone rewards them according to the measure of the Name with which they bestow grace."[78]

Ibn ʿArabī not only prioritizes merciful and compassionate interactions between human beings as a component of spiritual realization but also highlights the spiritual importance of attending to the needs of vulnerable segments of society. Because of divine love, God descends through subtle and mysterious grace amid human beings, replacing us in our hunger, thirst, and sickness:

> [God] sends himself down to us to stand in our place, so that when one of his servants is hungry, God says to the others, "I was hungry and you didn't feed me," and when one is thirsty, God says to his other

> servants, "I was dying of thirst and you didn't give me water." And when another of his servants was sick, God says, "I was sick and you didn't attend to me." And when those servants ask him about all of this, he says to them, "As for the one who was sick, if you had tended to him, you would have found me with him. And when someone was starving, if you had fed him, you would have found him with me, and so for the one who was thirsty, if you had given him water you would have found me there [*ḥadīth qudsī*]." And this report is true. This is one of the fruits of love when he comes down to us.[79]

Here, Ibn ʿArabī quotes the popular *ḥadīth qudsī* that indicates God's presence among "the least," those occupying marginal and liminal social spaces.[80] God's love and mercy are such that God partakes in the conditions of deepest human need. Here, the seeker is compelled to respond compassionately to the needs of those weakened through illness, hunger, and thirst, and such a response to other human beings is in effect a response to God's presence. Enacting compassion thus is not merely an act of extension to another human being but an act of connecting with the divine Beloved. Viewed from such a perspective, the benefactor is not simply the benevolent person who attends with merciful compassion to a poor, needy Other. In fact, the needs of a poor, hungry, and ill person provide a fertile opportunity for a fellow human being to encounter God. Moreover, such a person is not merely an intermediary, but in and through that person's predicament, God as the embodiment of love is fully present. Through his take on the spiritual dynamics of such a relationship, Ibn ʿArabī destabilizes the normative power relationship between giver and recipient. Both parties in this relationship give and receive divine mercy—the humanity and divinity of each are tied to the other, and all is a product of divine love. In such a framework, mercy is an integral manifestation of divine love.

For the seeker, Ibn ʿArabī prioritizes the embodiment of the *jamālī* qualities of mercy, compassion, and love. These attributes of similarity between God and creation provide the furnace for the transformation of the self into the divine form of *al-Insān al-Kāmil*. This view does not imply a disregard for Allah's *jalāl*; rather, the seeker attempts to dissolve the unrefined *jalālī* instincts of her *nafs al-ammāra* in the ocean of God's *jamālī* attributes. Through this process, the individual's *jalālī* dimensions can be safely harmonized; they have also been purified by receptivity to God and by having maintained the limit demanded by God's incomparability. Hence, it can be inferred that God's *jalāl* in humanity emerges out of the embodiment of God's *jamāl*. Human beings ascend through the grace of God to true vicegerency that entails a total and harmonious assimilation of all the divine qualities. Within this balance between *jamāl* and *jalāl*, the predominance of God's mercy—a *jamālī* reality—is ever-present and constantly evoked. A hermeneutic of mercy saturates Ibn ʿArabī's anthropological and cosmological framework and appears to pervade his interpersonal relationships.

This theological framework clearly illustrates that the assumption of *jamālī* attributes for human beings occurs in social contexts. A person's spiritual transformation occurs through embodying certain types of behavior in relation to other people. Character is refined by cultivating social interactions based on love, mercy, compassion, and gentleness toward fellow beings. Spiritual development consequently demands an ethics of care that is socially engaged; it is not a solitary, individualistic journey. Ibn ʿArabī's theological anthropology abounds with resources for socially engaged visions of spirituality that impel compassionate and just modes of human relationality.

Divine Attributes, the Gendered Insān, and Society

Ibn ʿArabī's foundational understandings of God and humanity have a number of implications for gender ideology. By foregrounding the *jamālī* aspects of humanity, this approach not only provides a general critique of social hierarchies and discriminatory ideologies but also rejects social structures that prize aggression and other unrefined *jalālī* qualities. In the contemporary world, this critique is extremely pertinent, given that these unrefined *jalālī* ways of engaging the world characterize the prevalent masculinist ways of being—not just in Islam—which continue to bring war, destruction, suffering, and death. Over and above providing a critique of these hostile social norms, Ibn ʿArabī's framework directs one to the alternatives in which the qualities of mercy, compassion, care, justice, generosity, patience, forbearance, and forgiveness are prioritized among human beings. His framework provides a rationale for cultivating societies that value peace and justice as a necessary context for, as well as a predictable result of, the cultivation of individual character. Ibn ʿArabī's theological anthropology is thus imminently social in its most rudimentary implications.

At this level, Ibn ʿArabī's teachings provide possibilities for a powerful, organic, and ontologically grounded critique of patriarchal power relations, in relation both to the individual and to social formations. This idea has great relevance for some of the contemporary challenges of gender inequality faced by Muslims in relation to traditional Islamic law (*fiqh*). As such, Ibn ʿArabī's framework raises the question of whether formulations of the law reflect an engagement with the foundational metaphysical principles of Islam. Sufism, with its prioritization of *jamālī* realities and where majesty (*jalāl*) always needs to be contained within an encompassing mercy (*jamāl*), potentially offers a crucial contribution to the development of a humane legal system that genuinely marries justice with mercy.

At a more specific level, Ibn ʿArabī's core concept of *al-Insān al-Kāmil* presents a pivotal understanding of human purpose that is significant in terms of its explicit gender inclusivity. Ibn ʿArabī repeatedly points out that *al-Insān al-Kāmil*, the most comprehensive standard for human realization, is ungendered, makes identical demands on men and women, and is attainable equally by both. For example, in a passage in which he describes forty-nine types of sainthood based on the Qurʾānic verse in *Sūrat al-Aḥzāb* (Q. 33:35), Ibn ʿArabī explicitly includes women as part of this discussion: "In each of these categories which we are speaking of there are men and women." He later adds, "There is no spiritual qualification conferred on men which is denied women."[81] After mention of each of the saintly categories, he adds the phrase "*min al-rijāl wa-nisāʿ* [from among men and women]," imitating the Qurʾānic verse 33:35 that delineates the various virtues of believers in both masculine and feminine terms. Referring to this verse, Ibn ʿArabī confidently declares that the Qurʾān confirms that each virtue, a particular portal to the process of spiritual refinement, is equally accessible to men and women. In addition, he points out that this gender-inclusive verse reflects a central Qurʾānic teaching on the complete ontological equality of men and women.

Ibn ʿArabī not only affirms the equal spiritual potential of men and women but also links these equal capacities to the realm of law and society. For example, he presents the case of Ḥājar, the wife of the Prophet Ibrāhīm, who ran between the hills of Ṣafā and Marwa in Mecca desperately searching for sustenance for her young child. Ḥājar's actions form the basis of the *saʿī* ritual, which is required of all Muslims performing the ḥajj. Ibn ʿArabī points out that the actions of this woman have become ritualized, forming the basis of a legal precedent applicable to the entire Muslim community, only because women, like men, possess the capacity for complete spiritual realization.[82] The gendered link between spiritual capacity and the ability to set communal legal precedents reflects an explicit connection between spirituality and law that characterizes Ibn ʿArabī's worldview.

In another example, Ibn ʿArabī provides his readers with a unique reading of women's legal testimony integrated with understandings of women's spiritual capacities. The normative position in Islamic law is that a man's legal testimony is generally worth that of two women.[83] However, Ibn ʿArabī reminds his readers of a view, not unknown among his peers, that in some situations, one woman's legal testimony is equal to that of two men, thereby reversing the normative gendered nature of legal testimony. These legal situations pertain to cases in which paternity of a child is being determined or in which the waiting period after divorce (*ʿidda*) before a woman can remarry is being determined. Ibn ʿArabī informs us, "In some cases, one woman can play the role of two men. Usually, a judge does not make a definite judgment except with the testimony of two men. Yet in some circumstances the testimony of one woman equals that of two men. For example, the judge's acceptance of her testimony about menstrual cycles as it related to the waiting period after divorce [*ʿidda*], or the husband accepting her statement about his paternity of the child—despite the uncertainty pertaining to such situations. [Another example of this] is the acceptance of her testimony that she is menstruating. So she occupies in such situations, the position of two reliable male witnesses just as the man occupies the position of two women in cases of testimony about debt."[84]

Here, Ibn ʿArabī points out that context and experience are principal considerations when determining gender-specific legal capacity. For a feminist reader, this approach might suggest that legal rulings appearing to favor men per se may in fact simply be responsive to the realities and pragmatics of the social arena.[85] Within his context, the ordinary woman's experience would have been limited primarily to the private realm of her body; men, conversely, were active in the public arena of commerce. The weight of their respective testimonies is related to these experiential and knowledge bases. Such a reading of the law resists the notion that male testimony is inherently superior. It invites the reader to link legal capacity to a person's expertise, knowledge, and experience.

This type of pragmatic reading not only helps to destabilize dominant notions of male superiority but also gives salience to women's agency and legal capacity and runs contrary to more patriarchal representations of men as primary agents. The underlying logic of this argument suggests that law is to be responsive to and informed by changes in contexts, experiences, and knowledge, a view that was not uncommon among premodern jurists but that seems to have been lost among many current proponents of Islamic law. Such a retrogression is unfortunate, especially as it affects issues of gender and women. Reclaiming a dynamic approach to *fiqh* as illustrated by Ibn ʿArabī opens up ways to contextually understand traditional legal rulings as well as to continue vibrant, socially engaged methods of formulating contemporary law. A return to this view allows contemporary Muslims critically to probe the ways in which legal rulings are premised on particular conceptions of religious anthropology.

Ibn ʿArabī's discussion subsequently takes a surprising and somewhat unexpected turn by introducing women's ability to become the ruling axial saint (*Quṭb*):

> Both men and women participate in all of the levels, even in being the axial saint [*Quṭb*]. Do not let yourself be veiled by saying of the messenger of God, on whom be peace and salutations: "A people who delegate governance to women will never ever prosper." For we are speaking about God's granting of authority, not peoples granting of authority [*tawliyat*]. The *ḥadīth* addresses one whom people have given authority. In tradition, if we received nothing concerning this matter except the saying of the Prophet that "women are the same as men in heritage," it would be enough. In other words, everything that a man can attain—spiritual stations, levels, or qualities—can be attained by women if God wills, just as they can be attained by men if God wills.[86]

So the reader follows Ibn ʿArabī as he moves directly from affirming a woman's capacity for full legal testimony to her capacity to assume the highest role of axial saint. He also defies dominant notions of women's unsuitability for leadership. In fact, at first blush, Ibn ʿArabī might be construed as an apologist for the popular *ḥadīth* report that "a people will never prosper that give a woman authority over their affairs." For many classical and even modern Muslim scholars, this report disqualifies women from political leadership. Situated in the heart of the canonical *ḥadīth* sources, this tradition has long buttressed patriarchal limitations on women's social power.

Ibn ʿArabī, in contrast, offers a radical new reading of this insidious and pervasive *ḥadīth* tradition. By summoning the powerful visage of a ruling female saint as a counterpoint, he opens up an unusual and refreshing ontological porthole on a *ḥadīth* that has otherwise become a rather monotonous refrain among guardians of Muslim patriarchies. Given that a *Quṭb* is the spiritual pivot in the hierarchy of saints, Ibn ʿArabī's assertion that women can assume this station is formidable. First, he limits the relevance of this *ḥadīth* to the realm of social rather than spiritual contingencies. He does so by arguing that this *ḥadīth* holds no relevance at the level of ontological reality, where a more relevant, superior, and comprehensive *ḥadīth* holds currency. According to that *ḥadīth*, "Women are the same as men in heritage." This idea, he notes, implies that all stations, levels, and attributes are equally accessible to men and women. Hence, while remaining faithful to textual canon, Ibn ʿArabī negotiates contradictory prophetic traditions by adroitly foregrounding gender inclusivity and women's full participation in the work of human existence.

His interpretation of these *ḥadīth* is not simply a way of dichotomizing the social from the spiritual, granting women access to the latter while restricting them from the former, as is evidenced by his understanding of the role of the axial saint. Contemporary scholar Souad Ḥakīm encapsulates Ibn ʿArabī's view of the station of axial saint (*quṭbiyya*) and the implications of a woman's assumption of such a position:

> We can say that once [she becomes] a Pole [axial saint], a woman becomes possessor of the moment [*waqt*], master of the time, God's vicegerent on his earth, representative of the Envoy in his community, heir to being chosen, cloaked [in] Adamic distinction. Around her the world turns: she arranges its governance and the needs of the entire world rest upon her. God is in solitude with her without the rest of His creation, and He beholds none but her during her time. She is the highest veil. [In the sphere of symbolic reality,] God erects for her a throne upon which He seats her, and then He bestows upon her all the Divine Names that the universe asks of her and she asks of Him/it. When she is seated upon the throne in the Divine Image, God orders the universe to pledge allegiance and to pay homage to her. Among her subjects are every being, high and low, except the highest of the angels, who are those lost in love [*muḥayyamūn*], and the singulars [*afrād*] of mankind, over whom she has no authority because they are like her, perfect, with the aptitude for what she has received of Polehood [*quṭbiyya*].[87]

The encompassing, universal scale of the *Quṭb*'s role clearly renders distinctions between the social and spiritual realms irrelevant. The axial saint is the human being par excellence, the true vicegerent of God, and the leader of humankind at the cosmic level, which pervades every other level of being. By this deft ontological move, Ibn ʿArabī effectively dislodges and dislocates notions of female inferiority. Given the ultimate priority of the spiritual realm within the Sufi framework, such an assertion of women's supreme spiritual capacities provides Ibn ʿArabī with a powerful means to combat prevailing views that women's purported social or legal incapacities can be related to ontological deficiency. Hence, his reference to the *ḥadīth* recognizes normative gender imbalances at the social level and expressly illustrates that such hierarchical social dynamics can blind people from the ultimate nature of human spiritual potentialities. In effect, his reading restricts, limits, and even subtly critiques the applicability of the *ḥadīth* that condemns women's leadership and explicitly reaffirms women's access to the highest of spiritual stations.

Ibn ʿArabī's explicit theoretical positions on the equal capacities of men and women were also informed by his experience of spiritual mastery among female Sufis. Ibn ʿArabī had extensive personal experiences with female spiritual teachers and disciples, and his powerful assertions of women's female spiritual capacities undoubtedly were influenced by his interactions with accomplished female savants, with significant implications for current understandings of gender within Sufism.

In discussing the standard view of two women's legal testimony being the equivalent of a single man's, Ibn ʿArabī performs the task of a hermeneutical acrobat, presenting the reader with a unique, subversive, and unparalleled reading of gender:

> You may also want to mention that God justifies making the testimony of two women equivalent to that of one man because of forgetfulness [*nisyān*], since he says, "So that if one of them errs, the other can remind her." . . . Forgetfulness, however, is also a characteristic of men. God, exalted is he, reported that Adam also was a victim of oblivion. The Prophet (peace be upon him) also said, "Adam forgot, and so did his descendants." . . . In the context of testimony, however, God described one of the two women with confusion [*ḥayra*] only, and he did not describe her of entire forgetfulness. Confusion is only half of forgetfulness, not all of it. See that God attributed complete forgetfulness to man, despite his readiness to reach spiritual completion, since he said about Adam, "But he forgot and we found no firm resolve on his part" (Q. 20:115). Therefore, the man can forget the testimony

> entirely while one of the women cannot forget, since she is the one who will remind the confused one. Since God asserts that one of the two women will remind the other, then we must believe that at least one of them will not forget, for God speaks only the truth. This means that one of the two women is characterized by one of the divine attributes, reported by Moses, and mentioned in the Qurʾān (20:52): "My Lord never errs, nor forgets."[88]

Here, Ibn ʿArabī completely reverses normative views of male superiority. This logic effectively makes a Qurʾānic argument for the ontological superiority of women, a genuinely iconoclastic interpretation of women's limited legal testimony. Ibn ʿArabī reinterprets a verse that historically and traditionally has diminished women's legal capacity, applying to it a revolutionary hermeneutic by drawing on the Qurʾān more holistically and arguing that the verse actually illustrates women's capacity for steadfastness, a divine attribute. He contrasts this statement with another Qurʾānic verse that describes men as forgetful and heedless. His explanation demonstrates a deep faithfulness to the literal text of the Qurʾān, and although this approach reflects Ibn ʿArabī's more mainstream or "orthodox" commitments, he draws out hitherto unanticipated emancipatory and heterodox meanings of law, gender, and human capacity that actively debunk normative notions of male superiority. Given that this discussion began as a commentary on women's restricted legal capacity, a topic generally invoked in assertions of women's inherent deficiencies, it is significant that Ibn ʿArabī has essentially turned the argument on its head, ending up with an assertion of women's ontological superiority.

To gauge fully the daring and dazzling originality of this argumentative process, a restatement of its three main discursive movements is useful. The discussion begins with his reference to particular cases, where contrary to the standard legal norms, one woman's testimony is equivalent to that of two men, illustrating that the seeming gender imbalance in legal testimony is not fixed but contingent, variable, and even reversible. Here, he is arguing as a legal technician. Second, he makes a case for gender equality by illustrating that women have access to the highest spiritual authority, wielding leadership as the axial saint of the day. In this move, we encounter Ibn ʿArabī the Sufi, whose extensive personal experience of women's spiritual mastery is used to swiftly debunk normative views of female deficiency. Third, he returns to the Qurʾānic verse on women's restricted legal testimony to provide a radical and unique subversion of gender categories, ultimately making a case for female superiority. In this final move, we discover Ibn ʿArabī, the exegetical virtuoso and iconoclast par excellence.

One reason why this unconventional reading of women's legal testimony is so important is the significant ways in which issues of limited female testimony have been used to embellish a discourse of the inherent flaws in women's nature. The particular *ḥadīth* regarding women's purported deficiencies in intellect and religion and the ensuing notion of limited female testimonial capacity provide the basis for the conventional view that women are less intelligent. In light of these dominant tropes of female inferiority evoked by the issue of female testimony, Ibn ʿArabī's hermeneutical interventions become especially meaningful and powerful.

In another discussion on gender and social roles, Ibn ʿArabī presents the reader with an ambivalent and provocative position. Commenting on the equal and shared spiritual capacities of men and women as reflected in Q. 33:35,[89] Ibn ʿArabī introduces questions of prophecy, prophetic mission, and status as an envoy. Quoting a *ḥadīth* that states that both Maryam, the daughter of Imrān, and Āsiya, the wife of Pharaoh, have attained complete spiritual realization or perfection (*kamāl*)—in this case, in relation to the station of prophecy (*nubūwwa*)—he informs the reader that men are exclusively privy to the station of "superlative perfection [*akmāliyya*]."

> Men and women come together at the level [*daraja*] of perfection [*kamāl*]. And men are given priority with superlative perfection [*akmāliyya*], not with perfection. For indeed they are both perfected with prophethood [*nubūwwa*]. However, the men are given priority with being envoys and with prophetic missions [*risāla wa baʿtha*]. And women have not achieved the level of envoys and prophetic mission. Despite the fact that men and women share in a particular station [*maqām*], some in that station have priority. . . . God has also said "Indeed we have given priority to some of the prophets over others" (Q. 17:55). And God has made men and women share in legal obligations. Women are obliged just as men are obliged. Even if women are specified with rulings that are not for men, then men are also specified with rulings that are not for women.[90]

Hence, despite basic levels of moral and spiritual correspondence between men and women, including the access to prophecy, Ibn ʿArabī notes that serving as envoys and pursuing a prophetic mission are attainable only by men. As such, the spiritual stations of some select male prophets carry with them a divinely designated responsibility to take forth a religious message into the social and political arena to transform communities.

Ibn ʿArabī attributes prophecy to women in the cases of Maryam and Āsiya, even though the consensus among his contemporaries regarded ideas of female prophecy as constituting heresy.[91] Ibn ʿArabī was thus among the minority of scholars who, like his Andalusian predecessor, Ibn Ḥazm, regarded prophecy as open to women. Ibn ʿArabī's view that women had access to this exalted level of spiritual attainment is an important assertion of female ontological capacity. Nonetheless, these assertions were still contained, constrained, and constructed within an androcentric world in which the positions of envoy and prophetic missionary remained the exclusive purview of men. This type of gender exclusivity reflects the ways in which patriarchal forms of power exclude women from particular positions of leadership. However, it is also possible to understand the gender-specificity of these two roles as functionally related to the pragmatic realities of male social power. Sending female envoys to societies where prevalent gender roles would reject them on the basis of biology would perhaps be a fruitless enterprise in the divine scheme of things.

Moreover, Ibn ʿArabī points out that very few male prophets have been designated as messengers and envoys. Particularly interesting is the way in which he presents this priority of "superlative perfection," informing readers that God has granted some prophets priority over other prophets. Ibn ʿArabī reminds his audience that although both men and women are subject to legal obligations, the particulars of such obligations might differ in varying contexts.

However, after the death of the Prophet Muḥammad, who, according to Muslim tradition, has sealed the station of prophecy, there is no difference in men's and women's access to all spiritual stations. In Islam, the belief that the Prophet Muḥammad was the final prophet and messenger implies that for all of his followers and thus the entire community of Muslims with the exception of its founder, there has never effectively been a spiritual station open to men from which women have been barred. Historically, therefore, Muslim women have always held exactly the same capacity and access to spiritual stations as have men. For Muḥammad's followers, then, an individual's state of attainment is purely the product of spiritual refinement and grace and is never the result of gender identity.

In light of this all-important theological position regarding the finality of the Prophet Muḥammad's mission, the assertion of men's exclusive access to superlative perfection becomes entirely theoretical or rhetorical. A feminist musing by an Ibn ʿArabī enthusiast might present the view that perhaps he was deliberately affirming his patriarchal audience's symbolical and psychological needs while presenting them with some unpalatable positions regarding women's actual complete spiritual equality that were almost heretically gender egalitarian. Or perhaps he was simply limited by his own subjectivity, which was always also enmeshed within a patriarchal symbolic universe. Whatever the case, Ibn ʿArabī accords to men only particular exclusive spiritual stations with particular social correlates that in reality are no longer applicable.

Another topic of social relations of gender, the issue of dressing and modesty, has become increasingly important in contemporary Muslim gender politics. Ibn ʿArabī again takes a very nuanced position. Rejecting discourses of fundamental gender difference in social responsibilities for physical modesty and the covering of nakedness (*ʿawra*), he states,

> Some people say that all of a woman's body, with the exception of her face and hands, constitutes the *ʿawra*. Another group excludes her feet from being *ʿawra*, while a third group considers all of her body without exception to constitute the *ʿawra*. . . . In our opinion, the only parts of her body that are *ʿawra* are her genitals. God, the exalted, says, "When they tasted of the tree, their shameful parts became manifest to them, and they began to sew together the leaves of the Garden over their bodies." God put Adam and Eve on equal footing regarding the covering of their shameful parts, which are their genitals. If women are still required to cover their bodies, and our school agrees with that position, it is for the sake of modesty, and not because their bodies are shameful.[92]

Again, with disarming logic and alacrity, Ibn ʿArabī debunks pervasive notions that women's bodies inherently and ontologically demand greater modesty than men's bodies. He incisively reminds his reader that all human beings are commanded to cover their genitals, the only part of men's and women's bodies that constitute the *ʿawra*. His statement implies that modesty requirements are not ontologically driven but rather socially and legally based. This element of social contingency is also reflected in the conditional "if" with which he begins this statement regarding the command for modesty. Ibn ʿArabī no doubt believed that women should abide by specific minimal legal and social standards of modest apparel, as reflected in his phrase "our [legal] school agrees with that position [of covering]." However, Ibn ʿArabī dismisses any assumptions regarding an innate or heightened sense of shame associated with women's bodies and opens up a more egalitarian and generous space in which his readers can engage with issues of dressing and embodiment. Moreover, his view that women's bodies do not constitute additional *ʿawra* also has profound implications for debates on whether women can lead mixed congregational prayers.

Since Ibn ʿArabī's discussion addresses the essential religious rationale underlying the *ḥijāb* debate, it offers contemporary Muslims a great deal of flexibility and dynamism in harmonizing religious requirements with cultural and social sensibilities on questions of physical modesty. Islamic feminists who condemn unfair social practices that require women to take on primary responsibility for containing public sexuality through their dressing can be nourished by Ibn ʿArabī's insights on the equal responsibilities accorded to men and women for modest physical self-presentation.

Ibn ʿArabī takes another particularly innovative position on women with regard to the leadership of ritual prayers, another topic that has occupied past as well as present-day Muslims. On this issue, he is clear:

> Some people allow the imamate of women absolutely before a congregation of men and women. I agree with this. Some forbid her imamate absolutely. Others permit her imamate in a congregation exclusively of women. How to evaluate this? The prophet has testified about the spiritual perfection [*kamāl*] of some women just as he witnessed of some men, even though there may be more men than women in such perfection. This perfection is prophethood. And being a prophet involves taking on the role of a leader. Thus, women's imamate is sound. The basic principle is allowing women's imamate. Thus, whoever asserts that it is forbidden without proof, he should be ignored. The one who forbids this has no explicit text [*naṣṣ*]. His only proof in forbidding this is a shared [negative] opinion of her. This proof is insubstantial and the basic principle remains, which is allowing women's imamate.[93]

Here again, Ibn ʿArabī links a public communal role—in this case, the position of imam—with an individual's spiritual capacity, an approach described by contemporary scholar Eric Winkel as "spiritual legal discourse."[94] Winkel observes that Ibn ʿArabī's spiritual legal discourse is about discerning divine guidance in ways that "illuminate the crossover from outward ritual to inward truth" in every moment to ensure the dynamic search for divine guidance.[95] Winkel finds precisely this approach in Ibn ʿArabī's views regarding women's imamate.[96]

Ibn ʿArabī explicitly connects the Prophet's affirmation of women's spiritual capacity to ritual leadership and explicitly disregards the position of scholars who reject women's imamate. In this case, complete spiritual realization implies equal and ungendered access to ritual leadership, a radically egalitarian position. While a few scholars had taken this position on the issue of women's imamate, including the much earlier Ṭabarī (d. 923), it was certainly not a popular viewpoint.[97] In fact, there are very few historically documented examples of women's imamate. Nevertheless, Ibn ʿArabī's discussion of this issue and his reference to other scholars' opinions prompts the question of whether women's imamate was perhaps an undocumented occurrence in certain communities. Whatever the case, discussions of these possibilities by leading Islamic intellectuals of the time illustrate that women's imamate was never relegated to the realm of the unthinkable. The Islamic legacy contains counternarratives of gender that destabilize patriarchal norms. In addition, implicit in Ibn ʿArabī's argument regarding women's imamate is the assumption and reality that communal prayer can and should occur in gender-inclusive spaces, though this idea is still contested in many contemporary Muslim contexts.

In reviewing these various legal positions, I am not simply arguing that Muslims possess a precedent for selecting gender-egalitarian ethics for reforming the traditional law in the areas of women's testimony, attire, and leadership of congregational prayers. Ibn ʿArabī's approach offers the resources to address deeper theological constructions underlying the formulation of the *fiqh* in much more fundamental ways. In particular, Ibn ʿArabī urges people to grapple with the nature of religious anthropology underpinning particular legal rulings that have evolved in Muslim legal thought. The religious constructions of "women" and "men" underpinning Muslim laws are crucially linked to the deepest metaphysical conceptions and the nature of human engagement with God that lie at the core of Islam. Consequently, ethics and laws that seek to enable and inspire Muslims to embody the primary archetype of the God-human relationship need explicitly to engage with the nature of theological and anthropological categories. As they evolve, Islamic legal formulations need to be illuminated by foundational theological considerations of the nature of God, human nature, and the gendered human being.

These insights might enable readers to approach particular legal rulings with a critical eye toward the underlying ways in which historical, cultural, and theological assumptions condition particular constructs of "men" and "women" as well as how gender-related laws are implicitly built on such assumptions. Thus, contemporary Muslims following Ibn ʿArabī's lead might suggest taking seriously the linkages between a religious anthropology premised on ungendered spiritual capacities, on the one hand, and particular legal positions, on the other. For Islamic feminists who seek to act with critical fidelity to the legal tradition, this approach provides a way to ground expansive notions of legal equality within a deeply embedded Islamic metaphysics and a spiritually imbued, nourishing religious anthropology.[98]

Ibn ʿArabī's conception of *al-Insān al-Kāmil* as representing a universal standard for complete human spiritual realization, one of the most pivotal tenets in his religious anthropology, is intimately linked to his vision of gender. It represents the universal and genderless ethical self to which all aspirants, male and female, are to aspire. This scholar's consistent point that gender is irrelevant to the pursuit of spiritual refinement reflects the normative Sufi assumption that one's inner state is the primary criterion of human worth. As he illustrates, this view also resonates fully with Qurʾānic teachings on human nature. The exoteric dimensions of human beings, including gender and biology, are considered irrelevant to the goal of spiritual attainment. Not all Sufis in all times have pushed these inherent gender positions to their logical conclusion. Since the central principles were and remain mediated and articulated by people within particular contexts, their interpretations likewise were and remain subject to the limitations of a contextual or individual perspective. Sometimes, their interpretations were (and are) sexist, regardless of current readings. It is thus necessary to subject these discourses to critical inquiry, measuring them against some of the central principles of Sufism.

Ibn ʿArabī's discussions on *al-Insān al-Kāmil* reflect pervasive and foundational Islamic principles relating to human nature, endeavor, and purpose that are explicitly gender-egalitarian. In particular, Ibn ʿArabī fully recognizes the equal agency, ability, and value of men and women, who can realize the ultimate goals of their religion; in addition, and more controversially, spiritual and ontological equality informs social and legal equality. These insights, which he justifies through his readings of the Qurʾān, offer Islamic feminism both a theoretical and methodological guide. By rigorously interrogating the gendered religious anthropology underlying legal positions as well as by engaging the law in ways informed by Sufism's elaborately articulated and holistic vision of submission, Islamic feminists can ensure that their search for Islamic ethics takes faith seriously. Doing so demands that we inform our sociopolitical lenses with a spiritual praxis that engages truth as an unfolding and dynamic process. Within this vision, law is about more than simple gender equality. It is about facilitating societies that foster the spiritual refinement of human character, a refinement to which gender equality is absolutely intrinsic. These rich resources within Sufism combine with feminist insights to allow for a radical and organic critique of patriarchal societies. Such a contemporary engagement with Sufism also opens up spaces for prioritizing alternative modes of equality-based relationships between all human beings. These alternative modes of gender relationships provide the focus for the next chapter.

Chapter Three

Mysticism and Gender

A Hermeneutic of Experience

Ibn ʿArabī's sophisticated cosmology, his profound understandings of human nature and the processes of spiritual transformation for men and women alike, and his sometimes radical gendered legal positions were birthed from within the complexities of his experience, both mystical and mundane. Using the insightful feminist adage that "the personal is political," this chapter explores aspects of Ibn ʿArabī's life and relationships as he presents them, imagining how these experiences created the background against which he received mystical insights and shaped his mystical understandings. For an epistemology of spiritual experience, mystical "openings" occur within a flesh-and-blood person whose personal disposition and life experience, in all their complexity and nuance, mediate the reception and formulation of these insights.

Given that I am foregrounding the category of "experience" as one epistemological entry point for analyzing Ibn ʿArabī's works, it is necessary to make some critical observations regarding this category. It is impossible empirically to verify most experiences discussed by Ibn ʿArabī, whether mystical or mundane, so I refer to Ibn ʿArabī's *representations* of his experiences. I thus creatively establish an internally cohesive set of connections between Ibn ʿArabī's reported experiences. Although I note specific narratives where his interactions with particular female characters are clearly tropological, I generally assume that his representations of relationships to women speak to his actual experience in the same way that his other representations of his relationships to men speak to actual experiences with men; in that manner, I accept his bona fide representations of his mystical experiences. Thus, with regard to both his "everyday experiences" and his "mystical experiences," I am dealing with Ibn ʿArabī's depictions and representations of these aspects of his life.

This chapter focuses on some of the textured layers of Ibn ʿArabī's interpersonal relationships, not as merely interesting contextual information about him but rather as central to the formulation of his worldview. In particular, exploring some of his relationships with women in the biographical sources might also help illuminate some of his understandings of human nature and gender. His understandings of human nature and possibilities were not simply the product of isolated mystical openings or even of subsequent theoretical abstraction but were also deeply informed by his interpersonal experiences.

Two aspects of the writings and experiences of Ibn ʿArabī beckon to any feminist scholar. First, amid the rich panoply of his mystical openings are some very radical conceptions of gender, atypical for much of the thirteenth-century male scholarly elite. These "egalitarian" narratives are nevertheless at times interwoven seamlessly with patriarchal elements normative within his context. Second, in perusing the biographical material on Ibn ʿArabī's life through a gender lens, the distinct and large presence of women in his life stands out: women were prominent in both his family and his religious and social circles. Given that premodern norms in many Islamicate cultures separated men and women in the social realm, Ibn ʿArabī's level of interaction with women outside of his family is noteworthy. He not only had female spiritual masters and disciples but also enjoyed an intense and enigmatic relationship with the beautiful Niẓām, who had boldly castigated him.

Did a connection exist between these two very unusual dimensions of Ibn ʿArabī's life—his mystical experiences, which rendered unique understandings of gender, and the flourishing presence of his personal and social experiences with women? Were his mystical experiences responsible for his openness toward alternative ways of understanding gender relationships? Or were his deep and intense interpersonal relationships with women responsible for his receptivity to particular forms of mystical insights on gender? These questions point to a number of relevant epistemological issues in both mysticism and feminism.

Formulating Subjectivities: Mysticism and Feminism

Mysticism and feminism share one significant epistemological concern: both have a deep interest in the way experience produces knowledge. Feminist philosophers have convincingly argued that knowledge production, notions of morality, and ethics are significantly shaped by the experiential matrix of its formulators. By exposing the partial, subjective contours of the knowledge project, feminist philosophers have deconstructed some of the assumptions about objectivity and universality in dominant patriarchal epistemological enterprises. In a rather different but parallel mode, mystics claim that knowledge gained in a mystical experience takes epistemological priority over purely rational deliberations. In varying ways, both feminist and mystical discursive traditions deconstruct rigid binaries of experience and theory, emotions and rationality, embodiment and knowledge, subjectivity and objectivity. Despite varying conceptions of the nature of subjectivity and questions about what constitutes the strata of "experience," both feminism and mysticism provide powerful alternatives to traditional ratiocentric epistemologies.

Premodern mystics and contemporary feminists present different epistemological assumptions in their respective discussions of experience. For many post-Enlightenment feminists, metaphysics might be entirely inconsequential to a conceptualization of human experience. Some of these feminists are even antimetaphysical, seeing religion as the handmaiden of patriarchy. Many feminists place on the agenda for epistemological reflection the vicissitudes of gendered human subjectivity, often in its everyday mundane realm.

For mystics, a metaphysical worldview is defining in every aspect of life. Sufis embrace the everyday mundane nature of human experience as the living canvas of spiritual praxis, an approach that allows for deep reflections on the nature and development of human subjectivity.[1] Simultaneously, Sufis present us with the category of mystical experience, which has a rather different epistemological status. These mystical states are often seen as the closest encounters with the one true reality, perhaps even as more true than everyday experiences. They are entirely Other yet simultaneously located in the deepest parts of the self. Mystical experiences are perceived to be given as an act of grace from the ultimate source of all things, having an immediate and personal "taste" of truth that is incontrovertible.

For mystics, these two levels of experience are profoundly connected. A person's receptivity to mystical experiences is in many situations at least partly contingent on his or her subjective spiritual state. Spiritual preparedness for receiving a mystical experience, in turn, happens as a consequence of the continual process of life experience, in which spiritual refinement is an everyday process permeating all of one's interactions and activities. In this framework, the spiritually transforming individual is the receptive nonbinary locus in which truth reveals itself on the subjective palate of the individual seeker, who simultaneously holds the human and the divine in a relationship of radical nonduality, transcending explicit categories of subject and object. Mystical experience incorporates the particular and the universal in a dialectical mode. I draw connections to feminist epistemology in terms of Sufism's integration of the individual seeker's particularity.

Feminists have brought into focus the organic relationship between gendered subjectivities and knowledge. They have debunked dominant assumptions that an individual can generate knowledge in a value-neutral way, independent of embodied experience.[2] Drawing on the feminist notion that embodied experience substantively shapes ideas and theory, I explore the possibility that Ibn ʿArabī's experiences with women in his life poured into his work. Experience, in its myriad forms, undoubtedly provides an epistemological base for Ibn ʿArabī's cosmology. However, many scholars of Ibn ʿArabī focus primarily on his mystical experiences to explain his gendered cosmology. Some scholars often present Ibn ʿArabī's multilayered relationships with his female teachers, wives, disciples, daughters, sisters, and friends as interesting but almost incidental biographical information. Others reinforce an impermeable binary between the pure transcendence of his "vertical" mystical experience as impervious to social and "horizontal" influences.[3] But one cannot discount all dimensions of his experiences, in particular, his relationships with women. In fact, Ibn ʿArabī's unitary worldview defies rigid separations between the different forms of human experience. In Ibn ʿArabī's framework, all experiences interpenetrate one another, collectively sculpting a mosaic of signs (*āyāt*) that point to the divine.

Ibn ʿArabī alludes to an interesting interface between his mystical and social experiences, particularly with regard to gender, when he reports that when he first embarked on the spiritual path, he intensely disliked women and sex. Lasting for about eighteen years, this state of aversion caused him great consternation, since he was aware of the *ḥadīth* stating that God made women lovable to the Prophet Muḥammad. According to this tradition, the prophetic love for women not only resulted from Muḥammad's natural inclinations but was a divinely bestowed love. Despising that which the Prophet loved, Ibn ʿArabī was deeply fearful of incurring the wrath of God. After Ibn ʿArabī beseeched the Almighty for help in this regard, his previous dislike of women and sex was removed: "When I became sincere with God in turning my attention to him in this due to my fear of God's anger because I despised what God made lovable to his prophet, this condition dissipated, thanks be to God! And God made them lovable to me, and I am the greatest of all creation in compassion toward them and in guarding their rights, because in this matter I am acting on insight [*baṣīra*], and it is from [women] being made lovable to me [by God] and not from love that proceeds from my own nature."[4]

Ibn ʿArabī is telling us that his gender lenses are in fact directly informed by his mystical insights and by his desire to emulate the prophetic example. Significant in this comment is his claim that love, compassion, and justice toward women are divine mandates incumbent on men based on prophetic example. These attitudes are thus not to be seen simply as the product of an individual disposition or the natural propensities of some men. He also makes explicit connections between love and justice: loving women for Ibn ʿArabī is not simply an asocial emotional experience but also directly impacts the protection of women's rights. Despite what might sound in a modern context as a somewhat condescending and paternalistic attitude toward women, Ibn ʿArabī is making a sweeping assertion in a patriarchal context. Claiming religious authority on the basis of both inspiration and prophetic example, Ibn ʿArabī demands that the men in societies characterized by gender asymmetry are obliged to relate to women with love and benevolence. More especially, this anecdote reflects the porous nature of the mystical and personal dimensions of human experience.

In addition, Ibn ʿArabī's comments about his early "aversion" to women must be juxtaposed with seemingly contrary evidence in which he extensively describes his devotion to female Sufi teachers early in his spiritual training. He describes his relationships as a young aspirant on the path with living exemplars of the Muḥammadan model—women teachers who epitomized a balance of both *jamālī* and *jalālī* attributes, Sufi role models who no doubt informed his constructs of human spiritual refinement, religious personhood, and ontology.

Teachers, Disciples, and Niẓām

Delving into the treasure trove of Ibn ʿArabī's writings, which collectively offer biographical insights about him, readers encounter a younger version of Ibn ʿArabī, traveling to various cities of learning in Andalusia, seeking out the learned and the wise, having already experienced mystical visions of

God. In the formative period of his life, he met, studied with, and served as a disciple to two women saints, Fāṭima bint Ibn al-Muthannā and Yasmīna Umm al-Fuqarāʾ.[5] He discusses his relationship to these spiritual savants in both his *Rūḥ al-quds* and his *Al-Durrat al-fākhira.*

He frequently visited Yasmīna, or "Shams," a woman in her eighties who lived at Marchena of the Olives, and although Shams generally concealed her spiritual state from others, she would reveal it to him on occasion since she considered him a student with unique capacities. He expresses his tremendous admiration for her many gifts: "Among people of our kind I have never met one like her with respect to the control she had over her soul. In her spiritual activities and communications, she was among the greatest. She had a strong and pure heart, a noble spiritual power, and a fine discrimination. . . . She was endowed with many graces. I had considerable experience of her intuition and found her to be a master in this sphere. Her spiritual state was characterized chiefly by her fear of God and his good pleasure in her, the combination of the two at the same time in one person being extremely rare among us."[6] He goes on to describe some of her supernatural abilities, including her ability to perceive things and communicate at great distances as well as the power to voice other people's thoughts. Ibn ʿArabī writes that Shams's "revelations were true, and I saw her perform many wonders."[7]

Ibn ʿArabī thus accords full recognition to the spiritual mastery of a woman adept, depicting her as superior in ability and attainment to many of her male contemporaries. She represents the prototypical spiritual aspirant and serves as a role model for her fellow Sufis. There is nothing exclusively or traditionally female in his description of her spirituality; she embodies not only gracious and merciful qualities but also mastery, strength, nobility, fine discrimination, and control of her soul. She epitomizes a balance of *jamālī* and *jalālī* qualities. Among Sufi masters, she is one among equals and is in fact distinctive in virtue and excellence. His comment about his frequent visits to her and deep pleasure at her private revelations of the secrets of her spiritual state suggests not only his high regard for her but also the intense interpersonal interaction among individual Sufi men and women in that context.

Ibn ʿArabī also spent two years serving Fāṭima of Cordova as a disciple.[8] Her intimate mentoring and nurturing teaching relationship with him is captured in her consideration of herself as his spiritual mother.[9] The young Sufi reports rather endearingly that when in the company of this ninety-year-old woman, "I was almost ashamed to look at her face when I sat with her, it was so rosy and soft."[10] In recounting Fāṭima's lofty spiritual station and singular devotion to God, he declares, "Although God offered her his kingdom, she refused, saying, 'You are all, all else is inauspicious for me.'" He also described her as "a mercy to the world" whose "spiritual influence was great"; she had been "given the power of the Qurʾānic chapter *Al-Fātiḥa* [The Opening] and was able to wield its power in any situation."[11]

Ibn ʿArabī's descriptions of his relationship with both of these female teachers carry tones of reverence and great admiration, conjuring up an image of an eager young disciple diligently striving to please his spiritual teachers and viewed very favorably by them. He jubilantly reports that Fāṭima described him as the most fully present and attentive of her students. Unlike some other disciples, who were preoccupied with other concerns while in her company, Ibn ʿArabī came to Fāṭima "with all of himself. When he rises up it is with all of himself and when he sits it is with his whole self, leaving nothing of himself elsewhere. That is how it should be on the Way."[12] The accounts of his special and deep relationships with these women are noteworthy; in his self-portrait, he saw himself as a diligent and devoted disciple of both of them.

Ibn ʿArabī's admiration of Sufi women was not restricted to his teachers; he also describes a number of his female cohorts. The *Rūḥ al-quds* contains an entry about a peer of his, an anonymous slave girl of Qāsim al-Dawla whom Ibn ʿArabī describes as "unique in her time," gifted with supernatural abilities to commune with mountains and trees and able to travel great distances quickly.[13] He admired her because her "spiritual state was strong" and because she adhered to the Sufi path with "unswerving sincerity." She was rigorous in self-discipline and frequently fasted through the day and night, earning Ibn ʿArabī's highest praise: "I have never seen one more spiritually chivalrous in our time."[14]

Ibn ʿArabī visited another prominent Sufi woman, Zaynab al-Qalʾiyya, in both Seville and Mecca. Despite being gifted with beauty and wealth, Zaynab had freely renounced the world. Ibn ʿArabī describes her as a "foremost ascetic of her day," known to levitate in the air during meditation; she was also "one of the most intelligent people of her time" and a companion of some of the most eminent male Sufis.[15] Ibn ʿArabī accompanied this great spiritual savant on a journey from Mecca to Jerusalem, observing that he had never seen anyone "more strict in observing the times of prayer than her."[16] In some contexts, therefore, unrelated Sufi men and women interacted freely in social spaces, even traveling great distances together.

Ibn ʿArabī also mentions a significant number of female disciples. In a series of short poems at the beginning of the *Dīwān*, Ibn ʿArabī supplies the names of fourteen people that he had invested with the *khirqa* (Sufi cloak); thirteen of these people were women.[17] Investing a disciple with the *khirqa* signified a binding initiatory relationship, characterized by transference of spiritual power from the master to the disciple.[18] Investiture of the *khirqa* enabled the process of inner transformation of the initiate, linking him or her to a chain of spiritual transmission (*silsila*) that originated with the Prophet Muḥammad. While he undoubtedly transferred the *khirqa* to many male disciples, it is noteworthy that the majority of named disciples are women. With the exception of Zumurrud, who elicited a critical poem from the *shaykh* for abandoning the *khirqa* he had passed to her,[19] all of these women are applauded as genuine aspirants on the path, with some described as exceptional:

You adorned Fāṭima with the garment of piety and guidance
  I do not see anyone more deserving of the apparel of virtue
You clothed her with the exalted and supreme mantle
  Casting all ills from her heart
Between substance and accident she learned virtue from me
  Suffering, by God, in discipleship
I asked God to give me a daughter
  And he obliged me with her
I beseech nothing for her, except him,
  So let her give thanks for the providence of the Compassionate.[20]

Many of his other poems in this collection also reflect the high regard with which he held his female disciples. Ibn ʿArabī clearly had not only impressive female spiritual teachers but also deep mentoring relationships with women disciples, all of whom clearly influenced his attitudes toward women and their spiritual capacities.

However, a Persian Sufi, Niẓām bint Makīn al-Dīn, remains by far the most intriguing woman depicted in his writings, not only for the window his writings open regarding this female personality but also for their revelations about the author. Although he had celebrated the great wisdom and beauty of his teachers and disciples, Niẓām appears to have had an indelible and unique impact on his being.[21] She provided the inspiration for some of the most spiritually devoted love poetry in his *Tarjumān al-ashwāq*.

Ibn ʿArabī became more closely acquainted with Niẓām through his association with her father, a distinguished scholar in Mecca, Makīn al-Dīn Ẓāhir ibn Rustam. According to Ibn ʿArabī, he had desired greatly to study traditions under Niẓām's aged aunt, the learned expert Fakhr al-Nisāʾ bint Rustam. However, she declined his request on account of her age, preferring instead to spend the winter of her life in devotion.[22] She agreed that her brother could write Ibn ʿArabī a general certificate of authorization (*ijāza ʿāmma*) for all the *aḥadīth* she had related, a fact that also suggests female expertise in traditional Islamic scholarship in Mecca at the time. Moreover, this story illustrates that female experts were also sought after as teachers for male scholars. In his contact with this family, Ibn ʿArabī was thus introduced to Niẓām. He writes,

> Now the Shaikh had a daughter, a lissome young girl who captivated the gaze of all those who saw her, whose mere presence was the ornament of our gatherings and startled all those who contemplated it to the point of stupefaction. . . . The magic of her glance, the grace of her conversation were such an enchantment that when on occasion she was prolix, her words flowed from the source; when she spoke concisely she was a marvel of eloquence; when she expounded an argument, she was clear and transparent. . . . If not for the paltry souls who are ever ready for scandal and predisposed to malice, I should comment here on the beauties of her body as well as her soul, which was a garden of generosity. . . . I took her as a model for the inspiration of the poems contained in the present book which are love poems . . . although I was unable to express so much as a part of the emotion which my soul experienced and which the company of this young girl awakened in my heart, or of the generous love I felt, or of the memory which her unwavering friendship left in my memory, or of the grace of mind or the modesty of her bearing, since she is the object of my Quest and my hope, the Virgin Most Pure. Nevertheless I succeeded in putting into verse some of the thoughts connected with my yearning, as precious gifts and objects which I here offer. I let my enamoured soul speak clearly, I tried to express the profound attachment I felt, the profound concern that tormented me in those days now past, the regret that still moves me at the memory of that noble society and that young girl. Whatever name I mention in this work it is to her that I am alluding. Whatever the house whose elegy I sing, it is her house that I am thinking. But that is not all. In the verses I have composed for the present book, I never cease to al-

lude to the divine inspirations, the spiritual visitations, the correspondences with world of the angelic Intelligences, in this I conformed to my usual manner of thinking in symbols; this because the things of the invisible world attract me more than those of actual life, and because this young girl knew perfectly what I was alluding to.[23]

This picture highlights Niẓām's exceptional qualities and charismatic presence. Ibn ʿArabī celebrates not only Niẓām's spiritual mastery, wisdom, and intellect but also her enchanting beauty and sensuality. Niẓām's distinguishing qualities that so profoundly affected Ibn ʿArabī—wisdom, beauty, intelligence, a magnetic presence, an exalted spirituality, and eloquence—together represent a very powerful image of womanhood in particular and of humanity in general. In Ibn ʿArabī's depictions, Niẓām epitomizes some of the most significant ungendered attributes of human refinement while being a real embodied woman. In such comprehensive descriptions, integrating dimensions of intellect, spirituality, and physicality, Ibn ʿArabī collapses some of the patriarchal stereotypes that isolate and bind women solely within the realm of the body. Simultaneously, however, he recognizes and celebrates in her the beauty and power of the female form.

Ibn ʿArabī's description of Niẓām's social behavior is also noteworthy. She appears assertive and uninhibited. She speaks at public gatherings, where people are riveted by her eloquence and beauty. She is unmarried and has friendships with unrelated males. She is clearly unveiled and dresses so that the beauty of her body is apparent, yet she remains modest. This woman is confident and, as discussed in chapter 2, does not hesitate to admonish Ibn ʿArabī, the greatest mystic of the day. Niẓām's understanding of the realities provides a learning opportunity for the great scholar and mystic as well as representing iconoclastic possibilities for women. Gender apparently does not constrain spiritual potential or attainment, an insight often echoed in Ibn ʿArabī's works. In social terms, Ibn ʿArabī's description represents Niẓām as independent and self-assured. Her behavior presents the antithesis of the ideal traditional woman, who stays quietly within the confines of her home, focusing on meeting the needs of her husband, father, and other male relatives and never engaging in any meaningful way with the public sphere.[24] Ibn ʿArabī's portrayal of Niẓām, in contrast, provides alternate imaginings of gender and female subjectivity.

This type of representation of women was nonconformist and even anathema to many of Ibn ʿArabī's male contemporaries, who accused him of dissembling erotic and sensual love to preserve his reputation. Following such censure, Ibn ʿArabī compiled a judicious commentary explaining the spiritual realities to which he was alluding in this work. This episode illustrates the interpenetrating nature of the mystical, the personal, and the political aspects of human experience. The outcry from some of Ibn ʿArabī's peers reflects a context in which representations of women combining and imbricating sensuality into spiritual discourse were considered immoral and cause for censure. These authorities found it difficult to see the relationship between human embodiment, sensuality, and spiritual truth.[25]

Ibn ʿArabī's unambiguous celebration of Niẓām's numerous gifts and talents illustrates how his views on women did not simply remain theoretical but were lived. His involvement with female spiritual authorities in his formative period, his later relationships with women such as Niẓām, his female disciples, and other peers contributed to his ability to relate to women as fully fledged aspirants along the Sufi path.

In light of such biographical revelations, it is appropriate to revisit Ibn ʿArabī's comment about his abhorrence of women and sex early in his spiritual career. In his recounting, these negative attitudes changed through divine intervention, with his newfound love for women in turn fueling a nobler goal of protecting their rights in the mold of the Prophet Muḥammad. The accounts of Ibn ʿArabī's various relationships with women Sufis contrast the reality of his early devotion to his female teachers with his purported "aversion" to women. What did he mean by "aversion" when he clearly had very strong and positive relationships with his early female Sufi teachers?

A number of possibilities emerge. This "aversion" might have related exclusively to sexually and emotionally intimate relationships with women. If so, Ibn ʿArabī, in the tradition of some earlier Sufis, did not relate to his female Sufi teachers as women per se but merely as spiritual teachers whose gender was an insignificant variable. If such was the case, his later spiritual "openings" toward women referred to women in general, not just his Sufi teachers. Another possibility is that his retrospective comment that his aversion to women had been transmuted through a mystical insight was a defensive claim, protecting him against possible accusations of eroticism, sensuality, and immorality made by detractors of the *Tarjumān*. His comment may have served even more broadly as an overall justification for his unusually large number of profound relationships with women and as a response to those resistant to his egalitarian readings of gender. A third possible explanation is the existence of all these dimensions—that is, his dislike of women was indeed dispelled by a spiritual transformation that he later invoked to defend himself against suspicions held by his peers about his numerous close relationships with women and to justify his unusually beneficent understandings of gender.

If his claims were in fact defensive, they point to particular social norms and forces that made such a defense necessary. The extent of Ibn ʿArabī's interactions with unrelated women is particularly noteworthy in light of recent scholarship on premodern Andalusian social norms. On the one hand, we certainly find interesting indications that a few other Andalusian thinkers appear to be sensitive to issues of gender in their works. For example, in a juristic work, *al-Muḥallā bil-āthār*, Ibn Ḥazm argues in favor of women's participation in certain public rituals, including praying in mosques, performing *iʿtikāf*, a form of devotion that involves seclusion in the mosque for prayer or fasting, and participating in funeral processions and visiting cemeteries.[26] However, one cannot read these legal positions as necessarily reflective of properly egalitarian social spaces. Historian María Luisa Ávila argues that despite some scholarly assertions about the freedom enjoyed by Andalusian women, this fact is not reflected in biographical dictionaries between the ninth and eleventh centuries.[27] Ávila concludes that relatively few women were involved in the acquisition of scientific and religious knowledge in Al-Andalus and that most women were active only in the sphere of the family; in the few exceptional instances when women were active outside of this sphere, social norms dictated that they stay as far away from men as possible.[28] If Ávila is correct about these gender norms, then Ibn ʿArabī's intense relationships with numerous nonkin women as well as the very powerful, socially visible Sufi women he describes gain even more significance.

In fact, Ibn ʿArabī refers to the fact that the male disciple is not supposed to have friendships with women until he reaches a particular state of spiritual maturity, at which point his soul becomes "feminine" in its receptivity to the divine.[29] After such a state of being is attained, relationships between the male disciple and women can be characterized by love without any risk of social or sexual impropriety. These collective sources might lead to the conclusion that close relationships between Sufi men and women of advanced spiritual stature were an acceptable exception to the social norm of gender segregation. This idea, however, does not detract from the powerful broader social implications of Ibn ʿArabī's statement about his spiritually changed state toward women. He makes an authoritative claim of a divinely mandated love for women, modeled on the prophetic example that men should deal lovingly with women and remain observant and protective of their rights.

Family Relationships

In addition to these more "public" relationships with female disciples, teachers, and spiritual luminaries, Ibn ʿArabī's writings offer significant details about his relationships with women in his family. While details about his mother are sparse, she regularly visited Fāṭima of Cordoba. In fact, according to Ibn ʿArabī, Fāṭima had often said to him, "I am your spiritual mother and the light of your earthly mother."[30] If nothing else, his biological mother's regular visits to Fāṭima indicate her inclination toward a Sufi teacher.

Ibn ʿArabī seems to have been a devoted and caring brother to his two sisters. Following the death of their parents, Ibn ʿArabī, the only son, faced family pressure to dedicate himself to supporting his two sisters. However, he seems to have managed to do so without sacrificing his religious life. He did not relinquish his responsibility to find them husbands to anyone else despite having received an offer for such assistance from no less than the "Prince of the Faithful," the ruler at the time.[31]

Ibn ʿArabī's profound love and tenderness toward his sisters is also reflected in a letter written to his elder sister on the occasion of their younger sister's death.[32] Ibn ʿArabī laments his sister's demise, describing her as the "best of ladies," a "white diamond." Praying fervently for her salvation, he hopes that he will be reunited with her in the afterlife. Addressing his surviving elder sister as "the honored mother-sister," his tender words of consolation at their shared loss reveal respect and deep caring.[33]

Possibly the most telling dimension of Ibn ʿArabī's relationship with his sisters is reflected in his description of a mystical vision of the Day of Resurrection.[34] In elaborate detail, he describes a conversation with God, who grants Ibn ʿArabī unreserved entry into paradise. Ibn ʿArabī then successfully appeals for intercession on behalf of the first people he sees, all of whom are women—his sisters, his wife, and another woman. He asks God to grant him intercession for all of his companions and relatives and then for all of those upon whom his gaze falls, without giving each one's name; God agrees. Striking in this account is the fact that the first four people—the only ones mentioned by name—are women whom he clearly loved and to whom he was deeply attached. Some of his earliest and most important interactions with females were positive, and he maintained a deep emotional and spiritual connection with women throughout his life.

The sources are unclear about exactly how many wives Ibn ʿArabī had. He had at least two and possibly more. He writes that his saintly wife, Maryam bint Muḥammad bin ʿAbdūn al-Bijāʾī, told him, "In my sleep I saw someone who often comes to visit me in my visions, but whom I have never met in the world of sense perception. He asked me, 'Do you aspire to the Way?' I replied, 'Most certainly, but I don't know how to reach it!' He said through five things, namely trust, certainty, patience, resolution, and sincerity."[35] Maryam shared Ibn ʿArabī's mystical orientation, and he obviously had great regard for her piety, as suggested by his descriptions of her as saintly. Their marital relationship appears to have been characterized by some significant shared priorities related to the mystical path.

Ibn ʿArabī's second wife was Fāṭima bint Yūsuf Amīr al-Ḥaramayn, the daughter of the custodian of the two holy mosques. She may have been the mother of one of Ibn ʿArabī's foremost disciples, Ṣadr al-Dīn al-Qūnawī. According to later sources, Ibn ʿArabī also married the daughter of the Mālikī *qāḍī*ʾ of Damascus.[36] Ibn ʿArabī describes an unnamed deceased wife to whom he dedicated his pilgrimage and fasting, beginning, "I had a wife whom I loved, but time separated us." He proceeds with a eulogy for her, describing her radiant smile and his great sense of loss at her death.[37] Ibn ʿArabī appears to have had deep emotional and spiritual connections to his wives, whether he was a polygynist (a cultural norm in Ibn ʿArabī's context) or a serial monogamist.

It is also difficult to determine exactly how many daughters Ibn ʿArabī had, especially since he often referred to some of his female disciples as daughters. He certainly had at least one biological daughter, Zaynab, about whom he writes with great affection. On one occasion, he had planned to meet his wife and young daughter in Mecca, where they had made the pilgrimage with his wife's brother. Their meeting makes for emotional reading and offers insights about his role and feeling as father: "My daughter caught sight of me and cried out: Mummy! It's Daddy!! Then her mother looked and saw me in the distance." Zaynab went on excitedly, calling, "There's my Daddy! There's my Daddy!" until one of her uncles called to him. According to Ibn ʿArabī, "When I came to her, she laughed and threw her arms around me, shouting, 'Daddy! Daddy!'"[38] In this account, Zaynab's response to him appears spontaneous, enthusiastic, and loving. The tone of the extract reflects great fatherly tenderness and affection.

In the *Futūḥāt*, Ibn ʿArabī narrates a noteworthy if unusual story set in a gathering of his family and disciples that depicts the young Zaynab's precocious intelligence: "One day I started questioning my daughter Zaynab in jest. She was only a year old and still at her mother's breast, and I asked her, 'When a man has intercourse with a woman without emitting sperm, what must he do?' She replied, 'He must perform the great ablution [*ghusl*]' to the amazement of all present."[39]

In this clearly tropological representation of his young daughter, Ibn ʿArabī appeals to the topos of Jesus speaking from the cradle. How might we understand this mimetic reproduction of Jesus in relation to Ibn ʿArabī's family? By depicting his one-year-old daughter as the pronouncer of a correct fatwa, Ibn ʿArabī appears to be critiquing the "real" jurists in his context, who understand little of true value. Invoking this trope simultaneously bolsters Ibn ʿArabī's reputation by signifying the unique gifts of his progeny.[40] Such a narrative construct incidentally also suggests Ibn ʿArabī's conceptual universe as one where discussions of sexuality are naturalized and boundaries between public and private spheres appear porous.

Finally, mention is made of a daughter, perhaps the same Zaynab, in a sad poem composed in the wake of her death. The poem expresses a father's profound sense of loss and suffering at burying the daughter of his "very flesh." In this poem, the personal experience of death and loss of a child leads to the father's universal reflections on the nature of human existence and the return to God.[41] Ralph Austin describes this elegy as a synopsis of almost all the most important teachings of Ibn ʿArabī's life.[42] As a father, his experience of intense grief, mourning, and melancholia grants him deeper insight into the nature of reality. Such relationships with members of his family depict a man profoundly, intimately, emotionally, physically, and spiritually connected to the women in his life.

Exploring Ibn ʿArabī's biographical details demonstrates that he enjoyed many different types of rich interpersonal relationships with women. He had deep, nurturing, and loving relationships not only with women in his family but also with others who were his spiritual teachers, peers, and disciples. In addition, given the extensive web of profound and transforming relationships that he shared with women throughout his life, it seems likely that reciprocal and mutually constitutive relationships existed among his mystical experiences, his personal interactions with women, and his understandings of gender. His reflections on women's equal spiritual capacities and his gendered positions on law and social norms seem to mimic his expansive modes of engaging women in his life.

A Relational Epistemology: Concluding Thoughts

In the wake of these glimpses into Ibn ʿArabī's life and his varied relationships with women, I now turn to his formal ideas on gender. His writings on gender are not always straightforward and clear cut; they often appear fluid and contingent. His notions of gender are part of an intricate web of spiritual apprehensions in which each understanding seems to have a ripple effect on others. In characteristic Sufi style, things are often not as they appear. In particular, Ibn ʿArabī's nuanced teachings on gender are integrally related to his essential assumptions about the nature of the human self as well as the paradigm of spiritual actualization explored. The narratives weave through one another in pervasive and subtle forms, constantly shifting perceptions of the nature of gendered realities. What Ibn ʿArabī writes in one place is often supplemented, reconfigured, or even contradicted in another. His writings suggest an iconic thinker who at times stretched and even flouted the gender norms of his era but at other times predictably reflected his cultural immersion in a deeply rooted patriarchy.

Two competing trends characterize Ibn ʿArabī's textured gender constellation if it is viewed through a critical linear lens. On the one hand, Ibn ʿArabī fully integrates women into the ultimate human quest for refinement, highlighting female agency both socially and spiritually and presenting "feminine" realities in radically innovative ontological terms, thereby destabilizing the traditional male-centeredness of hegemonic Muslim discourses. On the other hand, Ibn ʿArabī elsewhere articulates gender in ways that are enmeshed in traditional patriarchal assumptions premised on hierarchical relationships between men and women. At times, his gendered metaphors when describing macrocosmic principles appear to reinscribe this dominant and asymmetrical gender status quo.

Perhaps Ibn ʿArabī's seemingly conflictual readings of gender result partly from the interaction between his mystical visions as well as his reported personal relationships with women and the dominant gender mappings characterizing his social context. His mystical openings gave him experiential access to a profoundly unitary reality that, among other things, shattered prevailing conceptions of gender hierarchy. Given the nature of his teachings, these visions, together with his personal encounters with accomplished female mystics, appear to have fragmented some of his patriarchal social conditioning, though it continued to leave indelible traces in his ideas.

Until recently, academic debates on the nature of mystical experiences have been characterized by a tension between different approaches. In his *Varieties of Religious Experience* (1902), William James took a position premised on an essentialist assumption that all mystical experience has a universal and common core, often described as a state of "pure consciousness," underlying culturally specific articulations of such experience. In this type of framework, which other observers have subsequently articulated in varying ways, contexts of whatever kind are viewed as secondary or even incidental to the mystical experience—a mystical experience is viewed as a form of unadulterated access to reality. In this kind of purist approach, a mystic's gendered interpersonal relationships would be peripheral to understanding the nature of mystical insights. These assumptions also pervade the perennialist and traditionalist approaches in the study of Islam. My approach, through creatively suggesting connections between Ibn ʿArabī's mystical ideas and his interpersonal relationships with women, challenges some of the essentialist assumptions of the "common core" view of mystical experience.

The view that an unmediated universal core transcends different religious and cultural boundaries has already come under attack in Steven Katz's pioneering 1978 essay, "Language, Epistemology and Mysticism." His constructivist critique holds that there are no pure or unmediated mystical experiences but that a mystic's experiences are articulated only through a set of theological, epistemological, and metaphysical doctrines and that these different "languages" fundamentally condition the nature of such mystical experience. While I do not concur with Katz's radically constructivist view that mystical experiences are simply products of mediated theological doctrine in particular religious contexts, my approach to Ibn ʿArabī's is certainly enriched by attending to his personal context. Katz's sophisticated reflections on the epistemological process underlying the depiction of mystical experiences allow a contemporary reader to deliberate on the complex ways that Ibn ʿArabī's reported relationships with women might also inform his mysticism.

The most compelling contemporary approach on the relationship between context and mystical experience has been initiated by Frederick Streng and other scholars who have argued that both essentialist and constructivist positions are premised on the duality of human experience, a position that runs contrary to the writings of many mystics.[43] Instead, such scholars offer a dialectical approach to mysticism embracing the nonbinary character of mystical experience. Such an approach considers context and unconditional consciousness as an integral whole in ways that are more consistent with how many mystics assert the nonduality of their experiences. My reading of Ibn ʿArabī's mystical ideas, his life, and his relationships with women draws on this third dialectical approach, which refuses easy essentialist or constructivist approaches to understanding mystical experience. Such an approach does not exclude any dimension of human experience from the encompassing reach of its metaphysical situatedness, an approach that I think is most consistent with a *tawḥīdic* theology.

Chapter Four

Reading Gender and Metaphor in Ibn ʿArabī's Cosmos

Unsaying Gender: A Mystical Hermeneutic of Subversion

In engaging the tension between perspectives that challenge traditional gender stereotypes and those that reiterate normative conventions, feminist readers encounter a set of more nuanced methodological and theoretical considerations. At the outset, it is imperative to situate Ibn ʿArabī's teachings on gender within the assumptions of his worldview—that is, to take seriously the Sufi framework of his engagement with gender. As is characteristic of all Ibn ʿArabī's works, paradox, ambivalence, and contradiction are part of his mystical methodology. Since reality "as it really is" or mystical experiences give a glimpse into that which cannot be understood or captured in language and rational categorizations, Sufis employ a dialectical mode of discussion to overcome these limitations.

Jeffery Kripal, a scholar of mysticism, points out that mystical language often functions as "a dialectical attempt to transcend the distinction between form and formlessness."[1] In particular, the use of a dialectical mode allows Ibn ʿArabī to present within language, with all its limitations, insights that transcend normative and established patterns. Beginning with a shared symbol of traditional gender norms as one side of the dialectic is integral for meaningful communication within a given context. These norms are then countered by the other side—nonnormative, egalitarian gender narratives. The subsequent transcendence of the established positions through the dialectic opens up vast horizons for transforming fundamental assumptions on the nature of gender and its signification.

One might also discern within Ibn ʿArabī's dialectical presentations of gender hints of an apophatic method, a theological mode of "un-saying or speaking away" found in a variety of religious and mystical traditions.[2] According to Michael Sells, "Apophasis is a discourse in which any single proposition is acknowledged as falsifying, as reifying. It is a discourse of double propositions, in which meaning is generated through the tension between saying and unsaying."[3] In particular, Ibn ʿArabī's multiple and contrary formulations contain an "apophasis of gender," where the saying and unsaying of normative categories unhinge fixed understandings of gender, allowing for novel ways of imagining humanity beyond binary formulations.[4] His gendered imagination would certainly reflect Catherine Keller's observation that divinity "opens up" when we subvert "our most convenient binary oppositions, those dualisms that structure our certainties."[5] Within Ibn ʿArabī's cosmology, divinity opens up through an apophasis of gender precisely because *al-Insān al-Kāmil* (the complete human) is a comprehensive constellation of divine attributes that applies in full and equal measure to men and women alike.

Moreover, the dynamic methodology of saying and unsaying also suggests a mystical pedagogy—apophatic language both reflects and encourages a state of experiential openness and dynamism within the aspirant. Michael Sells discusses Ibn ʿArabī's *al-Insān al-Kāmil* as characterized by a state of perpetual transformation (*taqallub*).[6] This dynamic state simultaneously reflects the infinite nature of the real and of the microcosmic *al-Insān al-Kāmil*, never allowing for fixed and static notions of God or self. In fact, for Ibn ʿArabī, human nature is superior to the angels and able to manifest God's attributes most comprehensively precisely because of humanity's potential to embody a vibrant, perpetually transforming state. Despite their luminosity and elevation, the angels possess relatively limited capacities for apprehending the divine, a fact that explains why they initially questioned the divine command to prostrate before Adam and committed what Ibn ʿArabī calls an "error of binding [*taqyīd*]."[7] They erred in their belief that their particular conception, form, or understanding of God was the only way in which God is manifest. The angels could not perceive Adam's true nature as the reflection of the divine and consequently attempted to set a limit on God or fix God into their particular vision. Conversely, *al-Insān al-Kāmil* as a reflective mirror of the divine never limits or binds the divine or the self to a specific or particular determination.[8] This idea has important implications for readings of gender in Ibn ʿArabī, whose unsayings of gender are consistent with his core understandings of human nature as always transforming in line with the infinitely uncontainable mystery of the divine paradox. Ibn ʿArabī's work thus functions both as dialectical method and a state of spiritual dynamism. It serves as a harmonizing and constructive principle rather than a dualistic or divisive one.

Ibn ʿArabī's multiple interpretations of gender thus point to the fluid nature of a Sufi method where deeper layers of meaning are always present in seemingly fixed phenomena. In recognizing the always partial nature of human perceptions, a Sufi approach to knowledge carries the seeds of an organic hermeneutic of humility and openness. Knowledge is recognized as being infinitely layered and expansive—it reveals more or less of itself depending on the state of the seeker. Given this epistemological approach, where reality is constantly unfolding, a Sufi epistemology is theoretically more open to the ways in which truth claims are constantly shifting and are often reconstituted at different levels. In addition, Sufi methodology recognizes that language mediates between mystical truth and transient social realities and that such a mediatory process is inevitably dynamic and fluid.

Given this amalgam of personal and discursive influences on Ibn ʿArabī, his use of paradoxes might be seen as intentional—a clever, useful, and affirmative means of luring the reader into dismantling given assumptions and categories. For the reader, the act of interrogating Ibn ʿArabī's uses of paradoxes creates cognitive fissures, possibly allowing entirely different modes of engaging gender in his works. To borrow an apt description from contemporary scholar Fatemah Keshavarz's study of Jalāl al-Dīn Rūmī, "Searching for patterns in his work, will more often than not, lead to patterns that were created to be dismantled or transformed."[9] Ibn ʿArabī's dialectical gender motifs suggest to the probing investigator a hermeneutic of subversion through which he skillfully destabilizes normative constructs of gender by asserting dominant tropes while simultaneously reinterpreting them in radical and unusual ways. Such an approach suggests again Ibn ʿArabī's location as a "frontier thinker" who both integrates the given intellectual, cultural heritage of his time and forges new and novel paths of imagination.[10] Through these delicate discursive movements, he subtly shifts dominant gender constructs, opening up new horizons of interpretive possibilities.

Keshavarz comments on the Sufi deployment of paradox as a deliberate strategy for confounding standard attempts at categorization. While recognizing the value of structure and categorization, she points out that it is vital simultaneously to acknowledge the transitory nature of such analytical tools—maintaining the balance between the two aspects, she argues, is part of the productive challenge offered by mystical works.[11] When confronting paradoxes in Ibn ʿArabī's works, perhaps Keshavarz's crucial lead should be followed to treat mystical works as both "subjects of critical inquiry and tools for refining critical perception."[12] Capturing one of the central pedagogic impulses embedded within Rūmī's poetry, Keshavarz observes, "Serious works of art have always functioned as challenging opportunities for redefining norms and shifting familiar paradigms. Such opportunities come about when the horizons are expanded beyond the binary alternatives of discarding all defining notions, or remaining captives of definition. They come about through adopting a moving posture. Turning in circles in Rūmī's concentric universes, as he illustrated with whirling, is one way to stay centred while moving. From that whirling vantage point, his works are poetic cohabitations of stability and change. They are not one or the other."[13]

Keshavarz's image of whirling dervishes who move while remaining centered beautifully captures the plenitude of a discourse that simultaneously retains the seeds of tradition and bears fruit of a different taste and texture. When traversing Ibn ʿArabī's gendered imagination, readers are urged to embrace a nonbinary approach. Incorporating flavors of gender familiar to a traditional palate, he deftly introduces innovative gender motifs that constitute a radically transformative recipe. In so doing, he envisages new, dynamic landscapes for Muslim praxis that beckon readers, enabling creative conversations with the tradition.

Language and Metaphor: Theoretical Linkages

Ibn ʿArabī invokes sexuality and gender in discussions that range from understandings of the nature of the universe and the cosmos to that of the human realm. Engaging with his gender constellations demands a careful focus on the way in which he employs particular forms of language and imagery. In particular, his uses of metaphor are very evocative. Ibn ʿArabī uses gendered metaphors to describe all aspects of reality, including language about God, the macrocosmic configuration of the universe, and the microcosmic realm of human relationships. He uses terms such as "fathers" and "mothers," "female" and "male," "sexual union" and "offspring" in unique ways to signify different ontological phenomena and diverse relationships within God and the universe as well as within and between human beings.

Ibn ʿArabī appears to employ these gendered terms metaphorically in ways that reflect the normative gender symbolic while simultaneously transforming these conventional categories so that gender starts to become an open and malleable field of meaning.

Contemporary philosopher Paul Ricoeur provides some helpful insights regarding the uses and functions of metaphor in language. Metaphors are productive language tools that enable a reader to unfold the world of the text imaginatively, expanding its semantic field.[14] With their surplus of interpretive possibilities, metaphors demand an imaginative engagement, inviting latent, emergent forms of meaning continuously to arise. This creative figure of speech thus "does not destroy the referential dimension of language but rather [endows language] with a new kind of referential power: the power to re-describe reality."[15]

Philosopher Jacques Derrida further explains the nature of metaphor and its inherent presence in all language, which he describes as "radically metaphorical in character. . . . [W]hile literature is less deluded since it implicitly acknowledges its own rhetorical status, other forms of writing are just as figurative and ambiguous but pass themselves off as unquestionable truth."[16] From Derrida's perspective, metaphor is not simply one expressive dimension of language but an essential condition of language, which "works by transference from one kind of reality to another." While explicitly represented in metaphor, the flux and proliferation of meaning characterize the nature of all language.

Expanding the theoretical gaze on the general nature of language and its creative possibilities, Derrida discusses notions of textual polyvalence. He evocatively proposes that no text is a "finished product" and that textual meaning is "endlessly deferred" since "signifier and signified are continually breaking apart and re-attaching in new combinations . . . such that meaning moves along a chain of signifiers."[17] Here, he alludes to the dynamism and mobility of meaning making; words or signs are constantly "under erasure," being inadequate yet necessary in the endless play of signifiers that constitute language. In this conception of language, "any attempt to fix meaning is doomed in failure since it is in the very nature of meaning that is always already elsewhere."[18] Thus, Derrida asserts that all texts are unstable, "a ceaseless play of infinite meanings" that are pregnant with alternative possible worlds.[19]

In a fascinating comparison of respective hermeneutical approaches of Ibn ʿArabī and Derrida, Ian Almond alerts us to the fact that while both scholars might have similar approaches to the "play" of language as well as textual polysemy, they operate from fundamentally opposite philosophical assumptions.[20] For Derrida, a text is "infinitely poor . . . and draws its wealth from its surroundings, having nothing to offer of its own." Thus, as a consequence of this absence of inherent meaning and the irrelevance of the author, meaning roams freely.[21] For Ibn ʿArabī, God is the hermeneutical center, and the infinite abounding divine presence overflows not only the Qurʾān but all texts, causing meaning to multiply and creating a fullness that is never captured by particular formulations.[22]

Ibn ʿArabī's readings of gender are comprised of intertextual conversations among the Qurʾān, traditions, and multiple experiential contexts. Intertextuality, as originally outlined by feminist philosopher Julia Kristeva, sensitizes one to the dialogical and interweaving referential nature of texts—texts are always conditioned and mediated by other texts within a cultural system of signification.[23] In particular, Kristeva alerts the reader to the ways in which gender symbolism is always contextually defined and language imbricated in contesting power interests. When applying this idea to readings of gender in Ibn ʿArabī, it might be helpful to note Kristeva's view that instead of merely reflecting social relations, language is a productive system of signs that are always thrown open to varying appropriations and where "the power struggle intersects in the sign."[24] Language is one medium in which power is mediated, negotiated, and even reconstituted.

With these warnings, Kristeva draws the reader firmly into the realm of the material and the social. Nevertheless, despite Ibn ʿArabī's intricate gender subversions, his mystical openings and his radical—to some, even scandalous—positions on women, he remained a product of his era. Like every living human being, Ibn ʿArabī straddles the cultural and normative formulations of his time. Some elements of his writing are very clearly immersed in and reflective of a patriarchal imagination. For example, men are predominantly the subjects of his discourse, either implicitly or explicitly; their perspectives and realities are central, reflecting a pervasive masculinism in his work. These gender biases coexist with his radical and egalitarian views on gender, creating a "mixed" legacy that is a product of his historical condition.

Articulations of ontology and metaphysics within mysticism are always inscribed within the symbolic systems and languages of their interlocutors and thus always also incorporate a level of historical consciousness. Here again, a dialectical understanding is useful. While taking seriously the realm of "pure" or "unconditioned" consciousness as defining the mystical, one needs simultaneously to incorporate the fullness of the social, psychological, religious, and historical conditioning of the mystic. As Jeffery Kripal notes, "Context is not fluff or superimposition—it is the diaphanous stuff of the mystical."[25] When one reads the works of great mystics such as Ibn ʿArabī, the reader accesses them in language and expressions that are fully situated—that is, they are contextually and intertextually embodied. Thus, one of the goals of this book is to demythologize the remarkably tenacious assumption in much contemporary scholarship that Sufi articulations of ontology signify some pure and unsullied realm of reality unaffected by the historically conditioned nature of human embodiment.[26]

Ibn ʿArabī's predominantly patriarchal context must and does impact his language and formulations. It is not only pointless but somewhat immature to discount, excuse, or defend what might appear to a twenty-first-century reader those very androcentric formulations in the works of Ibn ʿArabī and other Sufis of his time. To the extent that those formulations might trap contemporary Muslims in a web of symbolic sexism, I subject such ideas, as they present in such historical works, to a rigorous critique. Yet I do so without holding these past thinkers hostage to contemporary sensibilities; to my mind, such anachronisms are not only intellectually and ethically immature but historically short-sighted.

In addition, given that my approach to Ibn ʿArabī's works is informed by both the post-Enlightenment feminist intellectual heritage and my embodied twenty-first-century understandings of Islam, which encompass a plethora of political, social, and intellectual vocabularies, I am acutely aware of Ebrahim Moosa's methodological caveat about the importance of reciprocity between different intellectual languages. "Reciprocity between languages," he cautions, implies "a transformation and deepening of each language in the mirror of the other," an approach that he adopts in his study of Ghazālī.[27] I bring feminism into conversation with Ibn ʿArabī, thereby enriching both Sufi discourse and feminist thought; perhaps in so doing, feminist conceptions of the subjectivity and self can be enhanced by the former's extraordinary anthropology of the human. Similarly, feminism has an opportunity to shine a light on elements of Ibn ʿArabī's gendered world that have remained in the shadows.

While Ibn ʿArabī was both a man of his time grounded in a patriarchal context and a human being whose mystical imagination mapped gender in ways that allow multiple readings and particularly expansive ways for understanding the human condition, his ideas offer emancipatory possibilities for contemporary Muslims. Ibn ʿArabī's gendered context did not represent an experiential monolith; despite his patriarchal social context, he simultaneously encountered and studied with women spiritual masters and adepts. These counterdiscourses of gender in his experience reflect more broadly Sufism's inherent discursive formation that foregrounds spiritual endeavor and realization as ultimately the sole criteria of human worth. Hence, his experience, together with his discursive context of Sufism, no doubt contributed to his continuous assertions that all spiritual capacities are as open to women as they are to men.

Some of his positions on women and gender relationships at both the practical and the ontological level were considered so iconoclastic by some of his contemporaries that they accused him of sexual depravity and immorality. In the Islamic legacy, nonnormative positions regarding gender relations have provoked and continue to provoke social resistance and accusations of immorality, particularly from those who are invested in established power structures. Nonetheless, the tensions between patriarchal norms and those that militated against such biases in Ibn ʿArabī's work reflect both a mystical dialectical mode that simultaneously integrates and transcends normative understandings and the ambivalences, tensions, and contradictions of his experiential context. By incorporating the normative symbolic system and simultaneously expanding the horizons of its meaning, Ibn ʿArabī opens up the dominant gender economy to rich interpretive possibilities, which are of tremendous value to the vision of Islamic feminism. While presenting the sophistication of his positions, I also subject them to critical scrutiny, interpretation, and reconstruction.

Metaphor, Macrocosm, and Microcosm

Activity and Receptivity in the Cosmos: A Model for Gender Relations?

In Ibn ʿArabī's framework, saturated as it is with a sense of unitary reality while reflecting a hierarchy of theophanic mirrors, gender pervades different levels of reality. For him, masculine and feminine principles suffuse the entire sphere of being; they are complementary and can operate only in relation to one another. Creation in every realm comes into existence through the interaction of these two principles. Within this framework, "maleness" reflects primarily the mode of activity, while "femaleness" is defined by receptivity to action and the capacity to be changed through such action.

An active or "male" reality has the power to act on the receptive or female reality, which, in receiving such activity, becomes the empowered, creative site of growth and manifestation.[28] So, all things that are receptive to the action of another are deemed "female." While femaleness and maleness function distinctively, they are ontologically inextricable as equal contributors in the creative process and are thus essentially relational.

Crucial to our understanding of Ibn ʿArabī's gender cartographies is the recognition that the principles of "maleness" and "femaleness" are not exclusively associated with biological males and females, respectively. All human beings are characterized by a combination of activity and receptivity in various spheres—in these terms, by the merging of "maleness" and "femaleness." Depending on one's nature, state of spiritual refinement, and the particular context, therefore, a biological man may be "female," or in a state of receptivity, while a biological woman might be "male," or in a state of activity. Not biology but rather a particular situation and relationship indicate whether one's state is characterized by activity or receptivity. From this perspective, Ibn ʿArabī's seemingly essentialized gender categories are effectively turned in on themselves to deessentialize the nature of gendered human beings. Moreover, when using gendered principles of activity and receptivity, there is no priority accorded to either one of the modes—they are interconnected and mutually create a single act.

Pointing to the universal application of these seemingly gender-specific principles, Ibn ʿArabī observes that all creation is ontologically female in relation to God, who impregnates each being with existence: "Other than the Creator, there is not in this universe a male," and those who are generally referred to as males are all "really female" since there is nothing in creation that is not acted on.[29] For Ibn ʿArabī, gender is refracted through an ontology that demands shifting and relationally defined categories.

Ibn ʿArabī's gendered images of the divine fall within a spectrum of Muslim approaches. At the most universal level, Muslim thought is characterized by belief that God is always beyond gender. However, in the discussions and reflections of the divine names or attributes, richly gendered analogies are often invoked. Sachiko Murata suggests that Muslim tradition is characterized by a tension between polar images of God.[30] On the one hand, theological and legalistic teachings stress God's power, incomparability, transcendence, and remoteness from humanity in ways that echo images of an authoritarian father. On the other hand, the spiritual and popular traditions invoke God's similarity, immanence, connectedness, and mercy in ways that invoke images of a loving mother. Nonetheless it is uncommon to find actual descriptions of God as "mother" or "father," particularly given the Christian resonance of the latter view. Ibn ʿArabī's explicit use of these terms is thus noteworthy.

Moreover, in describing the power generated by the merging of male and female principles in the universe, Ibn ʿArabī embroiders his metaphors more elaborately—he uses imagery of "sexual intercourse" between "mothers" and "fathers" who unite through the magnetism of "love" to bear "offspring." Again, these terms and principles describe phenomena and relationships not restricted to the human realm but relating to macrocosmic realities: "An act, when it gives rise to that which had no previous existence, assumes the quality of sexual intercourse [*nikāḥ*]. There is no act except that it causes [new things] in accordance with its reality and its way. So intercourse is the root of all things. Therefore it has comprehensiveness, superiority, and priority."[31]

Metaphors of sexual intercourse are thus employed to describe the relationship between the primal creative principles of the cosmos. The "sexual partners" are referred to as "fathers" and "mothers"—according to Ibn ʿArabī, "everything that exercises an effect is a 'father,' and everything that receives an effect is a 'mother,' while the fruit of their relationship is the 'child.'" The expansive range of Ibn ʿArabī's metaphoric use of gender is well illustrated in this discussion of speech: "The speaker is a father. The listener is a mother. The speech discourse between them is a marriage. What comes into existence from that [interaction] in the understanding of the listener is a child. Every father is high because he causes effects [in another] [*muʾaththir*], and every mother is low because she receives effects [*muʾaththar fīh*]. Every particular relationship between the two is a sexual act and or turning of attention. Every result is a child."[32]

In developing his relational construct of "fathers" as active and "mothers" as receptive, he invokes another example involving the relationship between an architect and an artisan. The architect, who communicates his knowledge and plan of design, is referred to as the "father," while the artisan, who receives this information, is the "mother." When the understanding of this communication has flowered in the artisan's imagination, it is the "child." Impressing on his reader the dynamic and changing nature of such relationships, Ibn ʿArabī adds that when the artisan undertakes labor to create this new product, he in turn becomes the "father." The wood then becomes the metaphoric "mother" on whom the artisan acts with his tools. Using sexual metaphors to describe the process of craftsmanship, Ibn ʿArabī states that when the artisan uses his tools to cut the wood, the act metaphorically reflects the manner of sexual coitus and the ejaculation of semen. The finished and final product of carpentry, the wooden chest, is the "child," a consequence of the "marriage" between the artisan and the wood.

These examples illuminate the complex and shifting ways that Ibn ʿArabī uses gendered metaphors to describe gender-neutral interactions between and active and receptive principles. Throughout his descriptions of the various "mothers" and "fathers" and their respective roles, he appears to map the underlying normative gender assumptions of his day onto varying types of relationships while constantly shifting the symbolism inherent in these terms. These examples prompt contemporary readers to align understandings of "fathers" as active and "mothers" as receptive principles in accordance with Ibn ʿArabī's particular framework rather than making essentialist associations of such relations between biological men and women.

In fact, if one were to apply these gendered principles to Ibn ʿArabī's relationship with his female teachers such as Shams or Nūna Fāṭima, one could map these same gender principles with interesting effect. In the context of the refining relationship of discipleship, these women "fathered" Ibn ʿArabī's learning. As a result of his feminine state of receptivity, he allowed their wisdom to penetrate him, thereby birthing his own deepening insight. For Ibn ʿArabī, the dynamic interactions between active and receptive principles in complementary modes constantly creating new realities pervade social and cosmological relationships.

The Primordial Sexual Act: Gendering the Macrocosm

Ibn ʿArabī employed sexual metaphors to describe the universal power of creativity. In this view, therefore, sexual unions pervade all of reality, from the plane of the divine One to every other echelon of existence, including unions between humans. In fact, Murata points out, one of Ibn ʿArabī's lost works bears the title *Kitāb al-nikāḥ al-sarīʿ fī jāmiʿ al-dharārī*, which can be translated as "The Book on the Sexual Act That Pervades All Atoms."[33]

METAPHORS FOR THE DIVINE REALITY

In Ibn ʿArabī's schema, the most sublime level of this "sexual union" is that of divine realities. He informs us that God originally existed as pure being, without otherness and reflection, in a state of undifferentiated wholeness prior to creation. In this state of solitude, God's longing to be known provided the impetus for the first macrocosmic act of sexual union. Ibn ʿArabī describes the primordial creative act where the possible things existed in God's knowledge, coming into existence through God's command of "Be."[34] At this, the highest level of the unitive principle, Ibn ʿArabī notes, "The first of the high fathers is the known. The first of the low mothers is the thingness of a possible but not yet existing thing, the first sexual act is the intent to do something. The first child is the existence of that essence of that thingness."[35]

He is, in fact, alluding to the famous *ḥadīth qudsī* where God said, "I was a Hidden treasure and I loved to be known, so I created the world in order that I might be known." Stephen Hirtenstein, a contemporary Ibn ʿArabī scholar, suggests that the divine "I" is the known, referring to the first "father," while the hidden treasure, buried as pure possibility and not yet existing within the divine "I," refers to the first "mother"; love is the creative force that calls these possibilities into existence, while the resulting creation is the "child" of this first act of sexual union at the level of divine realities.[36]

Ibn ʿArabī elaborates on the divine creative act as an unceasing sexual union that is forged whenever the real, lovingly and filled with desire, turns attention to the possible things, beckoning them into manifest existence.[37] In this intimate marriage, the "wife" is the entity of the possible thing, the divine attention as it turns to the possible thing steeped in loving desire is the "sexual act," and the "offspring" of this nuptial act is the conferral of existence on the entity of the possible thing. Ibn ʿArabī informs us that wedding feasts celebrate the most beautiful names (*al-Asmā al-Ḥusnā*), since the sexual union has conferred existence on the possible things so that the effects of divine names may be manifest. This marriage, he tells us, is constant and unceasing in existence—there can be no termination or repudiation of this marital contract.[38]

The primordial union thus occurs between different parts of the one God. The divine matrix of being is a unitary whole that abounds with inherent possibilities for all of existence to manifest. Through an ecstatic surge of desire, the real, as the "husband," approaches his "wife," who is the divine receptive nonexistent and virtual entities, and through their loving embrace, existence is bestowed on the divine names. This first division from within the undifferentiated whole of God as pure being is also a union. God is simultaneously the divine active "father," the divine receptive "mother," and the "child" of such union. With these metaphors of human sexual reproduction and traditional gender constructs, God is both feminine and masculine in this context.

Moreover, the description of fathers as "high" and mothers as "low" clearly does not signify any superiority in value for either dimension, since both exist within God. These adjectives convey the notion of pouring and receiving between different dimensions within the one reality. "High" and "low" are mutually constitutive and can only be conceptualized in relation to one another, symbolizing the creative relationship between the complementary dimensions of God.

In this rich narrative, the origin of all creation is God's desire and love. Macrocosmically, the heady power of divine love and desire catapults the process of God's staggering self-disclosure and manifestation. The reader encounters traces of this same divine desire shimmering through Ibn ʿArabī's portrayal of the love between men and women.

Ibn ʿArabī also uses analogies of pregnancy, labor, and birthing to describe God's primordial generativity. In his *Mahiyyat al-qalb*, he describes the nonexisting entities in the state of possibility as experiencing a metaphysical condition of pressure.[39] He uses the word *karb*, meaning "labor," to describe this state of distress. The divine creative force, the breath of the merciful (*nafas al-raḥmān*), releases them into the theater of existence.[40] This primeval union and birth are a result of the interactions of the active and receptive dimensions within the being of the one God who manifests. In the same way that women give birth to children, God births the cosmos. Ibn ʿArabī uses vibrant, pulsating images of marriage and sex, pregnancy, and birth to describe the processes through which God creates and self-discloses. Ibn ʿArabī's reproductive and sexual metaphors also point to the encompassing and rounded nature of many forms of premodern scholarship—science, philosophy, and poetry were integrated and woven into a single religious discourse of knowledge.

These enticing, elemental, and sensuous descriptions, where God loves and desires to be known, where divine self-disclosure is an imperative lodged within the nature of God and without which God experiences distress, and where metaphors of God include images of pregnancy and mothering, offer glimpses of this thirteenth-century scholar's central contribution to the destabilization of patriarchal theological constructs. God needs creation to complete and manifest divine potentiality. In particular, the notion of the divine need for completion through creation and humanity breaks down the hierarchy of traditional patriarchal images, where God is always Lord, above and entirely independent of humanity. Images of a distant, transcendent God are overcome by more immanent visages of the divine. Love, desire, and need define the divine creative spark, not simply unadulterated power and indomitable will that demand absolute obedience.

The female images of pregnancy, labor, and mothering also reconstitute some of the more hierarchical metaphors for God. They invoke a layer of intimate relation, nurture, and deep connection between God and humanity. Throughout Ibn ʿArabī's works, the reader discovers pervasive images of God that break down patriarchal dichotomies and present profound and intimate formulations of the God-human relationship. These images present radical shifts in the Muslim symbolic economy of the divine that allow for very different ways of relating to God, particularly from a feminist perspective. Such feminine images of God exist in contrast to Ibn ʿArabī's description of God as the only male in existence and creation as female. The gendered ways in which he describes God is contingent on the particular types of relationships he is attempting to depict at a given time. Each context and relational mode demands a different use of gendered metaphor, and Ibn ʿArabī is uniquely comfortable using conventionally "masculine" and "feminine" ways of describing God while simultaneously transforming the conventional way we might think about the symbolic field of these gendered categories.

However, this mythic and poetic integration of feminine dimensions cannot automatically be extended into an emancipatory social practice. As many feminist scholars of religion have illustrated, transformations in a symbolic system or in images of the divine are no guarantee of socially egalitarian gender practices or even more flexible social roles for women.[41]

Without inferring that feminine images of the divine by themselves translate into liberating social possibilities for women, ruptures of traditional patriarchal images of God are significant. Feminist Luce Irigaray, who responds primarily to a Jewish and Christian patriarchal symbolic dominated by male images of God, engages with Lacanian psychoanalysis to argue that for women to attain full and authentic forms of subjectivity, female images of the divine must be created and embraced.[42] Ibn ʿArabī's diverse and fluid gender images of God, including sexual metaphors and feminine visages for the divine, might be fruitful for feminists who want to explore alternative symbolic spaces.

While exploring these feminine symbolic spaces might provide a counterfoil for the more hierarchical images of the divine, becoming attached to any particular construction of God, whether masculine or feminine, is a fundamental spiritual error. Ibn ʿArabī is effectively working simultaneously at a number of different symbolic and metaphysical registers, so his images of God similarly function at multiple levels. To benefit from sojourning through his cosmology, readers, feminist or not, must avoid assuming one particular register of meaning. Doing so might mean missing some of Ibn ʿArabī's most profound insights and treasures regarding understandings of humanity and God.

Rather, readers should attempt to hold together and creatively engage the numerous registers in which Ibn ʿArabī uses gender-inclusive images of the divine. Following Irigaray's lead, Ibn ʿArabī's use of masculine and feminine images of God helps authenticate both male and female human subjectivities. This understanding resonates deeply with his consistent assertion that both men and women have equal and full access to the completed state of the *al-Insān al-Kāmil*, the individual who manifests all the divine attributes in perfect harmony. Irigaray's suggestions are therefore helpful in configuring some of the feminist and Sufi implications for Ibn ʿArabī's gendered images of God in relation to human identities.

However, when speaking at the register of the divine, Ibn ʿArabī does something even more powerful. His use of both masculine and feminine images of God presents us with another case of his mystical dialectic where he uses known gendered images in varying and contrasting ways to ultimately transcend all gendering of the divine. He cautions about vigilance against the "error of binding [*taqyīd*]," the attempt to delimit God in any particular way. He warns that people must never fix God into their own conceptual categories. Within a Sufi hermeneutics, all concepts serve as place holders to be used and discarded simultaneously to circumvent fixed constructions of God. Ibn ʿArabī's caveat is succinct:

> If you affirm transcendence you bind
> If you affirm immanence you define
> If you affirm both
> You hit the mark
> You are an imam and a master in the spiritual sciences.[43]

The real is in a state of perpetual transformation that cannot be captured in any one set of images. Ibn ʿArabī's metaphorical strategies thus create a mystical dialectic of both saying and unsaying the various gendered constructions of God that necessarily appear and must also necessarily disappear to remain faithful to the mystery of the divine. As a spiritual guide who points to God's immanent connection to all human beings, male and female, Ibn ʿArabī provides the reader with gender-inclusive images of God. As a chamberlain of monotheism, he points to God's transcendence of all gendered human binaries and the vast openness of the divine. In both affirming and unsaying gender in his descriptions of God, Ibn ʿArabī "hits the mark" exquisitely by embracing the plenitude of a simultaneous and paradoxical yes-and-no position.

NATURE

Ibn ʿArabī's nuanced gender images also extend to his descriptions of the creation of the world. His use of metaphorical strategy collapses dualistic binaries between spirit and matter: "All the spirits are fathers, and nature is a mother inasmuch as nature is a place [*maḥall*] of transformation [*istiḥāla*]. So the spirits turn their attention to the foundations that are the elements receptive to change and transformation. Then there manifests in nature the children, which are minerals, plants, animals, jinns, and human beings, who are the most perfect among them."[44]

Elsewhere, he similarly states, "God made between the sky [*samāʾ*] and the earth a symbolic synergy [*iltiḥām*] and a turning of attention toward the children—the minerals, plants, and animals—that God desired to bring into existence in this earth. And he made the earth like the wife and the sky the husband. The sky casts to the earth something of the command that God reveals in it, just as the man casts the fluid through sexual union in the woman. Upon this casting, the earth displays whatever the Real One has concealed in her of the existing beings in all their various levels."[45]

In his poetics of creation, where the macrocosm is birthed through the coitus between the sky and earth, Ibn ʿArabī employs mimetic metaphors of human sexuality and procreation. With these vivid images, he leads the reader into the world of God's perpetual creation and life-giving. The enduring cycle of fertility is the result of the generative union between the father/sky and the mother/earth, both essential for creation. The earth contains the precious treasures of all creation hidden within her by the real. Distinctly absent in his framework is a hierarchy that values the masculine as the positive heavenly spiritual pole and that degrades the feminine as the negative earthly corporeal realm. On the contrary, Ibn ʿArabī articulates a very rich appreciation for the dimension of the earth and corporeality:

> [The earth] gives all of the benefits from her essence [*dhāt*] and is the location [*maḥal*] of all good. Thus she is the most powerful [*aʾazz*] of the bodies. The movement of all things does not contest her own movement because they do not leave her sphere. Every foundation manifests in the earth its authority and she is the patient one [*ṣabūr*], the receptive one [*qābila*], the immutable one, the firm one. Her mountains still her quaking, mountains that God made to be her anchors. Whenever she moves from fearful awe of God, God secures her by means of these anchors. So she becomes still with the tranquility of those of faithful certainty. From the earth, the people of faith learn their certainty. Therefore, it is the mother from whom we come and to whom we return. And from her we will come forth once again. To her we are submitted and entrusted. She is the most subtle of foundations [*arkān*] in meaning. She accepts density, darkness, and hardness only in order to conceal the treasures that God has entrusted to it.[46]

In these forceful images, while the expansive sky casts the command of God from on high, the earth is prolific in its receptivity, stability, and subtlety. Through embodying particular divine qualities, the earth unfolds as a signifier of the spiritual state of faithful certainty. The earth thus provides a pedagogical archetype on which human aspirants can model their spiritual refinement. Ibn ʿArabī evokes a complex and beautiful resonance of some divine qualities in his description of the earth. He names the earth *al-Ṣabūr*, the Patient One, one of the ninety-nine beautiful names of God. The earth is the mother "from whom we come and to whom we return," evoking a similar Qurʾānic reference to God, "From Allah we come and to Allah we return." The earth conceals God's treasures, echoing the *ḥadīth qudsī* where God is depicted as a hidden treasure. The reference to the earth's essence as the source of all good and the most powerful of bodies resonates with Ibn ʿArabī's discussion of God's essence. This intricate symbolic lattice in which the earth immanently embodies the divine, abundantly manifesting God's qualities, represents a powerful shift in the dominant symbolic economy.

Again, Ibn ʿArabī wedges open a whole history of patriarchal imagination for feminist appropriations. His sublime portrayal of the earth offers a marked contrast to forms of patriarchal binary thought that view the earth as the lesser material principle, a necessary evil from which one seeks ultimate escape.[47] His favorable and positive understanding of the earth and its materiality extends to the closely related dimension of the human body. Ibn ʿArabī presents both father/sky and mother/earth as integral to the process of creative manifestation, with no intrinsic superiority accorded to either. By swathing (and at times cross-dressing) his cosmic creative principles in the normative gender categories of his time, he reconstitutes the nature of these categories.

Reflecting on Ibn ʿArabī's analogies of marriage, sexual union, procreation, and parenthood from a feminist position brings a number of issues to the fore. His understandings of what constitutes marriage, a marital relationship, the sexual act, mothering and fathering, and the respective attitudes of spouses are socially contingent. They are influenced by the specific historical and sociocultural norms of gender prevalent in his thirteenth-century context. Moreover, even the understandings of biology, sexual intercourse, and the procreative process, as well as each partner's physical contribution to procreation, are all subject to the knowledge of anatomy, prevailing medical technology, and social norms. When he uses these gender relationships as analogies for macrocosmic processes, he projects his own contextual understandings of these gendered relationships onto a metaphysical system. The problem arises when these socially, historically, and culturally bound and therefore contingent constructs of marriage and sexuality, procreation, and parenting are reified and cast as ontologically given, essential and unchangeable.

A too-literal reading of Ibn ʿArabī's gendered metaphors with a focus on his normative language in the absence of sufficient attention to the subtle ways in which he shifts the established parameters and meanings of accepted terminology could reduce his constructions of gender to a romantic defense of traditional patriarchy. If read thus, the notion of "fathers" as active and mothers as "receptive" reflects a cosmology that reinforces a patriarchal symbolic field, associating women primarily with receptivity and men with activity. Ideologically, this point of view can be interpreted to indicate fixed social roles and related power relationships, where male dominance as a manifestation of being "active" is normalized as an inherent quality of masculinity. Such interpretation of Ibn ʿArabī's work reinscribes the traditional gender stereotypes, keeping intact all their problematic social correlates.[48]

Such readings of his teachings are partial and incomplete, however. They silence the dynamic and subtle ways in which he incorporates the normative symbolic system while transforming its meanings. To recognize the prevalence of this feature in his writing is also to recognize that he opens up gender constructions to rich interpretive possibilities. His view that men and women are both simultaneously active and receptive and as such are "masculine" and "feminine" at different levels of reality reconfigures the basis of gender difference, a view that is indeed encountered in varying ways throughout his work. Finally, within this framework, all things are in relationships of receptivity to God, who is the only, ultimately real. All creation is relatively real, having received its existence on loan from God. If God is the only masculine, then all of creation is feminine. Simultaneously, the divine One births all of existence, a view captured through powerful female images of pregnancy, labor, and mothering. The divine and all creation are defined by paradox and pairing, not by hierarchy.

HUMANITY

From within Ibn ʿArabī's lush and verdant macrocosmic panoply, he offers similar intellectual offshoots, metaphorical strategies, and sensual images in his discussion of the creation of the human being:

> I am the son of fathers, pure spirits
> and of mothers, elemental souls.
> Between spirit and body lies our place of manifesting,
> from a union of mutual embrace and delight.
> I came not from one, that I should declare him one,
> but rather a host of fathers and mothers.
> They are for God, when you realize their task,
> like tools by which a craftsman produces things—
> such a relation is not one of product to carpenter.
> Thus has the Lord of creation granted us existence!
> Truly speaks the one who knows the unity of his Creator;
> truly speaks the one who establishes causes.
> If you look at the tools, long indeed for us
> is the chain of transmission reaching back to the Essence.
> If you look at Him, granting us existence,
> then we speak of His Oneness without the hosts.
> I am the child of the Unique One alone,
> all humanity have one father but different mothers.[49]

Here, Ibn ʿArabī offers his readers a powerful understanding of human nature. For the human being to emerge, the consorts—pure spirit and elemental soul—must merge in an amorous embrace. For him, the elemental soul signifies the soul permeated by the bodily elements. Invoking the same macrocosmic formula whereby the masculine "active" spirit fuses with the feminine "receptive" body, human beings emerge from these gendered unions between spirit and body. In this symbolic scheme, every human being, male or female, is comprised of both "masculine" and "feminine" dimensions. The "fathers" signify the property of spiritual activity in relation to the body, while "mothers" signify the body in its receptivity to the spirit.

Ibn ʿArabī provides clear directions on how readers should understand these "fathers" and "mothers"—they are instrumental, a "craftsman's tools," and not the ultimate state, not a completed "carpenter's product." These gendered strata are not ends in themselves but rather means to the creation of something greater. A multitude of these masculine and feminine radiations coalesce in the creation of a human being. Ultimately, however, all humanity and each creation are in a relationship of receptivity to God, who is uniquely active. In these gendered terms, according to Ibn ʿArabī, God is the only "father," and all creation, including seemingly masculine elements, are "mothers." He thus clearly sees gender as metaphorical, signifying different dimensions of reality. Remaining faithful to his schema requires a constant awareness that he uses gender metaphorically and an avoidance of conflating his notions of "masculine" and "feminine" with biological gender unless he explicitly makes such a connection.

Moreover, the creative imperative demands a mutual dependency between the two spouses, spirit and body. Human wholeness and completion are possible only through their union—each is an equally vital constituent in the nature of reality. This relationship between body and spirit is not only necessary but defined by "mutual embrace and delight." Such a conception of a joyful mutuality again transcends some of the more dichotomous Greek philosophical formulations of spirit and body, where spirit constantly struggles to transcend the body, a notion that existed among early ascetics but that also surfaced later in the writings of such Sufi thinkers as Shihāb al-Dīn Suhrawardī (d. 1191), the Shaykh al-Ishrāq. However, Ibn ʿArabī's positive framing of the value, function, and necessity of both body and spirit prioritizes their integrity as a connected pair, notions that also permeate his understandings of *al-Insān al-Kāmil*.

Ibn ʿArabī's depiction of *al-Insān al-Kāmil*, who manifests all divine attributes in his or her embodied state, affirms the complete integrity between body and spirit, as Ibn ʿArabī expressly recognizes in his commentary on the

Tarjumān al-ashwāq: "The soul loves the body because all of her knowledge of the Truth is gained through her imprisonment in the body and through her making use of it in order to serve God."[50]

The notion that a human being's knowledge of God can be gained by actively using the body for service is central. Knowledge is connected to action. Human beings know God through doing, and the unique human mode of doing is intrinsically related to existing within corporeal bodies. The body becomes a vehicle of knowing and manifesting the divine. From this perspective, embodiment is an instrumental and inherent part of human vicegerency and is specifically related to the unique human potential to be a complete reflection of divine attributes.

For Ibn ʿArabī, the distinctive theophanic possibilities of the human relates precisely to a unique synthesis of sensory corporeal realities as well as an inner knowledge of the real. In his chapter on Adam in the *Fuṣūṣ*, Ibn ʿArabī writes, "Know also that the reality has described himself as being the outer and the inner. He brought the cosmos into being as constituting an unseen realm and a sensory realm, so that we might perceive the inner through our unseen and the outer through our sensory aspect. . . . God unites the polarity of qualities only in Adam, to confer a distinction on him. Thus he says to Lucifer, *What prevents you from prostrating to one whom I have created with my two hands?* What prevents Lucifer is the very fact that [the human] unites in himself the two modes, the cosmos and the reality, which are his two hands. . . . His outer form he composed of the cosmic realities and forms, while his inner form he composed to match his own form. . . . It is only by virtue of this synthesis that he is superior [to all other beings]."[51]

Humans are distinctive in creation because of their uniquely synthesizing quality. God is both outer and inner, and Adam, as the archetypal human being, unites this polarity. Distinctively, the human being is the product of the "two hands of God," which Ibn ʿArabī defines as both the form of the world and the form of the absolute. He even describes God's creative act in language characterized by a primal physicality: "Since he created Adam with both hands, He named him *bashar* [human being] because of his 'touching' [*mubāshara*] him directly with the two hands that are attributed to him."[52] The embodied imagery reflects a unique intimacy that humanity shares with God, imbued as it is with the realms of both the outer and inner realities. Precisely this synergy gives the human being comprehensiveness within creation and an unparalleled capacity for intimacy and knowledge of God. In describing the state of the complete human being, Ibn ʿArabī provides a compelling portrayal of the attainment of God-human intimacy when he invokes a *ḥadīth qudsī*: "I love nothing that draws my servant near to me more than I love what I have made obligatory for him. My servant never ceases drawing near to me through superogatory works until I love him. And when I love him, I am his hearing through which he hears, his sight through which he sees, his hand through which he grasps, and his foot through which he walks."[53]

Thus, the path to spiritual completion for the human being who possesses a comprehensive constitution is connected to service and action. However, not only does one use the body to serve God, but through such service, the body becomes a locus of God's presence. In this ideal state, the human body is fully permeated with God's being, a view that radically resists inclinations of a body-denigrating theology.

Ibn ʿArabī's spiritual exaltation of embodiment surfaces again in another discussion of the relative status of humanity vis-à-vis the angelic order. For him, humanity's superiority over the angels is rooted in the fact that angels are purely spiritual (*rūḥiyya*), while human nature is "spiritual-bodily [*rūḥiyya badaniyya*]."[54] Elsewhere, he reiterates this point: "The human is superior to other beings of the 'elemental' species only by being a *bashar* of clay [the clay kneaded by the two hands of God]. Thus he is higher than all that have been created of elements without having being touched by his hands. So the human is in rank higher than all angels, terrestrial and celestial, although according to the sacred texts the archangels are superior to the human species."[55]

Humanity's composite nature, in which spirit is married to body, most completely manifests the divine. An embodied human state is superior to the purely spiritual disembodied realm of the angels. This position contrasts radically with some of Ibn ʿArabī's contemporaries, such as Suhrawardī al-Maqtūl, who presents a dualistic and hierarchical understanding of the body/spirit relationship within human beings. In Suhrawardī's view, the human being is essentially an angelic light trapped within the prison of a material body, constantly yearning toward its real primordial disembodied state of spiritual purity. Suhrawardī posits a world of dualisms, where the spiritual path involves transcendence of the "black pit," the world of matter and privation that conceals the human being's celestial angelic light.[56] In sharp contrast, Ibn ʿArabī robustly exalts the human as superior to the angel precisely because of human embodiment. This approach reflects a celebration of the body and materiality as intrinsic and vital dimensions of human spirituality.

Ibn ʿArabī thus sees human comprehensiveness as including not only the body but also human emotions. In the *Tarjumān al-ashwāq*, he describes desire, longing, passion, and loss in the pursuit of God as being a uniquely human station; the angels are unable to reach it because they lack the capacity for emotion. In the explanation accompanying this poem, he writes, "The riders are the angels [Q. 2:206]. They were unable to cross [this station] because these tears were shed in the grief of parting, and the heavenly hosts lack this emotion, for they are not veiled from God. Hence they are not allowed to traverse this station."[57]

Human emotions and passion generally linked to the condition of human materiality are depicted as crucial components in the search for the divine beloved. Longing, love, and yearning for God are essential ingredients in the human quest for spiritual completion. Such a compelling view of human emotions starkly contrasts with elements of stoic and other binary patriarchal philosophies that devalue emotions as a female, irrational realm that clouds sober, masculine intellectual pursuit of truth.[58] Again, Ibn ʿArabī welcomes the traditionally devalued and purportedly "feminine" dimension of emotion as integral to completion of the human self.

Within his nuanced and encompassing view of human nature, the mind and rationality are also important within appropriate boundaries. They are useful tools when trained and used correctly and are not synonymous with the spirit. Ibn ʿArabī cautions the seeker about potential limitations of the human mind, which, if misdirected, weaves a veil around the individual's consciousness, impeding human encounter with the divine. For him as for many other Sufis, the mind and rationality are not categorically prioritized over and above other dimensions of human existence. Ibn ʿArabī's spiritual anthropology reflects a multifaceted human being at its center. This human, whether male or female, harmoniously embraces and incorporates physical, spiritual, emotional, and mental realms, which together function as instrumental in giving humanity its unique station, the possibilities of becoming the most complete mirror of the divine.

Ibn ʿArabī's holistic approach to the human being challenges more dualistic anthropologies characterizing patriarchal thought across various religious and philosophical traditions. The latter often posit a hierarchically split human self, where the body and emotions are viewed as the descending and irrational female dimension of reality that obstructs the actualization of the spirit. In such perspectives, the spirit and its associate, the mind, depicted as male, constitute the exalted realms that are fundamentally opposed to the lower female sphere of the irrational body.[59] As such, the body and emotions are devalued as the corrupting aspect that threatens the higher, more spiritual dimensions of the human being.

Instead, Ibn ʿArabī's presents us with cosmology in which the interrelationship between body and spirit is essential for God's manifestation. His affirmation of the body has profound implications for conceptualizing gender and women. Since the diminution and devaluing of women traditionally have often been argued on the basis of biology and the body—reflected, for example, in positions that reject women as imams or that impose female segregation—an affirmation of the body in philosophical contexts such as those conceived by Ibn ʿArabī potentially translates into more fluid and possibly inclusive gendered spaces in the social context.

Ibn ʿArabī affirmed the embodied human being not only in his cosmological discussions but also in his poetry and biographical descriptions of people he knew, as in this poem dedicated to one of his female disciples:

A maiden was wrapped at our hand
  in a *khirqa* with which she attained
The essence of perfection
  An exalted religious *khirqa*
Elevating her to the station of men
  God wrapped her in a robe of glory, acceptance, and beauty
Illumination, radiance, temperance, splendor, and majesty
  Whenever I see her, I perceive her beauty and charm
So that it transports me away from myself
  May God help her to preserve her pledge
And it is incumbent on us to sustain her
  Through the difficulties of the path.[60]

Here, Ibn ʿArabī presents us with a living exemplar of his religious anthropology. This female human being has attained spiritual completion, a spiritual state that fully assimilates beauty and majesty. In an exquisite interplay of gender tropes, the young maiden is seen both to have reached the "station of men" and to possess power stemming from her feminine "beauty and charm," which captivate the poet.

His momentary response to the reality of her physical body, her "beauty and charms," is in fact a step to further advance a holistic affirmation of her. Her body is a signifier of the principles of divine reality as manifest in creation—in this case, the human female form, which is called to attention in the final three lines, which again affirm her spiritual majesty. Ibn ʿArabī offers an affirming perspective of embodiment; her form is appreciated at all levels of body, and body with spirit. None is denied. His male form, admiring and in power over the moment both as male observer-participant and as writer, is cognizant of its responsibility to render both her subjectivities through equal relation with the divine—all that has been given to both of them as man and woman—and all that is still being given by the refusal to objectify her by lowering her status in his gaze. Such a gaze and intention would paradoxically and ironically debase his form and spiritual position. Hence, nothing of the truth is denied—everything is affirmed through a pervasive consciousness of God.

Many of Ibn ʿArabī's writings on female disciples or teachers contain comments on their physical beauty within the context of the particular woman's spiritual attainment. This is not a case of physical or sexual objectification. His representations of these women signify an anthropology that assimilates women's physicality and spirituality in an integrated way.

Despite Ibn ʿArabī's normative gendered language regarding the female aspirants' "maleness" on the path, his portraits of women do not reflect disembodied women trying to be men—they are real, flesh-and-blood women, some even breathtakingly beautiful, who attain superlative spiritual heights. And Ibn ʿArabī effusively celebrates all dimensions of their beauty, both spiritual and physical. Moreover, by juxtaposing her "masculinity" on the path with her vividly feminine beauty, he enacts another moment of unsaying traditional gender categories. He also writes against the debasing of the body.

In another poem about a female disciple, Ibn ʿArabī actively counters some prevailing notions about women as the sexual snares of Satan or as primarily defined by a socially dangerous sexuality:

Wearing the cloak of the mendicants
  Ṣafiyya adorns herself with the raiment of trust
Surpassing all her peers in virtues acquired
  Discarding all vices
Sanctified by the harmony of character and creation
  She embodied the epitome of the names

"Little sister of the Virgin"
  Angels to her sanctuary announced
Untouched by suspicion, chaste
  Honored as the sister of the "red-cheeked one"
Nightly tidings from angels descending
  Bequeathed the legacy of the prophets to her.[61]

Ṣafiyya elevated spiritual attainments so that she "surpasses all her peers," epitomizing the harmony of the divine names, which culminates in nightly visitations by angels, who honor her with the revelatory legacy of the prophets. She is no ordinary disciple; she is unparalleled and outstanding among her contemporaries, both male and female. Equally significant is the clear defense of her sexual honor; she is associated with the chaste Mary, mother of Jesus, also a recipient of prophecy, as well as the innocent ʿĀʾīsha, wife of the Prophet Muḥammad. Ibn ʿArabī invokes the controversial social memory of two venerable women in the Muslim legacy, both of whom were wrongly accused of sexual impropriety.

By means of these historical associations, Ibn ʿArabī deflects any potential accusations of sexual misconduct that might be directed at this exceptional female disciple, perhaps because he recognized a social reality of the time—the predilection for vicious targeting of Sufi women of superior spiritual character that is so characteristic of patriarchal fury and envy. So while some may indeed interpret his stress on her chastity as reinforcing the dichotomy between the sexual and the spiritual, this strategy is not borne out in his approach more generally. In this context, the poet's spirited defense of Ṣafiyya may suggest that this woman was being slandered as ʿĀʾīsha had been, or perhaps there was controversy surrounding her association with Ibn ʿArabī, who had many female disciples. An emphasis on her unique and exalted spiritual station and invocations of ʿĀʾīsha and Mary effectively reject any associations with women characterized by sexual misdemeanor. Ibn ʿArabī uses his authority as a well-known scholar, mystic, and poet to render all four women in these two poems as subjects in their own right rather than as the objects of others' conservative constructions.

The approach in the poetic writings also presents a broader refutation of those aspects of the religious imaginary that present women and the female as the chaos-creating sexual principle, the embodiment of an enticing and dangerous sexuality that leads good men astray. In addition, Ibn ʿArabī's nuanced manner of integrating the physical and spiritual in gendered ways for these individual women mirrors his larger cosmological approach, which sees active and receptive, female and male, spirit and body as integrally related aspects of the cosmos.

In Ibn ʿArabī's spiritual cartography, gender categories are relative and fluid. The same reality is often "active" in one respect and "receptive" in another. Activity and receptivity are interdependent, since each mode requires the other to be fully functional and integrated. "Active" and "passive" realities combine, marry, and create offspring, who represent the union of these principles. Thus, the various levels of generative unions in the macrocosm are all directed in the final analysis to the manifestation of the human being, who is the ultimate objective of creation. Most important, the human being is a microcosmic reflection of ultimate reality and a combination of the masculine/active and feminine/receptive, of body and spirit, and of emotions and intellect, and this complete and full human reality is true for both men and women.

Chapter Five

The Poetics and Politics of Adam and Eve

Now that I have charted Ibn ʿArabī's gender principles macrocosmically, I proceed to explore some of his other teachings on men and women, including their relationships of love, desire, sexuality, and marriage. In particular, I focus on a number of interweaving creation narratives, primarily that of Adam and Eve, which form in the Abrahamic tradition the mythic center and site for discussions of intimate relationships between men and women. Within a variety of religious traditions, creation myths function as sacred stories of human origin, presenting religious communities with symbolic codes for understanding many dimensions of the human condition, including mappings of gender.[1] In particular, these gendered narratives present constructions of religious anthropology and personhood that are premised on particular understandings of the nature of men and women. Creation stories within various religious traditions generally constitute a foil against which religious communities decode and reinforce particular forms of gendered social structures and hierarchy.[2] Sacred creation stories invariably reveal significant dimensions of a religious tradition's gender imagination and are often open to a range of interpretive possibilities.

To contextualize Ibn ʿArabī's imaginative readings of the creation of Adam and Eve and related gender tropes, this chapter begins by examining some of the contrasting visions of Adam and Eve within the Qurʾānic text and the Muslim exegetical traditions. In exploring these gendered myths of origin, I journey from the voices of contemporary hermeneutic scholars to premodern exegetes. While my discussion of current interpretations enables a focus on some of the crucial gender implications of these Qurʾānic stories in the contemporary period, my survey of the premodern commentary enables readers to glimpse the dominant intellectual and imaginative landscapes informing Ibn ʿArabī's worldview. The first part of this chapter thus illustrates how Muslim creation myths are significant sites of gender contestation and provides a broader intellectual and exegetical context in which to understand Ibn ʿArabī's writings on gendered myths. I thus set the thematic and contextual stage for the discussion in the second part of this chapter and in chapter 6, which offer more detailed analyses of Ibn ʿArabī's specific commentaries on the creation narratives and other related texts.

Reading Qurʾānic Narratives: Multiple Horizons of Understanding

One of the most powerful Qurʾānic verses on human creation is, "O humankind! Be conscious of your Sustainer, who has created you from a single soul and from it created its mate and from them together have spread abroad a multitude of men and women" (Q. 4:1). The compelling assertion of a shared human essence between men and women within the creation process pervades the Qurʾānic view of the primordial human. That humanity was "created from a single soul and from it its mate" (for example, Q. 4:1, 7:189, 39:6) and that God has created human beings "in pairs—male and female" (for example, Q. 49:13, 53:45, 75:39) are repeated refrains in the Qurʾān. The Qurʾān also states that among God's signs to humanity is the creation of mates "from among yourselves" so that "you can find repose in them" (Q. 7:189, 30:21). So not only do men and women share a common existential identity, having originated in a single soul, but their respective as well as collective purpose is to provide each other with tranquility. Enigmatically, the Qurʾānic creation narratives do not specify the gender of the single soul that was first created. Elsewhere in the Qurʾān, the reader encounters the first man, Adam, and the first woman, his unnamed spouse, who according to later tradition is Ḥawwāʾ (Eve). So while the Qurʾānic text does not name Ḥawwāʾ, it also does not posit that Adam is primary and that she is secondary, nor is there any mention of her originating from Adam's rib, as some Jewish and Christian scriptural counterparts of this particular myth hold.[3]

Feminist Exegetical Trajectories

Contemporary feminist scholars have celebrated some of the gender-egalitarian elements of the Qurʾānic creation story that assert men and women as created from a single soul, noting that Muslim scripture does not present Eve as secondary to Adam in creation.[4] Riffat Hassan observes that the Arabic word for the original single soul, *nafs*, is grammatically feminine, while the mate, *zawj*, who derives from this original *nafs* is grammatically masculine. Within the context of the Qurʾānic narrative, she argues, these Arabic grammatical conventions function, among other things, to distance readers from inherited biblical notions that Adam was the first creation and Eve a derived and secondary creation and therefore ontologically inferior. Amina Wadud is clear that the Qurʾān neither posits the creation of humankind from a male person nor intimates that humanity originated from Adam or even from the *nafs* of the male Adam.[5] Instead, Wadud points out, the Qurʾān indicates that the partner (*zawjihā*) is created using the same process and pattern as the *nafs*. Accordingly, she suggests, the original pair of human beings is formed from "two co-existing forms of a single reality," in which each is contingent on the other, and the two are essentially equal.[6] Thus, the Qurʾānic narrative is open to a number of interpretations, including the view that God originally created a single, ungendered soul that subsequently split into two, the separated halves then becoming embodied as gendered human beings, male and female. In such readings, difference is posited as born from sameness.

Outside of the creation process, broader Qurʾānic narratives on the primordial couple are less egalitarian and contain rather more ambivalent gender tropes. Eve remains the unnamed partner of Adam. God speaks directly only to Adam while consistently referring to his wife as part of couple, using the dual grammatical form. Adam as a prophet is singled out for the covenant with God and is taught the divine names; the angels are commanded to prostrate themselves before him. Adam consequently occupies the center of these narratives, while Eve remains a silent presence in the background. If one interprets Adam and Eve as archetypes for gender, these narratives might justifiably be read as androcentric; however, they are certainly not misogynist.[7] Nonetheless, other Qurʾānic narratives depict Adam and Eve as equal agents: Both are equally responsible for events that occur in the garden, both are warned about the forbidden tree, and both are approached by the beguiling Satan (Q. 7:20–22). Moreover, both succumb to temptation and take jointly the consequences of their transgressions, and both are forgiven through their equal repentance.

In addition to the Qurʾānic reference to mutual action and responsibility, Adam is, however, twice singled out for bearing responsibility for transgression and disobedience (Q. 7:23–27). This central focus on Adam's presence and action is arguably linked to his station as prophet rather than to his identity as male.[8] The attribution of responsibility for sinning and transgression to both Adam and his spouse and then singly to Adam represents a clear and significant shift from some of the dominant gender tropes in traditional biblical exegeses regarding this particular myth of creation. Within the Christian tradition, many exegetes not only have attributed special culpability for humanity's expulsion from the garden to Eve but also have implicated her in a theology of the Fall in ways that have resulted in very negative consequences for the understanding of women in general. In this regard, the Qurʾānic narrative appears to be less accusatory of Eve, even at times seeming to place a greater burden of responsibility on Adam (Q. 7:23–27).

Nonetheless, it would be imprudent to view this as any kind of feminist victory. In his readings of exegetical narratives that place sole culpability and responsibility at Adam's feet, rabbinic scholar Daniel Boyarin points out that such renderings ironically and retrogressively suggest that the defining moment of cultural significance for a community is located in the actions of the male Adam, who becomes the mirror of power relations for its members. This, Boyarin notes, is a "powerful example of androcentricism at the same time that it subverts misogyny."[9] In effect, narratives that shift responsibility to Adam disable readings of Eve as the source of evil temptation and blame but also render invisible her role as agent in the story. Boyarin's analysis might also hold true to some extent for the Qurʾānic Eve, yet the Qurʾānic narratives do, in fact, at times present Eve as an equally liable, full partner to Adam. The Qurʾān includes depictions of Eve as an active agent who together with her husband sinned and took the consequences of sinning as well as depictions of her as a border presence, peripheral to the central actions of her spouse, Adam.

The Qurʾānic depictions of the primordial couple thus present diverse and sometimes ambivalent or paradoxical ways to read gender relations. The Qurʾānic narratives allow for fluid and varying interpretive spaces for understanding gender relations, and contemporary feminist scholars find solace in the gender-egalitarian threads of the Qurʾānic myths of origin. In particular, these scholars foreground narratives that reflect first the generic creation of man and woman from a single soul (and concomitantly the distinct absence of notions of male priority and female deficiency) and second depictions of both members of the primordial couple as agents in the events resulting in their expulsion from the garden. These egalitarian interpretations might indeed reflect particular contemporary gender lenses and specifically gender-sensitive readings, but they derive from a Qurʾānic text that is already open to diverse readings.[10]

Most (male) premodern scholars, however, inhabited a more patriarchal imagination and predictably projected very different gender assumptions onto the Qurʾānic creation narratives. In fact, contemporary Islamic feminists' focus on the relatively innocuous Qurʾānic creation narratives might be viewed as an implicit strategy of resistance to the gender-biased and at times even derogatory views of Eve that characterize traditional exegesis and *ḥadīth* traditions.[11] Islamic feminists develop notions of the equal nature and moral capacity of Adam and Eve as foundational figures for an emancipatory gender paradigm. These feminists consequently extrapolate from notions of the shared single soul from which the primordial pair was derived as well as their subsequent relationship of mutual action and accountability to elaborate a contemporary model of reciprocity and gender equality. This approach contrasts starkly with the hierarchical interpretations of the creation myth characterizing most premodern male exegesis, interpretations that work against women.

Premodern Exegetical Trajectories

Premodern exegesis and commentary discourses embroidered the relatively sparse Qurʾānic details on Adam and Eve by drawing on a multiplicity of other sources, among them *ḥadīth* literature, folklore, cultural norms, and the genre of prophetic tales (*Qiṣaṣ al-anbiyāʾ*), which draw heavily on Jewish and Christian (*Isrāʾīliyyāt*) sources. One *ḥadīth* that features prominently in many of the premodern exegeses on the creation narrative reads, "Adam dwelt alone in the garden without a companion. God caused him to fall asleep, and on awakening he found Ḥawwāʾ, whom God created from his left rib. He asked her, 'Who are you?' and she answered, 'Woman.' He asked, 'Why have you been created?' She replied, 'So that you might find tranquility in me.' The angels asked Adam, 'What is her name?' and he said, 'Ḥawwāʾ.' They said, 'Why was she called Ḥawwāʾ?' He said, 'Because she was created from a living thing [*ḥayya*].'"[12]

This interpretation creatively embellishes the original unadorned Qurʾānic story by developing a particular understanding of the nature and purpose of Eve in relation to Adam. While maintaining the notion of a deep intimacy between primordial man and woman, this *ḥadīth* presents a very distinct image of Eve as secondary and derived. She is created from the body of an already embodied Adam, is named upon his being, and is given the specific purpose of providing him with fulfillment and tranquility. Such a reading suggests a hierarchical ontological and existential scheme that situates Adam as the primary and central creation on whom Eve is dependent. Islamic feminists have illustrated that this *ḥadīth* does not merely embroider the Qurʾānic story of creation but significantly replots the narrative by rewriting the process of Ḥawwāʾ's creation. The image of Eve being created from Adam's rib gets further developed with an explicit gender ideology that is generalized to all womankind in another *ḥadīth* attributed to the Prophet Muḥammad: "I advise you to deal gently with women, for woman was created from a rib. The most crooked part of the rib is its upper part. If you attempt to straighten it, you will break it. If you leave it, it will continue to be crooked. Therefore, take good care of women."[13]

The view of woman created from Adam's rib and characterized by relative deficiency or "crookedness" in relation to him was firmly ensconced in the premodern imagination and thus became a "naturalized" part of the religio-cultural repertoire within which Ibn ʿArabī's ideas were framed. Moreover, premodern commentators borrowed heavily from those *Isrāʾīliyyāt* literary narratives that depict Eve as the first to succumb to Satan's insinuations and as subsequently tempting Adam into transgression. These "borrowings" on the nature of Eve are not surprising; many such views held by premodern scholars and commentators probably resonated with aspects of the dominant gender ideology characterizing those cultural worlds. Furthermore, premodern Muslim scholars viewed the *Isrāʾīliyyāt* literature as a body of information that ranged from acceptable to unacceptable to simply unknowable for Muslims.[14] Muslims incorporating aspects of the *Isrāʾīliyyāt* literature into their own literature often premised this practice on the implicit assumption that the Jewish and Christian traditions form part of the Islamic revelatory lineage; as such, these borrowings would have been viewed as intrinsically containing elements of truth. Such selective borrowings from these religious "ancestors" were, despite some intermittent debates, often considered acceptable, and depictions of Eve and Adam in the Muslim commentary traditions, drawing extensively on the Jewish and Christian biblical and exegetical narratives, followed in this tradition of scholarship.

Scholars such as Ṭabarī and Thaʿlabī thus enthusiastically portray a conniving Eve who entices an unwitting Adam into transgression by plying him with wine.[15] In such plots, a rather naive Adam, subject to the seductive wiles of a manipulative Eve, inebriated and thus not in possession of his rational faculties, unintentionally transgresses the boundaries for humans set by God. Eve, conversely, is characterized as a malevolent and purposeful offender, at times even as an accomplice of Satan. In so representing the primal female Eve, Ibn Kathīr clinches the negative judgment on all womankind by invoking another *ḥadīth*: "But for Ḥawwāʾ no female would be a traitor to her husband!"[16]

Echoes of Genesis 3 reverberate through Ṭabarī's exegesis describing Eve's additional punishment, the painful near-death experiences of childbirth, as well as her state of ritual impurity during menstruation as part of the divine punishment for corrupting Adam and tainting the human condition.[17] These vivid commentaries present a radical departure from the relatively bare Qurʾānic creation narratives, particularly in terms of gender tropes relating to transgression, blame, and accountability. In post-Qurʾānic theological tradition, the symbolic image of women as represented by Eve accrues a host of misogynist associations that form part of the dominant gender imaginary to which Ibn ʿArabī is heir.

Adam and Eve's Intertextual Companions

In the Muslim tradition, stories of Adam and Eve constitute one site on which constructions of gender and relations between men and women were and continue to be negotiated. In their gendered landscapes, premodern scholars produced a particular combination of Qurʾānic verses and *ḥadīth* traditions that simultaneously incorporated prevalent cultural norms and lived experiences to arrive at specific intertextual readings of the nature and relations of men and women. For example, one Qurʾānic verse (2:228) seems to have had extensive gender currency and was often cryptically transposed onto other discussions of gender: "Divorced women shall wait by themselves for three monthly periods, and it is not lawful for them to hide what God has created in their wombs, if they have faith in God and the last day. In such time their husbands have better right to bring them back if they wish for reconciliation. And [women] shall have rights similar to those [their husbands] have over them according to what is equitable. But the men have a degree over them. God is exalted and wise."

At face value, this verse appears specifically to relate to the contextual legal norms of divorce, with differing conditions, methods, and applications relating to men and women. However, a number of traditional commentators not only applied this male *daraja* (degree [over women]) to its Qurʾānic context of divorce laws but also expanded it in varying ways to other social, psychological, and legal applications. The final sentence of this verse, "Men have a degree above [women]," was often invoked as an isolated or standalone statement to bolster assumptions of a naturalized gender hierarchy, almost as if it were a Qurʾānic aphorism on the nature of male-female dynamics. Thus, this notion of a married man's "degree" over his wife was often interpreted and emphasized by readers conforming to an androcentric worldview as divine statement that reflected universal male advantage and priority over women. That notion from the past has carried over into the contemporary context among some Muslims.

In a lucid study on gendered premodern exegeses, Karen Bauer states that although there were some variations in interpretations of the notion of men's "degree" in earlier and later exegetical works, all Qurʾānic commentaries on the nature of this male *daraja* were nonetheless strongly influenced by the individual opinions and normative cultural assumptions of the exegetes.[18] Bauer notes that commonly understood interpretations of men's "degree" were summarized by the earlier exegete, Ṭabarī (d. 923). According to him, previous authorities handed down five major interpretations: (1) the surplus that God had granted to men rather than women relating to issues of inheritance and participation in *jihād*; (2) men's right to command and women's obligation to obey; (3) the dowry that men give to women and the differences in the procedures of *liʿān* for men and women;[19] (4) men give women their rights; and (5) men have beards, while women do not.[20] Later exegetes tended to incorporate more wide-ranging notions of men's superiority over women when interpreting the notion of "degree." Fakhr al-Dīn Rāzī (d. 1209) includes, inter alia, notions of men's superior rationality, men's superior legal capacities to become imams and judges, and men's right to take concubines.[21] Ibn Kathīr (d. 1371) asserts an encompassing inherent male superiority that includes advantage and preference over women in "creation [*khalq*], morals [*khulq*], status, obeying the order, spending, upholding the good, and preference in this world and the next."[22] Biqāʿī (d. 1408) claims that men have calmer minds than women and are more perfect in their religious observances.[23]

In light of these interpretations, it is clear that a Qurʾānic verse that arguably describes men's positions in relation to a specific context of divorce procedures has been significantly transformed. In particular, premodern exegetes expanded a potentially limited concept of male "degree" to a comprehensive position of men's superiority over women that encompassed realms of the legal and social as well as the psychological, moral, and intellectual. These pervasive notions of male priority and superiority over women were fortified by selective focus on particular *ḥadīth* traditions, including one on female deficiency in religion and intellect:

> Once Allah's Apostle went out to offer the *ʿĪd al-Aḍḥā* or *al-Fiṭr* prayer. He passed by the women and said, "O women! Give alms, as I have seen that the majority of the dwellers of Hell-fire were you [women]." They asked, "Why is it so, O Allah's Apostle?" He replied, "You curse frequently and are ungrateful to your husbands. I have not seen anyone more deficient in intelligence and religion than you. A cautious sensible man could be led astray by some of you." The women asked, "O Allah's Apostle! What is deficient in our intelligence and religion?" He said, "Is not the evidence of two women equal to the witness of one man?" They replied in the affirmative. He said, "This is the deficiency in her intelligence. Isn't it true that a woman can neither pray nor fast during her menses?" The women replied in the affirmative. He said, "This is the deficiency in her religion."

This *ḥadīth* suffused many of the premodern discussions on gender. Sufis such as Sulamī resisted this trope of female deficiency by explicitly and specifically designating female spiritual savants as exalted "in religion and intellect." In addition, a few premodern Muslim women held positions as jurists and *ḥadīth* scholars.[24] The invocation of these tropes of female deficiency thus operated in a context that ambivalently also facilitated and recognized female mastery in the fields of religion and intellect. Competing constructs of femininity and women existed but did so in the context of largely asymmetrical understandings of gender that calibrated the normative gender currency.

Ibn ʿArabī's interpretations of the Qurʾānic creation narratives of Eve and Adam must be situated among these established premodern intertextual glosses of gender, which selectively drew on the Qurʾān, *ḥadīth*, and exegetical commentary to fortify negative images of women as fundamentally lacking and inferior to men. The Qurʾānic verse on men's "degree" above women; the *ḥadīth* on Eve being created from Adam's rib (the rib *ḥadīth*); and the *ḥadīth* on female deficiency in religion and intellect (the deficiency *ḥadīth*) appear frequently in discussions of gender, and these sources and related interpretations fueled a patriarchal social imagination that is subverted even as it is articulated in Ibn ʿArabī's writings.

Contemporary readers can only truly begin to appreciate the real daring and originality of Ibn ʿArabī's interpretive provocations of the creation narratives and related gender tropes if they are appropriately contextualized within the prevailing views of his time. Read from a twenty-first-century feminist perspective, parts of Ibn ʿArabī's creation narratives might appropriately be critiqued for his problematic articulations of a number of gender constructs. However, situated in his own context and with his conceptualization of gender assessed as part of the premodern religious gender imagination, a rather different picture emerges. Ibn ʿArabī's works present a very different view of women and gender from that offered by a significant number of his predecessors and contemporaries, who sculpted onto the creation narratives layers of misogyny.[25]

I now turn to how Ibn ʿArabī transforms standard descriptions of Eve and, by extension womankind, as fundamentally lacking, deceitful, and weak into images of female power, plenitude, fecundity, receptivity, and enhancement. These transformations are effected even as he adheres to some of the dominant gender symbolisms of his context. Ibn ʿArabī characteristically presents the reader with multiple narratives of Adam and Eve, each one displacing its predecessor so that the result is a veritable house of mirrors where gender is never quite grasped definitively but is constantly shifting and opening up expansive spaces for understanding human nature.

Despite Ibn ʿArabī's creative, unique, and fluid understandings of gender, he was a man, primarily addressing a male audience in his works; his premodern social and cultural context was permeated by particular asymmetrical understandings of gender. Grasping some of the most critical implications of his work requires understanding that these contextual factors often condition some of the terms of his engagement as writer. Nonetheless, his works simultaneously resist dominant understandings and provide productive spaces to derive implications for women and for humanity in general.

Whirling with Ibn Arabī's Ontologies of Gender

Like a dervish, Ibn ʿArabī whirls with traditional narratives of women, thereby transforming dominant gender tropes in unanticipated ways. At times he uses the established patriarchal images of female deficiency and then skillfully spins them into stories of love, complementarity, identity, and spiritual synergy between men and women. At his most sublime and revolutionary, he infuses narratives of female power, strength, and capacity, presenting unique conceptualizations that value women and the "feminine" in surprising ways—indeed, at times even iconoclastically positing a female "degree" over men.

In my analysis of Ibn ʿArabī's texts on gender, I have identified three seemingly contrary but in reality intersecting positions that constitute his interpretative approach. First, on many occasions, his views reflect normative assumptions of male superiority. Second, Ibn ʿArabī presents his readers with universal notions of humanity, pointing to the inessential and peripheral designation of maleness and femaleness to the human condition while actively asserting the shared humanity (*insāniyya*) of both sexes at all levels of spiritual attainment. Third, he suggests women's superiority over men by presenting particular ways in which women uniquely or more powerfully manifest the divine. These different articulations of gender, arrived at in unpredictable and idiosyncratic ways, creatively destabilize most readers' assumptions about gender.

At the point in Ibn ʿArabī's writing when one might claim that he prioritizes one sex above the other, further writing follows in which he prioritizes the other; he then subverts the previous position. Thus, he is constantly employed in unsaying any form of gender privileging. At other times, the reader might discover all three different conceptions of gender interwoven within in a single passage in a work; as if that were not enough, Ibn ʿArabī then impishly further confounds the more categorically bent among his readers by at times blurring the borders among three seemingly contrary gender perspectives. By interposing porous boundaries between three apparently autonomous gender perspectives, he enables narratives of male superiority subtly to morph into notions of female superiority or human equality, and vice versa.

Through these fluid, ambivalent, and interweaving readings of gender, Ibn ʿArabī holds together the nuanced, paradoxical position that gender is both significant and ultimately irrelevant. He asserts gender difference in the human family, illustrating its enormous ontological significance, while simultaneously presenting the reader with the notion of a transcendence of gender. This transcendence is accomplished by embracing the fundamental universality of the human condition: the imperatives of human life are identical for each person, irrespective of gender. Ibn ʿArabī's powerful use of paradox enables fertile possibilities for interpretation; stretching and expanding the established limits of meaning, paradox serves as a potent literary device that opens up "safe" opportunities for readers to rethink given assumptions and ideas from within their own position. In this way, something can be and not be as well as can be and be more or different.

Ibn ʿArabī's predecessors and peers tended to interpret the Qurʾānic verse about men's "degree" over women (Q. 2:228) to signify men's fundamental superiority, whether by virtue of inherent intellectual or spiritual capacities, greater legal rights and obligations for men, or the pervasive power that men commanded in all aspects of social and legal life. In addition, many of these commentaries reflect the ways in which Qurʾānic creation stories relating to Adam and Eve were interpreted intertextually in light of particular *aḥadīth*. Particularly salient were the *aḥadīth* that suggested a secondary and diminished status for women, whether by arguing that Eve's origin from Adam's rib designated her to meet his needs, that she malevolently lured the unsuspecting Adam to transgress against God, or the pervasive tropes of female deficiency in religion and intellect. In light of a religiocultural milieu teeming with images of women as lacking, inadequate, and even "crooked" and traitorous, Ibn ʿArabī's approach to these canonical sources is conspicuous in its eschewing of misogynist and deprecating views of women, even in those articulations that maintain gender hierarchy. However, Ibn ʿArabī's perspectives on gender automatically assume a male subjectivity. Nonetheless, his ideas provide rich fertile spaces in which to derive implications for a female subject.

Readings of Adam and Eve: Intertextuality and Cosmology

Ibn ʿArabī distinctively draws *ḥadīth* and Qurʾānic sources into his cosmological framework, allowing for expansive readings of gender. He links the Qurʾānic notion of man's "degree" above women to the manner of Eve's creation from Adam. By using a complex analogy between macrocosm and microcosm, on the one hand, and Adam and Eve, on the other, Ibn ʿArabī both assimilates and reconfigures standard meanings of those Qurʾān and *ḥadīth* texts generally invoked to entrench ideologies of gender hierarchy.

> A) Given that "humanity" [*insāniyya*] is a reality shared by both male and female, then with respect to "humanity," men do not possess

an advantage [*daraja*] over women. Just as the human being and the macrocosm share the quality of "being a cosmos" [*ʿālamiyya*], in that respect, the macrocosm is not superior [*daraja*] to the human.

[Viewed from another register,] it is established that men do have a priority [*daraja*] over women. And it is incontrovertible that [the scale of] the creation of the heavens and the earth is larger than the creation of humans. Most people obviously do not realize that a homonym reveals its preferred [sense] through signifiers [*ḍalāla*] and signs [*ʿalama*]. So, when he said, "Is your creation more momentous than the heavens that we made?" he also went on to mention what was peculiar to [the making of the heavens]. Then, he followed it by mentioning the earth, its expansion, and its peculiarities.

All this is by way of [illustrating in this instance] the preference/superiority [of the heaven and earth] over humans. All this confirms that the advantage [*daraja*] the heaven and earth enjoy over humanity is identical to the superiority of the male over the female. The human is the recipient [*munfaʿil*] of the effect from heaven and earth; the human is generated between both and derived from both. And the point is that the recipient is not as strong as the actor from which it derived its strength.

B) Similarly, Eve is a recipient of Adam's act; she is derived and originated from the short rib. Hence, she fell short of reaching the level [*daraja*] of the one who acts upon her. Therefore, she reaches the [activity] level of the male bounded by the limit inscribed in the rib. Thus, Eve's perception of the reality of man falls short.

Similarly, the human being too is limited in knowledge of the cosmos by measure of the cosmos used for his existence. Nothing other. So the human being will never reach the level of the cosmos in its totality, even if he is an epitome of it.

Even though the human is an epitome of the cosmos, he will never reach its level in totality. Likewise, the woman can never reach the level [*daraja*] of the man, despite the fact that she is choicest [*naqāwa*] of the epitome.

C) The woman is analogous to nature in respect of being a locus for the reception of activity. Man is not like that. Indeed, man only casts semen into the womb. Nothing else. The womb is the locus of engendering and creation. Hence, the entities of this species become manifest in the female because she receives engendering via the transitions in the stages of creation, creative act succeeding creative act until finally a completed person emerges. Only to this extent are men distinct from women.

D) There is a reason why women were viewed as deficient in intellect compared to men [the deficiency *ḥadīth*]: women's understanding derives from the measure [of intellect] taken from primordial man during the root of configuration.

As to the women's deficiency in religion [the underlying logic is that] compensation follows the measure of action; action is preceded by knowledge. Knowledge is contingent on the amount it receives from the cosmos. Knowledge's reception of the cosmos is contingent on the amount of its preparation during the [period] of root configuration.

Woman's preparation falls short of the preparation of man [during the root configuration] because [at the time] she was incubated in man. Therefore, with respect to deficiency of religion, woman is distinct from man.

But this chapter demands the attribute in which men and women come together. That lies in what we mentioned: the fact that they stand in the relation of receiving activity. All of this in respect to the realities.[26]

In this passage, Ibn ʿArabī's interpretation works on multiple registers. In the first part, section A, he presents some of his primary cosmological principles, invoked to define and interpret gender relations. He offers two simultaneous perspectives on gender, one that asserts complete existential equality between men and women, and another that outlines difference between them, with the latter traditionally represented in the Qurʾānic notion of men's "degree" over women.

In this first section, Ibn ʿArabī informs his readers that one of the keys to understanding the different registers of gender is the homology between the macrocosm (universe) and the microcosm (human) on the one hand and men and women on the other. Section A presents an overarching framework, elucidating his cosmological principles, which are then elaborated in the rest of the passage. In section B, Ibn ʿArabī applies the cosmological principles outlined in section A to the *ḥadīth* on Eve's origin from Adam and to the *ḥadīth* on female deficiency. Section C illustrates how the cosmological principles apply to gender roles in the processes of reproduction and the generation of humanity. Finally, in section D, Ibn ʿArabī applies a cosmological reading to the deficiency *ḥadīth*, subtly transforming it from prevailing notions of essential female lack to one of active and receptive modes. So, while section A presents Ibn ʿArabī's statement of primary cosmological principles as related to gender, in the rest of the passage, he applies these principles to the three particular canonical sources on gender in the tradition. With this reading, he remains faithful to the text of the Qurʾān and *ḥadīth* while simultaneously reformulating them within a dynamic and fluid cosmological framework that allows for radically different, even subversive, understandings of gender.

Having mapped these broad textual movements, my focus shifts to a more detailed analysis of different sections of the passage. Section A begins with a clear and unambiguous statement that men and women share equally in the construct of humanity [*insāniyya*]. Men, Ibn ʿArabī unequivocally states, do not possess any degree of advantage over women in regard to *insāniyya* or humanity. Within the Sufi framework, *insāniyya* denotes the totality of human potential—that is, the complete existential possibilities inherent to being human. In the *Fuṣūṣ*, Ibn ʿArabī asserts that that which makes the human "human [*insān*]" is the breath of the merciful blown into him.[27] The *insān* is defined by the primordial inspiriting of human beings by God, a process that distinguishes and elevates human beings above other creation, designating their ultimate cosmic station and purpose. In relation to this defining criterion of being human, he emphatically states, "Men do not possess a degree over women in respect of *insāniyya*."[28] Given this semantic field of the word *insāniyya*, Ibn ʿArabī's assertion of human equality at this most foundational level suggests a statement of overarching principle within this passage. This incisive sage opens a discussion on gender with a clear assertion of gender equality at the most foundational level of human existence. For a discerning reader of Ibn ʿArabī's wider body of work, this assertion might conjure personal experiences with male and female spiritual masters who embodied the view that all human possibilities were attainable by men and women alike. This principle of equality is asserted just prior to a discussion on the Qurʾānic notion of men's "degree" over women, which has generally ushered in interpretive trajectories on fundamental and hierarchical gender distinctions.

In addition, in discussing the concept of being human (*insāniyya*), Ibn ʿArabī introduces a powerfully layered and deeply significant analogy on the nature of genderedness. This is an analogy between the relationship of Adam and Eve, on the one hand, and of the macrocosm and humanity, on the other.

In the same way that both the macrocosm and the human being share in each being a cosmos or a world without any degree of difference, so too do men and women share in the status of a complete human being, with no degree of difference. Thus, Ibn ʿArabī begins this discussion by resisting dominant interpretations of the male "degree" that often fundamentally diminish women's humanity. Multiple nuances are reflected in this rather carefully chosen analogy. His analogy reminds us that most people are oblivious to the rich layers of meaning carried by the homonym, noting that there are "preferred" understandings implicit in his use of analogy. Ibn ʿArabī suggests that readers seriously ponder the layers of signification implicit in the analogy between the macrocosm and the microcosm.

This analogy only offers up its range of possible meanings when placed within Ibn ʿArabī's worldview. Humanity's archetypal nature represents the refined and comprehensive embodiment of the divine names—hence the description of human beings as the "microcosm." Humans' capacity to be the all-embracing microcosm of the divine reflects their station as the ultimate and culminating link in the chain of creation. For this reason, Ibn ʿArabī describes the human being as the spirit blown into the body of the macrocosm, bringing the latter into existential completion. Humanity is thus vital to the macrocosm.

The macrocosm (the universe) also reflects all the divine attributes but does so in a more diffuse manner. It acts on human beings, mirroring to them the essential signs of their inner reality. From this perspective, macrocosm and microcosm (the human) are indispensable to one another. Each constitutes a part made whole by its complement. Simultaneously, each independently comprises a world, a full mirror of all the divine attributes, albeit in different modes.

Ibn ʿArabī further asserts that in the same way that both macrocosm and microcosm comprise a world that fully reflects the divine attributes, men and women each reflects all the divine attributes. There is, therefore, no distinction between men and women in the capacity to fully existentiate the divine attributes. This is why the notion of *insāniyya*, which culminates in the ideal human archetype, *al-Insān al-Kāmil*, applies to men and women alike, with no level of difference.

Having established this overarching first principle of men and women's equal *insāniyya* by using the intricate analogy of the macrocosm and microcosm, Ibn ʿArabī explains how "difference" functions in relation to these analogical pairs. When the macrocosm acts on the human being, it assumes a "degree over" the human being. Humanity receives the activity of the heavens and the earth; the human being is the receptive stratum on which these macrocosmic spheres act. Viewed from this perspective, the macrocosmic realities are granted a "degree" over the human microcosm. In an identical manner, according to Ibn ʿArabī, women receive the activity of men; hence, men's "degree" over women results from the latter's state of receptivity. This analogy principally reveals that Ibn ʿArabī interprets the "degree" of the Qurʾānic verse 2:228 as a difference in modes of activity and receptivity.

By stating that principles of activity and receptivity are the basis for understanding the notion of man's degree over woman, Ibn ʿArabī fundamentally reformulates the axis of gender difference. He shifts the entire signification of the Qurʾānic verse 2:228 to another register that is quite distinct from normative binaries of male superiority/female inferiority that characterized his cultural context. He also notes that this male degree is an ontological (*wujūdī*) level of difference that "does not disappear."[29]

So how does Ibn ʿArabī translate these ontological modes of activity and receptivity into the realm of human genderedness? In Ibn ʿArabī's framework, men and women may each embody active or receptive modes, contingent on their particular relationships at a specific juncture. Thus, in terms of gender constructs, he is clearly not referring to a generalized female receptivity or to a generalized male activity. What then are the specific cases of female receptivity to male activity for human beings?

Ibn ʿArabī answers this question clearly in sections B and C, where he expressly limits his application of these gendered modes of male activity and female receptivity to two particular instances: first, Eve received Adam's activity in the process of being created from his rib and derived from his being, a view quite consistent with other traditional perspectives on Eve's origin; second, Ibn ʿArabī tells the reader that during sexual acts between men and women, the woman receives her partner's semen. This act of female receptivity may restart the whole process of creation. So in the first case, Adam is cast as the material source for the creation of Eve; in the second case, woman generically is cast as the material source for human creation. Yet somewhat ironically, both the examples are intended to illustrate man's activity and woman's receptivity.

As section B relates, Eve received the activity of Adam, and the nature of her being is shaped and limited by the level of activity contained in his rib. The reader is also told that that which is a part (Eve, the human being) never reaches the totality of the whole (Adam, the cosmos) since the latter acts on the former. Ibn ʿArabī's use of terms such as "falls short" and "limited" invokes the deficiency *ḥadīth*, relating it to modes of activity and receptivity that characterize the way Eve was derived from Adam. In the same way that the magnitude of the macrocosm that acts on the human being is different from the human, Adam, the active source through which Eve is configured, is constitutionally of a different scale from his female partner. For Ibn ʿArabī, both the (in)famous "degree" and popular notions of female deficiency are morphed into relations of activity and receptivity that define the creation process of the primordial couple. Here, he appears to shift traditional ways of understanding patriarchal source texts while still adhering to the paradigm of gender hierarchy.

The critical, commendable, and most subversive part of this analogy, however, is contained in the end of section B. The notion that the human being comprises the epitome of creation echoes other aspects of Ibn ʿArabī's cosmology. The human being is the ultimate goal of creation and, from this perspective, despite the larger scale of the macrocosm, the human being supersedes the priority of the cosmos. By invoking the macrocosm/microcosm analogy, Ibn ʿArabī reveals a potent layer of signification. Humanity's privileged position as the epitome of the macrocosm intimates that women analogously occupy a position of privilege over men, women represent the "choicest" part (*naqāwa*) of humanity, a view that reverberates through other parts of his work. The term *naqāwa* used in this context to describe women generally carries associations of refinement, suggesting a distilled or purified essence. The notion that humanity is the epitome of creation is a crucial pivot that anchors not only Ibn ʿArabī's cosmology but also his religious anthropology. The introduction of a parallel notion that woman is the epitome of man is a radical assertion in a commentary purportedly on men's "degree" over women.

What exactly constitutes this female privilege over men? In what capacity does woman occupy a paramount position that surpasses her male counterpart? Ibn ʿArabī suggests in section C that this privilege relates to her fecund receptivity in the process of procreation. In Ibn ʿArabī's depiction of procreation, man actively deposits his seed into the receptive woman, and creation ensues. Noteworthy in this description are the particular ways in which male activity and female receptivity are depicted. A man's role in procreation is characterized by a singular and linear mode of activity that simply casts the seed into the womb, "nothing more." The one-dimensional and rather simple singular phallic male act presents a marked contrast to complex, layered, and multidimensional contribution of the female partner to the process. Pregnancy and birth are robustly generative processes embodied within the woman. She is the locus of receptivity, where receptivity is portrayed as prolific, engendering "creative act succeeding creative act until a completed person emerges." Here female receptivity is certainly not defined by inactivity or passivity. Ibn ʿArabī's depiction of women's receptive role as a dynamic process illustrates that receptivity in his framework is rich and fertile, productive and fruitful; women's wombs produce the ultimate microcosm of the universe, the human being. Such an articulation of the procreative process also creates porous boundaries between activity and receptivity as commonly understood.

This description of the procreative process illustrates Ibn ʿArabī's view that women are the choicest part of man, that they enjoy a subtle level of relational priority and refinement over men and the "masculine," a position that is a continuous thread in his thought. More important, introducing this notion of female priority over men even as he is purportedly discussing men's degree over women subverts gender hierarchy. In his description, the active reality possesses greater strength, while the receptive realities constitute the epitome and choicest part of these realities. This analogy introduces the idea that the supposed "degree" of gender difference might actually denote a distinction between scope and quality rather than a more hierarchical difference. In the same way that the macrocosm has a larger scope, so too does Adam have a more expansive and diffuse scope; women, like the microcosm, have a more concentrated and intense quality of manifestation.

In fact, Ibn ʿArabī does not attach an essential or enduring superiority to either the actor or the recipient. In the process of procreation, male activity might be linear and powerful, while female receptivity is a concentrated creative hub, dynamic and abundantly (re)productive. Ibn ʿArabī's discussions suggest different gendered modes of power reflected in the process of procreation. This example suggests that the "degree" between men and women pertains to substantial difference rather than to superiority, particularly the difference in their respective contributions to the procreative process. Furthermore, for Ibn ʿArabī, women's generative receptivity provides a microcosmic reflection of the divine feminine, the ultimate receptive matrix of reality that unites activity and receptivity and thereby gives rise to all of creation.

Until this point in passages C and D, the ontological differences between men and women concern their dominant modes of activity and receptivity. According to Ibn ʿArabī, these different modes relate to the creative imperative in terms of both the creation of Eve and the creation of all humanity. He has developed a rich notion of what the differences between activity and receptivity entail in ways that not only defy but also subvert normative hierarchies. Each reality is powerful from a certain relational perspective. Readers might, therefore, be quite disconcerted that after these very complex and nuanced understandings of gender, activity, and receptivity, Ibn ʿArabī proceeds to explain female deficiency.

Reading the entire passage, which begins by confounding normative gender constructs but concludes with a discussion of female deficiency, might cause some consternation and perhaps confusion. A cynic might reasonably suggest that Ibn ʿArabī is simply glorifying women's procreative capacities while diminishing their intellectual and religious capacities, as reflected by his allegiance to the deficiency *ḥadīth*. Perhaps this is true. However, by both recognizing and celebrating women's crucial contribution to creation and tying the *ḥadīth* on female deficiency in intellect and religion to the ways in which Eve was configured from Adam, Ibn ʿArabī draws this very problematic *ḥadīth* into his cosmological mappings of activity and receptivity. He has already explained his understanding of the "degree" of difference. By subjecting this *ḥadīth* to his much layered macrocosmic analogy, he compels readers subtly, albeit fundamentally, to shift normative understandings of gender and of the primordial female, Eve, while remaining faithful to the canonical sources. He ends with a statement that both men and women are receptive in relation to God, a view that reiterates the first, primary assertion about the equal *insāniyya* of men and women. Again, Ibn ʿArabī's juxtaposition of antithetical ideas produces an understanding of this point. Paradox allows for the emergence of higher syntheses that open up rather than limit the possibilities of understanding gender relations.

I do not deny the very problematic dimensions of the deficiency *ḥadīth*, with its primary focus on female lack as it relates to intellectual and religious capacities, and Ibn ʿArabī neither ignores nor refutes this *ḥadīth*. But Ibn ʿArabī incorporates even the most challenging of *ḥadīth* and Qurʾānic sources in dynamic ways. He consistently subjects the sources to his cosmology, which he would no doubt argue is derived from his mystical insights into the same sources. Through this cosmological framework, he reads gender in innovative ways, both asserting difference and maintaining an underlying shared humanity. His inclusion of all sources and the pro-

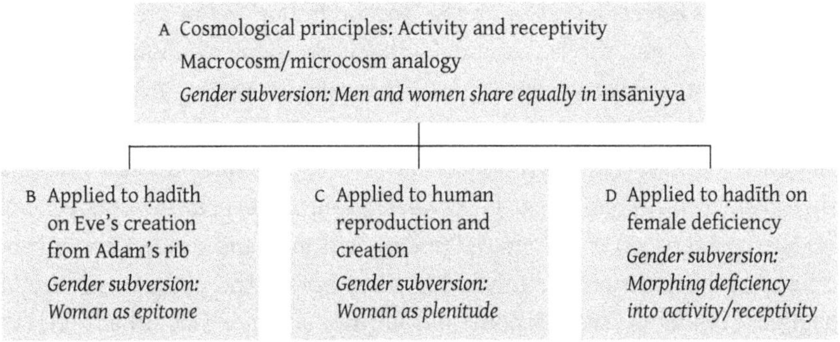

Figure 1. Ibn ʿArabī's Mapping of Gender through Cosmological Principles

cess of subjecting them to his cosmology reveal a scrupulous rigor, and his multiple approaches to gender are decidedly more complex and "difficult" than many of his contemporaries' rather straightforward, clichéd, and selective reflections. Figure 1 maps how Ibn ʿArabī subjects some of the textual sources and their gendered constructs to his cosmology.

Ibn ʿArabī thus assimilates dominant ideas while re-creating them in subtle yet significantly different ways. By so doing, he shifts the borders of established gender discourse, reconstituting the range and possibilities for understanding gender. He sows seeds of dissent to the given norms by subtly inserting radically unusual allusions to women as being the *naqāwa* of men in the same way that humanity is the epitome of creation, by providing novel ontological registers and understandings of female procreative roles, and by transforming dominant understandings of men's purported "degree" above women.

In another passage on the creation of Adam and Eve, Ibn ʿArabī again alludes to the Qurʾānic notion of men's "degree" or priority over women with a slightly different interpretive gloss: "The first of human bodies to come into existence was Adam. He is the first father of this [human] species. . . . He is the first that appeared by the command of God of this species, but as we have defined it. Then [God] separated from him a second father for us and named him a mother. So it is correct that this first father has a priority over her because his existence functions as a source/root for her. So the delegated authority of the circle of sovereignty should end with the likes of which it began, to remind us that all precedence is from the hand of God."[30]

While this passage reiterates many of the lessons of the previous excerpt, a few subtle new flourishes appear. Given Ibn ʿArabī's careful attention to language, his reference to Eve as the "second father" is not accidental. The terms "father" and the "masculine" inhabit the same symbolic constellation as activity, elevation, spirit, and luminosity. Imagining Eve as a father thus attributes to her all of these qualities. Here, then, Ibn ʿArabī's use of language suggests that at a foundational level of human creation, a primary shared ontological reality exists between Adam and Eve, a view that echoes his earlier assertion of the shared *insāniyya* of men and women. Ibn ʿArabī reiterates this position in many of his other works. And in the event that a negligent reader misses this point and wrongly assumes that either male (as first father) or female (as first mother) holds some type of ultimate priority over the other sex, the sharp-witted guide points out that "all precedence is from the hand of God." Both sexes are instrumental in a process of creation, inferring that neither one is fixed into a predetermined and unchanging station. Thus, even as he develops the position of seemingly hierarchical ontological gender difference based on male "degree" over women, he is sustaining contrary and deliberate discursive traces of a shared identity between Adam and Eve.

The reader is again exposed to Ibn ʿArabī's extraordinary poetics of subversion. By juxtaposing contrary gender constructs within the same narrative, he creatively enables the reader to "write in" the "absent" text of possibilities. Perhaps this strategy resulted from social conditions of censure or a context that might not otherwise be hospitable to such ideas. This is a "poetics" of abundance. Like poetry, it works in the main and most powerfully through association, opening up the text in expansive ways. These literary devices enable Ibn ʿArabī to forge dialogues with current readers, inviting them, centuries after he wrote his texts, to develop the ideas in them in new and germane ways—the concept of "future friendships." In addition, using these creation narratives, Ibn ʿArabī spawns a number of other rich understandings of the nature of male-female relationships.

Spinning Ribs into Love: Intimacy, Hierarchy, and Gender Difference

For Ibn ʿArabī, the myth of Eve's creation from Adam's rib becomes a primary nucleus from which he spins multiple stories on the nature of intimacy between men and women. Most significantly in this respect, Eve's emergence from Adam's body is the ontological basis for love and intimacy between men and women. Ibn ʿArabī writes,

> She was [created] from the rib because ribs are characterized by the quality of bending [*inḥināʾ*]. This is so that she might bend toward her child and her husband. The man bends in inclination toward the woman with a bending toward himself because she is part of him. The woman bends in inclination toward the man because she is created from the rib, and the rib has in it the quality of bending and sympathetic affection [*inʿitaf*]. And God filled the space within Adam from which Eve was extracted with desire [*shahwa*] for her because there never remains a vacuum in existence. So [God] filled him with desire, and he yearned for her, as a yearning for himself because she is a part taken from him. And she yearns for him out of homesickness for her place of origin. The love of Eve is love for a place of origin [homeland] and the love of Adam is love of himself. From this appears love of man for a woman because she was him in essence. And woman is given the power in loving man, a power expressed through her modesty or shyness [*ḥayāʾ*].[31]

Many of Ibn ʿArabī's contemporaries interpreted the rib *ḥadīth* to symbolize female "crookedness": the primordial woman's creation from the bent rib of Adam signified an implicit counterpoint to the straight and upright man. Ibn ʿArabī, however, draws very different conclusions. Reconfiguring the symbolic significance of the rib, he tells his reader that the quality of bending reflects woman's act of inclining toward her spouse and children, which is depicted as a positive and enriching quality showing sympathetic affection. For the reader, it invites an association of expansiveness and generosity with an Eve who bends and extends toward her family, an image that deflects normative visions of female deficiency and lack generally associated with the rib *ḥadīth*. Moreover, Ibn ʿArabī incorporates men into the same symbolic posture by describing them as possessing the same quality of bending. He does not just transform the meaning and symbolic constellation of the gendered "bent" rib from crookedness to munificence but turns the dominant gender ideology against itself by associating men with the same property of bending and inclining toward women. He seals this assertion of a shared identity between the sexes by noting that a man's love for a woman is born from the fact that "she was him in essence." In an androcentric world, such an assertion of sameness effectively counters a tradition of understanding women as different from and deficient relative to men. Thus, in this passage, a "rib nature" that bends and extends in love and yearning characterizes the self within all of humanity, and Ibn ʿArabī skillfully weaves this constant and intersecting thread of identity between men and women even as he enunciates gender differences.

In these creation myths, Adam and Eve are united in mutual love and desire for one another but are also divided by different kinds of desire. Adam's is the desire felt by an incomplete being for a lost part of itself; the chasm created in him by the "removal" of Eve (rib) is filled with and replaced by love and yearning for her. Eve's is the desire of the traveler for her home, for the birthplace of her being. Moreover, this mutual love is ontologically given, since it is part of the created condition of both the primordial man and woman. Ontologically embedded in one another, Adam and Eve both bend and incline toward one another. Ibn ʿArabī's final comment on the power of modesty in women's love presents an opportunity to reflect on the strength of a love that is kept within the sanctity of a private space, an inversion of normative views of power. Noteworthy however, is the specifically gendered depiction of a love defined by modesty.

Adam and Eve's deep existential intimacy is nonetheless still saturated with gender hierarchy; Adam is constructed as the primary "source" and Eve is the secondary "part," an aspect of his being. The idea of men and women being inextricably bound together by the reality of their createdness as well as a love that ensues as a consequence of such a created nature is significant. Such a reading provides a stark contrast to the dominant interpretation of the rib narrative as a means of consigning women to eternal "crookedness," deviance, and inherent moral inferiority to men.

The theme of intimacy and love between men and women is more fully developed in the final and most intriguing chapter of the *Fuṣūṣ al-ḥikam*, which focuses on the Prophet Muḥammad. Each chapter of the book is dedicated to a particular prophet, who embodies a specific facet of divine wisdom. Muḥammad is not only the final messenger and seal of the prophets but also the ultimate model of human spiritual realization in Ibn ʿArabī's terms, reflecting the divine wisdom of singularity. This masterly discussion presents the reader with one of Ibn ʿArabī's most compelling explanations of the nature of identity and intimacy between God and humanity and of human knowledge of God. Ibn ʿArabī's culminating chapter of the *Fuṣūṣ* simultaneously is devoted to the single-most-important figure in the Muslim tradition and offers extensive discussion on gender and male-female relationships. The Prophet Muḥammad occupies a central and pivotal role in Ibn ʿArabī's cosmology, serving as an archetypal and complete human being and providing a site for delving into some of the deepest dimensions of human nature and relationship with the divine as well as for articulating the core ontological category of "singularity." Gender is integrally woven into Ibn ʿArabī's cosmological fabric of ultimate value and existential significance, linked to the archetypal model of complete spiritual refinement, the Prophet Muḥammad. That "singularity" defines the central ontological dimension of male-female relationships in Ibn ʿArabī's schema presents an encompassing conception of humanity where the relationship between man and woman is integral to the manifestation of the divine One.

In the *Fuṣūṣ*, Ibn ʿArabī comments on a *ḥadīth* where the Prophet said, "Three things of this world of yours have been made lovable to me: women, perfume—while the coolness of my eye was placed in ritual prayer." He begins by informing his male audience that understanding the significance of women is central since woman "is a part of man in the very essence of her manifestation. So the human being's knowledge of himself preceded his knowledge of his Lord, thus his knowledge of his Lord is the result of his knowledge of himself. For this reason, the Prophet Muḥammad said 'Whosoever knows his soul knows his Lord.'"[32]

Addressing male subjectivities that might have been inclined to see women as defined by spiritual and moral deficiency, Ibn ʿArabī tears apart the cocoon of female inferiority and Otherness. Instead, he posits a radical ontological singularity defined by complete identity between men and women. In particular, he informs the dedicated male spiritual seeker that an understanding of women and gender relations is intrinsic to the foremost goal of the spiritual path, which is knowledge of the nature of the divine.

For Ibn ʿArabī, the turning point of the central *ḥadīth* on women, perfume, and prayer is that women were made lovable to the Prophet. The love that the Prophet Muḥammad felt for women was divinely endowed rather than being a willful love or a personal inclination on his part. According to Ibn ʿArabī,

> Women were made lovable to him—so he longed for them because the whole longs for its parts. This he explains as coming from the reality in the saying regarding the elemental human makeup, "And I breathed into him of my spirit." God describes himself as having deep longing for contact with man when he says to those who long, "O David, I long for them even more." . . . Since he has explained that he breathed of his spirit into man, he is yearning in reality only for himself. Consider,

> then how because of his spirit, his creation is in his own image. . . . That God should refer to the spirit through "blowing" alludes to the fact that it derives from the breath of the All-Merciful. The breath of the All-Merciful is within that which makes the human being human.[33]

Not only is the Prophet's love for women divinely bestowed on him but it is intimately linked to the relationship between God and humanity. Desire and love between men and women mirror God's love and desire for humanity. The analogy informs the reader that intimacy and longing between men and women is part of an existential blueprint originating in no less than God. Thus, Ibn ʿArabī provides a powerful spiritual sanctification for desire between men and women as emerging from the divine source.

This analogy between love and desire has consequences of a spiritual nature between the two corresponding sets of pairs. Humanity shares in the divine through God's breath; similarly, woman shares the same ontological source with man through his rib. Here again, Ibn ʿArabī earmarks God's inbreathing of spirit into a person as the ontological source of human identity (*insāniyya*). In light of his immediate male audience, for whom women and sexuality were often depicted as challenging obstacles to the spiritual life, his articulations on male-female relationships and desire become especially innovative.[34] Ibn ʿArabī elaborates,

> Then God split off from him a being in his own image, called woman, and she appears in his own image. So the man feels a deep longing for her, as something yearns for itself, while she feels longing for him as one longs for that place to which one belongs. Thus women were made beloved to him, for God loves that which he has created in his own image, and he made his angels, despite the grandeur of their power and rank and their lofty nature, prostrate to him. From here arises the connection. Image is the greatest, most glorious, and perfect connection. For it is a twin that made the being of the Real into two. In the same way, the woman through her existence makes man into two, making him into one of a pair.
>
> Thus triplicity is manifest: God, man, and woman. The man yearns for his Lord, who is his root, just as woman yearns for man. Thus his Lord made woman beloved to him just as God loves that which is in his own image. Hence, love arises only toward the one who is engendered from him. Or it may take place toward the one from whom a person is engendered, that is, the Real. This is why the Prophet said, "were made

> lovable to me." He did not say "I loved" from himself. His love is for his Lord in whose image he is, even his love for his wife since he loves her through God's love toward him, and thus qualified by the character of the divine.[35]

His analogy between men and women, on the one hand, and the divine-human relationship, on the other, provides the reader with ripe, vivid, and paradoxical gender discourses. These richly nuanced and uniquely layered passages may be interpreted in a number of ways. Utilizing a critical hermeneutic of suspicion, I first explore one interpretation that might present the most obvious gendered implications of his work for a feminist reader. I then supplement this reading by drawing on other discussions of gender by Ibn ʿArabī that might deepen the reader's hermeneutical lens.

NARRATIVES OF HIERARCHY

First and most starkly, this narrative can be understood to posit an explicit hierarchy in the chain of being where the relationship between man and woman corresponds to the nature of the relationship between God and man. Man loves God because he derives his being from the spirit of God, which is breathed into him, and thus God is his source and homeland. For God, the source of love for man relates to the fact that God's spirit resides in man. As such, God's love for man is none other than a love for God's self. Man is the part, and God is the whole. Accordingly, woman stands in a similar type of relationship to man. Woman, who derives her being from the rib of man, is part of him. As such, he is her source and her home, and she loves him. For his part, man feels love for the creation that emerges from his rib and is therefore part of him; his love for her is similarly a love for himself. Thus, while God represents the whole of which man is a part, man represents the whole of which woman is a part. Man is an image of God, and woman is an image of man. The parallels between God and man are clear.

In this type of interpretation, the most powerful underlying implication is that men are positioned as divine intermediaries if not demigods in relation to women. The notion that men represent the plenitude of being from which women are derived is clearly problematic. It renders the God-woman relationship secondary or mediated through man, whereas man has a direct and unmediated relationship with God. In this reading, man is the locus of God's disclosure and image, and woman is the locus of man's disclosure and image.

In such a discourse of spiritual hierarchy, God occupies the pinnacle; man, as the primary being who is the image of God, is at the center; and woman, who is the image of man, is subsequently a "degree" below men. Logically then, men are the necessary and connecting link between woman and God. Spiritual hierarchy here prefigures and prescribes gender and marital hierarchy, providing a metaphysical basis for male power and authority in relation to women. With this type of interpretation, the reader arrives at the notion of fairly benevolent and romanticized patriarchy, but a patriarchy nonetheless with a very problematic metaphysics that presents man as the primary image of God and woman as an image of man.

DIFFERENT ADAMS, ALTERNATIVE EVES: ONENESS AND DUALITY

Just as one might be tempted to rest confidently with such a feminist critique, Ibn ʿArabī whirls the reader away from any possible certainties by presenting different dimensions and images of Adam and Eve, traces of which are already present in the *Fuṣūṣ* passages cited earlier. Looking carefully at these passages, a discerning reader might glimpse a fleeting image of an androgynous Adam in addition to the male Adam. In fact, Ibn ʿArabī moves in his writings between two significantly different registers of Adam. There is the gender-inclusive androgynous first Adam who comprises both male and female. When the female part is separated and extracted from the first androgynous being, the second gendered Adam is thus created. The latter Adam is male, the primordial man who is what remains when Eve is taken from the compound whole. Evidence for an androgynous and gender-inclusive first human appears in a number of different passages in Ibn ʿArabī's works.[36]

> Nothing save itself divides one thing into two, be it in the sensory or intelligible realms. In the sensory realm, Adam was made two by that which opened up from his short left rib—that is, the form of Eve. He was one in his entity, then he became a pair through her, though she was none other than himself. *When she was in him, it was said that he was one.* . . . In the sensory realm, *Adam was made two by Eve*, who emerged from his essence. Then God "scattered abroad from the pair of them many men and women" (Q. 4:1) in the form of the pair. . . . God did not create from Adam and Eve an earth, a sky, a mountain, or anything other than their own kind. He created from them only their likes in

form and property. . . . Since the root is one and nothing made him two except himself, and since manyness only became manifest from his entity, everything in the cosmos possesses a sign denoting the fact that he is one.[37]

A nuanced gender-sensitive reading of Ibn ʿArabī faces the instinctive inclination to conflate these two Adams, yet it is imperative to keep them apart. The male Adam who remains after the creation of Eve is an ontologically different creature from the original, gender-inclusive, androgynous Adam created in the image of God. As if this were not complicated enough, Ibn ʿArabī at times uses the male Prophet Adam to signify the archetypal human being, with implications and applications to all humanity, men and women alike. Ibn ʿArabī therefore exposes the reader to three different levels of signification in the character of Adam: there is the all-encompassing, androgynous Adam who comprises male and female; the male Adam who is what remains after Eve is removed from the original androgyne; and the Prophet Adam, who despite his maleness is invoked in ways that represent the archetypal human condition.

These multiple Adams introduce the idea of a transformation of normative gendered archetypes symbolized in the primordial myth of creation; they disrupt "fixed" and "original" constructions of Adam and related gendered associations. Indeed, Ibn ʿArabī's language and style mimic this conceptual destabilization; his innovative and polyphonous narratives offer the reader an experience of the transformation in the Adamic figure, thereby interrupting the normative ideological positions associated with him. Through the literary devices of complex juxtaposition and paradox—that is, the multiple renditions of the creation narrative at which the reader can only arrive through the labor of multiple reading acts—Ibn ʿArabī leads his reader through a dynamic movement of thought, processing of logic, and experience of a new and possible gender imaginary. This is the experience of sought-after unfolding that Ibn ʿArabī's writing process mimics for the reader's reading process. Not only is this a highly effective strategy for rendering very complex ideological issues, but it is shrewd and thorough in that it works along with readers' possible assumptions while introducing them to an additional smorgasbord of new possibilities from which to choose. The neatness of this "trick" strategy for a writer laboring under narrowly circumscribed gender relations and possible conditions of censorship is that the writing as well as the unsaying are accomplished.

Moreover, embracing these multiple registers of Adam while clearly recognizing the different realities that Adam signifies in Ibn ʿArabī's thought is the crucial linchpin in a comprehensive reading of the gendered symbolism reflected in the primordial couple. To fully perceive the significance and crucial ontological dynamic presented in the analogy between God and humanity, on the one hand, and man and woman, on the other, readers must simultaneously keep in view all Adams, a veritable viewing trick in a house of mirrors. Doing so allows for a more nuanced reading of these texts, offering space and generosity to Ibn ʿArabī's most profound insights.

Throughout the chapter on Muḥammad in the *Fuṣūṣ*, the relationship between Eve and Adam is depicted as a microcosmic reflection of the relationship between God and humanity. The notion of humanity constituting a mirror to God echoes the *ḥadīth qudsī* of God as a hidden treasure who, desiring to be known, created the world. Without the mirror of creation and humanity in particular, God's manifestation and knowledge would be incomplete. Moreover, the analogy also informs the reader that in the process of creation, when humanity makes "the being of the Real into two," desire, love, and yearning are born. These feelings are a consequence of the original ontological identity between the separated parts that share in a primordial sameness, a sameness that paradoxically needed Otherness and separation to know itself. Yet Otherness is nothing but self. This analogy conveys the idea that the primordial human (the first Adam) encapsulates male and female and mirrors the divine.

Ibn ʿArabī's use of the male Prophet Adam to signify the archetypal human being has equal implications for men and women: both share the original heritage of being created in the image of God and thus can reflect the full amalgam of divine qualities. Ibn ʿArabī often refers to the male Adam in this universal way. For example, in his *Naqsh al-fuṣūṣ*, he explains that the central ontological dimension of Adam is the spirit that imbues the body of the world, adding, "and I mean by 'Adam' the existence of the human microcosm. And He taught him[Adam] the Names, all of them."[38] Thus, the figure of Adam here is representative not of male humanity but of the principle of humanity (*insāniyya*), which includes both men and women. The description of how God kneaded the clay for Adam's body for forty days before breathing into him God's own spirit signifies all of humanity's primordial constitution. Adam represents the prototypal gender-inclusive *insān*, who is constituted by the combination of body and spirit. In his *ʿUqlat al-mustawfiz*, Ibn ʿArabī states, "Maleness and femaleness are merely accidents and do not belong to the essence of *insāniyya*, which is one."[39] As he had also noted earlier, *insāniyya* is a reality that comprehends both male and female, so men do not possess a "degree" over women with respect to humanity.[40] Ibn ʿArabī's use of Adam as a signifier of all human possibilities, not only male realities, resonates with the Qurʾānic position. In the Qurʾān, Adam refers in twenty-one cases to human beings, male and female, in relation to their role as vicegerent; in only four cases does the signification refer to the particular male Adam as individual.[41]

In light of these multiple gendered significations of Adam, revisiting the *Fuṣūṣ* narrative describes the androgynous Adam as subsequently split into two, thereby introducing the notion of gender difference.[42] According to Ibn ʿArabī's analogy, in the same way that the Real becomes separated into two by the creation of the human being, the unitary male-female compound, the first Adam, is separated into two gendered beings. Ibn ʿArabī notes that woman makes humanity into two, reflecting and corresponding perfectly to her male counterpart. A key in the ontological dynamic presented by this analogy is the notion of triplicity. In the same way that the primordial gender-inclusive first human provides a mirror to God, woman, when removed from the first androgynous human, similarly provides a reflection of man. Rabia Terri Harris offers an insightful commentary on Ibn ʿArabī's dynamic of triplicity: "The human form has replicated, as the divine did before, and woman activates the self-awareness of humanity. Without woman the trick doesn't work. Without differentiation humanity could not see itself, could not locate its own capacities. What then would become of our service to the infinity of the divine? . . . Without women there is no dynamic."[43]

Ibn ʿArabī elsewhere explicitly outlines the crucial ontological significance carried by a dynamic of triplicity:

> Know that nothing is produced from the One [*al-aḥad*]. The first of the numbers is two, and nothing is originally produced from the two unless there is a third that brings them together and unites them. Thus, a thing that is produced through this union accords with the nature of the original two things, whether they were from the divine names, from the spiritual or perceptible cosmos, or any other thing. This is the nature of the matter at hand. It is the meaning of the name the Singular [*al-fard*] since three is the first [odd number]. Through this name, all possible existence becomes manifest. No possible thing is manifest from the One [*al-wāḥid*] except through a combination [*jamʿ*].

> The smallest combination is three, which is the singular, so every possible is contingent on the name the Singular [*al-fard*].[44]

Within this relationship, each of the triune is of equal significance to the ultimate ontological goal. Triplicity does not denote an interaction of lesser, derivative parts that emerge from the one, a notion that might appear obvious on a first reading of the *Fuṣūṣ* chapter on Muḥammad. Rather, to be manifest and conscious, divine oneness demands an intricate and equally weighted dynamic of threeness in which the being of each part is integral to the becoming of the whole. While each part that emerges from the whole also reflects the whole, their original identity within the whole creates the inclination toward its complementary part. This dynamic characterizes both sets of partners in the analogous creation narratives of the God-human relationship, on the one hand, and the Eve-Adam relationship, on the other. A position premised on such reciprocity between God and humanity might appear startling to those who see the divine-human relationship as simply defined by hierarchy. Particularly compelling in Ibn ʿArabī's cosmology is his ability to maintain the sovereignty of God above all creation while simultaneously presenting the deep and inextricable mutuality of the God-human relationship. His discussion of triplicity and its gender implications primarily reflects a theological perspective characterized by divine-human mutuality. The next chapter examines some of the more intricate and detailed gendered ways in which Ibn ʿArabī develops his understandings of the God-human relationship.

Chapter Six

Witnessing God in Women

A Different Story of Creation

This chapter explores the ways in which Ibn ʿArabī propels the reader into a different realm of imagining gender by presenting powerful antinomian images of the feminine, sexuality, and women. I begin by examining his depictions of the divine feminine and his related claim that God is most perfectly witnessed in women. His argument is peppered by constant invocations and references to the deep existential intimacy between man and woman as reflected in the primordial myth of Adam and Eve's creation. This leads us to examine Ibn ʿArabī's ideas on sex and sexual intimacy between men and women and how such experiences are also linked to knowledge of the divine. A heterosexual conception of sexuality frames Ibn ʿArabī's works, so I focus on heterosexual relations and identity. Finally, I examine Ibn ʿArabī's alternative narratives of creation that offer different and novel models for understanding gender. Here his innovative introduction of the creation stories involving Jesus' birth from the Virgin Mary serves as a foil against which to interpret the gender dynamics characterizing the dominant myth of Adam and Eve.

Creation and the Preeminence of the Divine Feminine

In the bezel of Muḥammad, Ibn ʿArabī amplifies, expands, and transforms his discussion on triplicity, gender, and creation by introducing his readers to yet another enormously significant creation story. Powerfully, he invokes God's mysterious essence (*al-dhāt*) as the source of all creation. More particularly, he invokes gender in a very deliberate manner, explicitly and distinctively describing this ultimate source as feminine and then drawing parallels to women. He introduces these dimensions of the debate by commenting on the symbolism carried by the grammatical gender of the words "women," "perfume," and "prayer" in the *ḥadīth* with the Prophet's announcement that "three things of this world of yours have been made lovable to me: women, perfume—while the coolness of my eye was placed in ritual prayer." According to Ibn ʿArabī,

> The Prophet gives precedence to the feminine over the masculine to give great importance to women. Thus he said "three things" in the feminine plural form and not in the masculine form. This is noteworthy since he also mentions "perfume," which is a masculine noun, and the Arabs usually make the masculine gender prevail [grammatically] over the feminine. Thus, one would say "Fāṭima and Zayd came" using a masculine plural verb, not the feminine plural. So the Arabs make the masculine gender prevail grammatically over the feminine even though there is only one masculine noun and women constitute the majority of the group. And the Prophet was an Arab. Hence he deliberately observed the specific meaning that he wanted to convey . . . and the prophet made the feminine gender prevail over the masculine gender by saying three things [in a way that indicates the feminine quality of the objects]. How insightful he is about the reality of things! How careful he is to protect the observance of rights! . . . Furthermore, he made the final term [prayer] correspond to the first term [women] in its femininity, and he placed the masculine term [perfume] between them. . . . Perfume stands between the two [feminine terms], just as the masculine stands between the two feminines in existence. Thus, the man is placed between the divine essence, from which he is manifested, and a woman, who is manifested from him. As such, he stands between two feminine entities: the substantive feminine of the divine essence and the other feminine in reality. . . . Between the two, perfume is like Adam between the divine essence from which he comes into existence and Eve, who comes into existence from him. If you want to say [that he does not come into being from the divine essence, but] from a divine attribute, "attribute" [*ṣifa*] is also feminine, if you want to say from the divine power, "power" [*qudra*] is also feminine. Indeed, whatever position you take, you will find that the feminine takes priority, even for those who claim that God is the cause of the cosmos, for "cause" [*ʿilla*] is also feminine.[1]

Given that Arabic is a gendered language, Ibn ʿArabī suggests that gendered grammar signifies aspects of ontology. Accordingly, he notes that not only is the Arabic term for the divine essence, *al-dhāt*, feminine, but so too are other significant terms indicating, for example, a divine attribute (*ṣifa*) or divine power (*qudra*). For him, the grammatically feminine forms describing God indicate the predominance and priority of the feminine dimensions of God in the processes of creation.

Particularly significant in this discussion is the skilful manner in which the narrative of Eve's creation from Adam is woven into a broader gendered mosaic of human creation from the divine feminine. God's essence, as the ultimate feminine source, precedes all else; from it emerges the first human being, who is subsequently separated into Adam and Eve. Thus, in Ibn ʿArabī's framework, Eve, as the receptive reality, emerges from the active principle embodied in Adam and is really the second step of the creation process. The ultimate creative ground of being is feminine, and from this first all-encompassing feminine source, all creation ultimately becomes manifest.

Ibn ʿArabī's position that men and the active dimensions of reality metaphysically reside between two feminines provides a strong argument for the primacy and dominance of receptive and traditionally feminine principles. Moreover, he transforms traditional conceptions of receptivity and femininity, presenting them as dynamic entities. The symbolic field of *al-dhāt* as the absolute source suggests a realm of being that is creative precisely because it encompasses both active and receptive qualities. His discussion of the feminine here raises an underlying theme in previous descriptions of women's procreative capacities: the creative feminine dimensions of reality encompass both activity and receptivity and are ultimately inescapable. The feminine, Ibn ʿArabī asserts, permeates all things ontologically, as is reflected in the fact that all abstract Arabic nouns referring to God are feminine. Through this position, he effectively relegates the argument about men's "degree above" women as secondary to a far more encompassing feminine reality that pervasively combines activity and receptivity, resulting in all creative possibilities. One glimpses a distinct view that at a different, more encompassing level of reality, women and the feminine occupy a "degree above" men and the masculine. In fact, following a discussion on women's capacity to assume all spiritual stations, including that of axial saint, Ibn ʿArabī notes that women in fact have a "degree over men." Again, he does so by invoking a reference to grammar, but somewhat obscurely this time: "Have you not examined God's wisdom in giving more to women than men in name. So God calls the male a man [*mar*ʾ] and calls the female a 'woman' [*mar*ʾ*a*]. And God increases by a syllable to the name 'mar' used to indicate a male. Therefore the female has a degree [*daraja*] over the man in this station [*maqām*] that the man does not have, in contrast with the degree given to man in the verse: 'Men have a degree above them' [Q. 2:228]. So the gap [established by this Qurʾānic statement] is filled by this increase granted to the woman."[2]

While he does not provide too much further clarity on what this female degree implies beyond the grammatical form here, elsewhere there is the clear sense that he foregrounds women and their particular ontological status. In his worldview, characterized as it is by a system of mirrors, he points to women's unique relationship to the divine feminine: "He who loves women as the Prophet loved them has loved God, who brings together all reception of activity. For he has been given knowledge by the objects of knowledge. Thus it can be said concerning him that he is the Knower. Hence he is the first to receive activity from the object of knowledge."[3]

In relation to men, women thus potentially mirror the image of God. He emphasizes the point that if a man loves a woman with the prophetic insight of the comprehensive nature of woman's reality, he has loved God. Women reflect that pervasive dimension of reality that brings together all reception of activity, a creative reality through which all knowledge and love becomes possible. This view of women provides a nuanced counter-narrative to the extract from the *Fuṣūṣ* examined in chapter 5, where Adam appears to be the mirror image of God to Eve. Moreover, the construction of women's encompassing capacities also reiterates the view that men are needy in relation to women, whom men actively seek out in order to know themselves and thus know God. In Ibn ʿArabī's cosmology, this unique correspondence between women and the creative feminine resonates with another unusual position that he takes—that is, the idea that women are the locus for the most perfect witnessing of God.

Women Divine

Within Ibn ʿArabī's cosmology, we have established that human beings are archetypically the most concentrated and refined locus for the manifestation of God's attributes. However, probably to the great consternation and bewilderment of his more misogynist peers, he adds that within humanity, women, over and above men, are the locus for the most perfect witnessing of God:

> When the man witnesses the Real in the woman, this is a witnessing within a locus that receives activity. When he witnesses him [God] in himself in respect to the fact that the woman becomes manifest from him, then he has witnessed him [God] in an active aspect. When he witnesses him [God] in himself without calling to mind the form of that which was engendered from himself, then this witnessing takes place in a locus that receives the Real's activity without intermediary. Hence his witnessing of the Real in the woman is the most complete and most perfect since he witnesses the Real in respect to the fact that he [God] is both active and locus of receiving activity. . . . This is why the Prophet loved women, because of the perfection of witnessing the Real within them. For the Real can never be witnessed disengaged from some material, since God in his essence is independent of the worlds. Since the situation is impossible in this respect and witnessing takes place only in some material, then the witnessing of the Real in women is the greatest and most perfect witnessing.[4]

Central in this passage is the notion that for men, women provide the most perfect locus of witnessing God because men can see in the female form both God's activity and reception of activity. Here, Ibn ʿArabī is weaving his understandings of the myth of Eve's creation from Adam's rib into a particular understanding of gender relations. As such, man witnesses God in women in the active mode in so much as the mythic Adam is the active intermediary for Eve's creation. And similarly, man can witness God in the receptive mode inasmuch as Eve is recipient to Adam's action. Without the primordial woman, man can simply witness his own receptivity, not both divine modes. So woman, as epitomized in Eve, becomes the most perfect source of witnessing God, since in her, the totality of divine modes is apparent. Since God as reality represents the union of opposites—God is both active/male and receptive/female—in women, men witness this *coincidenta oppositorium* as the most complete theophany of God.

While this position points to the more sublime representations of women's ontological potential in relation to men, the critical question that persists is the gendered nature of subjectivity. If the subject of this discourse is the male aspirant as witness and the object is the female theophany as the witnessed, how and where is female subjectivity articulated? If the reader instead posits woman as the spiritual aspirant, where might she find a perfect object of witnessing God? I concur with Rabia Terri Harris, who suggests that Ibn ʿArabī's answer to this question is, "Women take precedence only because they are the focus of receptivity, just as nature takes precedence over everyone that takes form from her. And nature in reality is none other than the breath of the Merciful. In her opens the forms of the universe, from the highest to the lowest, for the diffusion of the outbreath in primordial matter—specifically, in the world of the bodies."[5]

Woman, as the locus through which the "breath of the Merciful [*nafas al-Raḥmān*]" brings humanity into existence, embodies a distinctive and unique theophanic location combining receptive and active modes. Woman is simultaneously the primordial created and the maternal creator. By reflecting the "breath of the Merciful," woman assumes an agency through which all humanity is born. Here, therefore, female subjectivity and agency are articulated in relation to the most perfect witnessing of God. Given the station of primordial creativity and priority that woman occupies in relation to the human race, children, and by extension all humanity, this provides her the object for the perfect contemplation of God. In my reading, this witness is not limited to her occupying the role of mother in relation to biological children, a position that would exclude women who are unable to or choose not to have children, a category that included a number of early Sufi women, such as those who chose celibacy.

Rather, women witness God in all of human creation simply because they have received this pivotal archetypal and in many cases actual role in the unfolding of creation. Women receive this pivotal archetypal position by virtue of their capacity, or biological form, whether or not this potential is actualized in pregnancy and children. On deeper reflection, this position does not simply tie women to their biology; rather, it fully recognizes the stupendous weight of theophanic realities reflected in female procreative capacities, completely integrating body and spirit.

Given this isthmus role that women occupy in the existence of humanity, Ibn ʿArabī highlights their unique perfection: "The Prophet was made to love women because they are the locus of receiving activity [*infiʿāl*] for the purpose of bringing into being the most complete and perfect form. This is the human form [*al-ṣūra al-insāniyya*], and no other form is more perfect. Not every locus of receiving activity has this specific perfection. Thus, love of women was one of the things that God bestowed on his Prophet, so that he loved women although he had few children."[6]

This view resonates with his earlier suggestion that woman is the choicest part (*naqāwa*) of man; she reflects a distinctively refined aspect of the human microcosm. It also recalls the reader's earlier encounter with Ibn ʿArabī's moment of "conversion" to loving women, a crucial defining moment. In this instance, the reader receives another significant and spiritually compelling impetus for men loving women.

The depictions of women's unique theophanic location provides a noteworthy counterpoint to the earlier position that men alone can attain the station of superlative perfection, *akmāliyya*—that is, the roles of messenger and emissary. Ibn ʿArabī's characteristic prioritization and spiritualization of physical form, the notion that God can only be witnessed at the realm of materiality and can be best witnessed in the embodied reality of women, and the idea that women reflect the divine breath of the Merciful all provide clear inversion of patriarchal devaluations of women and their bodies.

Here, as in the previous chapter, the reader encounters views of woman as the most perfect divine disclosure by virtue of being a microcosmic reflection of the divine feminine, which combines the active and receptive principles in reality. Woman is the means through which the divine primordial matrix manifests Its creativity and births the perfect form—that is, the human being. In light of these equivalences and correlativity, the feminine is considered existentially prior and preeminent, and women are seen to provide a more perfect witnessing of God than men.

Women's capacity uniquely to embody particular divine attributes is also woven into another narrative describing the analogous relationship between Eve and Adam on the one hand and the womb and the All-Merciful on the other:

> The station of the woman in relation to the man in the root of coming into existence is the station of the womb in relation to the All-Merciful, because she is a branch from him, and she emerged in his form. Some traditions say, "God created Adam in the form of the merciful one." And it is established that the womb in us is a branch of the merciful one. So we have descended from the Merciful one in the station [*manzilāt*] of Eve [descending] from Adam. This station is the locus of procreativity and manifesting the potential for children. In a similar way, we are all the locus of the manifestation of action. The action, though it is God's, becomes manifest only by our hands. It is by sensory perception attributed only to us, nothing but us. If we were

> not a branch of the Merciful, then we could not accurately attribute [all actions] to the divine cause.[7]

Here, humanity in relation to the all-merciful One is placed in the station of Eve vis-à-vis Adam—that is, in the state of receiving activity. With this image, Ibn ʿArabī reiterates at a surface level the parallel between God and Adam. More significantly, however, by analogously situating humanity in the station of Eve, the latter symbolically signifies the generalized human experience. Like Eve, humanity as the receptive branch of the All-Merciful is the womb that engenders and manifests the acts of God. In particular, this imagery conveys in Ibn ʿArabī's terms the "feminine" or receptive nature of all humanity in relationship to God, again illustrating that "femininity" or receptivity is relational rather than gender-specific.

Furthermore, when Ibn ʿArabī speaks about the relationship between the All-Merciful as the root and the womb as the branch, the womb is not some metaphoric, disembodied entity but a physical organ that resides in the bodies of female humans. This idea again brings to the surface the unique relationship between God as All-Merciful and women, who are the loci of pregnancy and birthing. Moreover, the specific God-woman relationship signifies a more universal relationship that God shares with all of humanity, that of root to branch. So in this case, the God-woman relationship is the model of God-human relationship.

When Ibn ʿArabī subsequently uses the analogy of man as the root and woman as the branch, he conveys a more subtle point that Adam's identity as "root" is fundamentally predicated on the existence of Eve as branch. Accordingly, man's longing for woman is "the yearning of the root for the branch because the root nourishes and sustains the branch. And if it were not [for the branch], then the lordly power of nourishing and sustaining would not manifest in the root."[8]

While on one level, this viewpoint may be interpreted as another reiteration of male power over women, it simultaneously and paradoxically asserts that the relationship between them is the source of Adam's identity. Were it not for Eve, Adam could not realize and manifest fully his innate capacities. To this extent, man's purpose depends on woman, just as God depends on humanity for the complete manifestation of particular divine qualities. Further, the relationship signifies mutuality and emotional intimacy between men and women, "Because Eve is a branch from Adam, God made love and mercy between them, thereby informing us that between the womb and the

Merciful is love and mercy . . . so that the love that is made between the two spouses is the establishment of intercourse [*nikāḥ*] that leads to procreation [*tawallud*] and mercy. And the mercy that is placed between them is the yearning that each of the partners feels towards the other. So each yearns [*ḥanna*] for and finds repose in the other."[9]

This entire discussion is dominated by a focus on the divine attributes of mercy and love, *jamālī* attributes that have traditionally been associated with the feminine. Moreover, these *jamālī* attributes are generalized and applied to both men and women. Ibn ʿArabī reiterates the view that love between men and women is a reflection of the nature of love between the all-merciful God and humanity. This love and mercy between men and women culminates in sexual intimacy.

Ibn ʿArabī revolutionizes gendered ways of imagining human-divine relationships, providing unique associations of plenitude and divine presence with the traditionally female dimensions of reality. In tandem with exalting and sanctifying the feminine, he dethrones and humanizes the male by associating men with a profound dependence on women. For readers who might mistakenly still associate the male Adam with divine wholeness and completion and Eve with partiality and need in Ibn ʿArabī's creation narratives, we must attend to the various and sometimes subtle manner in which he unsays such associations.

Ibn ʿArabī unpicks the seams of an autonomous male: "As for women, it is the yearning of the part for its whole, and of the branch for its root and of the stranger for its home. And the yearning of the man for his wife is the yearning of the whole for its part because with it he can be truly called the whole and without it, this name [the whole], does not really belong to him."[10] With this statement, Ibn ʿArabī debunks notions of the male Adam as independently occupying the position of whole in relation to Eve, who is merely a part of him. In fact, each is a "part" in need of the other for completion, as intimated in the *Fuṣūṣ* when Ibn ʿArabī writes, "Woman through her existence makes man into two, turning him into one of a pair." This statement evokes a notion of gendered reciprocity, where man and woman turn each other into a pair of equal halves.

Such views interspersed in Ibn ʿArabī's texts also recall the idea that when the rib was taken from Adam, a vacuum was created in his being, an emptiness that caused yearning for a reuniting with that from which he had been separated. Readers who might infer a narcissistic tendency in this notion would be more prudent to reflect on how these constructions of Adam and Eve create opportunities for profound new ways of rethinking some of the dominant relationships between men and women and gesture toward more integral and generous ways to symbolize self and Other in gendered terms. This theme of the male as empty, needy, and incomplete without his female counterpart suffuses Ibn ʿArabī's gender imagination.

In all these cases, the male Adam signifies the male human being who is the leftover creature after Eve is separated from the primordial human creature. Maleness consequently is defined by a sense of loss or a privation of being, hence the yearning for his female counterpart. Their separation creates desire for return and union with one another. The subtle point underlying these depictions of a needy Adam is that Eve does not simply derive her being from the male Adam but is already a constituent part of the initial androgynous human being that is directly inspirited by God. Hence, Adam experiences a state of privation when Eve becomes separated from him. The androgynous Adam, the all-inclusive archetypal human, embodies all the divine names that seekers, men and women alike, attempt to emulate. Indeed, in the internal integration of the primordial Adam and Eve, the human becomes the microcosmic reflection of *al-Insān al-Kāmil*. This critical point disrupts the potential notion of gender hierarchy in the triplicity between God, man, and woman. In particular, it invites discussions on the idea, possibly quite novel in Ibn ʿArabī's context, that men are impoverished and destitute without women.

Elsewhere, in a highly unorthodox discussion of the divine attribute *Al-Qawī* (The Strong), Ibn ʿArabī again asserts that men stand in a position of lack and weakness without women:

> There is nothing in the created universe greater in power than women. This is a secret known only by those knowledgeable about how the universe came into existence and with what the Real [*al-Ḥaqq*] brought the universe into existence. It came through two prior principles [*muqaddima*] and [the universe] is the result. The active partner in intercourse is one who seeks. The one who seeks is poor and in need. The receiving partner in intercourse is sought or wanted. The one who is sought has the might [*ʿizza*] of being needed. And desire [*shahwa*] is overpowering. It is made clear to you the position of the woman in relation to all created things [*mawjūdāt*] and to what extent the divine presence looks upon her and by what means she manifests strength. So God informs us about the strength specifically attributed to women

in what God says about ʿĀʾisha and Ḥafsa: "If you back each other up against [the Prophet], then indeed God is his guardian, and Gabriel and the righteous believers and the angels after that are his supporters!" [Q. 66:4]. All of this is to counter the strength of two women! And God mentions only the strong ones, who possess power and strength. So the righteous believers act with conviction, and that is the strongest of actions. If you understand this you have set off on the path.[11]

In this passage, Ibn ʿArabī draws a parallel between women and the divine receptive realities, both of which, in his framework, enjoy a certain strength and primacy in the order of existence. This idea also resonates in another passage alluding to the divine feminine, when he speaks about the "possible entities" as the "wife" whom the divine masculine as "husband" seeks with desire and need; through their marriage, the entire cosmos is birthed.[12] Similarly, men as seekers need women, without whom they are "poor and needy." This statement again echoes the view that without women, men experience an existential privation of their being. Women, in being desired and sought after, represent to men fullness and completion. As such, women are in a position of power and strength vis-à-vis men. Ibn ʿArabī finds evidence for his position in the Qurʾānic verse where God invokes all the strong and powerful realities to support the Prophet Muḥammad in a dispute with two of his wives.

Utilizing an unconventional if imminently simple logic, Ibn ʿArabī suggests that God's invocation of all these powerful realities to counter two women in effect signals the latter's strength. This discussion presents one of Ibn ʿArabī's more astounding subversions of gender. On a surface level, this verse appears to castigate and reprimand the two recalcitrant wives of the Prophet. In fact, the next verse almost demands obedience from these two wives of the Prophet Muḥammad, with the threat that they might well be replaced by better women: "If he divorces you, maybe his Lord will substitute other wives in your place who are better than you; surrendering, believers, obedient, repentant, worshipping, pious, either previously married or virgins" (Q. 66:5). On the face of it, there seems to be little doubt that this Qurʾānic verse was upbraiding ʿĀʾisha and Ḥafsa.

Ibn ʿArabī, however, transforms this marital conflict into a testimony of women's power, depicting the Prophet's insubordinate wives who elicit God's admonition as role models of the divine attribute of strength. By invoking the example of the strength of ʿĀʾisha and Ḥafsa, he encourages believers to the path of strong conviction and action. This passage foregrounds the power of receptive realities through a positive reflection on female defiance.

The association of women with the *jalālī* divine attribute of strength again reveals Ibn ʿArabī's characteristic reversal of normative gender categories. This passage also alludes to the persistence of female power even within traditional social norms and broader structures of patriarchy that present men as pursuers and women as the pursued in love and sexual relationships. In a historical and cultural context that was defined by male power and dominance, the assertion that men are needy, lacking, and weak relative to women and that women reflect the attribute of divine strength most powerfully reflects an iconoclastic interrogation of particular patriarchal assumptions.

In various ways, Ibn ʿArabī unsays dominant understandings of men and women and the nature of gendered relationships. A central theme also emerging from many of these narratives focuses on ontological complementarity between men and women. This particular theme is most lucidly developed in Ibn ʿArabī's discussions on sexual relationships.

Divine Theophanies: Love, Yearning, and Sexuality

Fully contextualizing Ibn ʿArabī's understandings on sexuality requires reiterating some of the ideas from the *Fuṣūṣ al-ḥikam*. In Ibn ʿArabī's macrocosm, God's love to be known provided the impetus for God's self-disclosure as the hidden treasure in all creation, epitomized in the human being. Simultaneously, however, God's self-disclosure through the process of creation results in a separation and dispersion into multiplicity from the One. This separation paradoxically creates yearning for reunion, reflected in the human being's love and seeking for God. Love thus provides the impetus for striving on the path of spiritual cultivation that leads ultimately to a return symbolized in mystical union. Since love arises either toward one's ontological source or toward that which is ontologically engendered in one's own being, love is an eternal exchange between God and the human being. Similarly, men and women originated from a single soul (*nafsin wāḥidatin*) and, having then been separated, love and yearn for one another: this love and yearning culminate in sexual union. Thus, the love between human beings is a consequence of a shared ontological origin, which is why God made women lovable to the Prophet as well as to Ibn ʿArabī.

Ibn ʿArabī states, "Do you think that something that distanced him from his Lord would be made lovable to him? No, by God! That which brings him closer to his Lord is made lovable to him."[13] Despite the fact that his articulation reflects a male subjectivity, these formulations logically apply equally to women in relation to men. Because men and women are lodged in each other ontologically, their constitutions are interdependent. Hence, self-knowledge implies knowledge of one another, which, in turn, is necessary for knowledge of God. Their mutual love that impels them to come together is also based on this ontological model. Thus, their love for one another is not only modeled on the manner of divine love but is also a means of gaining knowledge of the divine. The love between men and women is, therefore, tied to the essence of human origins. It is a unique theophany that has the capacity to provide humans with an apprehension of the impetus for their individual and collective existences and relationships with God. As a result, women were *made* lovable to the Prophet, and his love for them is not simply a personal propensity. Perhaps for the same reason, Ibn ʿArabī also underwent this experience in his life.

Ibn ʿArabī posits that because of the full ontological correspondence between men and women, their love can fully absorb one another, which is why sexual union, when it occurs, is the "most complete union possible in love."[14] He elaborates on this mystical insight: indeed, sexuality offers a number of possibilities for spiritual realization. A man, he tells us, can completely and utterly merge with a woman based on a desire that suffuses every part of his being, which is why he needs to perform the major ablution so that "he might once again behold him [God] in the one in whom he dissolved, since it is none other than he [God] whom he sees in her."[15]

In this description of sexuality, Ibn ʿArabī uses ripe and redolent language to describe the all-consuming intensity of sexual experience; he employs the Sufi term *fanā*, often translated as "annihilation" or "extinction" and used to describe an extreme heightened spiritual state where the ego is dissolved or extinguished in the presence of God. At this apex of spiritual experience for the seeker, there is no longer an ego or an "I." This term signifies an extraordinary state of intense and overpowering union, a much-sought-after state for many seekers. Sexual intimacy, in Ibn ʿArabī's words, provides men and women with the possibilities for "total annihilation," because each is a locus of self-disclosure for the other. In these discussions, there is a complete interpenetration between spirituality and sexuality. In the *Futūḥāt*, Ibn ʿArabī explains,

> When something is a place of disclosure [*mujalla*] to a viewer, he sees nothing but himself in that form. When he, the viewer, sees in this woman himself, his love for her and attraction to her intensifies because she is his form. It has been clarified to you that his form is the form of the Real (*al-Ḥaqq*), through which he has been brought into existence. So he doesn't see anything but the real one but with desire of love [*shahwat al-ḥubb*] and taking delight in ecstasy [*iltidhādh waṣla*]. He dissolves [*yafnī fanāʾ*] in her with a real annihilation and sincere love. He encounters her with his essence in an absolute correspondence. For that reason, he dissolves in her. There is no part in him that is not in her. Love has suffused all his parts, so his entire being is interconnected [*tʾallaqa*] with her. For that reason, he dissolves in his likeness with a complete annihilation [*yafnī al-fanāʾ al-kullī*], in contrast to his love for anything that is not his likeness. He becomes one with his beloved so that he says, "I am the one I desire and the one I desire [*ahwā*] is I," and at the final point of this station says, "I am God [*anā Allāh*]." So when you love a person who is like you with such a love, then your witnessing [of the one you love] turns you back to God with such a return [*radd*]. Then you are among those whom God loves.[16]

Likeness and identity between men and women reflects the likeness and identity between God and humanity. In the experience of this correspondence with a sexual partner, the spiritual aspirant might behold the divine. When Ibn ʿArabī writes, "He encounters her with an absolute correspondence" and "there is no part in him that is not in her," one again hears potent reiterations of an ontological identity between men and women. The possibility for a "love that suffused all his parts" and "complete annihilation" is possible because men and women, in the physical act of coitus, might experience total spiritual correspondence. Such powerful affirmations of sexual and existential intimacy between men and women are predicated on notions of their interpenetrating identity, notions that significantly undermine normative views of female deficiency.

Ibn ʿArabī's vivid depiction of the profound, intense, and extreme intimacy between men and women during sex is unique and evocative. A relationship of such consuming intensity between two beings, characterized by inborn ontological correspondence and in which their complete beings become interconnected and they dissolve in one another, powerfully undermines any notion of female deficiency. Moreover, despite Ibn ʿArabī's male subjectivity, this passage implies that women too experience complete love and annihilation, since man represents a full spiritual correspondence to woman. Woman is not simply a romanticized and idealized object of man's witness of God, but both men and women are subjects *and* objects. Each is a locus of disclosure for the other, and given their common origin, the boundaries between subject and object are ultimately transcended, as is symbolized by the experience of orgasmic annihilation of the ego. This dissolving and melting into the beloved is a taste of the theophanic melting into God for those who are able to apprehend this reality.

Another particularly significant element in these discussions is that love is the impetus for sexual union between partners—in this instance, the love between men and women is part of the inherited human constitution. All human love is a theophanic reflection of God's love, which is the ultimate and ontological cause of human creation. Accordingly, in the more generalized heterosexual sense, love between men and women is an inherent aspect of loving God, bringing human beings closer to God. As such, marriage and union between a man and a woman fundamentally further their spiritual realization.

Ibn ʿArabī's views of male and female partners as providing a transformative spiritual canvas presuppose relationships based on strong, loving relationships. This point has as many implications for contemporary readers as it did for those in the past: It provides, for example, a profound critique of forced or coerced marriage, violent and abusive marital dynamics, and casual sexual relationships. The view that sexual and marital relationships are sites for profound spiritual experience and transformation engender a deep respect and reverence for self and Other among partners. Such weighting and value assigned to relationships defy any level of abuse or attitudes of nonchalance. As such, coercion and abuse as well as cavalier, careless approaches to sexual relationships become anathema.

Moreover, Ibn ʿArabī's descriptions of sexuality in male and female partnerships clearly refuted the views of those among his peers who constructed women as a distraction to men, causing deviation from the spiritual path. His understandings also differ substantially from those of Sufi thinkers who made more self-serving utilitarian and functionalist arguments in favor of marriage and sexuality. For example, Ghazāli promoted marriage, among other things, as a major strategy for providing the male aspirant with a housekeeper to free up his time for spiritual practice.[17] Ghazāli also viewed sex either as a desire that needs to be broken or as an appetite that needs cautious satisfaction to prevent it from absorbing the aspirant's energies, which are best saved for spiritual practice.[18]

On the contrary, Ibn ʿArabī sees sexual union as based on a deep existential love and as having the potential to be the greatest self-disclosure of God. However, the latter is a reality that only a small number of gnostics have genuinely realized.

> The axial saint [*quṭb*] knows of something of the self-disclosure of God through sexual union, and that incites him to seek it, being passionately enamored of it. Indeed he, along with others from among the sages, realizes his spiritual state of servanthood [*ʿubūdiyya*] through sex more than any other thing, more than eating or drinking or clothing that protect against harm. He doesn't desire marriage for personal progeny but only for desire and to populate the land with a new generation as a legal obligation. In his case, raising a new generation is a natural matter for preserving the continuation of the species in this world. So sex for the person of this spiritual station [*maqām*], is like sex for the people of paradise in that it is only for desire because it is the greatest self-disclosure of God, hidden from the world except for those whom God especially chooses from among his servants. Similarly, sex among animals happens only for desire [*shahwa*].
>
> Many of the sages are oblivious to this reality [of the spiritual importance of sexual desire]. Indeed it is one of the secrets that none know except a few of the people of divine favor [*ʿināya*]. What is it about sex that gives it its complete nobility, indicating the weakness that is demanded by the spiritual state of servanthood? It is nothing but the overpowering nature of pleasure that obliterates him of his strength and his self-importance. It is a delicious overpowering. Being overpowered [generally] precludes the one overpowered from delighting in the experience. Delight in the overpowering is a quality specific to the one who overpowers [*qāhir*] rather than the quality specific to one overpowered [*maqhūr*]. The exception is specifically this act [sex]. People remain oblivious to this nobility, making [sex] an animal appetite. They call it an animal appetite in order to keep themselves above it, despite the fact that they name it with the most noble of names

when they call it an "animalistic" [*ḥayawāniyya*] appetite. This means it is the special quality of animals [*ḥayawān*], who are endowed with life force [*ḥayāt*]. What is more noble than life? So what people believe according to themselves to be despicable is actually the essence of praiseworthiness in the view of the perfected sage.[19]

Accordingly, sex provides the mystic with the opportunity for one of the most comprehensive experiences of servanthood and receptivity. Since servanthood represents the highest human state in relation to God, sexual union provides the human being with the possibility of experiencing a penultimate state of receptivity. The pleasure experienced during sex intimates the pleasure of union with God, who is the ultimate beloved. Most people are unaware of the theophanic and pedagogic nature of sexual pleasure and do not apprehend the reality that God both takes and gives pleasure between man and woman.[20] Inherent in this perspective is a celebration and affirmation of the body and sexuality as intrinsic components of human spirituality. This conceptualization dislodges a tenacious gendered binary around sexuality often found in patriarchal societies, where women are either objectified as desired but dangerous sexual objects or venerated as religious beings devoid of sexuality.[21] Ibn ʿArabī specifically states that a woman might well occupy the spiritual station of ruling axial saint, logically implying that sexual experiences apply equally to male and female subjectivities. He is in no way promoting an unchecked male sexual dilettantism.

The act of reversing normative categories and perceiving underlying realities that transcend prevalent social evaluations is also reflected in his reinterpretation of the word *ḥayawān* (animal). Responding to those of his peers who had dismissed sex as a lower animal appetite to be overcome, he notes that *ḥayawān*, deriving as it does from the Arabic word for "living," indicates the higher and noble qualities of life. By arguing that sexual appetite is not a base characteristic but a noble life-giving desire and a spiritually energizing force, Ibn ʿArabī again overturns traditional patriarchal hierarchies. Life, the body, and sexual desire are affirmed and ennobled as integral to spirituality. He in essence presents the reader with a model of religious personhood that is liberated from the binaries of spirit and matter, piety and desire, sanctity and carnality, male and female. This is a holistic, embodied, and world-affirming spirituality par excellence.

Furthermore, in this extract, sexuality as a theophanic reality allows for the experience of the *coincidenta oppositorium*, which ultimately is also the nature of the reality of God. Ibn ʿArabī's framework dissolves the traditional divisions between *jamāl* and *jalāl*, and they are experienced simultaneously and become imbricated in one another. This epiphany of pleasure is a sense of being utterly overwhelmed, in a state of "weakness," stripped of any individual claims to power or strength; it is simultaneously a "delicious overpowering" and "complete nobility." The use of such contradiction or paradox suggests that the sexual act represents the possibility for experiencing such unitive intensity that boundaries between seemingly opposite states break down to merge into a whole in which both are contained and intertwined.

Moreover, Ibn ʿArabī's view that a state of "weakness" has spiritual value reflects a characteristic Sufi insight. For example, a similar concept is reflected in Qushayrī's interpretation of verse 2:228: "But men have a degree above them" in excellence, while women have the "advantage [*māziyya*] of weakness [*ḍaʿf*] and incapacity of mortal nature [*ʿajz al- bashariyya*]."[22] Hence, "weakness" is understood as an advantage since it allows the individual to perceive the reality of his or her dependency on God. Weakness in this context means humility and surrender. Commenting on Qushayrī's *tafsīr*, Sachiko Murata notes that the social experience of weakness may prevent an individual from becoming self-important and absorbed with his or her personal sense of power, which Murata sees as more likely to be a conceit of male social experience that keeps men veiled to the nature of their receptive relationship to God.[23] Women, conversely, experience weakness socially, which may paradoxically provide them with a greater ability to access this primary dimension of the God-human relationship. Thus, what may be considered a socially devalued attribute, when appropriately spiritually aligned, is a portal to human realization and apprehension.

While such a perspective holds some significance for spiritual teachings, it also invites a very dangerous social politics. On the one hand, in a Sufi framework, stripping oneself of socially accrued power and esteem is an essential part of the aspirant's practice. This prioritization of realizing one's dependency on God, the state of being bereft in the absence of God's grace and of spiritual poverty, is reflected in Sufi language, where the aspirant is called the *faqīr*, "the poor one." Such awareness facilitates a state of receptivity to which all Sufis aspire. In this regard, Sufism reflects an inversion of social norms, where the starting point for the Sufi path places greater value on weakness and dependency than on strength and independence. Moreover, in Sufism, the spiritual value of dependency on God might well involve experiences of weakness cultivated through social relationships. This idea presents a particularly stark contrast to the images of manhood cultivated in patriarchies. For Sufis, the realization of weakness is a spiritual strength. Perhaps Qushayrī is pointing more to men in patriarchies, arguing that the trappings of male power render them spiritually disadvantaged.

On the other hand, to embrace Qushayrī's description of the inner spiritual advantage of female weakness while discounting the outer structural inequalities on which it is predicated is also dangerous, potentially allowing for an apologetic legitimization of sociopolitical gender inequality. A subtle but distinctive difference exists between Sufi and patriarchal notions of self. While patriarchal power has only allowed for limited types of female subjectivity, often negating central human possibilities for women's selves, Sufism is premised on a different process. In Sufism, the diminution of the ego is not about the negation of self as much as it is about a process of self-mastery and detachment from the usual forms of social power that can create the ultimate state of receptivity to God. For this process to unfold in a healthy way, social spaces must be fostered that facilitate the formation of authentic female and male selves, and this authenticity must base itself on equality between the sexes and mutual respect, even while differences are valued. These factors have indeed presented all along as the preconditions for Ibn ʿArabī's recommendations for spiritual mastery on the *ṭarīqa*.

Ibn ʿArabī's overall formulations on sexuality also appear to reflect clear heterosexist underpinnings. However, elsewhere in his writings, he conveys a somewhat more ambivalent idea about human sexuality in general: "Love does not absorb the lover entirely unless his beloved is the Real [*al-Ḥaqq*] or someone of his own kind or a slave girl [*jāriyya*] or slave boy [*ghulām*]. Except for what has been mentioned, the love for anything else cannot fully absorb him. We say this because the human being in his complete essence does not conjoin with anything except one that is of his own form. When he loves that person, there is no part of him that doesn't have a [corresponding] likeness in the other. Then there remains nothing left over of him by which he can be sober for a single instant. He is enraptured, his outer form in the other's outer form, and his inner being with the other's inner being."[24]

Unless Ibn ʿArabī is suddenly introducing a female subjectivity when speaking about the slave boy, this extract creates an opening to investigate the implications for alternative sexualities in Ibn ʿArabī's framework. Is this a glimmer of acknowledgment that other types of sexuality might not be readily dismissed as fundamentally deviant and utterly problematic? His assertion that a complete joining is possible only when a lover is based on the "same form" certainly opens for contemporary readers some interesting possibilities that desire and love directed toward same-sex human beings are not in the realm of the unthinkable. Ibn ʿArabī's views on notions of complete correspondence between sexual partners as well as on identity and likeness between lovers are ripe areas of inquiry in terms of alternative sexualities.

Other Eves, Different Creation Myths

Ibn ʿArabī also presents his readers with a creation narrative based on a somewhat different understanding of the process through which Eve, the primordial woman, was created. Particularly salient is the description of Eve directly receiving the spirit of God: "So [God] formed in that rib all of what God formed and created in the body of Adam. And Adam's body was created in the image of God just as a potter creates from clay and firing. And the creation of Eve's body is the creation of a carpenter in what he carves of an image in wood. So when God carved her into the rib and established her form, proportioned her and balanced her [Q. 82:7], God breathed into her of God's spirit. Then she stood up alive, speaking, a female. So that God would make of her a place of sewing and tilling for the bearing of fruit [*inbāt*] which is giving rise to a new generation [*tanassul*]. So Adam rested in her and she rested in him, and she was a garment for him and he was a garment for her."[25] This creation narrative provides us with another dimension of understanding the relationships among God, man, and woman. Here, God forms, balances, and blows spirit into Eve. There is a direct and unmediated relationship between God and the primordial woman; Adam's function here has been to provide some of the material source for the creation of Eve.

In Ibn ʿArabī's view, God's inbreathing of the divine spirit into the human being is the foundational dimension of what constitutes *insān*. As stated by Ibn ʿArabī, "because of [God's] spirit, his creation is in his own image."[26] Collectively, these narratives reiterate that women, like men, are fully *insān*. Ibn ʿArabī adeptly both deploys and transforms the standard patriarchal topoi: Eve still emerges from the rib of man, but God specifically carves, forms, proportions, balances, and inspirits this primordial woman. In this description, there is nothing derivative or ontologically secondary about her creation. She, like Adam, is created as a primary image of God, thus reflecting a complete microcosmic world.

However, Ibn ʿArabī's descriptions of the two different process of material creation are evocative and suggestive. Adam's body is molded in the same way that a potter kneads wet, malleable clay into a particular form, baking it to a state of readiness. Then God breathes his spirit into this first being. Eve's creation follows a different type of fashioning: like a carpenter, God carves into the original rib, whittling and shaving it until the form of Eve emerges. This process evokes Ibn ʿArabī's earlier description of women as the choicest part (*naqāwa*) of the human condition. Emerging from the rib, Eve has in some sense already undergone Adam's material creation. This description suggests that she is the product of an additional process of divine creation, involving a further refinement and distillation of the rib, where excess is removed and spirit is again blown in. This image explains why Ibn ʿArabī describes Eve as the *naqāwa* of the human condition.

Moreover, this narrative also foregrounds the dimension of mutuality between Adam and Eve. They "rested" in one another and were "garments" for each other, pointing to their reciprocal need, intimacy, and complementarity. His reference to the Qurʾānic metaphor of spouses as "garments" to one another evokes a rich symbolism of relationship. Garments are right up against our skin, an apt metaphor for the deep intimacy and closeness that marriage can bring. In addition, in the same way that garments cover what is private and needs protection from the public eye, spouses ought to maintain the sanctity of each other's innermost being. Garments protect our bodies from the withering influence of the elements; so, too, marriage ideally provides protection from the harshness that life sometimes presents. When appropriate, spouses also cover or defend one's vulnerabilities and weaknesses. Garments beautify wearers, suggesting the ways in which spouses might accentuate each other's more beautiful qualities. Ibn ʿArabī's allusion to Adam and Eve as resting in each other and being garments for one another thus conjures associations of an intimate relationship between the primordial couple that is animated by qualities of mutual protection, nurture, sanctification and beautification—virtues that inspire all of us in our intimate relationships.

If so much of the God-human relationship unfolds through the origin of the male-female form and subsequent relationships and then heightens in sexual union and might culminate in procreation, do marriage, sexuality, and procreation constitute the prescribed model for all human beings? Are there no choices and opportunities for realization outside such a "model?" Some of the real relationships in which Ibn ʿArabī and other Sufis were involved offer answers. Ibn ʿArabī's relationship with Niẓām shows the reader a different or alternative relationship: they were neither married to nor sexually intimate with each other, yet the relationship between them was profound and spiritually transforming for Ibn ʿArabī. Niẓām also independently embodies a different model: from all accounts, she remained single and was clearly a highly spiritually attained individual, as were Rābiʿa and other celibate Sufi women and men.

Ibn ʿArabī's reflections on sex, marriage, and procreation thus provide one significant model of attainment, particularly in many contexts where marriages between men and women were and continue to be widely shared human experiences. Hence, his promptings toward engaging marriage and sexuality as the living canvas of spiritual refinement and experience is no doubt profound and meaningful to many people, married or not. His ideas urge those involved in heterosexual marriages to strive for deeper and more nourishing relationships. However, his teachings in this regard are clearly not prescriptive and in no way limit any level of spiritual attainment to marriage and heterosexual sexuality.

Ibn ʿArabī's images here significantly differ from the images of a hierarchical triplicity discussed in chapter 5. While Adam's physical creation process and material source may have differed from Eve's, each, having been inspirited by the same source, equally embodies a capacity for spiritual realization, a point that Ibn ʿArabī reiterates even more explicitly: "That woman's degree is below man has nothing to do with attainment of completion—the 'degree' in question is simply that of coming into being since she was created from him. Now, the relationship of Adam to that from which he was created—namely, the earth—is the same as that of Eve with respect to Adam. Yet this relationship [of Adam] to the earth does not in any way deny the completion which is affirmed about him."[27]

This analogy between Adam's creation from earth and Eve's creation from Adam's rib is significant. It presents their respective creation stories as reflecting different material processes, with possibly some ontological significance, while retaining the common ontological end of complete spiritual attainment. In Ibn ʿArabī's cosmology, human beings' capacity to manifest all the divine names is the reason that they are considered the ultimate microcosm, the epitome of creation. Thus, at one very significant ontological register, inasmuch as Adam symbolizes the human microcosm, he is greater than all other created realities, including the earth. And just in case the reader had mistakenly thought that Adam represented the ontological capacities of the male and not the gender-inclusive human, Ibn ʿArabī reminds us that Eve's material creation from Adam's rib does not detract from the same ontological capacities.

Thus, Ibn ʿArabī spins the "Eve from rib" myth into multiple gender narratives. For this Sufi teacher, this myth accounts for the popular Qurʾānic "degree" that men have above women and for the prophetic *ḥadīth* referring to women as deficient in religion and intellect. Ibn ʿArabī morphs these traditionally negative associations of the female as rib into narratives of Eve's rib nature as comprising a complete mirror to Adam. Here, Ibn ʿArabī explicitly reinforces a shared identity between the two: "God formed within that rib everything that he had formed and created in the body of Adam."[28] For Ibn ʿArabī, a "rib nature" symbolizes bending, inclination, and love, characteristics shared by women and men in their relationships toward one another. Concurrently, his depiction of Eve as constituting the choicest part of humanity signifies a degree of female refinement over males.[29] Hence, the varying ways in which traditional understandings of Eve as rib constitute a site for Ibn ʿArabī's saying and unsaying of gender norms. While his discussions often reflect an androcentric male subjectivity, his shifting narratives of human creation present a fundamental disruption of misogynist views of Eve and women as fundamentally weak and lacking, views prevalent among many of his peers.

Different Gender Paradigms of Origin: Jesus and Mary

In addition to subverting and transforming the gender significance of the Eve/Adam myth with his multiple versions of the story, Ibn ʿArabī presents the reader with completely different creation models, including Jesus' birth from the Virgin Mary, that further undermine dominant gender norms. In fact, in his writings, the Adam and Eve story is actually part of a larger concatenation of creation narratives. In this regard, he interweaves four different creation stories: first, Adam created from the earth; second, Eve created from Adam; third, Jesus created from Mary; and fourth, the rest of humankind created from both men and women. He writes,

> [With regard to] the origin of human bodies [*jusūm*], . . . they are of four kinds: the body of Adam, the body of Eve, the body of Jesus, and bodies of [all other] human beings [*banī ādam*]. Each body from among

these four kinds has an origin that is different from the origin of the others in causality [*sababiyya*] despite their commonality in bodily and spiritual forms [*ṣūra jismāniyya* and *rūḥāniyya*]. Indeed, I expound this and emphasize it so that one who is weak in intellect should not imagine that divine power [*qudra ilāhiyya*] or that spiritual realities [*ḥaqāʾiq*] are limited to providing human origin by only one [mode of] causality in bringing this origin from the divine essence. God dispels this doubt by revealing the human origin in Adam by a means which the body of Eve did not appear and revealed the body of Eve in a manner that the body of other human beings did not appear, and revealed the body of other human beings in a manner that the body of Jesus did not appear. Yet the name human [*insān*] is applied to each one of them in its definition and its spiritual reality. Indeed, God does that so that one might know that God knows all things and is capable of all things.

Indeed, God included all four types of creation in one verse of the Qurʾān, *Sūrat al-Ḥujarāt* [Q. 49:13]. God said, "We created you all," indicating Adam; "from a male" indicating Eve; "and from a female" indicating Jesus; and from the joining of male and female, indicating the rest of humanity, by means of intercourse [*nikāḥ*] and procreation. This verse is from the most comprehensive discourse and the most decisive speech that was given to Muḥammad.[30]

Drawing on a powerful Qurʾānic verse, Ibn ʿArabī presents the reader with alternative accounts to understand the nature of human creation and gender. Despite the different modes of origin, the final product of each of the four creation processes is the human being, who shares equally in the complete array of physical and spiritual realities constituting *al-Insān.*[31]

In particular, he directs his audience to the varying gender constructs underlying the different creation sequences—the creation of Jesus from a female (Mary) without a male proposes a gendered counterpoint to the creation of Eve from a male (Adam) without a female. So in a parallel way, Eve was created from a man, without a mother, while Jesus was created from a woman, without a father. However, Ibn ʿArabī summarily informs the reader that both these stories are exceptional, since the rest of humanity are a result of the joining of male and female. Particularly interesting is Ibn ʿArabī's comment on why he is invoking these different Qurʾānic creation models—that is, to avert "the weak-minded" from creating idolatrous mythologies that exclusively associate God's creativity with a particular mode of gender relationships. This rationale is particularly effective in demanding that the audience does not attach itself to the Adam/Eve creation as the definitive and exclusive way of imagining divine creativity. By holding up these alternative narrative mirrors, Ibn ʿArabī whirls readers in new directions, demanding intellectual suppleness, creative malleability, and spiritual receptivity.

Ibn ʿArabī expands and elaborates on these different models of creation, particularly on the Jesus/Mary dyad as an alternative ontological model of relationship between men and women. He presents multiple readings of the story of Jesus' creation from Mary without the intermediary of a man, readings that present ambivalent and contradictory valences of gender, again depriving his audience the comfort of certainty.

In one passage on Jesus and Mary, Ibn ʿArabī reiterates the traditional position that men are the sole active agents in the creative process: "Since God said 'Men have a priority [*daraja*] over them,' he did not make Jesus receptive to the activity from Mary lest the man would receive activity from the women in the same way that Eve [received the activity] from Adam. So Gabriel or the angel 'appeared to her in the likeness of a well formed man' [Q. 19:17]. And he said to her, 'I am a messenger of your Lord to give to you a boy most pure' [Q. 19:19]. And he gave Jesus to her. Thus Jesus received the activity from the angel that appeared in the likeness of a man's form. And he emerged on the form of his father—a male, a human, a spirit."[32]

Commenting again on the verse 2:228, Ibn ʿArabī weaves the Jesus/Mary story into his more standard readings of the Adam/Eve story that highlight man's activity and woman's receptivity in the process of origin. Noteworthy in this invocation of the Qurʾānic verse on Jesus' conception is that the angel Gabriel, despite appearing in the likeness of a male form, is in reality not a man but a spirit. Nonetheless, this formulation reflects a more traditional gender viewpoint that appears to cast men and women in exclusive and distinctive modes of activity and receptivity.

Ibn ʿArabī also revisits the narrative with a novel interpretation of the Mary/Jesus relationship that provides an explicit contrast to the traditional Adam/Eve model. He states that the degree of difference between men and women cannot be accounted for by the creation of Eve from Adam's rib, since this incident reflects only the particular case of these two individuals and it is countered by the conception of Jesus in Mary without the intermediary of a man. In the *Futūḥāt*, Ibn ʿArabī argues, "Some people claim that the degree is the fact that Eve came into existence from Adam so she became manifest only through him. Hence, he has the degree of being secondary cause, and she can never reach him in that. But this is the situation in a particular entity [Eve], and we could counter it with [another particular entity,] Mary in relation to the existence of Jesus. Hence the degree is not that he is the secondary cause of her becoming manifest. The fact is that the woman is the locus that receives activity, while the man is not like that. The locus that receives activity does not possess the level of activity, so it falls short. But in spite of falling short there is dependence upon it and inclination toward it."[33]

Here, Ibn ʿArabī makes the subtle but important point that the degree between men and women is related to modes of activity and receptivity rather than to the mythic notion that Eve was created from Adam. However, Ibn ʿArabī subsequently reverses these gendered notions of activity and receptivity and whirls the reader into yet other articulations of gender. He writes, "God brought Jesus into existence from Mary. Hence Mary settled into the station of Adam, while Jesus settled in the station of Eve. For just as a female came into existence from a male, so a male came into existence from a female. Hence God finished with the likes of which he began, by bringing into existence a son without a father, just as Eve came to be without a mother. Hence, Jesus and Eve are two siblings, while Adam and Mary are their two parents."[34]

Ibn ʿArabī further elaborates that "Jesus' reception of activity from Mary became manifest opposite Eve's reception from Adam. 'Surely in that is a reminder for one who has a heart.' Thereby such a person can understand God's words: 'O People! we have created you from a male,' as in the case of Eve, 'and a female,' as in the case of Jesus, and from both together, as in the case of the rest of the offspring, the children of Adam. This encompasses the creation of all people."[35]

Ibn ʿArabī thus specifically states that Jesus receives the activity of Mary—that is, a male receives the activity of a female in a particular creation myth. These new perspectives confound the traditional gender dimensions that he previously attributed to modes of activity and receptivity in relation to human origin. By increasing the spectrum of possibilities for understanding gender relations, his differing arguments lend enormous fluidity and breadth to his gender framework. Ibn ʿArabī's four models for human creation provide readers with different conceptualizations of gender relations. These distinct creation models are theophanic, reflecting the varying modes of being in the greater reality. That Jesus receives the activity of Mary and is engendered from her destabilizes and undermines the construct that in creation, men exclusively are the active principle in relation to woman and that women are never the active principle in relation to men.

Ibn ʿArabī intentionally and explicitly presents the Mary/Jesus model as a counternarrative to his Adam/Eve model. By reversing the dominant gender narrative, Ibn ʿArabī effectively breaks mythological ideas of gender embedded in traditional discourses on Eve's creation from the rib and the related derogatory understandings of female deficiency.

However, he casts the creative process in the Adam/Eve and Mary/Jesus models as particular and exceptional cases, stating that the rest of humanity was created from men and women together. This strategy suggests that the way in which activity and reception of activity are gendered for the rest of humanity does not reproduce either of these two exceptional models of engenderment. Rather, the rest of humanity is created from men and women, both of whom are active and are recipients of activity, with no gender-specific modalities identified.

Ibn ʿArabī deconstructs the gender of active and passive modalities and the notion of these modalities as distinct. The traditional boundaries between these different modes are then perforated: "Humanity [*insāniyya*] is a category that encompasses the male and the female. How can one category include the reality of the active one [*fāʾil*] and the receptive one [*munfaʿil*] who receives the influence of the active one. The active one does not act except in one corresponding to its own constitution [*fī mushākili hi*]. This is because he is the first within whom receiving activity happens. Subsequently, a form manifests in him that can exert influence on another. By that strength, that which receives activity receives activity. This is like the divine names Originator, Creator, and the Real."[36]

Hence, each modality of being is embedded within the other. Being receptive implies containing the seeds of activity; Eve was already actively present within Adam in his original state; Adam's constitution was seamlessly configured by the existence of Eve, and vice versa. This idea reiterates the earlier position that the original Adam was both male and female and that the subsequent gender-specific differentiation made both Adam and Eve into parts of the original whole. Despite this separation, each contained both the modalities of the whole within them—that is, each retained activity and receptivity corresponding to their source, the original Adam.

This view also mirrors the reality of the Godhead, in which the "Immutable Entities" as receptive realities within God acted on God, and, therefore, God as Originator actively realizes their possibilities. All of these are configured within the oneness of God's being. Hence, Ibn ʿArabī collapses some of the traditional distinctions between active and passive that he has elsewhere set up as the benchmark of gender differentiation. The relationship between activity and receptivity is then porous, interconnected, and interconstitutive. In the final analysis, these are not independent modes of being. Most important, activity and receptivity are not gendered in exclusive and discrete ways.

Ibn ʿArabī's alternative creation narratives—that is, the Mary/Jesus stories as well as the *al-Dhāt*/humanity dyad—relativize the earlier creation model of Eve created from Adam's rib. At the ontological level, the priority accorded to Adam (and thus men) is counterposed by the priority given to Mary (and thus women) as well as to preeminence of the divine feminine, *al-dhāt*, over Adam and all creation. Each of these multiple creation narratives refine and edify, contaminate, and complicate gender discourses contained in the others; by also presenting paradoxes, contradictions, and ironies, they deconstruct some of the traditional gender constructs in the established religious imagination. They further constitute Ibn ʿArabī's method of "unsaying" the metaphysical correlates of traditional gender norms.

So, why then, have the rib narrative and the "degree" that men have above women been so pervasive in Ibn ʿArabī's work? At the most basic level, these phenomena reflect his faithfulness to the Qurʾānic text, his commitment to the inherited canon of *ḥadīth*, and his immersion within a contextually defined symbolic world. At another level, however, his particular interpretations of this narrative limit and circumscribe some of its more patriarchal implications. Given that he introduces alternative creation models and comments on the nongeneralizablity of the two exceptional models, the primary significance of the rib narrative in his teachings is not simply the "degree" of difference between men and women. The notion of fundamental difference between men and women had already been given in his context. By providing variant readings of this creation story, he reinvents the gender constructs implicit in the traditional rib narrative. This approach reflects the innovative aspects of his gender philosophy, especially when in his teachings the rib comes to signify the shared humanity of men and women. In his exegeses, unlike those of many of his predecessors, the "degree" morphs into positions that illustrate ontological identity and love, a shared human nature, and a complementary relationship between men and women.

Ibn ʿArabī's view that men and women are both different and similar is a not a binary opposition but rather a both/and relationship. For Ibn ʿArabī, ontology and the related natures of men and women are connected to a mythic creation narrative of Adam and Eve; consequently, the introduction of these alternative creation models provides critical openings for conceptualizing different ontological possibilities for gender and the related constructions of men and women. In reading these multiple stories together, it is clear that his approach constantly finds nuances in boundaries and gender categorizations while maintaining a shared humanity for men and women.

Ibn ʿArabī's Gender Mappings

Given the complexity of Ibn ʿArabī's varying and sometimes seemingly contrary formulations of gender, I conclude with a brief mapping of the three discursive modes of gender that characterize his approach. This simplified representation will enable a more nuanced view of the relationships between the different representations of gender in his writings.

1. Men's superiority: This gender construction is reflected in some of Ibn ʿArabī's discussions of the three source texts—that is, (1) the *ḥadīth* on Eve being created from Adam's rib, (2) the Qurʾānic verse about men's "degree" over women (Q. 2:228), and (3) the *ḥadīth* on female deficiency in religion and intellect. Readers may see glimpses of this perspective in Ibn ʿArabī's discussions of the exclusively male station of envoy and prophetic missionary vis-à-vis women's access to prophecy alone and in particular narratives where he employs parallels between the God-human relationship and the male-female relationship.
2. Universal *insāniyya*: The second set of gender narratives is reflected in Ibn ʿArabī's assertions on the shared humanity (*insāniyya*) of men and women; depictions of Eve that foreground her constitutional similarity to Adam; statements about the inessential and peripheral designation of maleness and femaleness to the human condition; assertions of men and women's equal access to complete spiritual realization; the comment that God formed in Eve all that was formed in Adam; a reference to Jesus' creation from Mary as a gendered counterpoint to Eve's creation from Adam; and finally

the surprising and rather helpful assertion that the creation model represented in Adam and Eve is unique and exceptional, since the rest of humanity follows a different model of creation that relies equally on men and women.

3. Female superiority: Here, one encounters Ibn ʿArabī's notions of women as constituting the epitome of human creation; a narrative on women as embodying the divine attribute of strength in ways more powerful than men; an analogy between the essence of God as a receptive feminine matrix and women's receptive capacities; associations between the womb and God as the all-merciful; and the assertion that God is witnessed most completely in women.

By positing these three distinctive readings with regard to gender, Ibn ʿArabī presents a universal way of understanding human nature while presenting clear notions of gender difference. The challenge of reading his shifting tales of gender involves evading reification: readers who try to fix him into any one aspect of his articulation will miss entirely the meaning presented by the variety of his formulations, which skillfully assert a notion of ungendered human universality (*insāniyya*) while embracing both the male and the female in distinctive ways. Even as he speaks the language of the dominant gender imagination, at times in ways that are explicitly hierarchical, he simultaneously fragments, subverts, and reconstitutes these articulations in ways that open up fresh and creative vistas for conceptualizing human nature and possibilities. All three gender motifs interweave through Ibn ʿArabī's varying albeit interconnected writings on gender.

Chapter Seven

Ibn ʿArabī and Islamic Feminism

In this final chapter, I outline how my approach to gender in Ibn ʿArabī's work differs from other contemporary interpretations of his work. In the process, I highlight and reiterate how his central teachings offer unique ways to engage the process and goals of Islamic feminism. I conclude with some reflections on how Sufism in general and Ibn ʿArabī's teachings in particular shift the foundations of the debates in relation to both Islamic and secular feminism, offering enriching ways to engage questions of gender.

Engaging Traditionalist Interpretations

Given the nuanced and often subtle manner in which Ibn ʿArabī's approach both incorporates and transforms traditional gender constructs, his work is open to multiple readings. My interpretation of him differs significantly from some of the standard ways in which contemporary scholars have engaged with him. I believe my approach provides unique ways to grapple with and overcome some of the substantial limitations of the prevalent traditionalist interpretations of his work, which effectively reinforce patriarchy. Two prominent contemporary scholars of Ibn ʿArabī who exemplify this approach are Seyyed Hossein Nasr,[1] and Sachiko Murata,[2] a former student of Nasr. Their approaches are selective, highlighting one dimension of his work while marginalizing other aspects of his writings. These interpretations and invocations reflect a partial and incomplete perspective on Ibn ʿArabī's work and do not adequately engage his varying positions. Moreover, their approaches present gender constructs as articulated by Ibn ʿArabī and other specific premodern Sufis as signifying an ontological reality outside of historical and sociological mediation. Scholars such as Nasr and to a more limited extent Murata ultimately are committed to reading gender essences into the Sufi writings. Consequently, they often reify such gender constructs instead of allowing them the fluidity and deconstructive potential inherent particularly in Ibn ʿArabī's writings. In varying ways, both Nasr's and Murata's approaches universalize particular elements in Ibn ʿArabī's work as part of building a broader traditionalist gender paradigm, but these elements reflect his own contextual constraints and language culture. In contrast, my reading addresses some of these aporias in the traditionalist approach and therefore opens up possibilities for rethinking gender relationships in ways that remain grounded in the soil of Islamic spirituality.

Nasr and Traditional Gender Complementarity

Seyyed Hossein Nasr, a prominent academic scholar of Sufism and a recognized *shaykh* of the contemporary Maryamiyya Sufi order in the United States, draws on, among other works, the writings of Ibn ʿArabī. While Nasr maintains the idea of a shared humanity between men and women, he argues for fundamental ontological differences between them. His work features a pervasive notion that men and women microcosmically embody and reflect different divine qualities that are complementary. As such, men and women are to have harmonious but distinct social functions. Nasr then translates these gendered constructs into practical and social realms: "God is both Absolute and Infinite. Absoluteness—and Majesty, which is inseparable from it—are manifested most directly in the masculine state; Infinity and Beauty in the feminine state. The male body itself reflects majesty, power, absoluteness; the female body reflects beauty, beatitude and infinity."[3]

Whereas Ibn ʿArabī's references to "masculine" and "feminine" states relate to active and receptive modes, respectively, and are not restricted to biological gender, Nasr directly links these states to men and women. So, according to Nasr, majesty and other *jalālī* qualities are not only related to a "masculine" state—that is, a spiritual state of activity in Ibn ʿArabī's terms—but are also reflected in the nature of a man's body and being. Similarly, beauty and other *jamālī* qualities are not simply related to a "feminine" state—that is, a state of receptivity—but are reflected in the body and being of a woman. In such a gendered landscape, one finds a narrow and traditional construct of complementarity in which qualities of majesty are associated with men and qualities of beauty with women.

Despite referring to the attainments of some eminent women in Islamic history, Nasr pursues a hierarchical construct of gender complementarity into the personal-political realms. He thus asserts the ontological normativity of male power and its corollary, female obedience: "This [gender] complementarity was rooted in equity rather than equality and . . . on the human levels it recognized the role of the male as the immutable pole around which the family was constructed and in whose hand responsibility for the welfare of the woman and child, as well as protection of God's law and social order were placed. . . . [Man] has been entrusted with this task as the *imām* of God and His vicegerent whose soul is surrendered to Him. . . . The revolt of the female sex against the male did not precede but followed in the wake of the revolt of the male sex against Heaven."[4]

For Nasr, therefore, ontological gender differences translate into men's social power, authority, and religious and social agency and the defense of women, who are under the authority of the male head of family. He sees the "revolt" of women to men's authority in terms of the latter's misuse of their power. For Nasr, essential ontological differences between men and women exist at the level of embodying the divine names. These differences, in turn, demand a patriarchal social structure and particular modes of gender power relations at the level of interpersonal and societal relationships. Effectively, women's religious vicegerency is restricted to an ineffable inwardness that demands a dutiful subservience to men's supremacy in the external realms of family, society, and politics. Moral agency and human vicegerency translate into fundamentally different social realms for men and women.

Nasr effectively dichotomizes God's *jamālī* and *jalālī* qualities in gender-specific and exclusive ways. While Nasr notes in passing that men and women "contain something of both the male and female principles within themselves," he reverts to the superordinate principle that "in men, the male principle, and in women, the female principle, is dominant."[5] He superimposes a simplistic notion of patriarchal complementarity onto a Sufi conception of human nature that is complex and nuanced. The result is a reductionist vision of gender that cannot account for some substantive Sufi concepts as articulated in Ibn ʿArabī's teachings. Nasr's argument about gender-specific manifestations of the divine names lacks the richness and sophistication of Ibn ʿArabī's views on the nature of *al-Insān al-Kāmil*, which Ibn ʿArabī presents as a universal ideal that makes the same demands of men and women as well as resulting in a harmonious integration of both *jamālī* and *jalālī* qualities for men and women alike.

Ibn ʿArabī and the Integration of Gender: A Rejoinder to Nasr

Since Ibn ʿArabī states that men and women alike share in all levels and stations of spiritual attainment,[6] the theophanic realities of a particular station are by definition ungendered. This position is also practically illustrated in his biographical reflections with descriptions of various women spiritual aspirants who clearly embody both *jamālī* and *jalālī* attributes (see chapter 3). Thus Nasr's gendered bifurcation of *jalāl* and *jamāl* presents a view that runs contrary to Ibn ʿArabī's explicitly gender-inclusive depictions of spiritual stations and his descriptions of Sufi adepts as well as to his universal conception of the human archetype, *al-Insān al-Kāmil*.

Furthermore, Nasr's simple gendering of *jamāli* and *jalālī* dimensions in human beings also fails to attend to the ways in which a thinker such as Ibn ʿArabī sets up a fundamental hierarchy between the divine names and their interrelationships within the human being. As discussed in chapter 2, Ibn ʿArabī prioritizes *jamālī* attributes for all human beings and is wary of the possible misuse of *jalālī* qualities. In this framework, the *jalālī* names belong primarily to the realm of incomparability for the seeker, while the *jamālī* names belong to the realm of similarity. To progress toward intimacy with God, the seeker responds with absolute receptivity to God's *jalālī* qualities. Ibn ʿArabī cautions that stepping over the limits of a designated name can result in banishment from the realm of closeness to God; this danger is most salient in the case of *jalālī* names. If one were to react to God's commands with an assertion of individual and ego-centered *jalāl*, alienation results, as exemplified in Iblīs's refusal to submit to God's command to prostrate before Adam on the basis that he was better than the human. Unrefined *jalāl* is not receptive to the divine and is thus excluded from the realm of divine intimacy. Similarly, Ibn ʿArabī states that one who assumes superiority over others because of his or her powerful social position or possession of a certain noble quality fails to heed the reality of his or her servanthood and might thus easily descend into ignorance and "repugnant negligence."[7] Hence, for an individual to assign superiority to him- or herself and assume power over others is a potentially hazardous affair in spiritual terms.

Ibn ʿArabī's insights in this area also provide the basis for a far-reaching critique of the patriarchal claims that de facto associate majesty and power with men as the rightful order of reality. Instead, according to Ibn ʿArabī, superiority claimed on the basis of biology or social location constitutes spiritual negligence and heedlessness, the fruits of which are spiritual destruction. Within this very finely tuned spiritual psychology, the claims of the *nafs al-ammāra* to superiority over others are never to be indulged—on the path of purification, there is no space for false deities, male or otherwise. In Ibn ʿArabī's framework, one clearly needs to be very wary and cautious in relation to *jalālī* qualities, since misalignment with them is perilous to seekers.

Whether or not a concentration of *jalālī* qualities exists among some men as a consequence of either social power or innate capacities is ultimately insignificant. On the spiritual path, the real issue is the process of refinement and purification, so that the heart can increasingly become a polished mirror able to reflect a perfectly balanced combination of the divine qualities. Contemporary Sufi and scholar Rabia Terri Harris incisively makes this point: "Perhaps the raw materials for *jalālī* attributes are more naturally concentrated in males than in females, in the 'powerful' than in the 'powerless.' If so, it does not matter. Raw material is not the point. When we consider spiritual stature—which means attunement to the divine order—the natural starting point is irrelevant. One half ounce of pure gold is worth a small mountain of unrefined ore. The possession of extra resources, of any kind, is not a sign of divine favor. The real question is, 'How will they be used?' It is refinement versus un-refinement and not male versus female—or any other dichotomy that counts."[8]

On the Sufi path, therefore, the crux of the matter relates to the purification of the heart, which occurs in large part through refusing to submit to the inclinations of the *nafs al-ammāra*, with all its attachment to power and prestige—that is, the raw *jalālī* qualities. The seeker, enamored and assuming a state of servanthood, proceeds on the path. The qualities of mercy, love, and compassion, together with the work of self-purification, are demanded of the seeker. These are grounding and receptive realities that facilitate one's spiritual growth, which ultimately allows one entry into the realm of intimacy with the Beloved. *Jamālī* qualities are not only epistemologically prioritized along the path but also ontologically prioritized in God's statement, "My mercy precedes my wrath."

The process of spiritual actualization in Ibn ʿArabī's framework thus demands that the seeker observes the correct boundaries and relations to the divine names, recognizing servanthood as the highest human state as well as foregrounding the *jamālī* over the *jalālī* qualities. Embodying the attributes of similarity—qualities of mercy, compassion, and love—provides the basis for the alchemical transformation of the self into the divine form of *al-Insān al-Kāmil*. I am not discounting Allah's *jalāl*. Instead, one purifies and calibrates the more instinctive *jalālī* tendencies, which are otherwise vulnerable to the machinations of the *nafs al-ammāra*, within the safety and balance of God's *jamālī* attributes. This process facilitates human receptivity to God while respecting the boundaries demanded by God's incomparability. In the journey of balancing the embodiment between *jamāl* and *jalāl*, the priority of God's mercy is crucial.

In chapter 2, I have noted the significance and potential implications of Ibn ʿArabī's approach, which involves a harmonious balance of divine attributes premised on the foregrounding of *jamālī* attributes, for contemporary societies. This approach offers a profound critique of some of the ways in which human societies and global politics are often premised on interactions characterized by the unrefined qualities of aggression, domination, and violence. Ibn ʿArabī suggests a very different modus operandi, encouraging an ethics of mercy and care. This framework facilitates integrity between the refinement of the individual and the cultivation of social virtue while providing rich resources for a critique of patriarchal values.

By simplistically highlighting *jamāl* as female and *jalāl* as male, Nasr misses a crucial part of this Sufi understanding of the nature, construction, and interrelationships between the divine names for the spiritual aspirant. The notion that *jalālī* qualities can be exhibited without being fundamentally grounded in and related to the *jamālī* dimension ignores a central principle in the process of human transformation, a process reflected incisively by Ibn ʿArabī's cosmology. Ibn ʿArabī's foundational position holds that human comprehensiveness is uniquely defined by integrating and manifesting all the divine names, thereby reflecting God's image most fully among creation. Hence, if men were only *jalāl* and women only *jamāl*, they would lack the criterion of *kamāl*, the distinctive human capacity for refined comprehensiveness. Nasr's approach to gender dichotomizes and desiccates the very rich and holistic nature of human spirituality in the Sufi paradigm superbly articulated by Ibn ʿArabī and thereby denies both men and women the completeness inherent in this paradigm.

Moreover, Nasr's inference that as repositories of *jalāl*, men rightfully take on the roles of authority over women at both the family and the social level has profound ideological and political implications. This position clearly reinforces gender power imbalances in the family and society, resulting in the structural marginalization of women as well as presenting a rather limited view of women's agency on numerous levels. His articulation of gender complementarity where Muslim men are entrusted solely with the "responsibility for the protection of God's law and the social order" effectively constructs women as political and social minors. This type of mind-set can and has resulted in political structures that are fundamentally prejudicial and unjust to women. One trajectory of this type of gender ideology played itself out in the aftermath of the 1979 Iranian Revolution, a context that was equally inhospitable to Nasr. In that instance, male clerics as emissaries and protectors of God's law progressively disempowered women through the imposition of a draconian legal system that deprived women of their social and spiritual agency in numerous ways.[9]

Murata: Ideology, Language, and Society

The other traditionalist thinker, Sachiko Murata, presents a far more complex and nuanced view of Sufi gender constructs. In her pioneering and thorough account of gender in premodern Islamic thought, *The Tao of Islam*, Murata exquisitely illustrates a variety of complex gender mappings characterizing what she describes as the "sapiential" traditions of Islam—that is, Sufism and to a more limited extent philosophy. Like many other scholars of gender and Sufism, I am profoundly indebted to Murata for this landmark contribution on the subject. Her work has strongly influenced some of my formative ideas on Sufism and gender. My critical approach to her work comes as a genuine and deep engagement with some of the extremely thoughtful, sophisticated, and provocative ideas she has presented. While much of her work offers a very nuanced and dynamic view of cosmological gender, I am focusing here mainly on particular aspects of her work that I find problematic and that reinforce more essentialized gender conceptions.[10]

In much of her interpretation, Murata argues that gendered differences are foundational in Ibn ʿArabī's works while maintaining that biological men and women are not always correlated with the categories of male/masculine and female/feminine as well as their relevant discourses. Throughout her work, however, she embraces patriarchal stereotypes implicit in traditional constructs of "masculine" and "feminine" and the related ideologically embedded nature of language as mediator. Even more problematic is her argument, based on readings of Sufi texts, for women's complete spiritual equality with men while embracing gender hierarchy at the social level.

Murata seeks to illustrate that traditional Islamic gender discourses were motivated not by their authors' will to power but rather by a solid understanding of Islamic metaphysics and the nature of reality.[11] While she often reflects the dynamic ways in which gender is understood in Sufi cosmology, her reading of gender as it relates to the social realm of human gendered relationships is relatively static. She marginalizes and at times even silences the fluid and iconoclastic ways that Ibn ʿArabī deals with human gendered relationships. She appears to be committed to reinstating and defending the traditional parameters of understanding gender. In this regard, she writes, "On the social level Islam affirms the primacy of God as King, Majestic, Lord, Ruler. It establishes a theological patriarchy. . . . On the spiritual level the picture is different. In this domain many Muslim authorities affirm the primacy of God as Merciful, Beautiful, Gentle, Loving. Here they establish a spiritual matriarchy."[12] Murata later concludes, "My 'feminist agenda' is to help those Muslims who are so inclined to re-establish the vision of the divine feminine, which is the essence of God. The sapiental perspective allows people to see feminine qualities at the peak of reality. The Real in Itself is receptive to every entification. It gives birth to the bipolar God who is both merciful and wrathful, yin and yang, mother and father. The mercy of this bipolar God preceded Her Wrath, which is to say that Her femininity is more real and fundamental than Her masculinity."[13]

Despite this important and accurate valorization of the feminine principles of reality, Murata's articulation of the gendered nature of the divine reflects an uncritical acceptance of the nature of these categorizations. In particular, she conflates aspects of Ibn ʿArabī's contextually situated vocabulary with the substantive content of his insights while neglecting the critical manner in which he simultaneously unsays traditional gender positions. Hence, she reinscribes and naturalizes traditional categories of "masculine" and "feminine" without either acknowledging the contingent nature of such contextual language or sufficiently interrogating some of the implications of these dichotomous formulations. For example, it is unproblematic to accept that a balance exists between the active principles and receptive principles in the universe. However, the problem arises when a reader in the contemporary period uncritically accepts the general association of activity with the male principle and receptivity with the female principle. In those cases where Ibn ʿArabī appears to have used a more binary gendered formulation of these active and receptive principles, he might well merely have been reflecting the normative understandings of gender characterizing his premodern context; for us in the present, however, it becomes imperative to explore these binary conceptualizations more critically and fully in light of their contemporary implications.

Within Ibn ʿArabī's thought it is imperative to hold the tensions consistently within his writings—that is, simultaneously to engage his traditional gender symbols vis-à-vis his counternarratives of gender. Instead of merely accepting the normative symbolic system, it must be interrogated ideologically. Contemporary readers must ask why, if male and female principles or qualities are not to be confused with men and women (as Murata illustrates), we should continue the use of such gendered terminology. When we call the active principle a "masculine principle" and the female principle a "receptive principle," these gendered understandings of reality are not socially innocuous. They reinforce a social imagination in which the associations of passivity with women and activity with men imply power differentials that perpetuate clear patterns of discrimination.

Instead of justifying such gendered language as reflective of the nature of Islamic metaphysics, Ibn ʿArabī's usage of this type of language must be explored in all its complexity and divergence. Only then is it possible to create a map of the realities to which his gendered symbolic alludes metaphorically and to speak about these realities outside of his contextually bound gendered language. Moreover, it is imperative critically and systematically to analyze the ideological and social implications of using gendered language to describe the nature of reality.

This process involves the application of bipolar divine attributes to the human level. Within Islam, the categorization of God's qualities into categories of majesty (*jalāl*), with attendant associations of wrath, thereby inspiring awe in humanity, and categories of beauty (*jamāl*), with attendant associations of mercy, thereby inspiring love in humanity, is deeply rooted within the tradition and gives rise to a rich and complex metaphysical schema. However, the problem arises when one uncritically labels all the related qualities of the one face of God (the merciful) with a feminine principle and all the related qualities of the other face of God (the majestic) with a masculine principle. To say that the qualities of mercy are feminine and those of majesty are masculine does a disservice to all humanity.

Uncritical employment of traditional gender categories to label visions of ultimate reality has repercussions in the social world. It reinforces the essentialist view that the feminine (women) are gentle, merciful human beings who inspire love and that the masculine (men) are powerful and wrathful human beings who inspire awe. Simplistically, the implication is that women are to be loved and men are to be feared. Not only do such notions suggest fundamentally different spiritual and emotional capacities among men and women, making relationships of mutuality quite difficult, they also facilitate hierarchical power relationships between them.

Such constructs particularly limit the possibilities for either men or women to fully existentiate the full array of divine attributes and are thus ontologically reductionist. If one were to argue that one gender of the human species is predominantly associated with a specific divine mode and the other with its polar mode, then one could say that any gendered human being reflects only part of divinity. However, this implication runs contrary to Ibn ʿArabī's view of the microcosmic totality represented by *al-Insān al-Kāmil.*

By accepting fundamental metaphysical distinctions between masculine and feminine principles without critically engaging their social relevance, Murata facilitates a continued projection of patriarchal constructs onto the level of ontology. Despite the feminist importance of asserting the centrality of the qualities reflected in the "divine feminine," Murata does not develop a full-blown critique of some of the central ways that patriarchy has destroyed precisely such values at the social level. In addition, she methodologically retains the same essentialist formulation as patriarchy but inverts the evaluation of the feminine instead of seriously examining the foundational suppositions and implications of such categories. Even when she does point out that full spiritual possibilities are open to both men and women in Sufism, her discourse appears to remain at the level of some type of asocial spiritual practice. She explicitly does not extend these openings to critically engage issues of genderedness and social spaces in Islam.

On the contrary, Murata states that in the Islamic view, God establishes distinct and strictly defined social roles.[14] According to her, the social teachings of Islam are characterized by relationships of separateness and essential differences, while the spiritual teachings are characterized by relationships of mutuality and interconnectedness. Murata argues that the sapiential tradition accepts the first approach as the valid and even necessary starting point for the second.[15] She states, "The patriarchal view of God is normal for the *Sharīʿa* that pertains to all Muslims but the matriarchal view pertains to the spiritual path, the *Ṭarīqa*, so not everyone can appreciate it."[16] Elsewhere, Murata argues, "Islamic spirituality . . . places divine mercy and compassion, the divine *yin* at the pinnacle of value. Again this primacy of *yin* cannot function on the social level since it undermines the authority of the law. . . . In the Islamic perspective, the revealed law prevents society from degenerating into chaos. One gains liberty not by overthrowing hierarchy and constraints, but by finding liberty in its true abode, the spiritual realm."[17] In reflecting on her approach, Murata informs her readers, "Nowadays some people may assume that a woman's duty in writing a study of Islam is to help undermine Islam's patriarchal structure. In a sense I am doing that since I have brought out the 'matriarchal' elements in Islamic thought clearly enough. But to bring out the feminine stress of Islamic spirituality does not necessarily mean criticizing the masculine stress of the *Sharīʿa* and *Kalām*."[18]

Murata's constructs of theological patriarchy and spiritual matriarchy do not simply concern a human being's submission to God as a prerequisite for a relationship of intimacy with God. Her position also validates social hierarchies between men and women as a necessary starting point for subsequent relationships of complementarity and connectedness. She explicitly argues that hierarchy in the social order is necessary for communal stability, while overthrowing hierarchy in one's inward life is the way to spiritual realization.[19] This idea implies that women are to be fulfilled with a freedom and liberty in the spiritual realm while outwardly observing social hierarchies and a male-dominated interpretation of *Sharīʿa* as the accepted order of things. This view also assumes that the *Sharīʿa* is de facto masculine and thus primarily concerned with *jalālī* elements.

Such an approach to *Sharīʿa* is quite widespread in the contemporary Muslim world and constitutes a serious problem. Dominant discourses regarding *Sharīʿa* have been and continue to be articulated primarily by men and are generally defined in terms of unmitigated harshness rather than interpreted in ways that marry justice to mercy. It is not coincidental that reformers and critics of contemporary formulations of *Sharīʿa* law are people with inter alia commitments to gender justice, given that women are particularly vulnerable under dominant androcentric interpretations of the *Sharīʿa*. For Murata to give legitimacy to the "masculine stress" of the *Sharīʿa*, as if it exists as some ideal ahistorical reality, fails to recognize the levels of social injustice implicit in most current male-dominated applications of *Sharīʿa* law. Many contemporary applications of *Sharīʿa* law are characterized both by extreme gender discrimination and by an inability to respond effectively and justly to changing circumstances and legal sensibilities. Women in particular are on the receiving end of these interpretations of *Sharīʿa* and might suffer enormously.[20] Murata's idealization and uncritical reification of *Sharīʿa*, with no clear acknowledgment of its historicity, of the dominance of male experience and power in its formulation, or of its sexist contemporary applications, are ideologically complicit with patriarchy. Her approach inadvertently undermines the work of Muslim feminists who problematize and critique many contemporary interpretations of *Sharīʿa* for their gender biases and propose alternative legal positions, ethics, and applications that are more women-friendly and humane.[21]

Furthermore, Murata's notion that men and women are spiritually and morally equal before God but have fixed and different roles at the social level is clearly problematic. It is premised on a dichotomy between spirituality and social life that is in conflict with Ibn ʿArabī's approach. Ibn ʿArabī explicitly links spirituality and social praxis, arguing that men's and women's equal spiritual potential has a number of practical implications: women can set legal precedents, can lead mixed congregations in prayer, can be teachers and leaders on the *Ṭarīqa* with both women and men as disciples, can attain the highest level of leadership by being the axial saint (*quṭb*) of a period, and so forth.

Elsewhere, Ibn ʿArabī also points to the contextual and therefore socially contingent determinants of certain *Sharīʿa* rulings. For example, he argues that the normative legal position that two women's testimony is worth that of one man is countered by particular situations where one woman's testimony is in fact sufficient or is equal to that of two men (that is, legal cases involving parentage and the subject of *ʿidda*). Hence, Ibn ʿArabī presents the *Sharīʿa* as informed by the realities of the social context, including the experiences that are associated with traditional gender roles.

With all these discussions of women's agency in the social and legal realms, Ibn ʿArabī contends that men and women's equal access to spiritual completion is enacted in society. Murata does not engage any of these teachings but simply omits some of the most important and revolutionary sociolegal ideas on gender written by the Shaykh al-Akbar. Although large portions of her book are devoted to gender in the works of Ibn ʿArabī, Murata fails to include his perspective on Ḥājar as creator of legal precedent, his novel discussion of legal testimony, or his views regarding women's capacity to lead mixed prayer congregations. By excluding these perspectives from within Ibn ʿArabī's corpus, Murata effectively censors and suppresses an impetus toward social justice that emerges inherently from Ibn ʿArabī's view of human spirituality. Thus, Murata's dichotomization between spiritual equality and sociolegal equality, together with her reification of the *Sharīʿa* as an ahistorical phenomena, reflects her biases and selectivity. These separations between the spiritual and the social cannot be attributed to Ibn ʿArabī, who explicitly connects and integrates these two dimensions of human life, presenting fairly radical understandings on the nature of women's agency in the social realm.

Murata's position, like many other traditionalist versions of romanticized patriarchy that accord women spiritual equality without any effective translation into society, runs counter to a foundational dimension underlying the broader Islamic tradition. In Islam, morality and spirituality are not restricted to acts of private worship (*ʿibādāt*) but include social actions (*muʿāmalāt*). Both the prophetic example and the Qurʾān state that the enactment of faith through moral agency is fundamentally and simultaneously rooted in the individual, social, and communal realms. If men and women are seen to have equal moral and spiritual capacity, then both should logically have equal access to enact such capacities in the world, and both should take the full consequences of adopting this vicegerency. This idea is also enshrined in the Qurʾān, which states,

> The Believers, men and women
> are protecting friends of one another [*awliyāʾ*];
> They enjoin what is just and forbid what is evil;
> they observe regular prayers, practice regular charity
> and obey God and the Apostle.
> On them God will pour mercy,
> for God is exalted in power, Wise.
> God has promised Believers, men and women,
> Gardens under which rivers flow, to dwell therein,
> And beautiful mansions in gardens of everlasting bliss,
> But the greatest bliss is the good pleasure of God.
> That is supreme felicity. (Q. 9:71–72)

Thus, gender differences are irrelevant to the central concerns of religious practice, spiritual development, and moral agency. Moreover, men and women are charged with mutually overseeing one another; they are not pitted against or above one another. Murata's notion that women's spiritual equality is unrelated to the imperative of gender justice and human equality in sociopolitical terms runs contrary to the basic tenets of Islam, its *Tawḥīdic* integrity, and its comprehensive view of human agency. Many contemporary Muslim women find it untenable to bow at the altar of abstract and theoretical possibilities for their sex without translating these possibilities into the practical realm of gendered power relationships. These insights, drawn from fundamental Islamic teachings and exemplified in Ibn ʿArabī's teachings and interactions with women, reflect a dimension critical to Islamic feminism—that is, spirituality and sociality, the personal and the political, faith and action are integrally connected and form an inextricable whole. Since God is whole, creation is whole, and the actualization and harmonization of the divine qualities is demanded of human beings in all spheres of life. It is imperative to integrate this *Tawḥīdic* worldview into our politics and our social formulations. Living with patriarchal binaries that fragment reality into disconnected hierarchies is inconsistent with Islamic spirituality.

While differences between men and women exist, Ibn ʿArabī teaches that the goals of human life are universal and ungendered. These ends make equal demands on men and women in terms of process. With varying degrees of sophistication, Nasr and Murata articulate gendered social hierarchy in reified, stable, and ontologically determined ways that have profoundly conservative and even repressive political implications for women. In keeping with their traditionalist assumptions, these scholars' readings of Ibn ʿArabī also reflect a dismissal of the dimension of historicity implicit in his articulations of gender. The result is a decontextualization of Ibn ʿArabī's language and imagery as well as a marginalization of the dynamic and shifting ways in which the scholar articulates gender categories.

In trying to understand why Nasr and Murata ultimately prioritize essentialized, hierarchical understandings of gender in Ibn ʿArabī and other Sufi works, I turn to Laury Silvers. Commenting on the *Tao of Islam*, Silvers, a former student of Murata, pays tribute to her superior scholarship and unparalleled contribution to analyzing gender in early and classical Islamic thought. However, Silvers argues that Murata's interpretations of and arguments for "statically relational and hierarchical" formulations of gender and the social submission of women reflect more strongly Murata's intellectual formation and genealogy than the texts she is analyzing.[22]

Silvers is alert to the influence of Murata's former teachers, among them Nasr and Henry Corbin, whose views on traditionalism include an elitist and hierarchical view of reality.[23] For my purposes, the most significant of Murata's and Nasr's traditionalist assumptions relate to a rejection of modernity, materialist sciences, and profane understandings of history, as well as to an embrace of rigid divisions between the sacred and the profane, while foregrounding the esoteric and the inner and the idea that the advocacy of ahistorical and perennial truths lies at the core of all religions. Silvers notes that through their idealization of the past, these traditionalist scholars understand "pre-modern racial, gender and class distinctions [to] reiterate a harmonious celestial order."[24]

In fact, Silvers's point is borne out in Nasr's other writings, where, for example, he argues that humanity, in addition to being divided into male and female, is also divided into "castes and races, both of which must be understood in their essential reality and without the pejorative connotations which have become associated with them in the modern world."[25] The "traditional science of man," as Nasr explains, employs the concept of caste to distinguish between different human types. He further maintains that innate temperament and disposition correspond to varying social roles, ranging from those who are born to lead to those whose "virtue it is to follow and to be led."[26] Similarly, the four races—"the yellow, the red, the black and white"—represent essential and distinctive aspects of the "pontifical" human condition. For Nasr, the range of essential human differences reflected in gender, caste, and racial distinctions points to an ultimate primordial unity of mankind. According to Nasr, this view of unity can only be comprehended by a traditional science of mankind "without reducing this unity to a uniformity and a gross quantitative equality that characterizes so much of the modern concern for man and the study of human state."[27] So for many traditionalists, including Nasr and Murata, the ways in which contemporary Islamic feminists might lobby for social justice are incompatible with a worldview that sees hierarchy as essential to the nature of reality and of Islam. While these contemporary traditionalist scholars reflect some of the ways that Ibn ʿArabī's gender legacy has been invoked, his body of work as a whole opens up far more liberating possibilities that demand to be engaged in more critical, constructive, and extensive ways.

Ibn ʿArabī, Spirituality, and Contemporary Gender Ethics

Ibn ʿArabī's works offer Islamic feminism possibilities for engaging fundamental questions of human value and existence in a manner that has profound implications for understandings of gender difference and equality. Developing the emancipatory potential inherent in his approach requires bearing in mind that there are two dimensions to the fluidity and tensions in his writings with regard to questions of gender and male-female relationships.

First, in cases where he employs patriarchal imagery, he is reflecting, both consciously and unconsciously, the prevalent gender constructs of his time. He is very much a product of his time, using a vocabulary, mythology, and worldview shared by his coreligionists and fellow intellectuals. In so doing, he is, like any person in general, communicating in the prevailing language, constructs, and codes of his time. This aspect of his writing is reflected, for example, in his views about men's ontological "degree above" women, as inferred from the Genesis narrative of Eve's derivation from Adam; his belief that masculinity signifies the category of active and femininity the category of receptive; and his use of the term *rijāl* (men) for female aspirants. These notions indicate some of the dominant and normative constructs of his time. Such language and imagery reveal his situatedness. Indeed, his usage of common idiom and symbolism enabled him to communicate effectively with his audience, whose members could relate to notions that resonated with their own heritage of ideas and norms.

Second, he inverts many of the normative understandings of prevalent constructs and radically reinterprets prevalent categories of gender. He often seems to contradict some of his earlier positions. In such instances, Ibn ʿArabī offers very iconoclastic presentations of women and men, of feminine and masculine, of the nature of God and reality, thereby deconstructing many established gender norms. He transforms the tradition while still retaining a connection to it. This strategy is evident, for example, in writings in which he associates women (specifically the two wives of the Prophet, ʿĀʾisha and Ḥafsa) with the stereotypically masculine and *jalālī* divine name *Al-Qawī* (The Strong) and when he speaks about the priority of the feminine principle in reality despite the prevalent social norms that evaluated masculinity as paramount. These dimensions of his work present possibilities that can inform a genuinely transformative vision for Islamic feminism.

Providing a comprehensive interpretation of Ibn ʿArabī's approach to gender requires keeping both his modes of articulation, the normative and counternormative, in conversation with one another. Some of his counternormative positions shift the paradigm of patriarchy, thereby offering Islamic feminism foundational ways of reconstituting gender constructs. Three related positions are of particular note here: Ibn ʿArabī's deconstruction of the duality between God and humanity, men and women, and the spirit and body.

Ibn ʿArabī's depictions of God present radical alternatives to the dominant images characterizing patriarchal theology. He views the ultimate source of reality, whether God's essence (*al-dhāt*) or God's attributes (*ṣifāt*), as "feminine" receptive realities that predominate. He describes God's primordial creativity via images of pregnancy, labor, and birthing that reflect complete divine involvement in the process. Here, creation and humanity emerge from within the depths of God's being, characterized by a relationship of fullness, identity, connection, and interiority vis-à-vis God.

This approach presents a very different representation than exists in the traditional view of God as sovereign king who imperiously bids existence into being with the royal command, "Be." With the latter hierarchical model, creation occupies a very different level of being from the Creator, with a relationship between the two of remoteness, difference, separateness, and exteriority. By instead using creative maternal images for the God-human relationship, Ibn ʿArabī prioritizes alternative ways of being. He emphasizes intimacy, connectedness, and continuity as a foundational matrix of relationship, thereby displacing patriarchal norms of separation, autonomy, and hierarchy.

In particular, Ibn ʿArabī's presentation of a cosmogonic myth where at the very beginnings, the nonexisting entities within the Godhead experienced distress and an urgent need to be born into existence implies the divine need for creation as intrinsic to God's realization. Similarly, humanity needs God to actualize humanity's own reality, source, and goal. Hence, the notion that mutual need defines the relationship between God and humanity presents an additional conception of the divine-human relationship that simultaneously embraces, complements, extends, and reconfigures the more popular conception of the Lord/servant dynamic. From this perspective, hierarchy is overcome by mutuality and reciprocity.

Similarly, Ibn ʿArabī reconstitutes the nature of relationships between men and women, transforming the standard hierarchical understanding of Eve coming from Adam's rib into the view that the rib signifies the level of shared humanity, ontologically rooted love, and completion between men and women in relation to the divine. Love between God and humanity results from their original unity; the love between woman and man is similarly rooted in their ontological identity having originally been created from a single soul. Hence, the love between men and women provides a microcosmic model for understanding the nature of human origin and divine love. More especially, his view that man is needy and incomplete without woman, and vice versa, establishes mutuality as a fundamental basis for intimate relationships. So the completion that men and women experience in one another also reflects and is connected to their ontological completion in relation to God.

Hence, Ibn ʿArabī provides a lens that radically turns assumptions of gender hierarchy on their head by illustrating the depth of shared identity and mutual love that draws men and women together, although he is occupied by a heterosexual focus. The final chapter on Muḥammad in the *Fuṣūṣ*, the "Bezel of Singularity," connects the oneness between God and humanity to the oneness between man and woman. Here, Muḥammad, who is the seal of all messengers, thereby culminating the fullness of prophetic wisdom and divine communication with humanity, links the God-human identity with the man-woman identity. Women were made lovable to the Prophet because a relationship with a woman enabled him to comprehend, through personal experience, the nature of his relationship and love with God. Similarly, such relationships between men and women provide humans with a sign about the nature of their existence. Here, men and women are made lovable to each other precisely because their unity brings them closer to the Source, with each providing the other with a taste for their existential state of oneness with God. Some of the most intense tastes of this oneness between human beings may be experienced during sexual intercourse, when the dissolution of the self into the Other echoes the mystical state of *fanāʾ* (annihilation) in the Beloved. On the divine canvas of theophany, such relationships reveal the deepest level of meaning of human existence and thus provide a window on the nature of reality.

This position presents heterosexual gender relationships, marriage, and sexuality informed by mutual respect and interdependence as loci for experiencing and realizing the most sacred of realities. As such, it offers Islamic feminism a way of conceptualizing intimate relationships between men and women as an avenue of spiritual realization; such relationships demand the highest level of cultivation of character and good qualities. If men and women approach their relationships with an eye toward the spiritual realities they hold within and among themselves, they will relate to one another with the due reverence, respect, and humility with which anyone approaches the sacred. Doing so fosters a recognition of male-female relationships as a potent workshop for refining some of the most noble possibilities in character and attitude, making it possible to overcome hierarchy with a reverential mutuality.

Furthermore, Ibn ʿArabī's complex exegesis on verse 2:228 ends up radically limiting the relevance of man's "degree above" women to essentially a difference in procreative capacities. By arguing that the active/receptive mode of creation evident in the Adam/Eve narrative is countered by that of Mary/Jesus, both of which, in any case, are particular and nongeneralizable creative modes, he effectively degenders the active/receptive modes in the creation model for humanity more generally. By stating that man's "degree above" woman is primarily about active and receptive modes and then defining these modes in relation to very specific and circumscribed realities of procreation, Ibn ʿArabī effectively domesticates, circumscribes, and defangs the verse's potential for interpretation as a basis for gender hierarchy. Furthermore, his rich description of women's procreative receptivity and fecundity presents this role not only as positive but also as reflective of women's unique theophanic capacities. Ideologically, this approach values dominant female experiential realities in the deepest possible sense.

In addition, Ibn ʿArabī's vision of *al-Insān al-Kāmil* fully integrates all facets of the human being, including the body, mind, emotions, and spirit, as intrinsic to complete spiritual realization. In particular, the notion that embodiment is fundamentally connected to humanity's capacity for comprehensiveness completely discards traditional patriarchal dualisms that denigrate the body. The historical association of women with the "lower" material, physical dimensions and of men with the "higher" spiritual, intellectual dimensions has locked many thinkers into forms of religious anthropology that unjustly denigrate women and undiscerningly venerate men. With his construction of corporeality and the body as well as the attendant physiological processes of pregnancy and birth as intrinsically spiritually imbued and necessary loci for manifesting God's qualities and realities, Ibn ʿArabī breaks down such dualisms of body and spirit. In this way, women and men, with their physiological differences and spiritual correspondences, are affirmed in the fullness of their embodiment.

Ibn ʿArabī's conceptualization therefore genuinely dismantles some of the foundational binaries of patriarchal hierarchy both theologically and socially. He offers integrated and holistic ways of understanding the relationships between God and humanity, man and woman, body and spirit. These insights relating to theology and religious anthropology collectively provide Islamic feminism with an array of possibilities for critiquing gender-discriminatory social and religious hierarchies.

Ibn ʿArabī's ideas offer a plethora of possibilities for Islamic feminism that both enable the deconstruction of foundational patriarchal narratives and posit egalitarian alternatives. Although his foundationally heterosexist assumptions arguably limit his work, the complex manner in which he bends normative notions of gender and his focus on a universal ethical ideal that exists outside of biological gender constitute an arena for further research and critical analysis.

I conclude this discussion with a reflection on the overall paradigmatic implications of Ibn ʿArabī's teachings for Islamic feminism, with a particular view to his unique contributions. Many feminist critiques of patriarchy, whether religious or secular, often operate primarily within the discourse of rights. The constraints of discourse focused solely on rights may be its pragmatic attention to the immediate consequences of structural gender inequality rather than detailed, critical scrutiny directed at the source of such structures. So, rights-based discourses may end up unintentionally defined by dominant power structures.

Within Islam, many female legal scholars operate within a rights-based discourse in their critique of gender inequality. These feminist reformers, inter alia, highlight that traditional *fiqh* discourse offers women more rights than societies practically afford to them[28] or stress that the variability and multivocality of the traditional *fiqh* discourse in the premodern period allowed Muslim women far more freedom than is available in current permutations.[29] In addition, they prioritize traditional legal positions that favor women, such as maintenance and dower.[30] The goal, then, is to retrieve rights for women that have been marginalized within dominant interpretations of the Qurʾān and *Sharīʿa*. This effectively translates into a discourse of competing equalities—that is, men and women are granted rights by traditional approaches to the *Sharīʿa*; men have generally been granted their rights, but the same has not always held true for women. Hence, the goal is balance, according women parallel if not always equal rights based on established legal traditions.

These rights-based approaches followed by many feminist Muslim scholars are strategically and pragmatically necessary. However, scholars also urgently need to engage in a comprehensive theological critique that actively interrogates the foundational premises and nature of dominant *fiqh* structures. A pure rights-based discourse is limited by the fact that it often deals with the symptoms of inherited structures of patriarchal discourse without necessarily or rigorously interrogating the nature, roots, and assumptions of the structures—in other words, the causal factors informing such structures.[31] A rights-based discourse often inadvertently internalizes the hegemony of inherited structures and is thus more vulnerable to reversions to patriarchal articulations in strained and conflicted social and political contexts. For example, in the current geopolitical environment, where Muslim identity in different contexts may be perceived as under threat, reversions to patriarchal *fiqh* as the benchmark of Muslim identity and authenticity become particularly salient and charged.[32] Thus a feminist rights-based discourse needs to be firmly wedded to a clear and strong interrogation of core principles and values at a foundational level.

Developing a more structural and theologically robust critique requires foregrounding the constructed nature of *fiqh* as a historically evolving interpretation of *Sharīʿa* that is intended to actualize particular ideals, values, and visions of reality and that is not an end in itself. A structural critique of the established *fiqh* canon would involve asking some fundamental questions relating to the nature of *Sharīʿa* and its historical interpretations: What are the ideological implications of using the terms *Sharīʿa* and *fiqh* interchangeably? What is the continuing impact of context and historical circumstance on the formation of Islamic law? In particular, what is the notional content of the terms "human being," "society," and "God" that underlie dominant positions in the *fiqh* literature? Most significant, it is imperative to look at the nature and constitution of *fiqh* in relation to a deeper vision of ultimate reality and human purpose. Such a reevaluation needs to ask how the inherited *fiqh* as a discourse manifests and enacts that reality and whether in fact it really does so.

Particularly in relation to issues of gender, scholars and others must ask critical questions about the nature of human beings and gender differences assumed within the traditional *fiqh* discourse. Since the established legal canon implicitly operates on particular understandings of the nature of men and women and the relationships between them, it is necessary to interrogate the basis of such understandings. Doing so illustrates that many of the specific understandings of gender relationships assumed by dominating discourses in the *fiqh* canon reflect the contingent and contextual constructs of their premodern formulators. These discourses need to be reexamined and reformulated to be relevant and not discontiguous.[33]

Any such rethinking cannot develop exclusively on the basis of contemporary social sensibilities. For Muslims, it must also be informed by metaphysical sensibilities that foreground the God-human relationship in developing an ethics. Sufism organically addresses these deeper levels of meaning and human existential positioning. A comprehensive analysis and critique of social structures requires focusing on both the types of prevalent gendered practices and their underlying religious rationale. Holding the underlying issues of values, principles, and human purpose—areas of Sufi concern—consistently in view enables the inquirer to arrive at different possibilities from the dominant *fiqh* discourse.

The debates on the relationship between *Sharīʿa* and *Ṭarīqa* have a long history in Islamic thought. In some Sufi groups, adepts with advanced capacities for ethical judgment exercised their discretion in observing the law. Others insisted that religiously acceptable behavior should always be determined by the letter of the law; in fact, in the modern period, contestations of the nature of what constitutes proper Sufi teachings and practice resulted in an intensified focus by some major Sufi groups on asserting the primacy of the *Sharīʿa* in relation to Sufi practice.[34] Most of these discussions, however, generally accept the dominant *fiqh* canon, with all of its gendered assumptions, as accurate expressions of *Sharīʿa*. I question such assumptions, particularly some of the problematic presuppositions on the nature of men and women that underlie much of the inherited and socially conditioned *fiqh* canon. While for most legal scholars, it is a theoretical commonplace that the *fiqh* canon represents limited human attempts to express the *Sharīʿa* and that the *fiqh* is the product of dynamic human processes, more ideologized and simplistic conflations between *Sharīʿa* and *fiqh* often appear in popular discourse and in the statements of some Muslim religious leaders. This phenomenon continues to have detrimental consequences for gender justice and women's rights in many contemporary Muslim societies.

My argument here also challenges the dominant gender constructions that underlie much of the traditional *fiqh* canon, since I believe that they deviate from the ontological assumptions intrinsic to the *Sharīʿa*. Hence, I am not engaging in the older debate regarding the primacy of *Sharīʿa* over the *Ṭarīqa*, or vice versa. Rather, I am arguing that certain Sufi discourses may present more faithful readings of the *Sharīʿa* and the related assumptions of human nature as reflected in the Qurʾān than do the dominant *fiqh* discourses. By exploring Sufi metaphysics, this book suggests a different nexus between *taṣawwuf* and *Sharīʿa*, offering a fundamental ontological ground for reshaping gender ethics in emerging feminist *fiqh*. Sufism, with its prioritization of *jamālī* realities, where majesty (*jalāl*) always needs to be contained within an encompassing mercy (*jamāl*), potentially offers a crucial contribution to the development of a humane legal system.

At the same time, many strands of contemporary secular feminism do not deliberately and consciously interrogate conceptions of the self, society, and reality in ways that deeply engage questions of human purpose and value. Vacillating and relativist constructions of self often are unable to withstand more insidious ideological forces such as capitalism and consumerism. In *The Whole Woman*, Germaine Greer has pointed to this profound crisis of identity characterizing feminism and Western society. In my view, her work demonstrates that the lack of a coherent and ontologically grounded vision of the human self and society has resulted in a dangerous relativism of all ethics.[35] As a consequence, there is an absence of ontologically grounded values against which one's constructs of gender and self can be measured.

Greer points out that this crisis and its resulting ethical vacuum have been invaded by hegemonic discourses such as capitalism, with its focus on the consuming acquisitive and insatiable self. For all practical purposes, these forces have perpetuated, if not heightened, gender discrimination and structural inequality. Greer illustrates these realities by pointing to the intensified way in the twentieth and twenty-first centuries in which the continuing structures of capitalism and male dominance have colluded to produce realities that create women as objects of self-serving corporate structures such as the fashion, pharmaceutical, and pornographic industries.[36] The central point in this observation is that feminist discourses, whether secular or Islamic, that do not carefully address foundational questions of the nature of the self in relation to a thoroughly grounded understanding of human values are bound to be influenced and colonized by prevailing ideological forces that are voracious, avaricious, and destructive in the extreme.

In this regard, Sufism as well as mysticism in other traditions have great spiritual riches to offer feminist analyses of the problem, enabling the interrogation of dominant conceptions of the self and society and the proposal of alternatives. However, as scholar of gender and Christian mysticism Grace Jantzen points out, the contemporary tendency to privatize spirituality—that is, to frame spirituality as primarily internal, personal, and individual—obscures its relation to social justice.[37] Jantzen notes that this dynamic of privatization reinforces the status quo, since intellectual and religious energy are directed toward internal religiosity rather than transformative sociopolitical action. She adds, "This has the net effect not only of turning the attention of those seeking deepened spirituality away from issues of justice but also of leaving the efforts for justice to those who have abandoned concern with spirituality, seeing it as having nothing to offer in the work for structural change."[38] It is thus imperative for those interested in the more comprehensive implications of mysticism for justice to rethink the ways that mysticism might offer a different, deeply rooted approach to current gender dilemmas, addressing integral questions of ontology, spiritual refinement, and social ethics.

Ibn ʿArabī and Sufi discourse more broadly, by their nature, address reality and the nature of human beings, society, and God at a foundational ontological level. Comprehensively analyzing and critiquing core social structures require asking not simply the "how" but also the "why" of gender relations. This book, in conversation with Ibn ʿArabī's ideas, asks some of these core perennial religious questions, including, Who am I? What is the nature of the universe? Why am I here? How do I live correctly? What are my criteria for measuring value? It does so while simultaneously foregrounding gender as a central category of analysis at a foundational level of religious meaning. Such an engagement allows us to arrive at very different answers than the ones proposed by dominant paradigms. Indeed, the teachings of Ibn ʿArabī and Sufism in general have much to offer in the way of a comprehensive framework within which to interrogate a politics of gender.

From a Sufi perspective, and particularly in Ibn ʿArabī's worldview, the ultimate goal of any politics must be the constant movement of the individual and the society toward God. Moreover, this movement is conceptualized in relation to a particular understanding of God and human beings where the ideal self is defined as the universal *al-Insān al-Kāmil*, who harmonizes and manifests the divine names. This is a preexisting ideal ethical self to which gender, in the ultimate sense, is irrelevant. There is no crisis of identity, and the same standard is set for all. Even having articulated these realities in a language and context where prevalent values were already partially plotted onto gender identities, Ibn ʿArabī spoke not only to these narratives but also simultaneously to the wholeness and inclusivity of human identity as well as to those who would succeed him long in the future. As such, this approach tears away the veils of gender constructs to reveal a self that can access complete spiritual realization and whose object it is to know God.

This worldview is rooted in a particular metaphysics where the goals of human life make equal demands of men and women.

These constructs of human spiritual refinement and God are replete with firm criteria for existentiating, evaluating, and valuing human qualities, attributes, character, behavior, social interactions, and legal structures. Sufism offers both a vision and a practical methodology. Here one undertakes to purify the self and society of things that pull us to the inclinations of the *nafs al-ammāra*, including the discriminatory attachments of patriarchy, and to realize an innate spiritual capacity where the value of every human being is defined solely by level of inner refinement and God consciousness. Moreover, legal and social structures are to be held accountable to these norms. This is freedom and gender equality par excellence.

Using a critical and holistic approach to Ibn ʿArabī's work, this book demonstrates the nuanced richness of his gender mosaic. His ideas and methodologies are remarkably generative, characterized by a delicate balance between conventional categories and alternative possibilities. Although they reflect the normative gender assumptions, language, and constructs of his specific context, his writings fragment patriarchal binaries and destabilize reified gender categories. This dialectical method captures a multivalent ambiguity that "enables the reader to break out of habituated ways of perception" to facilitate fresh insights.[39] Ibn ʿArabī's remarkable immersion in language—as a poet, mystic, and legal scholar—mirrors the human capacity to whirl its way to a level of human attainment that is comprehensively spiritual in nature, with organic and powerful social implications.

Ibn ʿArabī also uses the dialectical method as a means to transcend the limitations of language in communicating a unitary *Tawḥīdic* reality. This vision of unity more especially fractures and disrupts normative gender dichotomies and evaluations. By adhering to fundamental Sufi assumptions that prioritize humans' inner state over their biology and that posit a single spiritual and ethical ideal for all humans, Ibn ʿArabī's approach offers a primary basis for the critique of sexual discrimination. He complexly configures the nature of gender difference while providing rich interpretive possibilities for his disciples and readers. Maximizing the egalitarian potential of his ideas requires that we not treat his constructs in a reified manner and thereby limit their inherent fluidity and deconstructive potential.

Because Ibn ʿArabī's Sufi framework offers a comprehensive understanding of the nature of human beings, their purpose in the world, the ethical self, and criteria for value and meaning, questions of gender can be addressed not only at the level of rights but also at the foundational level of value and meaning. With his conceptualizations, Ibn ʿArabī pushes normative gender categories to new registers, thus rendering them mobile, fluid, and multivalent. His approach thus provides novel insights, enabling contemporary Muslims to rethink gender and its articulations in new contexts while remaining firmly rooted in Islam's spiritual heritage. By offering a critical lens that sees with both eyes, embracing the contextual and the transcendental, Ibn ʿArabī's teachings offer a twenty-first-century audience Copernican possibilities for transformation.

Appendix

Selected Poems from the *Dīwān Ibn ʿArabī*

In a set of poems that inaugurate the *Dīwān* (pp. 54–60), Ibn ʿArabī pays tribute to some of his female disciples. Translations of some of these poems appear in chapters 3 and 4. To my knowledge, the poems in this appendix have not previously been translated and published.

I adorned my daughter, Dunyā,
  With the garment of faith and reverence.
Perchance I will see her grow by what God had compelled.
  Surely this world of yours,
Is an abode of trials and tribulation
  If you drink the water of life to quench your thirst.
Instead, if you merely breathe it in,
  It will be more joyous and nourishing,
Truly slaking your thirst.

I wrapped Siti al-ʿAysh in the
  Same *khirqa* of God's friends
Which the people of piety and bounty
  Had enveloped me within.
The one who wears
  The honorable *khirqa* of God's friends
Is beyond reproach,
  On condition that she wears it
In the manner of the virtuous ones.
  Her station is one that

Reaps felicity, success, and prosperity
in all that she seeks.

We invested our mantle
In the daughter of Zakī al-Dīn.
After a refining discipleship
Cultivated in divinity
She burnished her tributaries
And sanctified her essence
from all uncertainty.
Suffused with knowledge, you its quintessence
Derived from a sincere teacher and father
So let the daughter bestow our mantle,
Spreading his will,
Having reached the divine names
And an exalted lineage,
To all humans and jinns who in discipleship
Follow the teachings in my books.

Zumurrud requested to wear the *khirqa.*
After I responded to her appeal, she wore it.
Then she went to Egypt with her daughter
Desiring to satisfy her need.
After she was gratified, she deserted the *khirqa*
seeking the land of Jillaq [Damascus]
In a state of abasement.
On her return, her state
Was characterized by misconduct.
She thought herself too proud [to return]
Since she had indulged her whims.

Jamīlah is unparalleled.
Adorned by an exalted garment
I bestowed on her a momentous *khirqa.*
When she turned to me as her trustee

Since accompanying us [on the path],
She has cultivated the good [qualities].
Now her actions are all beautiful.
If truth be told, it is not my teaching
That is the catalyst.
Since I am not in reality, the responder [to the inner needs]
Truly my Lord is the caretaker.

I bestowed upon my daughter, Safarī
A *khirqa* possessed by the people of refinement [*adab*].
I clothed her in a robe of piety
Comprised of every pleasing virtue.
"Oh, daughter!" I said, "Follow my path and my legal school [*madhhab*].
My way is the *Sharīʿa* of the Arab Hashemite prophet."
Thus the garment that I bestowed on her
Encompasses [the knowledge] of every noble teacher.
I say this and I am Muḥammad Ibn al-ʿArabī.

When you, the ultimate point of my pain,
And you, the best of people in meaning and form,
Adopted my good qualities
And you, the best of people in meaning and in form
And her[1] qualities had already possessed my heart,
and if you wanted to verify that
In itself it would be a piece of news.
From the most illumined of garments
I wrapped her in the raiment of piety,
That raised her above gender.
She received from the very robes of Al-Khidr
All beautiful qualities and character [*adab*]
As well as the morals embedded
In the verses and chapters of the Qurʾān.
The pledge between us is that
She does not reveal [these gifts] to any other person.
This will allow her growth in sincerity and singular dedication
And protect her from harm.

Notes

INTRODUCTION

1 My creative rendition of this story is based on an anecdote chronicling Ibn Taymiyya's response to Shaykha Fāṭima's preaching, recorded by Safadī, *Aʿyān al-ʿasr wa-aʿwān al-naṣr*, 4:28.

2 For Maqrīzī's description of Shaykha Fāṭima, see *Al-Mawāʿiz wa al-ʿiʿtibār bi dhikr al-khitat wa al-ʿathar*, 3:602–3.

3 ʿAsqalāni, *Al-Durar al-kāmina fī aʾyān al-miʿa al-thāmina*, 3:226.

4 For this incident, see Safadī, *Aʿyān al-ʿasr wa-aʿwān al-naṣr*, 4:28–29.

5 Ibid.

6 Hashmi, "Women" analyzes the complex roles and social relationships in the lives of women religious leaders (including Fāṭima) in Mamluk Cairo and Damascus.

7 A *muftī* is a Muslim jurist who issues formal albeit unbinding legal opinions (*fatāwa*) on particular issues based on his or her expert interpretations of Islamic law in relation to a particular issue presented by either a judge or an individual.

8 Women's access to mosques varies in different parts of the Muslim world. In South Africa, for example, a number of mosques simply do not permit female worshipers, while other mosques have some reserved spaces for women—in some cases, rather beautifully decorated upper floors of the mosque; in others, spaces in adjacent buildings, small cordoned-off sections at the rear of the mosques, or dark and unwelcoming spaces in the basement. The Claremont Main Road Mosque has the central space divided front to back by a single rope so that men and women pray separated but alongside one another, with relatively equal visual and auditory access to the prayer leader or other speakers.

9 Following Wadud's *khuṭba*, members of the Muslim Youth Movement expanded the gender egalitarian momentum within their Johannesburg office by discretely initiating a mixed Friday prayer where women not only delivered sermons but also led the entire congregation of men and women in the *jumuʿa* prayer. The youth movement continued this practice of female ritual leadership in South Africa for two years before its members made a strategic decision to join local mosques and work for broader gender transformation.

10 Stowasser, "Religious Ideology," 262–96.

11 For a comparative exploration of the politicization of the veil in contemporary France and Iran, see Hoel and Shaikh, "Veiling, Secularism, and Islamism."

12 Abu-Lughod, "Feminist Longings," 3.

13 Tucker, "Gender and Islamic History," 38–39. For a discussion on the various realities currently experienced by Muslim women from different parts of the world, see Hibri, "Islamic Law."

14 Feminists such as Rosemary Radford Ruether have paid much attention to the gendered category of "theological anthropology" within Christianity. See, for example, Ruether's *Sexism and Godtalk*, 93–95. While the term "anthropology" focuses on understanding human experience, a "theological" or "religious" anthropology foregrounds the impact of religion on the way in which human nature might be understood. While the term "religious personhood" seems to be gaining some currency in contemporary scholarship, I prefer to retain "religious anthropology" for its suggestive and more holistic connotations.

15 Gracia, *Metaphysics*, 147–48.

16 From the eighteenth century on, the term "cosmology" has been used increasingly in the areas of physics and astrophysics, with a focus on the physical origin and evolution of the universe. This usage differs from its usage as religious "cosmology," an established category of inquiry within a variety of religious traditions. The latter seeks to understand the nature of the universe in relation to specific metaphysical and religious assumptions. For a perspective on Muslim cosmologies that integrates both science and theology in the premodern period, see Nasr, *Introduction*.

17 While there is no evidence that Ibn ʿArabī was a practicing jurist, Eric Winkel and Michel Chodkiewicz illustrate that *fiqh* is integral to Ibn ʿArabī's entire vision, demonstrating the extensive legal thinking and jurisprudence found in Ibn ʿArabī's *Al-Futūḥāt al-makkiyya*. See Winkel, *Ibn ʿArabī's Fiqh*; Winkel, *Islam and the Living Law*; Chodkiewicz, *Ocean without Shore*.

18 Ibn ʿArabī, *Al-Futūḥāt al-makkiyya*, 1:447.

19 Here, I am drawing on Scott Kugle's translations of *islām*, *imān*, and *iḥsān*, which I find most precise and comprehensive (*Rebel*, 12).

20 Ibid.

21 Ernst, *Shambhala Guide*, 26.

22 The phrase "The personal is political" was coined by Hanisch in "The Personal," 76.

23 For a helpful discussion of these issues, see Pateman, *Sexual Contract*.

24 See Sulamī, *Early Sufi Women*.

25 For this approach, see Ḥujwīrī, *Kashf al-maḥjūb*, 363–65.

26 Sufism in fact adheres to an encompassing spiritual hierarchy with deep-rooted power differentials between masters and disciples. For an in-depth if partial reading of the nature of hierarchical power dynamics in master-disciple relationships, see Malamud, "Gender and Spiritual Self-Fashioning."

27 The most thorough current biography on Ibn ʿArabī is Addas, *Quest*.

28 Hirtenstein, *Unlimited Mercifier*, 10.
29 For a rich history of the intellectual currents and social dynamics of Andalusia, see Fletcher, *Moorish Spain*.
30 Landau, *Philosophy*, 15.
31 Ibid.
32 For his biographical entries on these two female spiritual masters, see Ibn ʿArabī, *Sufis of Andalusia*, 142–46.
33 Ibn ʿArabī, *Al-Futūḥāt al-makkiyya*, 8.
34 Nasr, *Three Muslim Sages*, 96.
35 Landau, *Philosophy*, 16.
36 Nasr, *Three Muslim Sages*, 98.
37 Cited in Chittick, *Sufi Path*, 13.
38 Ibn ʿArabī, *Fuṣūṣ al-ḥikam*, 45.
39 Knysh, *Ibn ʿArabī*, 11.
40 For a discussion of the impact of Ibn ʿArabī's work, see Hirtenstein, *Unlimited Mercifier*, 6–8; Nasr, *Three Muslim Sages*, 90–91.
41 Knysh, *Ibn ʿArabī*, 1.
42 Kugle, *Rebel*, 79.
43 For an excellent summary of Ibn Taymiyya's criticism of Ibn ʿArabī's legacy, see Knysh, *Ibn ʿArabī*, 87–111.
44 Ibn ʿArabī did not use the phrase "*waḥdat al-wujūd*" in his work.
45 Based on his epithet "Shaykh al-Akbar," scholars have used the term "Akbarian" to describe influences deriving from Ibn ʿArabī's ideas and works.
46 See especially Knysh's discussion of Ibn Taymiyya's challenges to immanentist proclivities in Sufism in *Ibn ʿArabī*, 90–92.
47 For a contextualization of Ibn ʿArabī's notion of divine transcendence and immanence vis-à-vis some of the dominant theological schools, see Almond, "Shackles of Reason."
48 Knysh, *Ibn ʿArabī*, 139.
49 Ibid., 4.
50 Homerin, "Ibn Arabi."
51 Ibid.
52 Baldick, *Mystical Islam*, 174.
53 For an array of varying responses to Sufis in specific historical and political contexts, see De Jong and Radtke, *Islamic Mysticism Contested*; Sirriyeh, *Sufis and Anti-Sufis*.
54 Peskes, "Wahabiyya and Sufism," 151.
55 Ernst, "Between Orientalism and Fundamentalism," 115.
56 Ibid., 108–23.
57 See also Ernst, *Shambhala Guide*, 3–5.
58 Ernst, "Between Orientalism and Fundamentalism," 108–18.
59 For a broad overview of Sufism in the contemporary world, see Ernst, *Shambhala Guide*, 199–228.

60 See Yavuz, "Matrix."

61 Amina Wadud has described feminism as the "radical notion that women are human beings" (*Qurʾan and Woman*, xviii).

62 I developed this definition of feminism in Shaikh, "Transforming Feminisms," 148. A significant part of my argument here draws on that article.

63 Clearly, neither the "Muslim world" nor the "West" exists as homogenous or discrete entities. I am simply using them as descriptive categories to the extent that they reflect perceptions of shared identity among the members of their respective communities.

64 For such critiques, see Moraga and Anzaldúa, *This Bridge Called My Back*; Mohanty, Russo, and Torres, *Third World Women*. Mohanty astutely reflects on the imbalanced power relationship between Western feminists and many women in the Third World, writing, "Power is exercised in any discourse when that discourse sets up its own authorial subjects as the implicit referents, that is, the yardstick by which to encode and represent cultural Others" (55).

65 Much of the critical and vigilant work among Western feminists addressing issues of representation, difference, and authority emerged in the latter part of the 1980s and in the 1990s. Such works include Spelman, *Inessential Woman*; Caraway, *Segregated Sisterhood*; Russo, "We Cannot Live." This type of nonhierarchical scholarship was limited and marginal during the formative period of second-wave Western feminism.

66 There are also smaller groups of secular feminist women who prefer to approach religion as a private matter, outside discourses of women's rights. See, for example, Moghissi, *Feminism and Islamic Fundamentalism*. This perspective, while important, is not my primary concern, since I am focusing on feminist approaches from within an Islamic framework.

67 The concept of "multiple critique" as articulated by Cooke, *Women Claim Islam*, captures Islamic feminists' vigilance in relation to varying types of political hegemony.

68 For discussions of different categories of feminism among Muslim women, including the ways in which tensions and alliances between different groups have developed within specific geographic, national, and political contexts, see Karam, *Women, Islamisms, and the State*; Cooke, *Women Claim Islam*; Mir-Hosseini, *Islam and Gender*.

69 For varying scholarly approaches to this dissonance between Islamic ideals and realities on questions of gender relations, see Hibri, *Women and Islam*; Webb, *Windows of Faith*.

70 See Hassan, "Islamic Perspective"; Hassan, "Muslim Women"; Mir-Hosseini, "Construction of Gender"; Mir-Hosseini, *Islam and Gender*; Mir-Hosseini, "Muslim Women's Quest"; Wadud, *Inside the Gender Jihad*; Wadud, *Qurʾan and Woman*.

71 See Ahmed, *Women and Gender*; Mernissi, *The Forgotten Queens*; Mernissi, *The Veil and the Male Elite*; Wadud, *Inside the Gender Jihad*; Wadud, *Qurʾan and Woman*.

72 See Ali's incisive approach and reflections in *Sexual Ethics*. In addition, drawing on Ibn ʿArabī's ideas, Silvers has exquisitely argued an Islamic feminist theo-

logical position on the complexities and burdens of human choice when engaging revelation ("'In the Book'").

73 See for example, Gottlieb, *She Who Dwells Within*; Ruether, *New Woman, New Earth*. In "Braiding the Stories," Kahf, harvests a number of premodern Islamic literary and historical genres to uncover women's voices and their contestations of androcentric norms in early Islam. In the contemporary period, Moi's *Sexual/Textual Politics* addresses some of the debates surrounding questions of gender and authorship, exposing the complexities of studying gynocentric and feminist-authored texts vis-à-vis the traditional patriarchal "canon" in Western literature (74–77).

74 Gross, *Buddhism after Patriarchy*, 17–24.

75 Ibid., 20.

76 Ibid., 23.

77 See West, "Silenced Women Speak," 76–77; Fiorenza, *Bread Not Stone*, 6.

78 Among Muslim feminists, the various works of Amina Wadud and Fatima Mernissi reflect the use of both a hermeneutics of suspicion and a hermeneutics of reconstruction. Some biblical scholars have reflected more explicitly on such feminist methodologies in the study of the Bible. See, for example, Sakenfield, "Feminist Uses," 166.

79 Spivak, "French Feminism," 177–78.

80 Kristeva, *Desire in Language*, 69.

81 Culler, *Pursuit of Signs*, 105.

82 Boyarin, *Unheroic Conduct*, 25–27.

83 For two excellent contemporary approaches to constructive Christian theology, see Jones and Lakeland, *Constructive Theology*; Kaufman, *In Face of Mystery*.

84 Such arbitrary gendered linguistic conventions are clearly illustrated by the fact that the Arabic word for chair (*kursī*) is masculine while the word for table (*ṭāwila*) is feminine, while there are two different Arabic terms for the word "window," one (*nāfidha*) grammatically feminine and the other (*shubbāk*) grammatically masculine.

85 Sells, *Approaching the Qurʾan*, 202; Scott Kugle, appendix 2 in Iskandarī, *Book of Illumination*, 370–76.

86 Scott Kugle, appendix 2 in Iskandarī, *Book of Illumination*, 375.

87 I carefully unpack these dialectical theological constructs in great detail later in chapters 4 and 6.

88 Ibn ʿArabī notes his occasional use of the feminine pronoun for God in relation to the divine feminine in *Al-Futūḥāt al-makkiyya*, 1:424. Sensitive to the nuanced gender metaphors at play in Ibn ʿArabī's work, Murata, *Tao of Islam*, astutely renders the feminine pronoun "She" for God when translating a passage from Kāshānī's commentary on Ibn ʿArabī's discussion of the divine feminine (197–98).

89 Moosa, *Ghazālī*, 38–63.

90 Ibid., 40–45.

91 *Uwaysī* relationships are a developed trope in Islamic thought. The term refers

to inspirational relationships with someone who is not present physically, possibly also involving relations across time. For a discussion of this concept, see Moosa, *Ghazālī*, 43.

CHAPTER ONE

1 Stoddart and Nicholson, *Sufism*, 28.
2 For a more detailed discussion of mechanics of the Sufi path as reflected in the different *ṭuruq*, see Trimingham, *Sufi Orders*.
3 I am using the term "psychology" in its more classical Greek sense, which is the study of the self. Earlier notions of the self or the psyche were more holistic and included notions of the spirit, soul, mind, personality, emotions, and behavior. For an understanding of how the "psyche" was understood in ancient Greece, see Rohde, *Psyche*. Reed, *From Soul to Mind*, provides an absorbing genealogical discussion on how the term "psyche" has been progressively narrowed to the study of the mind in the development of modern psychology.
4 Schimmel, *Mystical Dimensions*, 191. She refers to these tripartite components on the basis of the reflections of some of the major Sufi thinkers, including Jaʿfar al-Ṣādiq, Rābiʿa al-ʿAdawiyya, Qushayrī, Bisṭāmī, and Junayd.
5 Chittick, *Sufi Path*, 17.
6 Sulamī, *Early Sufi Women*, 118.
7 Ḥujwīrī, *Kashf al-maḥjūb*, 202.
8 Sulamī, *Early Sufi Women*, 244.
9 Chittick, *Sufi Path*, 7.
10 Muḥāsibi (d. 857) developed a complex moral psychology that provided the seeker with ways to understand egoism and vigilantly monitor one's responses. See selections of his writings in Sells, *Early Islamic Mysticism*, 171–95.
11 For discussions on what constitutes Sufi practice, see Sells, *Early Islamic Mysticism*.
12 Ghazālī, *Iḥyāʾ ʿulūm al-dīn*, 12.
13 In addition to using the word "Islam" to refer to a religion, the term "*islām*" also refers to the process of an individual's submission to God.
14 Safadī, *Aʿyān al-ʿaṣr wa-aʿwān al-naṣr*, 4:28.
15 Schimmel, "Eros," 124. See also Cornell, "'Soul.'"
16 Schimmel, "Eros," 124.
17 Makkī, *Qut al-qulūb*, 2:409.
18 Bukhārī, *Saḥīḥ al-Bukhārī*, 7:1.
19 Goldziher, *Introduction*, 122.
20 There are also a few traditions in which the Prophet forbade men who had so requested from castrating themselves. See Bukhārī, *Saḥīḥ al-Bukhārī*, 7:6–8.
21 See Walther, *Women in Islam*, 143–52; Ahmed, *Women and Gender*, 83–87. The ʿAbbāsid caliph al-Mutawakkil had four thousand concubines, while one of his predecessors, Hārūn al-Rashīd, had hundreds of concubines. See Hitti, *History*, 342.
22 Arberry, *Sufism*, 33–34.

23 Early Christian monastic attitudes rejecting the world and the flesh filtered to some extent into early Sufism, as a consequence of the generally amiable relations between Muslims and Christians during the Umayyad dynasty. See Andrae, *In the Garden*, 39.

24 Ghazālī, *On Disciplining*, 23–24; Andrae, *In the Garden*, 7–32.

25 Andrae, *In the Garden*, 45.

26 Ibid., 48.

27 Sarrāj, *Kitāb al-luma fī taṣawwuf*, 199. Ibn Adham, however, candidly noted that his choice of celibacy was based on his lack of desire for marriage as well as the rather helpful self-awareness that his disposition would most likely cause distress to a wife in need of love and devotion.

28 Ghazālī, *Proper Conduct*, 52.

29 Ibid., 74.

30 Schimmel, *Mystical Dimensions*, 428.

31 Ibid., 428.

32 Cited in Andrae, *In the Garden*, 49.

33 Sulamī, *Early Sufi Women*, 36.

34 For the exceptional extant autobiographical writings of a fifteenth-century female Sufi, ʿĀʾisha al-Bāʿūniyya, see Homerin, "Writing Sufi Biography."

35 In this context, the term "accuracy" refers not to objective historical facts but to a set of historical religious representations.

36 Sulamī, *Early Sufi Women*, 46, 70.

37 Ibid., 46–47.

38 Ibid., 63.

39 Mojaddedi, *Biographical Tradition*, 25–39.

40 Homerin, "Writing Sufi Biography," 389.

41 Roded, *Women*, 92.

42 Sulamī, *Early Sufi Women*, 43.

43 Silvers makes this case convincingly in "Statistical Analysis." Dakake, "'Guest,'" demonstrates how early Sufi women often used the language and metaphor of domesticity to describe their relationships to the divine Beloved in ways that were distinctive from their male counterparts.

44 For glimpses of "alternative" social roles and lifestyles among some Sufi women, see Sulamī, *Early Sufi Women*; for an overview of Sufi women's varying practices, see 62–65. These practices are further evidenced in many of the entries from Sulamī and Ibn al-Jawzī translated in the rest of the manuscript. See also entries of the Sufi women in Ibn ʿArabī, *Sufis of Andalusia*, especially 142–44, 154. More generally, the debate regarding premodern Muslim women's participation in various facets of social life is complex and nuanced. Roded, *Women*; Hambly, *Women*; and Sonbol, *Beyond the Exotic*, illustrate that women in varying periods and contexts of Muslim history were often engaged both directly and indirectly with the social sphere and in public discourses in ways that challenge commonplace assumptions about Muslim women's historical silence and invisibility. In reflecting on Roded's assessment that "female seclusion was

an ideal that may have been more honored in the breach," Silvers argues that the relevant historical reports might suggest that realities of relative freedom and mobility would not have applied to the average women in average circumstances. Rather, she argues, the women who enjoyed these freedoms were "either exceptional women or average women in exceptional circumstances" ("Statistical Analysis," 11). Yet other studies show that lower-class women have historically enjoyed greater freedom and mobility than upper-class women. See Hambly, *Women*.

45 Cornell, "Introduction," in Sulamī, *Early Sufi Women*, 60–64.

46 Ibid., 61.

47 Sulamī, *Early Sufi Women*, 88.

48 Cornell, "Introduction," in Sulamī, *Early Sufi Women*, 64.

49 Ibid.

50 Ibn al-Jawzī, [*Ṣifāt al-ṣafwa*], in Sulamī, *Early Sufi Women*, 310, 320.

51 She apparently informed a male cohort, "I was walking in Baysān (a village in Palestine to the south of Tiberias) when a fierce dog approached me. When it came close to me, I looked at it and said, 'Come on, dog! If this is your lucky day, then devour me!' When he heard my words, he barked and turned away to leave" (ibid., 320).

52 See Cornell, "Introduction," in Sulamī, *Early Sufi Women*, 65; M. Smith, *Rābiʿa*, 140–42; Ibn al-Jawzī, [*Ṣifāt al-ṣafwa*], in Sulamī, *Early Sufi Women*, 300–303. In addition, Ḥujwīrī, *Kashf al-maḥjūb*, 362, talks approvingly of a devout married couple who had loved each other dearly and had remained in a celibate union for sixty-five years.

53 Ibn al-Jawzī, [*Ṣifāt al-ṣafwa*], in Sulamī, *Early Sufi Women* , 316.

54 Sulamī, *Early Sufi Women*, 126.

55 Ibn al-Jawzī, [*Ṣifāt al-ṣafwa*], in Sulamī, *Early Sufi Women*, 268.

56 ʿAṭṭār, *Muslim Saints*, 173–74.

57 Ibid., 173.

58 Ḥujwīrī, *Kashf al-maḥjūb*, 119.

59 Schimmel, *My Soul*, 40.

60 ʿAṭṭār, *Muslim Saints*, 174–75.

61 M. Smith, *Rābiʿa*, 16.

62 Cornell, "Introduction," in Sulamī, *Early Sufi Women*, 59.

63 Nurbakhsh, *Sufi Women*, 162.

64 Ibid.

65 ʿAṭṭār, *Muslim Saints*, 174–75.

66 Cornell, "Introduction," in Sulamī, *Early Sufi Women*, 59–60.

67 Ibid.

68 Ibn ʿArabī, *Al-Futūḥāt al-makkiyya*, 2:588.

69 Cornell, "Introduction," in Sulamī, *Early Sufi Women*, 66.

70 Qushayrī, *Sufi Book*, 201.

71 Ibid. In addition, Cornell points out that the Sufi practice of *futuwwa* is closely

related to the notion of *adab*, or appropriate behavior. See her "Introduction," in Sulamī, *Early Sufi Women*, 67.

72 Murata, *Tao of Islam*, 268.

73 See, for example, Sulamī's description of Fāṭima al-Khānaqahiyya in *Early Sufi Women*, 256; Ibn ʿArabī's description of the slave girl of Qāsim al-Dawlah is in *Sufis of Andalusia*, 154.

74 Cornell, "Introduction," in Sulamī, *Early Sufi Women*, 65–69.

75 ʿAṭṭār, *Muslim Saints*, 39–51.

76 Ibid., 40.

77 Ibid.

78 Cited in M. Smith, *Rābiʿa*, 2.

79 Elias, "Female and the Feminine," 221.

80 Ibid., 212.

81 Jantzen, *Power, Gender, and Christian Mysticism*, 16.

82 Schimmel, *Mystical Dimensions*, 426.

83 ʿAṭṭār, *Muslim Saints*, 66. Rābiʿa's reproach echoes the Qurʾānic condemnation of Pharaoh's statement, "I am your lord" (79:24).

84 ʿAṭṭār, *Muslim Saints*, 45. While it is unlikely that Ḥasan and Rābiʿa ever in reality met, since they did not live at the same time, the endurance of these narratives provides some indication of the gender imaginary present in Sufism.

85 Karamustafa, *Sufism*, 4.

86 For Rābiʿa's contribution to the Sufi notion of sincere love for God, see M. Smith, *Rābiʿa*, 89–111.

87 Sells, *Early Islamic Mysticism*, 163.

88 Ibid., 162.

89 Nicholson, *Mystics*, 183.

90 Schimmel, *Mystical Dimensions*, 45.

91 Andrae, *In the Garden*, 48.

92 Ḥujwīrī, *Kashf al-maḥjūb*, 363–64.

93 Ibid., 364.

94 Andrae, *In the Garden*, 49.

95 Ibid., 48.

96 Schimmel, "Eros," 129.

97 The relevant Qurʾānic verse reads, "And among His signs is this, that He created for you mates from among yourselves, that you may dwell in tranquility with them. And He put love and mercy between your [hearts]. Verily in that is a sign for those who reflect" (30:21).

98 Schimmel, *Mystical Dimensions*, 294–301.

99 Nicholson, *Mystics*, 110.

100 Schimmel, "Eros," 128.

101 For a detailed discussion of Rūmī's views on love, see Chittick, *Sufi Path*; Nicholson, *Rumi*.

102 See Ḥujwīrī, *Kashf al-maḥjūb*, 200–206, 416.

103 Schimmel, *Mystical Dimensions*, 289.
104 Ḥujwīrī, *Kashf al-maḥjūb*, 416.
105 Bellamy, "Sex and Society," 35.
106 ʿAṭṭār, *Muslim Saints*, 220.
107 Schimmel, *Mystical Dimensions*, 299.

CHAPTER TWO

1 This is my creative reading of the encounter between Ibn ʿArabī and Niẓām referred to in the *Tarjumān al-ashwāq* and depicted in Corbin's discussion thereof (*Creative Imagination*, 139–45).
2 Ibn ʿArabī, *Tarjumān al-ashwāq*, 15. I have used Corbin's translations with some modifications (*Creative Imagination*, 140).
3 Corbin, *Creative Imagination*, 143–44.
4 For a detailed discussion of the relationship between Ibn ʿArabī and Niẓām, focusing especially on the latter as symbolizing "sophianic wisdom," see ibid., 136–45.
5 Clark, "Lady Vanishes," 23–24.
6 Ibid., 24–30. Wider, another feminist historian challenges scholars who suggest that Diotima was a fictitious character invented by Plato. While arguing that Diotima existed, Wider nonetheless asks how much of the celebrated position on the nature of Platonic love articulated by the character of Diotima in Plato's *Symposium* represents "the view of the historical Diotima, and how much if any is the view of Socrates, and how much if any Plato's view" ("Women Philosophers," 45).
7 Clark, "Lady Vanishes," 31.
8 See Wider, "Women Philosophers," 45–48.
9 While there are no additional outside sources to verify Niẓām's empirical existence, in all likelihood she was probably a real woman given the types of details Ibn ʿArabi supplies about her and his relationship with other members of her family (see chapter 3). It is likely that Niẓām is both a tropological figure and a real woman who inspired Ibn ʿArabī.
10 Chittick, *Sufi Path*, xviii.
11 Landau, *Philosophy*, 18.
12 Fakhry, *History*, 222.
13 These debates about "philosophy" refer mostly to a narrow form of Aristotelianism dominant at the time. They do not incorporate the breadth of philosophical thought current in our context, which embraces more expansive and diverse approaches to epistemology and existence.
14 Ibn ʿArabī, *Al-Futūḥāt al-makkiyya*, 1:153.
15 Coates, *Ibn ʿArabī and Modern Thought*, 27.
16 The veracity of this exchange reported by Ibn ʿArabī cannot be confirmed by sources outside his biographical notes. Dominique Urvoy, a scholar of Ibn Rushd, argues that this exchange is fictitious and is inconsistent with Ibn Rushd's psychology, since he explicitly states in two of his books that Sufis have

"troubled minds" (*Averroes*, 168). Urvoy contends that the opportunistic Ibn ʿArabī bolstered his reputation by exploiting Ibn Rushd's fame and prestige.

17 See Ibn ʿArabī, *Al-Futūḥāt al-makkiyya*, 3:99, 2:319.

18 For insightful discussions of the implications of the exchange between Ibn ʿArabī and Ibn Rushd, see Stelzer, "Decisive Meetings."

19 Ibn ʿArabī, *Al-Futūḥāt al-makkiyya*, 1:153.

20 Ibid., 1:325.

21 Ibid., 2:523.

22 Rosenthal, "Ibn ʿArabī," 15–16.

23 Ibid., 35.

24 While Ghazālī is often recognized as the pioneering scholar who foregrounded major epistemological debates on the relationship between philosophy and mysticism, Ibn ʿArabī's teachings are among the first Sufi works to include a complete theoretical discourse on metaphysics.

25 Chittick, *Sufi Path*, xii.

26 Izutsu, *Sufism and Taoism*, 241.

27 Chittick, *Sufi Path*, xii.

28 Ibn ʿArabī, *Al-Futūḥāt al-makkiyya*, 1:120.

29 Ibid., 3:334.

30 Both Winkel, *Islam and the Living Law*, and Chodkiewicz, *An Ocean without Shore*, discuss the very traditional Islamic foundations of Ibn ʿArabī's work as well as illustrating the integral relationship between the *Sharīʿa* and the *ṭarīqa* in his framework.

31 Morris, *Orientations*, 13.

32 Schimmel, *Mystical Dimensions*, 268.

33 Ibn ʿArabī, *Al-Futūḥāt al-makkiyya*, 2:230.

34 Izutsu, *Sufism and Taoism*, 219.

35 Ibn ʿArabī, *Fuṣūṣ al-ḥikam*, 54.

36 Ibn ʿArabī describes this divine creative process in detail in the chapter on Adam in the *Fuṣūṣ al-ḥikam*, 48–58.

37 Chittick, *Sufi Path*, 10.

38 For an excellent discussion of Ibn ʿArabī's views on God's "necessary" existence and the overlap with related discussions in philosophy, see Izutsu, *Sufism and Taoism*, 239–40.

39 Ibn ʿArabī, *Fuṣūṣ al-ḥikam*, 49.

40 See Ibn ʿArabī, *Meccan Illuminations*, 96.

41 Ibid.

42 Ibn ʿArabī, *Al-Futūḥāt al-makkiyya*, 3:274, 276.

43 Ibid., 2:160.

44 Ibn ʿArabī summarizes his views on the macrocosm and microcosm in the chapter on Adam in his *Fuṣūṣ al-ḥikam*, 48–58.

45 Ibid., 49.

46 Coates, *Ibn ʿArabī and Modern Thought*, 3–4.

47 Ibn ʿArabī, *Fuṣūṣ al-ḥikam*, 48–49.

48 Given these associations, I have decided to primarily use Sells's translation of the term *kāmil* in the context of *al-Insān al-Kāmil* as meaning "complete" rather than "perfect" (*Mystical Languages*, 79–81). Sells argues convincingly and compellingly that while earlier, more ascetically inclined Sufis tended to view spiritual perfection as a transcendence of the human condition, becoming "as like the angels as possible," for Ibn ʿArabī, *kāmil* denotes a deepening cultivation of the human to the point of actualizing his or her complete, all-embracing capacities for divine manifestation. Drawing on the *Fuṣūṣ* chapters on the prophets Idrīs and Ilyās, Sells observes that the process of spiritual completion includes not just an ascent but also a descent into the realms of the "animal, vegetable and mineral reality and finally into pure elementality" (251–52). Thus, Sells notes that the complete human encompasses movement in both directions, not just the traditional notions of spiritual "perfection" as simply a process of ascent. I do in some instances retain the term "perfect" or "perfection" when translating *kāmil* or *kamāl*. I do so with an awareness of the complex, nuanced, and all-embracing and expansive nature that such a process of spiritual realization entails.

49 Ibn ʿArabī, *Al-Futūḥāt al-makkiyya*, 2:67.

50 For lucid discussion of these topics, see Chittick, *Imaginal Worlds*, 31–35.

51 Ibid., 34.

52 Ibid.

53 Ibn ʿArabī, *Fuṣūṣ al-hikam*, 272.

54 Ibid.

55 Izutsu, *Sufism and Taoism*, 236.

56 Ibid., 238.

57 Ibid.

58 Ibid.

59 Schimmel, *Mystical Dimensions*, 419.

60 Izutsu, *Sufism and Taoism*, 237.

61 Ibid.

62 Ibn ʿArabī, *Al-Futūḥāt al-makkiyya*, 2:134; Chittick, *Sufi Path*, 241.

63 Ibn ʿArabī discusses his understanding of the divine names in *Al-Futūḥāt al-makkiyya*, 3:397, 2:300.

64 Ibid., 2:203.

65 Ibid.

66 Ibid., 303.

67 For discussions of the hierarchy among the names, see ibid., 2:527, 608.

68 Ibid., 1:216, 2:391.

69 Ibid., 1:259.

70 Ibid., 4:3.

71 Ibid., 2:57.

72 Ibid., 3:380.

73 Ibid., 2:596.

74 For a discussion on the pervasive dimension of mercy in Ibn ʿArabī 's thought, see Beneito, "Presence."

75 Ibid.

76 Ibid.

77 For a helpful discussion on the element of divine mercy, see Chittick, *Ibn ʿArabī*, 123–44.

78 Ibn ʿArabī, *Al-Futūḥāt al-makkiyya*, cited in Beneito, "Presence," 7.

79 Ibn ʿArabī, *Al-Futūḥāt al-makkiyya*, 2:596.

80 This *ḥadīth qudsī* strongly echoes Matthew 25:34–45 in the Bible.

81 Ibn ʿArabī, *Al-Futūḥāt al-makkiyya*, 2:35.

82 Ibid., 1:708.

83 Legal scholars have based this gender imbalance regarding legal testimony on the Qurʾānic verse 2:282: "O you who believe! When you contract a debt for a fixed term, record it in writing. Let a scribe record it in writing between you in [terms of] equity. . . . But if the debtor is of low understanding, or weak, or unable himself to dictate, then let the guardian of his interests dictate in [terms of] equity. And call to witness, from among your men, two witnesses. And if two men be not [at hand] then a man and two women, of such as ye approve as witnesses, so that if the one errs [through forgetfulness] the other will remind her. And the witnesses must not refuse when they are summoned."

84 Ibn ʿArabī, *Al-Futūḥāt al-makkiyya*, 3:89.

85 For a thorough and incisive analysis of the ways in which some premodern jurists negotiated the gendered component of women's witness and other legal capacities, see Fadel, "Two Women."

86 Ibn ʿArabī, *Al-Futūḥāt al-makkiyya*, 3:89.

87 Hakim, "Ibn ʿArabī's Twofold Perception," 3.

88 Ibn ʿArabī, *Al-Futūḥāt al-makkiyya*, 3:89–90.

89 The verse reads, "For men who surrender unto Allah and women who surrender unto Allah, for believing men and believing women, for devout men and devout women, for truthful men and truthful women, for men and women who are patient and constant, for men and women who are humble, for men and women who give charity, for men and women who fast, for men and women who guard their modesty, for men and women who are God-conscious—for them, Allah hath prepared forgiveness and a great reward" (Q. 33:35).

90 Ibn ʿArabī, *Al-Futūḥāt al-makkiyya*, 3:87.

91 Stowasser, *Women in the Qurʾan*, 77.

92 Ibn ʿArabī, *Al-Futūḥāt al-makkiyya*, 1:408.

93 Ibid., 447.

94 Winkel, *Islam and the Living Law*, vii.

95 Ibid., 23–24.

96 Ibid., 40–41.

97 In *Bidāyat al-mujtahid*, Ibn Rushd, an Andalusian contemporary of Ibn ʿArabī, also presented the view that among the various legal positions on women's

leadership of congregational prayer, there existed one that allowed women to lead mixed congregations.

98 In developing this approach more fully, it is possible to address some of the structural problems of gender in the traditional law, as outlined in Ali, "Progressive Muslims"; Ali, *Sexual Ethics*.

CHAPTER THREE

1 For an example of the ways in which Sufi psychology promotes a persistent state of awareness and vigilance with the self, see the works of Muḥāsibī in Sells, *Early Islamic Mysticism*, 171–95.

2 Longino, "Subjects, Power and Knowledge," 398.

3 Nasr, *Three Muslim Sages*, 100–101.

4 Ibn ʿArabī, *Al-Futūḥāt al-makkiyya*, 4:84.

5 For his biographical entries on these two female spiritual masters, see Ibn ʿArabī, *Sufis of Andalusia*, 142–46.

6 Ibid., 142.

7 Ibid., 143.

8 Ibn ʿArabī, *Al-Futūḥāt al-makkiyya*, 1:274.

9 Ibn ʿArabī, *Sufis of Andalusia*, 26.

10 Ibid., 143.

11 Ibid., 143–45.

12 Ibid., 143.

13 Ibid., 154.

14 Ibid.

15 Ibid., 154–55.

16 Ibid., 155.

17 Ibn ʿArabī, *Dīwān Ibn ʿArabī*, 54. In addition, there are also poems addressed to three unnamed women and two unnamed men in this section. The appendix presents selected translations of these poems.

18 For an informative discussion on the significance of the *khirqa*, see Elias, "Sufi Robe," 275–89.

19 Ibn ʿArabī, *Dīwān Ibn ʿArabī*, 59.

20 Ibid., 54.

21 For a detailed discussion of the relationship between Ibn ʿArabī and Niẓām focusing on the theophanic realities and "sophianic wisdom" that Niẓām symbolizes, see Corbin, *Creative Imagination*, 136–45.

22 Ibn ʿArabī, *Tarjumān al-ashwāq*, 3.

23 Corbin, *Creative Imagination*, 136–38.

24 For precisely this type of depiction of ideal womanhood, see Ghazālī, *Proper Conduct*, 92–95.

25 The challenges of conceptualizing female personhood in ways that integrate embodiment and spirituality continue in the contemporary Muslim world. Coercive social practices that constrain and restrict women's lives, mobility, and behavior are evident in contexts such as Iran, where the state enforces specific

forms of modest dressing on women, and Saudi Arabia, where women are prohibited from driving cars or traveling without the permission of their male guardians. Underlying such practices are problematic patriarchal conceptions of the gendered relationship between spirit and body.

26 Adang, "Women's Access."
27 Ávila, "Women."
28 Ibid., 159.
29 Ibn ʿArabī, *Al-Futūḥāt al-makkiyya*, 2:192.
30 Ibn ʿArabī, *Sufis of Andalusia*, 26.
31 Ibid., 75–76. In *Sufis of Andalusia*, Austin suggests that the ruler at the time must have been Abū Yaʿqub Yūsuf, the Almohad.
32 Addas, *Quest*, 85–86.
33 Ibn ʿArabī, *Rasāʾil*, 374–78.
34 For a full description of this encounter, see Addas, *Quest*, 84–85.
35 Ibid., 86.
36 Ibid.
37 Ibn ʿArabī, *Kitāb muḥadarāt al-abrār*, 2:58.
38 Ibn ʿArabī, *Al-Futūḥāt al-makkiyya*, 4:117, cited in Austin, "Two Poems," 3.
39 Addas, *Quest*, 264.
40 I am indebted to one of my anonymous reviewers for this incisive interpretation of this incident.
41 Austin, "Two Poems."
42 Ibid., 4.
43 See Streng, "Language and Mystical Awareness."

CHAPTER FOUR

1 Kripal, *Kali's Child*, 17.
2 Sells, *Mystical Languages*, 2.
3 Ibid., 12.
4 See also Sells's analysis of the "apophasis of gender" in relation to the works of medieval Christian mystics Meister Eckhart and Marguerite Porete in *Mystical Languages*, 180–205.
5 Keller, "Apophasis," 918.
6 Sells, *Mystical Languages*, 90–115.
7 Ibid., 78.
8 See the chapter on the Prophet Adam in Ibn ʿArabī's *Fuṣūṣ al-ḥikam* for the limitations of angels, as well as the chapters on the Prophets Shuʿayb and Noah for discussions of a heart that is perpetually transforming. Sells provides an erudite and compelling commentary on these concepts as they appear in the *Fuṣūṣ* (*Mystical Languages*, 90–115, 78–81).
9 Keshavarz, "Pregnant with God," 91.
10 For a conceptual discussion of "frontier thinkers," see Moosa, *Ghazālī*, 38–63.
11 Keshavarz, "Pregnant with God," 91.
12 Ibid.

13 Ibid.
14 See Ricoeur, "Interpretation Theory."
15 Thompson, "Paul Ricoeur."
16 Sarup, *Introductory Guide*, 46.
17 Ibid., 33.
18 Ibid.
19 Ibid., 53.
20 Almond, "*Meaning of Infinity*."
21 Ibid., 104–5.
22 Ibid., 102.
23 See, for example, Kristeva, *Desire in Language*.
24 Moi, *Sexual/Textual Politics*, 158.
25 Kripal, *Kali's Child*, 18.
26 Two contemporary writers whose analyses of Ibn ʿArabī's gender constructs embody this assumption are Nasr and Murata (see chapter 7).
27 Moosa, *Contrapuntal Readings*, 3.
28 Ibn ʿArabī, *Al-Futūḥāt al-makkiyya*, 1:507.
29 Ibid., 6:445.
30 Murata, *Tao of Islam*, 9.
31 Ibn ʿArabī, *Al-Futūḥāt al-makkiyya*, 2:167.
32 Ibid., 1:139.
33 Murata, *Tao of Islam*, 147.
34 Ibn ʿArabī, *Al-Futūḥāt al-makkiyya*, 1:139.
35 Ibid. See also Hirtenstein, *Unlimited Mercifier*, 45.
36 Hirtenstein, *Unlimited Mercifier*, 45.
37 Ibn ʿArabī, *Al-Futūḥāt al-makkiyya*, 3:516.
38 Ibid.
39 Cited in Austin, "Feminine Dimensions," 8–9.
40 Ibid., 9.
41 See, for example, Jantzen, *Power, Gender, and Christian Mysticism*, 28; Wolfson, *Language, Eros, and Being*, 58–59.
42 For a detailed argument of this position, see Irigaray, "On Becoming Divine."
43 Cited in Sells, *Mystical Languages*, 100.
44 Ibn ʿArabī, *Al-Futūḥāt al-makkiyya*, 1:138.
45 Ibid., 1:131.
46 Ibid., 2:455.
47 For an example of patriarchal binaries between spirit and body in Greek philosophy and the theology of the early church fathers, see Hein, "Liberating Philosophy."
48 Seyyed Hossein Nasr follows precisely this ideological route in his interpretation of Ibn ʿArabī's views on gender. See Nasr, "Male and Female." See also Moris, "Sufi Perspective."
49 Cited in Hirstenstein, *Unlimited Mercifier*, 41.
50 Ibn ʿArabī, *Tarjumān al-ashwāq*, 139.

51 Ibn ʿArabī, *Bezels*, 55–56.
52 Cited in Izutsu, *Sufism and Taoism*, 231. See also Ibn ʿArabī, *Bezels*, 180.
53 Cited in Murata, *Tao of Islam*, 253. See also Ibn ʿArabī, *Bezels*, 182–84.
54 Izutsu, *Sufism and Taoism*, 231.
55 Ibid., 232.
56 Webb, "Human/Angelic Relation," 80.
57 Ibn ʿArabī, *Tarjumān al-ashwāq*, 126.
58 See Kotzin, "Ancient Greek Philosophy," 15.
59 Carr, *Transforming Grace*, 117.
60 Ibn ʿArabī, *Dīwān Ibn ʿArabī*, 55.
61 Ibid., 54.

CHAPTER FIVE

1 For an interesting array of Jewish and Christian readings of the creation myth and to a more limited extent Muslim interpretations, see Kvam, Schearing, and Ziegler, *Eve and Adam*.
2 Ibid., 9–10.
3 The Qurʾānic creation story is closer to the more universal and gender-inclusive creation narrative in Genesis 1 than to the very distinct gender hierarchies characterizing Genesis 2.
4 In an analysis of the commentary tradition of the Qurʾānic creation story, Jane Smith and Yvonne Haddad write that the ungendered nature of the Qurʾānic narratives is celebrated not only by modern women scholars but also by male scholars who might otherwise adhere to fairly traditional gender norms ("Eve," 143–44).
5 Wadud, *Qurʾan and Woman*, 20.
6 Ibid., 21.
7 See Gross's incisive discussions on the differences between androcentricism and misogyny in *Buddhism after Patriarchy*, 22. She notes that the term "androcentricism" describes a mode of consciousness that consistently defines women in relation to a male-centered scheme of reality, while misogyny suggests a more intense form of "hatred (or fear) of women and femininity." Androcentricism, therefore, does not always imply misogyny.
8 J. Smith and Haddad, "Eve," 136. The same point is made by Hassan, who observes that twenty-one of the twenty-five Qurʾānic references to the Prophet Adam signify the prototypical human rather than the prototypical man ("Muslim Women").
9 Boyarin, *Carnal Israel*, 89.
10 J. Smith and Haddad, "Eve," points to the commentary on the creation narratives by a modern male writer, Ibrāhīm Zakī al-Saʾī, that reflects both traditional hierarchical perspectives on gender relations and a more complex view of the equal character and moral capacity of Adam and Eve, critiquing other traditional views that depict Eve as the source of the human predicament.
11 Hassan's approach reflects one clear case of a contemporary Islamic feminist

who resists the more negative depictions of women in the *ḥadīth* and the commentary tradition by prioritizing the contrasting egalitarian gender perspectives available in the Qurʾān. Similarly, J. Smith and Haddad's discussion of traditional literature on the Adam and Eve myth suggests that the related Qurʾānic narratives are not essentially discriminatory with regard to women, whereas the traditional literature betrays gender biases against women. Wadud's *Qurʾan and Woman* and Barlas's *"Believing Women"* also reflect a foregrounding of the Qurʾān as distinctly more egalitarian than the traditional commentary literature.

12 Ibn Kathīr, *Al-Bidāya wa-nihāya fi-tārīkh*, 80.

13 Ibid.

14 Von Denffer, *ʿUlūm al-Qurʾān*, 133.

15 See J. Smith and Haddad, "Eve," 139.

16 Ibn Kathīr, *Al-Bidāya wa-nihāya fi-tārīkh*, 84.

17 J. Smith and Haddad, "Eve," 140.

18 Bauer, "Room for Interpretation," 64.

19 *Liʿān* refers to the process of mutual oath-swearing that can result in the judicial dissolution of marriage. The husband alleges without legal proof that his wife has committed adultery, and the wife swears under oath to the contrary, ultimately leading to the dissolution of the marriage.

20 Cited in Bauer, "Room for Interpretation," 69. Bauer also notes that Ṭabarī uniquely introduces the notion that the male "degree" over the female is a prescription for a husband's good behavior rather than a description of a husband's rights. Accordingly, men who engage women with generosity and magnanimity then possess a "degree" over them. However, as Bauer demonstrates, Ṭabarī's rather refined and considered view in this instance did not seem to carry much weight with subsequent exegetes, who did not incorporate his view into their commentaries.

21 Ibid., 95.

22 Ibid., 100.

23 Ibid., 102.

24 See, for example, Abou Bakr, "Teaching."

25 I am not suggesting that Ibn ʿArabī was unique in dissenting from the dominant elements of the patriarchy in his context. In other areas of Muslim thought, a handful of male thinkers challenged, albeit ambivalently, one-sided negative views of women. For an analysis of premodern Sunnī legal discourses that expertly demonstrates the tensions and ruptures within dominant gender ideology among medieval jurists in relation to questions of female participation in the law, see Fadel, "Two Women."

26 Ibn ʿArabī, *Al-Futūḥāt al-makkiyya*, 3:87.

27 Ibn ʿArabī, *Fuṣūṣ al-ḥikam*, 216.

28 Ibn ʿArabī, *Al-Futūḥāt al-makkiyya*, 3:87.

29 Ibid., 2:171.

30 Ibid., 1:136.

31 Ibid., 1:124.
32 Ibn ʿArabī, *Fuṣūṣ al-ḥikam*, 210.
33 Ibid.
34 For negative depictions of women and sexuality in other Sufi works, see Cornell "'Soul.'"
35 Ibn ʿArabī, *Fuṣūṣ al-ḥikam*, 216–17.
36 The notion of an androgynous Adam in Ibn ʿArabī's works has been mentioned, albeit not discussed extensively, by a number contemporary scholars. See Chittick, *Essential Seyyed Hossein Nasr*, 182–83; Chodkiewicz, *Ocean without Shore*, 39; Dakake "Walking," 125; Lutfi, "Feminine Element,"13.
37 Ibn ʿArabī, *Al-Futūḥāt al-makkiyya*, 3:314; Chittick, *Sufi Path*, 358–59.
38 Chittick, "Ibn ʿArabī's Own Summary," 35.
39 Chodkiewicz, "Female Sainthood," 15.
40 Ibn ʿArabī, *Al-Futūḥāt al-makkiyya*, 3:87.
41 Hassan, "Muslim Women."
42 The idea of an androgynous first Adam who is subsequently separated into male and female is also reflected in early Christian and Jewish exegetical commentaries on the Genesis narrative. See Boyarin, "Gender." Given Ibn ʿArabī's interreligious discursive context, it is likely that these constructs were familiar to him.
43 Harris, "One Degree," 16.
44 Ibn ʿArabī, *Al-Futūḥāt al-makkiyya*, 3:126.

CHAPTER SIX

1 Ibn ʿArabī, *Fuṣūṣ al-ḥikam*, 219–20.
2 Ibn ʿArabī, *Al-Futūḥāt al-makkiyya*, 3:89.
3 Cited in Murata, *Tao of Islam*, 185.
4 Cited in Murata, *Tao of Islam*, 192. For an incisive analysis of this extract in relation to female agency, see Harris, "One Degree," 29–30.
5 Ibn ʿArabī, *Fuṣūṣ al-ḥikam*, 219; Harris, "One Degree," 29–30; see also Ibn ʿArabī, *Bezels*, 277.
6 Ibn ʿArabī, *Al-Futūḥāt al-makkiyya*, 4:243.
7 Ibid., 3:88.
8 Ibid.
9 Ibid.
10 Ibid.
11 Ibid., 2:466.
12 Ibid., 3:516.
13 Ibid., 2:190.
14 Ibn ʿArabī, *Fuṣūṣ al-ḥikam*, 217.
15 Ibid.
16 Ibn ʿArabī, *Al-Futūḥāt al-makkiyya*, 4:454.
17 Ghazālī, *Proper Conduct*, 29–30.
18 Ghazālī, [*Kitāb kasr al-shahwatayn*], in *On Disciplining*, 171–82.

19 Ibn ʿArabī, *Al-Futūḥāt al-makkiyya*, 2:574. While premodern Muslim thinkers generally recognized the importance of procreation, most premodern legal schools permitted contraception, and a significant number of them permitted abortion before the pregnancy reached 120 days. For related discussions, see Shaikh, "Family Planning."
20 Ibn ʿArabī, *Fuṣūṣ al-ḥikam*, 217.
21 The virgin/whore binary, which finds varying expressions in different societies, represents precisely this kind of irreconcilable split between female sexuality and female spirituality. Such a binary posits the idealized, pure, and nonsexual woman against the fully sexualized, defiled, and promiscuous woman.
22 Qushayrī, *Laṭāif al-ishārāt*, 1:193, cited in Murata, *Tao of Islam*, 177.
23 Murata, *Tao of Islam*, 177.
24 Ibn ʿArabī, *Al-Futūḥāt al-makkiyya*, 3:325.
25 Ibid., 1:124.
26 Ibn ʿArabī, *Fuṣūṣ al-ḥikam*, 273.
27 Cited in Chodkiewicz, *Female Sainthood*, 15.
28 Ibn ʿArabī, *Al-Futūḥāt al-makkiyya*, 1:124.
29 Ibid., 3:87.
30 Ibid., 1:124.
31 For additional discussions of the radically different form and spiritual constitution of Jesus according to Ibn ʿArabī, see Hakim, "Spirit."
32 Ibn ʿArabī, *Al-Futūḥāt al-makkiyya*, 3:182.
33 Ibid., 2:471; Murata, *Tao of Islam*, 180.
34 Ibn ʿArabī, *Al-Futūḥāt al-makkiyya*, 1:136; Murata, *Tao of Islam*, 178.
35 Ibn ʿArabī, *Al-Futūḥāt al-makkiyya*, 4:84; Murata, *Tao of Islam*, 185–86.
36 Ibn ʿArabī, *Al-Futūḥāt al-makkiyya*, 4:84.

CHAPTER SEVEN

1 Nasr, "Male and Female." While this is a fairly short article that draws on Ibn ʿArabī's ideas as well as those of other Sufis, it is particularly useful in encapsulating a powerful trend in broader traditionalist approaches to the gendered nature of spirituality and sociality. In this article, Nasr exemplifies an interpretation of Sufi writings on gender that reinforce hierarchy coupled with a romanticized notion of patriarchal complementarity. The same trend is also reflected in Murad, "Islam, Irigaray, and the Retrieval of Gender"; Moris, "Sufi Perspective."
2 Murata, *Tao of Islam*.
3 Nasr, "Male and Female," 49.
4 Ibid., 54.
5 Ibid., 53.
6 Ibn ʿArabī, *Al-Futūḥāt al-makkiyya*, 2:35.
7 Ibid., 3:380.
8 Harris, "Reading the Signs," 188.
9 Nasr was a proponent of the Pahlavi regime and opposed the revolutionaries,

but their imposition of strict gender laws arguably reflects some of the harsh practical realities that could be derived from Nasr's rather romanticized gender vision.

10 For a full picture of Murata's other very nuanced views on gender, see *Tao of Islam*.

11 Ibid., 321.

12 Ibid., 79.

13 Ibid., 324.

14 Ibid., 174.

15 Ibid., 10.

16 Ibid., 208.

17 Ibid., 79.

18 Ibid., 322.

19 Ibid., 324.

20 In 2002, the legal trial of a Nigerian Muslim woman, Amina Lawal, came to international prominence. A divorced woman who had conceived a child out of wedlock, Lawal was initially prosecuted on the charge of adultery, which carried the penalty of being stoned to death if found guilty. However, the man that she named as the father of the child was relieved of any accountability after simply denying paternity. The decision was subsequently overturned in the *Sharīʿa* appeal court partly on the basis that traditional Mālikī law allows for a period of five years between conception and birth and that Lawal had been married five years prior to the birth of her child.

21 See, for example, Mir-Hosseini, *Islam and Gender*; Hibri, "Islamic Law."

22 Silvers, "Good, the Bad, and the Ugly," 2.

23 For a detailed and extensive discussion of both Nasr and Corbin's intellectual genealogy, see Wasserstrom, *Religion after Religion*.

24 Silvers, "Good, the Bad, and the Ugly," 4.

25 Chittick, *Essential Seyyed Hossein Nasr*, 183.

26 Ibid., 184.

27 Ibid., 185.

28 See, for example, Quraishi, "Her Honor."

29 See, for example, Sonbol, *Women, the Family, and Divorce Laws*.

30 See, for example, Hibri, "Introduction."

31 Ali lucidly makes this case in her analysis of contemporary "feminist-apologist" approaches to Islamic law, "Progressive Muslims."

32 An example of such politically charged implementation of *Sharīʿa* law happened in northern Nigeria in 2000.

33 For the problematic nature of premodern legal formulations of gender, see especially Ali, *Sexual Ethics*.

34 For a detailed discussion of these debates in the modern world, see Sirriyeh, *Sufis and Anti-Sufis*.

35 Murad, "Boys Will Be Boys," 1, also refers to Greer in highlighting some of the current crises of gender. While I share some of his views regarding the types of

current gendered dilemmas and the need to engage these problems at a deeper level, my approach clearly embraces a very different analytical and ideological lens to imagine alternatives based in Sufism. Murad, like Nasr and Murata, interprets Sufism to argue for gender complementarity and essentialism in ways that justify traditional patriarchal social structures. In this regard, see also Murad, "Islam, Irigaray and the Retrieval of Gender."

36 Greer, *Whole Woman*, 23–38, 181–201.

37 Jantzen, *Power, Gender, and Christian Mysticism*, 21.

38 Ibid.

39 Sells, *Mystical Languages*, 93.

APPENDIX

1 The sudden shift from second- to third-person pronoun while referring to the same subject is a common rhetorical technique known in Arabic poetry as *iltifāt*.

Bibliography

Abou Bakr, Oumaima. "Teaching the Words of the Prophet: Women Instructors of the Hadith (Fourteenth and Fifteenth Centuries)." *Hawwa: Journal of Women of the Middle East and the Islamic World* 1, no. 3 (2003): 306–28.

Abu-Lughod, Lila. "Feminist Longings and Postcolonial Conditions." In *Remaking Women: Feminism and Modernity in the Middle East*, edited by Lila Abu-Lughod, 3–34. Princeton: Princeton University Press, 1998.

Adang, Camilla. "Women's Access to Public Space According to *Al-Muḥallā bil-āthār*." In *Writing the Feminine: Women in Arab Sources*, edited by M. Marin and R. Deguilhem, 75–94. London: I. B. Tauris, 2002.

Addas, Claude. *Quest for the Red Sulphur: The Life of Ibn ʿArabi*. Cambridge: Islamic Texts Society, 1993.

Ahmed, Leila. *Women and Gender in Islam*. New Haven: Yale University Press, 1992.

Ali, Kecia. "Progressive Muslims and Islamic Jurisprudence: The Necessity for Critical Engagement with Marriage and Divorce Law." In *Progressive Muslims: On Justice, Gender, and Pluralism*, edited by Omid Safi, 163–89. Oxford: Oneworld, 2003.

———. *Sexual Ethics in Islam: Feminist Reflections on Qurʾan, Hadith, and Jurisprudence*. Oxford: Oneworld, 2006.

Almond, Ian. "The Meaning of Infinity in Sufi and Deconstructive Hermeneutics: When Is an Empty Text an Infinite One?" *Journal of the American Academy of Religion* 72, no. 1 (2004): 97–117.

———. "The Shackles of Reason: Sufi/Deconstructive Opposition to Rational Thought." *Philosophy East and West* 53, no. 1 (2003): 22–38.

Andrae, Tor. *In the Garden of Myrtles: Studies in Early Islamic Mysticism*. Albany: State University of New York Press, 1987.

Arberry, Arthur John. *Sufism: An Account of the Mystics of Islam*. Mineola, NY: Dover, 2002.

Al-ʿAsqalānī, Aḥmad b. ʿAlī b. Hajar. *Al-Durar Al-kāmina fī aʿyān al-mia al-thāmina*. Vol. 3. Beirut: Dār al-Jīl, 1993.

ʿAṭṭār, Farīd al-Dīn. *Muslim Saints and Mystics: Episodes from the Tadhkhirat al-awliyāʿ (Memorial of the Saints)*. Translated by A. J. Arberry. London: Routledge and Kegan Paul, 1966.

Austin, Ralph. "The Feminine Dimensions of Ibn ʿArabī's Thought." *Journal of the Muhyiddin Ibn ʿArabī Society* 2 (1984): 5–14.

———. "Two Poems from the Diwan of Ibn ʿArabī." *Journal of the Muhyiddin Ibn ʿArabī Society* 7 (1988): 1–16.

Ávila, María Luisa. "Women in Andalusi Biographical Sources." In *Writing the Feminine: Women in Arab Sources*, edited by M. Marin and R. Deguilhem, 149–63. London: I. B. Tauris, 2002.

Baldick, Julian. *Mystical Islam: An Introduction to Sufism*. New York: New York University Press, 1989.

Barlas, Asma. *"Believing Women" in Islam: Unreading Patriarchal Interpretations of the Qurʾan*. Austin: University of Texas Press, 2002.

Bauer, Karen. "Room for Interpretation: Quranic Exegesis and Gender." Ph.D. diss., Princeton University, 2008.

Bellamy, James A, "Sex and Society in Islamic Popular Literature." In *Literary Heritage of Classical Islam: Arabic and Islamic Studies in Honor of James A. Bellamy*, edited by M. Mir, and J. E. Fossum, 23–42. Princeton, NJ: Darwin, 1993.

Beneito, Pablo. "The Presence of Superlative Compassion." *Journal of the Muhyiddin Ibn ʿArabī Society* 24 (1998): 53–82.

Bhabha, Homi K. "Unsatisfied: Notes on Vernacular Cosmopolitanism." In *Text and Nation: Cross-Disciplinary Essays on Cultural and National Identities*, edited by L. Garcia-Moreno and P. C. Pfeiffer, 191–207. Columbia, SC: Camden House, 1996.

Boyarin, Daniel. *Carnal Israel: Reading Sex in Talmudic Culture*. Berkeley: University of California Press, 1993.

———. "Gender." In *Critical Terms for Religious Studies*, edited by Mark C. Taylor, 117–35. Chicago: University of Chicago Press, 1998.

———. *Unheroic Conduct: The Rise of Heterosexuality and the Invention of the Jewish Man*. Berkeley: University of California Press, 1997.

Al-Bukhārī, Muḥammad ibn Ismaʿīl. *Saḥīḥ al-Bukhārī*. Translated by Muhammad Muhsin Khan. Ankara: Hilal Yaginlari, 1979.

Caraway, Nancy. *Segregated Sisterhood*. Knoxville: University of Tennessee Press, 1991.

Carr, Anne. *Transforming Grace: Christian Tradition and Women's Experiences*. San Francisco: Harper and Row, 1988.

Chittick, William C., ed. *The Essential Seyyed Hossein Nasr*. Bloomington, IN: World Wisdom, 2007.

———. *Ibn ʿArabī: Heir to the Prophets*. Oxford: Oneworld, 2007.

———. "Ibn ʿArabi's Own Summary of the *Fuṣūṣ*: The Imprint of the Bezels of the Wisdom." *Journal of the Muhyiddin Ibn ʿArabi Society* 1 (1982): 30–93.

———. *Imaginal Worlds: Ibn ʿArabī and the Problem of Religious Diversity*. Albany: State University of New York Press, 1994.

———. *The Sufi Path of Knowledge: Ibn Al-ʿArabī's Metaphysics of Imagination*. Albany: State University of New York Press, 1989.

———. "The Way of the Sufi." *Sufi: A Journal of Sufism* 14 (Summer 1992): 5–10.

Chodkiewicz, Michel. "Female Sainthood in Islam." *Sufi: A Journal of Sufism* 21 (1994): 12–19.

——. *An Ocean without Shore: Ibn ʿArabi, the Book, and the Law*. Translated by David Streight. Cambridge: Islamic Texts Society, 1993.
——. "Le Proces Posthume d'Ibn ʿArabī." In *Islamic Mysticism Contested: Thirteen Centuries of Controversies and Polemics*, edited by Frederick De Jong and Bernd Radtke, 93–123. Leiden: Brill, 1999.
Clark, Elizabeth A. "The Lady Vanishes: Dilemmas of a Feminist Historian after the 'Linguistic Turn.'" *Church History* 67, no. 1 (1998): 1–31.
Coates, Peter. *Ibn ʿArabī and Modern Thought*. Oxford: Anqa, 2002.
Cooke, Miriam. *Women Claim Islam: Creating Islamic Feminism through Literature*. New York: Routledge, 2001.
Corbin, Henry. *Creative Imagination in the Sufism of Ibn ʿArabī*. Princeton: Princeton University Press, 1969.
Cornell, Rkia. "'Soul of a Woman Was Created Below': Woman as the Lower Soul (*Nafs*) in Islam." In *World Religions and Evil: Religious and Philosophical Perspectives*, edited by Hendrik M. Vroom, 257–80. New York: Rodopi, 2007.
Culler, Jonathan. *The Pursuit of Signs: Semiotics, Literature, Deconstruction*. London: Routledge and Kegan Paul, 1981.
Cutrufelli, Maria. *Women of Africa: Roots of Oppression*. London: Zed, 1984.
Dakake, Maria Massi. "'Guest of the Inmost Heart': Conceptions of the Divine Beloved among Early Sufi Women." *Comparative Islamic Studies* 3, no. 1 (2007): 72–97.
——. "'Walking upon the Path of God Like Men'?: Women and the Feminine in the Islamic Mystical Tradition." *Sophia: The Journal of Traditional Studies* 8, no. 2 (2002): 117–38.
De Jong, Frederick, and Bernd Radtke, eds. *Islamic Mysticism Contested: Thirteen Centuries of Controversies and Polemics*. Leiden: Brill, 1999.
Elias, Jamal. "Female and the Feminine in Islamic Mysticism." *Muslim World* 78 (1988): 209–24.
——. "The Sufi Robe (Khirqa) as a Vehicle of Spiritual Authority." In *Robes and Honor: The Medieval World of Investiture*, edited by Stewart Gordon 275–89. New York: Palgrave, 2001.
Ernst, Carl. "Between Orientalism and Fundamentalism: Problematizing the Teaching of Sufism." In *Teaching Islam*, edited by Brannon Wheeler, 108–23. New York: Oxford University Press, 2003.
——. "Mystical Language and the Teaching Context in the Early Lexicons of Sufism." In *Mysticism and Language*, edited by Steven Katz, 181–201. New York: Oxford University Press, 1992.
——. *The Shambhala Guide to Sufism*. Boston: Shambhala, 1997.
Esack, Farid. "In Search of Progressive Islam Beyond 9/11." In *Progressive Muslims*, edited by Omid Safi, 82–93. Oxford: Oneworld, 2003.
Fadel, Mohammad. "Two Women, One Man: Knowledge, Power, and Gender in Medieval Sunni Legal Thought." *International Journal of Middle East Studies* 29, no. 2 (1997): 185–204.

Fakhry, Majid. *A History of Islamic Philosophy*. New York: Columbia University Press, 1983.
Fiorenza, Elizabeth Schussler. *Bread Not Stone: The Challenge of Feminist Biblical Interpretation*. Boston: Beacon, 1995.
Fletcher, Richard. *Moorish Spain*. Berkeley: University of California Press, 2006.
Al-Ghazālī, Abū Ḥāmid. *Ihyā ʿulūm al-dīn*. Cairo: Matbaʿat al-ʿAmīrat al-Sharafiyya, 1909.
——. *On Disciplining the Soul (Kitāb riyāḍat al-nafs) & on Breaking the Two Desires (Kitāb kasr al-shahwatayn)*. Translated by Timothy Winters. Cambridge: Islamic Texts Society, 1995.
——. *The Proper Conduct of Marriage in Islam (Adab al-nikāḥ)*. Translated by Mukhtar Holland. Fort Lauderdale, FL : Al-Baz, 1998.
Goldziher, Ignaz. *Introduction to Islamic Theology and Law*. Princeton: Princeton University Press, 1981.
Gottlieb, Lynn. *She Who Dwells Within: Feminist Vision of a Renewed Judaism*. San Francisco: HarperOne, 1995.
Gracia, Jorge. *Metaphysics and Its Tasks: The Search for the Categorical Foundation of Knowledge*. Albany: State University of New York Press, 1999.
Greer, Germaine. *The Whole Woman*. New York: Random House, 1999.
Gross, Rita. *Buddhism after Patriarchy*. Albany: State University of New York Press, 1993.
Al-Hakim, Souad. "Ibn ʿArabī's Twofold Perception of Woman: Woman as Human Being and Cosmic Principle." *Journal of the Muhyiddin Ibn ʿArabī Society* 39 (2006): 1–13.
——. "The Spirit and the Son of the Spirit: A Reading of Jesus According to Ibn Arabi." *Journal of the Muhyiddin Ibn ʿArabi Society* 31 (2002): 1–29.
Hambly, Gavin, ed. *Women in the Medieval Islamic World: Power, Patronage and Piety*. New York: St. Martin, 1998.
Hanisch, Carol. "The Personal Is Political." In *Notes from the Second Year: Women's Liberation*, edited by Shulamith Firestone and Ann Koedt, 76–78. New York: New York Radical Feminists, 1970.
Harris, Rabia Terri. "One Degree: The Bezel of Muhammad and the Gender Dilemma." Paper presented at the Ibn ʿArabī Society Symposium, New York, 1992.
——. "Reading the Signs." In *Windows of Faith: Muslim Women Scholar-Activists in North America*, edited by Gisela Webb, 172–94. Syracuse: Syracuse University Press, 2000.
Hashmi, Irfana. "The Women of the Medieval Minbar." Paper presented at the international meeting of the American Academy of Religion, Washington, DC, 2006.
Hassan, Riffat. "An Islamic Perspective." In *Women, Religion and Sexuality*, edited by Jeanne Becher, 93–128. Philadelphia: WCC, 1990.
——. "Muslim Women and Post-Patriarchal Islam." In *After Patriarchy: Feminist Transformations of the World Religions*, edited by Paula Cooey, William R. Eakin, and Jay B. McDaniel, 39–64. New York: Orbis, 1991.

Hein, Hilde. "Liberating Philosophy: An End to the Dichotomy of Spirit and Matter." In *Women, Knowledge, and Reality: Explorations in Feminist Philosophy*, edited by Anne Gary and Marilyn Pearsall, 437–53. London: Routledge, 1996.
Al-Hibri, Azizah. "Introduction to Muslim Women's Rights." In *Windows of Faith*, edited by Gisela Webb, 51–71. Syracuse: Syracuse University Press, 2000.
——. "Islamic Law." In *A Companion to Feminist Philosophy*, edited by Alison M. Jaggar and Iris M. Young, 541–49. Cambridge, MA: Blackwell, 1998.
——, ed. *Women and Islam*. Oxford: Pergamon, 1982.
Hirtenstein, Stephen. *The Unlimited Mercifier: The Spiritual Life and Thought of Ibn ʿArabi*. Oxford: Anqa and Ashland, OR: White Cloud, 1999.
Hitti, Phillip. *History of the Arabs*. London: Macmillan, 1940.
Hoel, Nina, and Saʾdiyya Shaikh. "Veiling, Secularism, and Islamism: Gender Constructions in France and Iran." *Journal for the Study of Religion* 20, no. 1 (2007): 111–29.
Homerin, Th. Emil. "Ibn Arabi in the People's Assembly: Religion, Press, and Politics in Sadat's Egypt." *Middle East Journal* 40, no. 3 (1986): 462–77.
——. "Writing Sufi Biography: The Case of ʿAʾisha Al-Baʿuniyah (D. 922/1517)." *Muslim World* 96, no. 3 (2006): 389–99.
Al-Ḥujwīrī, ʿAlī bin ʿUthmān. *The Kashf al-maḥjūb: The Oldest Persian Treatise on Sufism*. Translated by R. A. Nicholson. Reprint, London: Luzac/Gibb, 1976 (New Edition, 1936).
Ibn ʿArabī, Muḥyī al-Dīn. *The Bezels of Wisdom*. Translated by R. W. J. Austin. New York: Paulist, 1980.
——. *Dīwān Ibn ʿArabī*. Cairo: Būlūq, 1855.
——. *Fuṣūṣ al-ḥikam*. Beirut: Dār al-Kutub al-ʿArabī, 1946.
——. *Al-Futūḥāt al-makkiyya*. Cairo: N.p., 1911.
——. *Kitāb muḥadarāt al-abrār wa musāmarat al-akhyār.* Damascus: Dār al-Yaqazah al-ʿArabiyya, 1968.
——. *The Meccan Illuminations: Selected Texts*. Translated by William C. Chittick, Michel Chodkiewicz, Cyrille Chodkiewicz, Denis Gril, and James W. Morris. Paris: Sindbad, 1989.
——. *Rasāʾil Ibn al-ʿArabī.* Beirut: Dār Ṣādir, 1997.
——. *Sufis of Andalusia: The Rūḥ al-quds and Al-Durrat al-fākhira*. Translated by R. W. J. Austin. Roxburgh: Beshara, 1988.
——. *Tarjumān al-ashwāq*. Translated by R. Nicholson. London: Theosophical Publishing House, 1911.
Ibn Kathīr, Ismaʾīl ibn ʿUmar. *Al-Bidāya wa-nihāya fī-tārīkh*. Edited by Muḥammad ʿAbd al-ʿAzīz al-Najjār. Vol. 1. Cairo: Matbaʿat al-Saʿada, 1932.
Ibn Rushd, Abū al-Walīd Muḥammad. *Bidāyat al-mujtahid wa-nihāyat al-muqtasid*. Cairo: Dār al-Kutub al-Islāmyya, 1983.
Irigaray, Luce. "On Becoming Divine." In *Women, Knowledge, and Reality: Explorations in Feminist Philosophy*, edited by Anne Gary and Marilyn Pearsall, 471–84. London: Routledge, 1996.

Al-Iskandarī, Ibn ʿAṭāʾ Allāh. *The Book of Illumination (Kitāb al-tanwīr fī isqāt al-tadbīr).* Translated by Scott Kugle. Louisville, KY: Fons Vitae, 2005.
Izutsu, Toshihiko. *Sufism and Taoism: A Comparative Study of Key Philosophical Concepts.* Berkeley: University of California Press, 1983.
James, William. *The Varieties of Religious Experience.* Glasgow: Collins Fount, 1960.
Jantzen, Grace M. *Power, Gender, and Christian Mysticism.* Cambridge: Cambridge University Press, 1995.
Jones, Serene, and Paul Lakeland, eds. *Constructive Theology: A Contemporary Engagement with Classical Themes.* Minneapolis: Fortress, 2005.
Kahf, Mohja. "Braiding the Stories: Women's Eloquence in the Early Islamic Era." In *Windows of Faith: Muslim Women Scholar-Activists in North America*, edited by Gisela Webb, 147–71. Syracuse: Syracuse University Press, 2000.
Karam, Azza M. *Women, Islamisms, and the State: Contemporary Feminisms in Egypt.* New York: St. Martin, 1998.
Karamustafa, Ahmet T. *Sufism: The Formative Period.* Edinburgh: University of Edinburgh Press, 2007.
Katz, Steven. "Language, Epistemology, and Mysticism." In *Mysticism and Philosophical Analysis*, edited by Steven Katz, 22–74. New York: Oxford University Press, 1978.
Kaufman, Gordon. *In Face of Mystery: A Constructive Theology.* Cambridge: Harvard University Press, 1995.
Keller, Catherine. "The Apophasis of Gender : A Fourfold Unsaying of Feminist Theology." *Journal of the American Academy of Religion* 76, no. 4 (2008): 905–33.
Keshavarz, Fatemeh. "Pregnant with God: The Poetic Art of Mothering the Sacred in Rumi's Fihi Ma Fih." *Comparative Studies of South Asia, Africa, and the Middle East* 22 (2002): 90–99.
Knysh, Alexander D. *Ibn ʿArabi in the Later Islamic Tradition: The Making of a Polemical Image in Medieval Islam.* Albany: State University of New York Press, 1999.
Kotzin, Rhoda Haddassah. "Ancient Greek Philosophy." In *A Companion to Feminist Philosophy*, edited by Alison Jaggar and Iris Young, 9–20. Malden, MA: Blackwell, 1988.
Kripal, Jeffrey John. *Kali's Child: The Mystical and the Erotic in the Life and Teachings of Ramakrishna.* Chicago: University of Chicago Press, 1995.
Kristeva, Julia. *Desire in Language: A Semiotic Approach to Literature and Art.* Edited by Leon Roudiez. New York: Columbia University Press, 1980.
Kugle, Scott. *Rebel between Spirit and Law: Ahmad Zarrūq, Sainthood, and Authority in Islam.* Bloomington: Indiana University Press, 2006.
Kvam, Kirsten E., Linda S. Schearing, and Valarie H. Ziegler, eds. *Eve and Adam: Jewish, Christian, and Muslim Readings on Genesis and Gender.* Bloomington: Indiana University Press, 1999.
Landau, Rom. *The Philosophy of Ibn ʿArabī.* London: Allen and Unwin, 1959.
Lapidus, Ira. *A History of Islamic Societies.* Cambridge: Cambridge University Press, 1988.
Longino, Helen E. "Subjects, Power, and Knowledge: Description and Prescription

in Feminist Philosophies of Science." In *Feminist Epistemologies*, edited by Linda Alcoff and Elizabeth Potter, 101–20. London: Routledge, 1993.
Lutfi, Huda. "The Feminine Element in Ibn ʿArabī's Mystical Philosophy." *Alif: Journal of Comparative Poetics* 5 (1985): 7–19.
Al-Makkī, Abū Ṭālib. *Qut al-qulūb fī- muʿāmalāt al-maḥbūb wa-waṣf ṭarīq al-murīd ilā maqām al-tawḥīd*. Beirut: Dār al-Kutub al-ʿIlmiyyah, 1997.
Malamud, Margaret. "Gender and Spiritual Self-Fashioning: The Master-Disciple Relationship in Classical Sufism." *Journal of the American Academy of Religion* 64, no. 1 (1996): 89–117.
Mamdani, Mahmoud. *Good Muslim, Bad Muslim: America, the Cold War, and the Roots of Terror*. New York: Pantheon, 2004.
Al-Maqrīzī, Aḥmad ibn ʿAlī. *Al-Mawāʿiz wa al-ʿiʿtibār bi dhikr al-khitat wa al-ʿathār*. Vol. 3. Cairo: Maktabat Madbuli, 1998.
Massignon, Louis. *Essay on the Origins of the Technical Language of Islamic Mysticism*. Notre Dame, IN: University of Notre Dame Press, 1997.
Mernissi, Fatima. *The Forgotten Queens of Islam*. Minneapolis: University of Minnesota Press, 1993.
——. *The Veil and the Male Elite: A Feminist Interpretation of Women's Rights in Islam*. Reading, MA: Addison Wesley, 1991.
Mir-Hosseini, Ziba. "The Construction of Gender in Islamic Legal Thought and Strategies for Reform," *Hawwa: Journal of Women of the Middle East and the Islamic World* 1, no. 1 (2003): 1–28.
——. *Islam and Gender: The Religious Debate in Contemporary Iran*. Princeton: Princeton University Press, 1999.
——. "Muslim Women's Quest for Equality: Between Islamic Law and Feminism." *Critical Inquiry* 32 (2006): 629–45.
Moghissi, Haideh. *Feminism and Islamic Fundamentalism: The Limits of Postmodern Analysis*. London: Zed, 1999.
Mohanty, Chandra Talpade, Ann Russo, and Lourdes Torres, eds. *Third World Women and the Politics of Feminism*. Bloomington: Indiana University Press, 1991.
Moi, Toril. *Sexual/Textual Politics*. London: Routledge, 1985.
Mojaddedi, Jawid A. *The Biographical Tradition in Sufism*. Richmond: Curzon, 2001.
Moosa, Ebrahim. "Contrapuntal Readings in Muslim Thought: Translations and Transitions." *Journal of the American Academy of Religion* 74, no. 1 (2006): 107–18.
——. *Ghazālī and the Poetics of Imagination*. Chapel Hill: University of North Carolina Press, 2005.
Moraga, Cherríe, and Gloria Anzaldúa. *This Bridge Called My Back: Writings by Radical Women of Color*. Watertown, MA: Persephone, 1981.
Moris, Zailan. "The Sufi Perspective on the Feminine State." *Islamic Quarterly* no. 36 (1992): 46–57.
Morris, James Winston. *Orientations: Islamic Thought in a World Civilisation*. Cambridge: Archetype, 2004.
Murad, Abdal Hakim. "Boys Will Be Boys." 2001. http://www.masud.co.uk/ISLAM/ahm/boys.htm. 29 December 2009.

——. "Islam, Irigaray, and the Retrieval of Gender." 1999. http//www.iol.ie/~afifi/Articles/gender.htm. 29 December 2009.
Murata, Sachiko. *The Tao of Islam: A Sourcebook on Gender Relationships in Islamic Thought*. Albany: State University of New York Press, 1992.
Nasr, Seyyed Hossein. *An Introduction to Islamic Cosmological Doctrines*. Albany: State University of New York Press, 1993.
——. "The Male and Female in Islamic Perspective." In *Traditional Islam in the Modern World*, 47–58. London: KPI, 1987.
——. *Three Muslim Sages: Avicenna, Suhrawardī, Ibn ʿArabī*. Delmar, NY: Caravan, 1976.
Nicholson, Reynold A. *The Mystics of Islam*. London: Routledge and Kegan Paul, 1962.
——. *Rumi: Poet and Mystic*. London: Allen, 1950.
Nurbakhsh, Javad. *Sufi Women*. London: Khaniqahi-Nimatullahi, 1990.
O'Fahey, R. S., and Bernd Radtke. "Neo-Sufism Reconsidered." *Der Islam* 70 (1993): 52–87.
Özdalga, Elisabeth. *Naqshbandis in Western and Central Asia*. Richmond: Curzon, 1999.
Pateman, C. *The Sexual Contract*. Cambridge: Polity, 1988.
Peskes, Esther. "The Wahhabiyya and Sufism in the Eighteenth Century." In *Islamic Mysticism Contested: Thirteen Centuries of Controversies and Polemics*, edited by Frederick De Jong and Bernd Radtke, 145–61. Leiden: Brill, 1999.
Quraishi, Asifa. "Her Honor: An Islamic Critique of the Rape Laws of Pakistan from a Woman-Sensitive Perspective." In *Windows of Faith*, edited by Gisela Webb, 102–35. Syracuse: Syracuse University Press, 2000.
Al-Qushayrī, Abuʾl Qāsim. *Sufi Book of Spiritual Ascent (Al-Risāla al-Qushayrī)*. Translated by Rabia Terri Harris. Chicago: ABC, 1997.
Reed, Edward S. *From Soul to Mind: The Emergence of Psychology, from Erasmus Darwin to William James*. New Haven: Yale University Press, 1998.
Ricoeur, Paul. *Interpretation Theory: Discourses and the Surplus of Meaning*. Fort Worth: Texas Christian University Press, 1976.
Roded, Ruth. *Women in the Islamic Biographical Collections: From Ibn Saʿd to Who's Who*. Boulder, CO: Rienner, 1994.
Rohde, Erwin. *Psyche: The Cult of Souls and the Belief in Immortality among the Greeks*. London: Routledge and Kegan Paul, 1925.
Rosenthal, Franz. "Ibn ʿArabī between 'Philosophy' and 'Mysticism': 'Sūfism and Philosophy Are Neighbors and Visit Each Other.'" *Oriens* 31 (1988): 1–35.
Ruether, Rosemary R. *New Woman, New Earth: Sexist Ideologies and Human Liberation*. New York: Seabury, 1975.
——. *Sexism and Godtalk*. Boston: Beacon, 1983.
Russo, Ann. "We Cannot Live without Our Lives: White Women, Antiracism, and Feminism." In *Third World Women and the Politics of Feminism*, edited by Chandra Talpade Mohanty, Ann Russo, and Lourdes Torres, 297–313. Bloomington: Indiana University Press, 1991.
Al-Safadī, Khalīl ibn Aybak. *Aʿyān al-ʿasr wa-aʿwān al-naṣr*. 6 vols. Beirut: Dār al-Fikr al-Muʿasir, 1998.

Said, Edward. *Freud and the Non-European*. London: Verso, 2003.
Sakenfield, Katherine. "Feminist Uses of Biblical Materials." In *Feminist Interpretations of the Bible*, edited by Letty Russell, 55–64. Philadelphia: Westminster, 1989.
Al-Sarrāj, Abū Naṣr. *Kitāb al-luma fī taṣawwuf*. London: Gibb, 1914.
Sarup, Madan. *Introductory Guide to Poststructuralism and Postmodernism*. Athens: University of Georgia Press, 1989.
Sayyid-Marsot, Afaf Lutfi. *Society and the Sexes in Medieval Islam*. Malibu, CA: Undena, 1979.
Schimmel, Annemarie. "Eros in Sufi Literature and Life." In *Society and the Sexes in Medieval Islam*, edited by Sayyid-Marsot Afaf Lutfi, 119–41. Malibu, CA: Undena, 1977.
———. *My Soul Is a Woman: The Feminine in Islam*. New York: Continuum, 1997.
———. *Mystical Dimensions of Islam*. Chapel Hill: University of North Carolina Press, 1975.
Sells, Michael Anthony. *Approaching the Qur'an*. Ashland, OR: White Cloud, 1999.
———. *Early Islamic Mysticism: Sufi, Qurʿan, Miʿrāj, Poetic and Theological Writings*. New York: Paulist, 1996.
———. *Mystical Languages of Unsaying*. Chicago: University of Chicago Press, 1994.
Shaikh, Sa'diyya. "Family Planning, Contraception and Abortion in Islam." In *Sacred Rights: The Case for Contraception and Abortion in World Religions*, edited by Daniel C. Maguire, 105–28. New York: Oxford University Press, 2003.
———. "In Search of *Al-Insān*: Sufism, Islamic Law, and Gender." *Journal of the American Academy of Religion* 77, no. 4 (2009): 781–822.
———. "Knowledge, Women, and Gender in the Hadīth." *Islam and Christian-Muslim Relations* 15, no. 1 (2004): 99–108.
———. "Transforming Feminisms: Islam, Women, and Gender Justice." In *Progressive Muslims: On Gender, Justice and Pluralism*, edited by Omid Safi, 147–61. Oxford: Oneworld, 2003.
Silvers, Laury. "The Good, the Bad, and the Ugly of 'Creative Imagination': Constructivism, Neo-Traditionalism, and Neo-Romanticism in North American Islamic Intellectual History." Paper presented at Breaking apart the Monolith: The Many Ways of Being Muslim Conference, Princeton University, 2007.
———. "'In the Book We Have Left Out Nothing': The Ethical Problem of the Existence of Verse 4:34 in the Qur'an." *Comparative Islamic Studies* 2, no. 2 (2006): 171–80.
———. "Representations: Sufi Literature." In *Encyclopedia of Women and Islamic Cultures*, 5:535–40. Leiden: Brill, 2007.
———. "Representations: Sufi Women, Early Period, Seventh–Tenth Centuries." In *Encyclopedia of Women and Islamic Cultures*, 5:541–43. Leiden: Brill, 2007.
———. "Statistical Analysis, Comparison, and Close Readings: Getting at the Data on Early Pious and Sufi Women." Paper presented at the international meeting of the American Academy of Religion, Philadelphia, 2005.
Sirriyeh, Elizabeth. *Sufis and Anti-Sufis: The Defence, Rethinking, and Rejection of Sufism in the Modern World*. London: Curzon, 2003.

Smith, Jane, and Yvonne Haddad. "Eve: Islamic Image of Woman." *Women's Studies International Forum* 5, no. 2 (1982): 135–44.
Smith, Margaret. *Rābiʿa the Mystic and Her Fellow Saints in Islam*. London: Cambridge University Press, 1928.
Sonbol, Amira El-Azhary, ed. *Beyond the Exotic: Women's Histories in Islamic Societies*. Syracuse: Syracuse University Press, 2005.
——. *Women, the Family, and Divorce Laws in Islamic History*. Syracuse: Syracuse University Press, 1996.
Spelman, Elizabeth V. *Inessential Woman: Problems of Exclusion in Feminist Thought*. Boston: Beacon, 1988.
Spivak, Gayatri Chakravorty. "French Feminism in an International Frame." *Yale French Studies* 62 (1981): 154–84.
Stelzer, Steffen. "Decisive Meetings: Ibn Rushd, Ibn ʿArabī, and the Matter of Knowledge." *Alif: Journal of Comparative Poetics* 16 (1996): 19–55.
Stoddart, William, and Reynold Nicholson. *Sufism: The Mystical Doctrines and the Idea of Personality*. Delhi: Adam, 1998.
Stowasser, Barbara F. *Women in the Qurʾan, Traditions, and Interpretation*. New York: Oxford University Press, 1994.
——. "Religious Ideology, Women and the Family: The Islamic Paradigm." In *The Islamic Impulse*, edited by Barbara Freyer Stowasser, 262–96. Washington, DC: Center for Contemporary Arab Studies, Georgetown University, 1987.
Streng, Frederick. "Language and Mystical Awareness." In *Mysticism and Philosophical Analysis*, edited by Steven Katz, 141–69. London: Sheldon, 1978.
Al-Sulamī, Abū ʿAbd al-Raḥmān. *Early Sufi Women (Dhikr al-niswa al-muta ʿabbidāt al-ṣūfiyyāt)*. Translated by Rkia Cornell. Louisville, KY: Fons Vitae, 1999.
Thompson, John B. "Paul Ricoeur." In *Routledge Encyclopedia of Philosophy*, edited by E. Craig. London: Routledge, 1988. http://www.rep.routledge.com. Accessed 13 June 2011.
Tlili, Sarra. "Women in Ibn ʿArabī's Life and Work." Unpublished paper. University of Pennsylvania, 1999.
Trimingham, John Spencer. *The Sufi Orders in Islam*. Oxford: Clarendon, 1971.
Tucker, Judith. "Gender and Islamic History." In *Islamic and European Expansion*, edited by Michael Adas, 37–75. Philadelphia: Temple University Press, 1994.
Urvoy, Dominique. *Averroes*. New York: Routledge, 1991.
Von Denffer, Ahmad. *ʿUlūm al-Qurʾān: An Introduction to the Sciences of the Qurʾān*. Leicester: Islamic Foundation, 1989.
Wadud, Amina. *Inside the Gender Jihad: Women's Reform in Islam*. Oxford: Oneworld, 2006.
——. *Qurʾan and Woman: Rereading the Sacred Text from a Woman's Perspective*. New York: Oxford University Press, 1999.
Walther, Wiebke. *Women in Islam: From Medieval to Modern Times*. Princeton, NJ: Wiener, 1993.
Wasserstrom, Steven M. *Religion after Religion: Gershom Scholem, Mircea Eliade, and Henry Corbin at Eranos*. Princeton: Princeton University Press, 1999.

Webb, Gisela. "The Human/Angelic Relation in the Philosophies of Suhrawardī and Ibn ʿArabī." Ph.D. diss., Temple University, 1989.
——. *Windows of Faith: Muslim Women Scholar-Activists in North America*. Syracuse: Syracuse University Press, 2000.
West, Gerald. "Silenced Women Speak: Biblical Feminist Hermeneutics." In *Women Hold Up Half the Sky*, edited by Denise Ackerman, 76–90. Pietermaritzburg: Cluster, 1991.
Wider, Kathleen. "Women Philosophers in the Ancient Greek World: Donning the Mantle." *Hypatia* 1, no. 1 (1986): 21–62.
Winkel, Eric. "Ibn ʿArabi's *Fiqh*: Three Cases of the Futūhāt." *Journal of the Ibn ʿArabi Society* 13 (1993): 54–74.
——. *Islam and the Living Law: The Ibn Al-Arabi Approach*. New York: Oxford University Press, 1997.
Wolfson, Elliot. *Language, Eros, and Being: Kabbalistic Hermeneutics and Poetic Imagination*. New York: Fordham University Press, 2005.
Yavuz, Hakan. "The Matrix of Modern Turkish Islamic Movements: The Naqshbandi Sufi Order." In *Naqshbandis in Western and Central Asia*, edited by Elisabeth Özdalga, 129–46. Richmond: Curzon, 1999.

Index of Qurʾānic Verses

To differentiate sura and verse numbers from page numbers, sura and verse numbers are given in boldface type (for example, **2:30** for sura 2, verse 30).

2:30 77

2:206 135

2:228 152, 176, 201

4:1 142, 168

7:20–22 143

7:23–27 143, 144

7:156 79

7:189 142

9:71–72 215

12:53 37

15:29 37

17:55 88

17:85 37

19:17 197

19:19 197

20:115 86

30:21 142

33:35 82, 88, 245

35:15 76

39:6 142

49:13 142, 196

53:45 142

66:4 183

66:5 183

75:2 38

75:39 142

82:7 192

89:27 38

Index of Traditions (*Aḥadīth*)

Adam dwelt alone in the garden without a companion. God caused him to fall asleep, and on awakening he found Ḥawwāʾ, whom God created from his left rib . . . , 145–46, 149, 152, 154, 161, 163, 200, 201
After two hundred years, celibacy shall be permitted in my community, 42
But for Ḥawwāʾ no female would be a traitor to her husband, 147
The first thing that God created was my light, 74
God created Adam in God's own form, 77
God created Adam in the form of the Merciful one, 179
God has seventy thousand veils of light and darkness. If they were lifted, the glories of the divine visage would annihilate all things perceived by the eyes of the creatures gazing upon it, 70
God is beautiful and loves beauty, 59
The heavens and earth contain Me not, but the heart of my faithful servant contains Me, 35, 38
I advise you to deal gently with women, for woman was created from a rib. The most crooked part of the rib is its upper part. If you attempt to straighten it . . . , 146, 149, 152, 163, 200, 201
I am Aḥmad without the *mīm*, 74
I fast and I break my fast, I pray and I sleep, I also marry women. This is my example. Those who are averse to my example are also averse to me, 41
If you want to be a Christian monk, join them openly. If you are one of us you must follow our example and our example is married life, 41
I love nothing that draws my servant near to Me more than I love what I have made obligatory. My servant never ceases drawing near to Me through superogatory works until I love . . . , 35, 134
I was a Hidden treasure and I loved to be known so I created the world in order that I might be known, 69, 124, 129, 170
I was a prophet even while Adam was between water and clay, 73
I was hungry and you didn't feed Me, 79–80, 245 (n. 80)
Many have attained complete spiritual realization (*kamāl)* among men, but among women, only Maryam, the daughter of Imrān, and Āsiya, the wife of Pharaoh . . . , 88–89
My mercy precedes my wrath, 79
A people who delegate governance to women will never ever prosper, 84

Three things of this world of yours have been made lovable to me: women, perfume—while the coolness of my eye was placed in ritual prayer, 98, 165, 174
Women are deficient in intelligence and religion . . . , 46, 149, 154, 158, 160, 161, 163, 195, 201
Women are the same as men in heritage, 84

General Index

ʿAbbāsid empire, 41–42, 59
ʿAbd al-Wahhāb, Muḥammad ibn, 19
Abrahamic prophecy, 74
Abū Yaʿqub Yūsuf, the Almohad, 247 (n. 31)
Active/activity, 52–53, 72–73, 182; in relation to receptive/receptivity, 31, 39, 73–74, 77, 120–25, 130–31, 132–33, 139, 153–55, 157–62, 175–80, 197–200, 204, 210–11, 218, 221
Adam: made of clay, 73, 134, 170, 192–93; second to Muḥammad, 73–74; as archetype, 77, 133, 170; and Iblis/Lucifer, 78; Adamic distinction, 85; and forgetfulness, 86; and angels, 114, 133; as first father, 161; yearns for Eve, 163–66, 170, 180–82; as androgynous, 168–69, 171, 182, 251 (nn. 36, 42); as part, 181, 199
Adam and Eve, 32, 90, 141–47, 149–50, 152–55, 157; ambivalent gender tropes, 143, 144; equal agency, 143, 144; transgression, 143–44, 146–47, 152; expulsion from garden, 144; as microcosmic reflection of God-human relationship, 154, 156, 170; love and yearning, 163–64, 166–67; mutual love, 164, 185, 220; as garments to one another, 192–93
Al-ʿAdawiyya, Muʿādha, 48, 50
Agency: moral, 7, 9, 24, 93, 110, 205, 215; and women, 83, 110, 178, 209, 214, 215, 251 (n. 4)
Al-aḥad/aḥadiyya (the One/Unity), 70, 74, 171
ʿĀʾisha, 138, 183, 218
Akmāliyya (superlative perfection), 88, 179
Ali, Kecia, 253 (nn. 31, 33)
ʿAlī, Umm, 37
ʿAlī Fāṭima, Umm, 50
Almond, Ian, 117–18
Andalusia: and Ibn ʿArabī, 13–14, 99, 106
Androcentrism: misogynism compared to, 143, 249 (n. 7); and narratives of primordial couple, 143–44; and *Sharīʿa*, 213–14. *See also* Patriarchal social context
Angels/angelic, 37, 85, 104, 114, 134–35, 138, 143, 145, 166, 183, 197, 244 (n. 48), 247 (n. 8); archangels, 134
Animals, 37, 128, 188, 189, 244. See also *Hayawān/hayawāniyya*
Apartheid, 4
Arabic language: and gender, 29–30, 51, 143, 174, 175, 237 (nn. 84, 88)
Aristotelianism, 64–65, 242 (n. 13)
Aristotle, 67
Ascetism: and Sufism, 36, 40, 59; origins of, 41; and culture of empire, 41–45, 59, 239 (n. 23); and Sufi women, 47–48, 56; and love mysticism, 57, 59
ʿAṭṭār, Farīd al-Dīn, 52–53
Austin, Ralph, 109, 247 (n. 31)
Averroes. *See* Ibn Rushd, Abū al-Walīd Muḥammad

Avicennian philosophical tradition, 64
Ávila, María Luisa, 106
ʿ*Awra* (nakedness), 90–91
Al-Azhar University, 3

Baqlī, Rūzbihān, 58
Barlas, Asma, 250 (n. 11)
Bauer, Karen, 148, 250 (n. 20)
Beauty. See *Jamāl* and *jalāl*
BenCheikh, Sohaib, 3
Bible, 237 (n. 78)
Al-Bijāʾī, Maryam bint Muḥammad bin ʿAbdūn, 108
Biqāʿī, 148
Al-Bisṭāmī, Bāyazīd, 50, 51, 53
Boyarin, Daniel, 28, 144
Breath of the merciful (*nafas al-raḥmān*), 73–74, 79, 125, 155, 178, 179

Capitalism, 225
Cartesian dualism, 8
Celibacy: and Sufism, 36, 40, 59; and culture of empire, 42–43, 239 (n. 27); and Sufi women, 49, 56, 178, 194, 240 (n. 52); and love mysticism, 57, 58
Child/children, 47, 58, 82, 83, 109, 122–25, 128, 131, 147, 163, 178–79, 198, 205, 253 (n. 20)
Chittick, William C., 64, 67, 68, 70, 72–73
Chodkiewicz, Michel, 234 (n. 17), 243 (n. 30)
Christianity: and God-human relationship, 17, 122; and female subjectivity, 25; and constructive theology, 29; and asceticism, 49, 62, 239 (n. 23); and mysticism, 54; creation narratives of, 142, 144, 145, 146, 251 (n. 42); theological anthropology within, 234 (n. 14)
Claremont Main Road Mosque, 4, 233 (n. 8)
Clark, Elizabeth, 62–63
Coates, Peter, 65, 72
Coincidenta oppositorium, 177, 189
Collective memory, 25–26
Colonialism, 20, 22
Concubines, 42, 148, 238 (n. 21)
Consumerism, 225
Cooke, Miriam, 236 (n. 67)
Corbin, Henry, 216
Cornell, Rkia, 46, 47, 51, 52, 240–41 (n. 71)
Cosmology: and gender equality, 7; of Islam, 7, 9; and gender, 11, 13; of Ibn ʿArabī, 11, 13, 15, 17–18, 28, 31, 68, 69, 71, 72–73, 75, 76, 79, 81, 95, 98, 114, 120–23, 127, 130, 136, 139, 152–55, 158, 160–61, 164–65, 172, 176, 194, 208, 210, 219; as term, 234 (n. 16)
Creation narratives: Abrahamic creation narratives, 32, 141; and God as hidden treasure, 69, 70, 76, 124, 129, 170, 184; and gender, 141, 142; and Qurʾān, 141, 142–50, 152, 196, 197, 200, 221, 249 (nn. 3, 4), 250 (n. 11); and Christianity, 142, 144, 145, 146, 251 (n. 42); and Judaism, 142, 145, 146, 251 (n. 42); and Ibn ʿArabī, 142, 146, 149–52, 173–76, 181, 192–202, 218, 221; and ontology, 143, 146; four types of, 195–96, 198

Dakake, Maria Massi, 239 (n. 43), 251 (n. 36)
Al-Daqqāq, Abū ʿAlī, 52
Daraja. See Male *daraja*
Al-Dārānī, Abū Sulaymān, 42, 46, 59
Dard, Khwāja Mīr, 58
Deficiency, female, 46–47, 86, 87, 144, 146, 149, 150, 152, 154–55, 158, 160–61, 163, 165, 186, 187, 199, 201
Degree. *See* Male *daraja*
Derrida, Jacques, 32, 117–18
Al-dhāt (divine essence): and Ibn ʿArabī, 69, 70, 79, 173, 174, 175, 200, 219; as feminine, 173–75; and humanity dyad, 200
Dhūʾn-Nūn al-Miṣrī, 51, 53, 54, 56–57

Divine essence. See *Al-dhāt*
Divine feminine: and Ibn ʿArabī, 32, 159, 173–76, 179, 183, 200; and Murata, 210, 212, 237 (n. 83)
Divine names or attributes: and God-human relationship, 29, 75–81; and gender, 29, 81, 87, 114, 121, 124, 127, 137–38, 156, 179, 181, 182, 194, 199, 205–8, 211, 212, 226, 230; and Ibn ʿArabī, 69–70, 71, 75–81, 124, 129, 156, 206, 207–8, 244 (n. 63); and *ḥadīth* tradition, 70, 77; and *al-Insān al-Kāmil* (The Complete Human), 71–72, 75, 76, 114, 127, 132–33, 194, 226; and Adam, 77, 143, 182, 194–95; and *Quṭb*, 85; and embodiment, 132–33, 205, 207
Divine reality (*ḥaqīqa*), 35
Divorce waiting period (*ʿidda*), 83, 147, 214
Dīwān Ibn ʿArabī (Ibn ʿArabī), 102, 229–31
Al-Durrat al-fākhira (Ibn ʿArabī), 100

Earth, 35, 38, 74, 85, 128–30, 153, 157, 168, 194, 195
Eckhart, Meister, 247 (n. 4)
Egypt, 18
Embodiment: contestation of, 3, 4; and moral obligation, 10; and Ibn ʿArabī, 17, 131–39, 189; women identified with bodily principle, 17, 136, 137, 138–39, 221; and God-human relationship, 17, 170, 192–93; and culture of empire, 43; and divine names or attributes, 81, 132–33, 205, 207–8; and experiences, 98; spirituality integrated with, 105, 131–39, 189, 219, 221, 246–47 (n. 25); and women as theophany of God, 178, 179, 180
Epistemology: and gender, 5–6, 11, 27–28, 45, 96–99, 110–12; and philosophy, 63–67; and Sufism, 63–68, 97, 115, 242 (n. 13); and divine attributes, 77, 79, 207; and mysticism, 95, 96–99, 110–12; and experience, 95–99, 110–12; and Ghazālī, 243 (n. 24)
Ernst, Carl, 20
Ethics: of *ṭarīqa*, 10; of gender justice, 11; and Ghazālī, 12; of gender, 68; ideal ethical self, 72, 226, 227; of mercy and care, 75–81; implications for Islamic law, 81–84, 86–87; and God-human relationship, 224; relativism of, 225
European Orientalism, 20, 22
Eve: no mention of rib-origin in Qurʾān, 142; unnamed in Qurʾān 142, 143; border presence, 144; named Ḥawwāʾ, 145; creation from Adam's rib, 145, 146, 152, 153, 157, 161, 162–67, 168, 177, 181, 192–93, 194–95, 197, 199, 200, 201, 219; conniving and malevolent, 146–47; as *naqāwa* (choicest part), 153, 158, 161, 179, 193; as second father, 161–62; shared essence/identity with Adam, 163, 165, 170–71, 186, 191; yearns for Adam, 163, 166; inbreathing of God's spirit into, 192; as primary image of God, 192
Experience: and gendered subjectivity, 25–27, 61–63; Ibn ʿArabī's representations of, 31, 95; Ibn ʿArabī's mystical experiences, 95–96, 98, 99–100, 107–8, 110–11; and knowledge production, 96–97, 98; and feminism, 97–99; and mysticism, 97–99, 112, 113; duality of, 112

Al-Faḍl, Wahaṭiyya Umm, 51
Fanāʾ (annihilation), 185–87, 220
Faqīr/fuqarā (spiritual seekers as impoverished or needy), 76, 100, 190
Fatā (spiritual warrior), 52
Father(s), 14, 30, 41, 103, 104, 108–9, 116, 121–25, 128, 130–32, 161–62, 197–98, 210, 230, 248 (n. 47), 253 (n. 20)
Fāṭima, Shaykha, 1–2, 39
Fāṭima of Cordova, 14, 100–101, 107
Fāṭima of Nishapur, 51, 53, 54, 56

Feminine/femininity, 8, 11, 25, 135–37, 218, 237 (n. 84), 249 (n. 7); of the divine, 30–31, 125–27, 159, 173–76, 179, 180–81, 183, 200, 202, 210–12, 219, 237 (n. 88); as mode, 39, 151; constructs of, 82, 110, 131–32, 149, 151, 179, 204, 209, 213, 218; and soul, 106, 143; principles, 110, 120, 123, 128, 132, 139, 180, 212; priority of, 159, 162, 174–75, 178, 200, 218; two feminines, 173–76
Feminisms: and private/political binary, 11; definition of, 21–22, 236 (n. 61); Third World feminism, 22; Western feminism, 22, 236 (nn. 64, 65); reconfiguration of, 22–23; and hermeneutics, 23–28; and textual canon, 24–26; and subjectivities, 96–99, 119; and mysticism, 96–99, 225; and perspectives on gender, 113; and images of divine, 126; and Qurʾānic creation narrative, 142; secular feminist women, 225, 236 (n. 66). *See also* Islamic feminisms
Fiqh, 82–84, 92–93, 222–24, 246 (n. 98), 253 (n. 31). See also *Sharīʿa*
Friends of God (*awliyā*), 72
Al-Fuqarāʾ, Yasmīna Umm, 100, 123
Fuṣūṣ al-ḥikam (The Bezels of Wisdom) (Ibn ʿArabī): and Prophet Muḥammad, 15, 75, 164–65, 170, 172, 220; and Adam, 133, 168, 171, 176, 181, 243 (n. 44), 247 (n. 8); and humanity, 155; and Eve, 168, 176, 181; and sexuality, 184; and spiritual completion, 244 (n. 48)
Al-Futūḥāt al-makkiyya (The Meccan Openings) (Ibn ʿArabī), 14–15
Future friendships, 32–33, 162
Futuwwa (young manliness), 52, 240–41 (n. 71)

Ganj-i Shakar, Farīd al-Dīn, 53
Gender: politics of, 4–5, 7–11, 90; essentialist views, 6, 8, 123, 210–12; and religious anthropology, 6, 8–9, 10, 11, 12, 36, 53; and moral capacity, 6–7, 148, 205, 214, 215; and ontology, 9, 10, 11, 175, 212, 216, 225; and Ibn ʿArabī, 10–11, 13, 31, 32, 62, 74, 75, 95, 96, 98–99, 110–12, 113, 114–20, 123, 150–52, 201–2, 203, 214, 216, 218, 226–28; and Sufism, 10–13, 24, 31, 35, 36, 38–41, 43, 53–54, 59, 60, 209, 226, 241 (n. 84); and inner path (*ṭarīqa*), 12, 38–41, 51, 214; narratives of, 26, 27, 28; and Arabic language, 29–30, 51, 143, 174, 175, 237 (n. 84); unsaying, 30, 113, 114, 127, 128, 137, 151, 169, 195, 200; counternarratives on, 54–56, 92, 120, 211, 241 (n. 83); and spiritual capacity, 82–90, 92, 93, 110, 120, 149, 152, 154, 175, 209, 212–15, 245 (n. 89); and paradoxes, 115–16, 131, 144, 151–52, 160, 167, 169–70, 180, 184, 190, 200; and metaphors, 116–20, 122, 123, 126, 127, 130, 132; and activity and receptivity, 120–23, 130–31, 132, 139, 153–54, 157–62, 175, 177, 178, 179–80, 182–83, 198–200, 204, 210–11, 218, 220; complementarity, 151, 184, 193, 204–5, 209, 213, 252 (n. 1), 254 (n. 35)
Gender difference: and Ibn ʿArabī, 156–57, 159, 162, 163–64, 200–201, 202, 209–10, 217, 227; and Nasr, 204–5, 208–9, 217, 252–53 (n. 9); and Murata, 209–10, 212–13; and Qurʾān, 215; and *fiqh* discourse, 223
Gender equality: contestation of, 3, 5–6; and moral capacity, 6–7; and cosmology, 7; and Sufism, 12, 60; and feminism, 22; and Islamic feminisms, 23–24, 222; and Ibn ʿArabī, 28, 82–94, 96, 105, 118, 150, 151, 154, 155, 217, 222, 250 (n. 25); and ontology, 82, 85, 86, 87, 89, 120; and Qurʾānic creation narrative, 142–45, 249 (n. 4), 250 (n. 11)

Gender justice: global context of, 5; ethics of, 11; and Sufism, 12, 24; and feminisms, 22; and Islamic feminisms, 23–24, 217; and textual tradition, 25; and masculine pronouns for God, 30; and *Sharīʿa*, 213–14, 224; and Ibn ʿArabī, 214; and Murata, 215; and mysticism, 226
Gender norms: and Sufi women, 12, 47, 48–49, 50, 56, 60, 149; in Andalusia, 106; and Ibn ʿArabī, 115, 117, 120, 125, 130–31, 195, 200, 218, 227, 228
Gender relations: power relations, 21–22, 147–49, 205, 208–9, 211, 212, 216; and Qurʾānic narratives, 144; and *Isrāʾīliyyāt* literary narratives, 145, 146; and *ḥadīth* tradition, 145–47, 149, 153, 154; rib *ḥadīth*, 146, 149, 153, 154, 157, 162–64, 166, 167, 168, 177, 181–82, 192–95, 197, 199, 200, 201, 219; traditional hierarchical perspectives on, 147–48, 159, 160, 164, 168, 203–5, 209–12, 216–17, 221, 249 (n. 10), 252 (n. 1); deficiency *ḥadīth*, 149, 154, 155, 158, 160, 195, 201; and Ibn ʿArabī, 151–72, 210, 218, 219, 221; and intimacy, 162–66, 173, 180–81, 185–87, 219–20; and God-human relationship, 165–68, 170, 172, 181, 192–95, 201; and androgynous Adam, 168–69; and divine feminine, 173–76; and women as theophany of God, 176–84; and ontology, 184–87, 194–95, 200, 204, 205, 219, 220; and Murata, 209–10, 213, 216; and Nasr, 216; and Islamic feminisms, 220–21
Al-Ghazālī, Abū Ḥāmid: and ethics of justice, 12; Moosa's study of, 32, 119; and love mysticism, 58; and Sufi teachings, 63; and Qurʿānic truths, 64; and marriage, 187–88; and epistemology, 243 (n. 24)
God: beyond all similitude, 29; God-language, 29–31, 116, 121, 125; oneness of, 35, 64, 131, 172, 200; friends of, 51, 52, 72; beauty of, 59, 69, 210; transcendence and immanence of, 68–69, 121–22, 127–28; as hidden mystery, 69; as needy, 69; as pure being, 69, 124; hidden essence of, 69–71; veils of, 70; as light, 70–71, 74; names of, 75–76; similarity of , 76–77; incomparability of, 77; as All-Merciful, 79, 166, 179, 180, 181, 202; present in conditions of deepest human need, 79–80; as embodiment of love, 80; as perpetually transforming, 114, 127; as father, 124–25, 132; longs to be known, 124–25, 165, 184; as birthing creation, 125–26; two hands of, 133–34; human body as locus of presence of, 134; witnessed in women, 177–79, 186; as *Al-Qawī*, 182, 218; sexual union as self-disclosure of, 186–88; breathed her own spirit into Eve, 192; Immutable Entities within, 199–200. See also *Al-dhāt*; Divine feminine; *Jamāl* and *jalāl*; *Tawḥīd*
God-human relationship: and gender, 9, 11; and Sufism, 10, 29, 35, 36, 39, 224; and Ibn Taymiyya, 16–17; and Ibn ʿArabī, 16–18, 68, 69–71, 92, 125–26, 127, 165–68, 170, 172, 200, 218–19; and God's transcendence, 17, 18, 68, 69, 121; and God's immanence, 17, 18, 68, 121–22; and Islamic feminism, 22; and jurisprudence, 29; and Sufi women, 55; and divine names, 75–81; and gender relations, 165–68, 170, 172, 181, 192–95, 201; God-woman relationship as model of, 180; and ethics, 224
Greco-Roman civilization, 13, 64, 132
Greer, Germaine, 225, 253 (n. 35)
Gregory of Nyssa, 62
Gross, Rita, 25–26, 45, 249 (n. 7)

Haddad, Yvonne, 249 (nn. 4, 10), 250 (n. 11)

Ḥadīth qudsī: and God's love for devoted servant, 35; and heart as spiritual center, 38; and God as hidden treasure, 69, 70, 76, 124, 129, 170; and God's mercy, 79, 80
Ḥadīth/aḥadīth: interpretation of, 5, 10; and asceticism, 41; and Sufi women, 46; and gender, 51; and divine names, 70, 77; and Prophet Muḥammad, 73, 74, 98; and women's spiritual capacity, 84–85, 86, 88; and premodern exegesis, 145, 149; and Islamic feminisms, 145, 250 (n. 11); and gender relations, 145–47, 149, 153, 154; and Qurʾānic creation narrative, 152; and Ibn ʿArabī, 152, 155, 200
Haeri, Shaykh Fadlallah, 20
Ḥafsa, 183, 218
Ḥājar, 214
Al-Ḥakīm, Souad, 85
Al-Hamadhānī, ʿAyn al-Quḍāt, 58
Al-Ḥaramayn, Fāṭima bint Yūsuf Amīr, 108
Harris, Rabia Terri, 171, 178, 207
Hārūn, Umm, 48, 240 (n. 51)
Ḥasan al-Baṣrī, 42, 55
Hashmi, Irfana, 233 (n. 6)
Hassan, Riffat, 143, 249 (n. 8), 249–50 (n. 11)
Hayawān/hayawāniyya (animals/animalistic), 37, 188–89, 244 (n. 48)
Heart (*qalb*), 37–38, 39, 55, 67, 68, 207
Heaven/heavenly, 35, 38, 50, 128, 135, 153, 157, 205
Heedlessness, 78, 87, 207
Hermeneutic: of suspicion, 26–27, 167–68; of reconstruction, 27, 47, 237 (n. 78); of recovery, 45; of mercy, 79–81; of subversion, 113–20, 237 (n. 78)
Heterosexual, 8, 173, 187, 194, 220
Ḥijāb (head scarves), 5, 6, 91
Hirtenstein, Stephen, 124
Homerin, Th. Emil, 18
Homoerotic elements: of love mysticism, 58–59
Al-Ḥujwīrī, ʿAlī bin ʿUthmān, 37, 50, 57, 58–59, 240 (n. 52)
Ḥukayma of Damascus, 46, 48, 49, 51
Ḥulūl (incarnation), 17, 58
Humanity (*insāniyya*): as vicegerent of God, 39, 85, 171, 205; Ibn ʿArabī on, 131–39, 151, 152–53, 155–56, 158, 160, 162, 165, 166, 170–71, 179–80, 199, 201–2
Hurst, 21

Iblīs, 206
Ibn Adham, Ibrāhīm, 42–43, 239 (n. 27)
Ibn al-ʿArabī, Muḥyī al-Dīn: on women's ritual leadership, 3, 9–10, 84, 91–92, 214; as jurist, 9, 87–88, 91, 234 (n. 17); on women's imamate, 9–10, 91–92; and Sufism, 10, 16–18; and gender, 10–11, 13, 31, 32, 62, 74, 75, 95, 96, 98–99, 110–12, 113, 114–20, 123, 150–52, 201–2, 203, 214, 216, 218, 226–28; cosmology of, 11, 13, 15, 17–18, 28, 31, 68, 69, 71, 72–73, 75, 76, 79, 81, 95, 98, 114, 120–23, 127, 130, 136, 139, 152–55, 158, 160–61, 164–65, 172, 176, 194, 208, 219; education of, 13; and Spain, 13, 14; Arab lineage of, 14; visions of, 14, 15, 67, 111; interactions with women, 14, 31, 95, 96, 98, 99–110, 111, 112, 120, 137, 138, 179, 185, 216, 246 (n. 17); and Niẓām, 14, 61–62, 63, 66, 96, 104–5, 194, 242 (n. 9); works of, 14–16, 32, 68, 99–107; and paradoxes, 15, 17, 113, 115–16, 128, 131, 151–52, 160, 167, 169, 180, 184, 190, 200; and Prophet Muḥammad, 15, 73–75, 164–66, 170, 172, 220; contesting of, 16–18; and God-human relationship, 16–18, 68, 69–71, 92, 125–26, 127, 165–68, 170, 172, 200, 218–19; metaphysics of, 17, 68–69, 211, 243 (n. 24); ʿAbd al-Wahhāb on, 19; and *Sharīʿa*

Sufism, 20; and Beshara School, 21; depictions and images of women in works of, 27–28; feminist reading of, 27–28; mystical concepts of, 28, 31, 65–68, 113, 114, 116, 119–20, 127–28; and gender equality, 28, 82–94, 96, 105, 118, 150, 151, 154, 155, 217, 222, 250 (n. 25); and divine attributes, 30–31, 68, 69–70, 71, 72, 76, 77–81, 114, 124–25, 128, 156, 176, 179, 208, 219, 237 (n. 88); and theological language of gender, 30–31, 227; religious anthropology of, 31, 63, 68, 71, 75–81, 83, 92–93, 135, 136, 137, 158, 221–22; and divine feminine, 32, 159, 173–76, 179, 183, 200; and female deficiency, 46, 158, 160, 163, 165, 187, 195, 199, 201; and realization of *rujūliyya*, 51; and Sufi women, 52, 86, 100–101, 105, 106, 123; world-affirming approach of, 57; and divine beauty, 59; and epistemology, 63–66; philosophical language of, 64, 67; biographical accounts of, 65; and Ibn Rushd, 65, 66–67, 242–43 (n. 16); and ethics of gender, 68; and divine independence (*istighnāʾ*), 69; and divine essence (*al-dhāt*), 69, 70, 79, 173, 174, 175, 200, 219; and divine names, 70, 71, 75–81, 124, 129, 156, 206, 207–8, 244 (n. 63); and macrocosm and microcosm, 71–73, 114, 116, 123–39, 152–53, 154, 155–58, 160, 179, 184, 243 (n. 44), 244 (n. 48); eschatology of, 72; and social engagement, 81, 83; and axial saint (*Quṭb*), 84–87, 175, 188, 189, 214; and dressing and modesty, 90–91; mystical experiences of, 95–96, 98, 99–100, 107–8, 110–11; and family relationships, 107–10; wives of, 108; daughter of, 108–9; and apophatic method, 114; and gendered metaphors, 116–20, 122, 123, 126, 127, 130, 132; and gendered principles of activity and receptivity, 120–23, 130–31, 132, 139, 153–54, 157–62, 175, 177, 178, 179–80, 182–83, 198–200, 204, 210–11, 218, 220; and divine reality metaphors, 123–28; and nature metaphors, 128–31, 178; and humanity metaphors, 131–39, 151, 152–53, 155–56, 158, 160, 162, 165, 166, 170–71, 179–80, 199, 201–2; and gendered creation narratives, 142, 150–52, 173–76, 181, 192–202, 218, 221; and Qurʾānic creation narrative, 146, 149–52; and gender transcendence, 151; and gender difference, 156–57, 159, 162, 163–64, 200–201, 202, 209–10, 217, 227; and triplicity, 166, 171–72, 173, 182, 194; and androgynous Adam, 168–71, 182, 251 (nn. 36, 42); and male Adam, 169–70, 182; and Prophet Adam, 169–71; and Jesus and Mary as creation models, 195–201, 221; traditionalist interpretations of, 203–17; and gender integration, 206–9; linking of spirituality and social praxis, 214. *See also* specific works
Ibn al-Ḥawārī, Aḥmad, 49, 58
Ibn al-Jawzī, Abū al-Faraj, 46–47, 48, 239 (n. 44)
Ibn al-Muthannā, Fāṭima bint, 100
Ibn Ḥazm, 89, 106
Ibn Kathīr, Ismaʾīl ibn ʿUmar, 147, 148
Ibn Rushd, Abū al-Walīd Muḥammad, 14, 65, 66–67, 242–43 (n. 16), 245–46 (n. 97)
Ibn Rustam, Makīn al-Dīn Ẓāhir, 103
Ibn Taymiyya, Taqī al-Dīn, 2, 16–17, 20, 39
Iḥsān (virtuous excellence), 10
Īmām (inward faith), 10
Incarnation (*ḥulūl*), 17, 58
Incomparability (*tanzīḥ*), 77
Inner path (*ṭarīqa*): ethics of, 10; and gender, 12, 38–41, 51, 214; and Khidr, 14; goal of, 35, 36, 44, 52, 60, 69, 191;

and Sufi women, 37; and mysticism, 68, 243 (n. 30); and Murata, 212; and *Sharīʿa*, 224
Al-Insān al-Kabīr (The Big Human), 71
Al-Insān al-Kāmil (The Complete Human): as archetype, 71–72, 75, 182, 205; and divine attributes, 72; and Prophet Muḥammad, 73–74, 164–65; and divine names, 75, 76, 226; transformation of self into, 80, 208; gender inclusivity of, 82, 93, 114, 127, 156–57, 170–71, 192, 194, 205, 206, 214; and perpetual transformation, 114; as microcosm, 114, 139, 182, 192, 194, 212; and integrity between body and spirit, 132–34, 135; and embodiment, 221; translation of, 244 (n. 48)
Insāniyya, 151, 152, 155–56, 160–61, 162, 166, 170–71, 199, 201, 202
Inshaʾ al-dawāʿir (The Description of the Encompassing Spheres) (Ibn ʿArabī), 15
Intellect, 8, 46, 64–67, 73, 88, 104, 139, 149, 152, 154, 160
Intimacy: and Ibn ʿArabī, 162–66, 173, 180–81, 185–87, 219
Iran, 21, 246–47 (n. 25)
Iranian Revolution of 1979, 209, 252–53 (n. 9)
Irigaray, Luce, 126, 127
Al-Iṣfahānī, Abū Nuʿaym, 46, 47
Ishārā al-qurʾān fi ʿālam al-insān (Allusions of the Qurʾān in the Human World) (Ibn ʿArabī), 15
Ishrāqi (Illuminationist) school of philosophy, 64
Islam: generalizations of, 5; gender debates of, 5–6, 9, 28–29; and morality, 6–7; cosmology of, 7, 9; patriarchal discourses of, 12, 23, 24; ideals of, 23, 24, 27, 215–16; and female subjectivity, 25, 237 (n. 73); metaphysics of, 211–12; social teachings of, 212–13; and *Tawḥīdic* worldview, 215–16. *See also* Sufism
Islām (outward conformity), 10, 38, 238 (n. 13)
Islamic feminisms: and Ibn ʿArabī, 21, 120, 217–22; definition of, 22; range of gender activism within, 23; and multiple critique, 23, 236 (n. 67); and gender justice, 23–24, 217; and reading traditional texts, 25–27; and Sufism, 26, 32; and *Uwaysī* friendship, 33, 237–38 (n. 91); and dressing and modesty, 91; and legal equality, 93–94; and Qurʾānic creation narrative, 145; and *ḥadīth* tradition, 145, 250 (n. 11); and *Sharīʿa*, 214, 222–23; and spirituality and sociality, 216; and gender relations, 220–21
Islamophobia, 22
Isrāʾīliyyāt literary narratives, 145, 146
Ittiḥād (union with God), 17
Izutsu, Toshihiko, 67, 73

Jamāl (beauty) and *jalāl* (majesty), 76, 78–82, 211; and Dhūʿn-Nūn al-Miṣrī, 56; in men and women, 78, 204–8, 211; and prioritizing *jamāli* qualities, 78–82, 207–8, 225; women epitomizing balance of, 99–100; and love and sexuality, 181, 190
James, William, 111
Jāmī, ʿAbd al-Raḥmān, 58
Jantzen, Grace, 54, 225–26
Jesus, 32, 53, 109, 138, 173, 195–201, 221, 252 (n. 31)
Jihād (struggle), 37, 60
Judaism: and female subjectivity, 25; creation narratives of, 142, 145, 146, 251 (n. 42)
Junayd of Baghdad, 57
Jurists: Ibn ʿArabī as jurist, 9, 87–88, 91, 234 (n. 17); and Sufism, 18; and God-human relationship, 29; and women's legal testimony, 46, 83–84, 86–87, 245 (n. 83). See also *Fiqh*

Kahf, Mohja, 237 (n. 73)
Kalām, 213
Kamāl (complete spiritual realization or perfection), 88, 91, 208, 244 (n. 48)
Kāshānī, 52
Kashf (unveiling of divine Beloved), 56
Katz, Steven, 111
Keller, Catherine, 114
Keshavarz, Fatemah, 115–16
Al-Kharrāz, Abū Saʿīd, 59
Khawāṭir, 38
Khidr, 14
Khiḍrūya, Aḥmad, 50
Khirqa (Sufi cloak), 102, 136
Kitāb al-nikāḥ al-sarīʿ fī jāmiʿ al-dharārī (Ibn ʿArabī), 123
Knowledge production: and experiences, 96–97, 98; and action, 133
Knysh, Alexander, 15–16
Kripal, Jeffery, 113, 119
Kristeva, Julia, 27–28, 118
Kugle, Scott, 30, 234 (n. 19)

Lacanian psychoanalysis, 126
Landau, Rom, 13
Language: Arabic language and gender, 29–30, 51, 143, 174, 175, 237 (n. 84); God language, 29–31, 116, 125; masculine language and Sufi women, 51–54, 137, 218; and metaphor, 116–20; reciprocity between languages, 119; and gender, 209, 211
Law, 3, 5, 12, 16, 18, 31, 68, 74, 82–84, 87, 92–94, 110, 147, 148, 205, 209, 213, 223, 224, 233 (n. 7), 234 (nn. 13, 17), 243 (n. 30), 246 (n. 98), 250 (n. 25), 252 (n. 9), 253 (nn. 20, 31, 32). See also *Fiqh*; *Sharīʿa*
Lawal, Amina, 253 (n. 20)
Layla and Majnūn, 59
Legal capacity: of women, 46, 83–84, 86–88, 92, 95, 110, 149, 209, 214, 245 (n. 83); of men, 148, 152
Liʿān (mutual oath-swearing), 148, 250 (n. 19)
Linguistic theory, 27
Love: conception of, 11; Prophet Muḥammad's love for women, 98–99, 105, 107, 165–67, 174, 176, 177, 178, 185, 220; and Ibn ʿArabī, 141, 164, 165–66, 181, 184–85, 186, 187, 191, 219–20
Love mysticism, 56–59, 60

Macrocosm and microcosm, 7, 71, 110, 116, 120, 122–25, 128, 130–32, 139, 141, 152–53, 155–61, 184, 243 (n. 44)
Mahiyyat al-qalb (Ibn ʿArabī), 125
Majesty. See *Jamāl* and *jalāl*
Al-Makkī, Abū Ṭālib, 40, 43–44
Male *daraja* (degree [over women]): in Qurʾān, 147; and premodern exegetes, 148–49; Ibn ʿArabī on, 152–59, 160–62, 171, 175–76, 194–95, 197–98, 200–201, 218, 221; and spiritual hierarchy, 168; and Qushayrī, 190; and Ṭabarī, 250 (n. 20)
Mālikī law, 253 (n. 20)
Marriage: conception of, 11; and Sufism, 35–36, 40–41, 59–60, 187–88; origins of, 41; and culture of empire, 42–44, 239 (n. 27); and Sufi women, 49–50, 56, 240 (n. 52); and love mysticism, 57–58, 60; and Qurʾān, 58, 241 (n. 97); and Ibn ʿArabī, 130, 141, 187, 193, 194, 220; and critique of abuse, 187; engaging as spiritual refinement, 194
Mary (mother of Jesus), 32, 88–89, 53, 138, 173, 195–201, 221
Masculine/masculinity, 11; and language, 29–30, 51–52, 82; of the divine, 30–31, 125–27, 183, 210, 218; as mode, 39; principles, 120, 128, 130, 131, 135, 159, 174–75, 183, 204, 209, 211–13, 218; of spirit, 132; of men and women, 132, 137, 139, 159, 174–75, 204, 209; and soul, 143; and Eve, 162; between two feminines, 173–76

Master-disciple relationship: and Sufism, 234 (n. 26)
Materiality: and Ibn ʿArabī, 17, 129–30, 135, 179; and Sufi women, 50; and Sufism, 57. *See also* Embodiment
Men: as authority, 39, 78, 84, 161, 168, 205, 208, 213; as needy in relation to women, 176, 182–83, 184, 220. *See also* Male *daraja*; *Rijāl/rujūliyya*
Mercy: hermeneutics of, 75–81; as social ethic, 81–82, 208; to world, 101; as maternal, 122, 179; between Adam and Eve, 180–81; preceding wrath, 207–8, 210–12, 225, 245 (nn. 74, 77). See also *Jamāl* and *jalāl*
Mernissi, Fatima, 237 (n. 78)
Misogyny: in Sufi literature, 39; androcentrism compared to, 143, 249 (n. 7); and post-Qurʾānic theological tradition, 147; and creation narratives, 150; Ibn ʿArabī disrupting, 195
Modernism: and Sufism, 20
Modesty, 90–91, 103, 163–64, 245 (n. 89)
Mohanty, Chandra Talpade, 236 (n. 64)
Moi, Toril, 237 (n. 73)
Mojaddedi, Jawid A., 47
Moosa, Ebrahim, 32, 119
Moral capacity: and religious anthropology, 6–7, 9; and gender, 6–7, 148, 205, 214, 215; and metaphor of embodied human being, 10; and *khawāṭir*, 38; and Qurʾānic creation narrative, 145
Mosaic of signs (*āyāt*), 98
Mosques: women's access to, 4, 8, 9, 233 (n. 8)
Mother(s), 12, 14, 30, 48, 49, 53, 100, 107–9, 116, 122–26, 128–32, 138, 161–62, 178, 196, 198, 210
Muftī: definition of, 233 (n. 7)
Muḥammad, Prophet: and Ibn Taymiyya, 2, 39; and Ibn ʿArabī, 15, 73–75, 164–66, 170, 172, 220; and Sufism, 20; and asceticism, 41, 57, 238 (n. 20); and qualities of true spiritual warrior, 52; and love for women, 57, 98–99, 105, 107, 165–67, 174, 176, 177, 178, 185, 220; and marriage, 59; when Adam was between water and clay, 73; *al-rūḥ al-muḥammadī*, 73; as *al-Insān al-Kāmil*, 73–75, 164–65, 220; *al-nur al-muḥammadī*, 74; and *farḍiyya* (singularity), 75, 164, 165; as final prophet, 89–90, 220; and women's spiritual capacity, 92; and *khirqa*, 102; wives of, 138, 183–84; on woman created from Adam's rib, 146. *See also* Singularity
Muḥāsibi, 238 (n. 10)
Muhyiddin Ibn ʿArabī Society, 21
Al-Murabit, Abdalqadir as-Sufi, Shaykh, 20
Murabitun, 20
Murad, Abdal Hakim, 253–54 (n. 35)
Murata, Sachiko, 121, 123, 190, 203–4, 209–17, 237 (n. 88), 248 (n. 26), 254 (n. 35)
Muslim fundamentalism, 20
Muslim women: and gender politics, 4–5; representations of, 5; and Western feminism, 22. *See also* Islamic feminisms; Sufi women
Muslim Youth Movement, 233 (n. 9)
Al-Mutaʿabbida, Lubāba, 46
Mysticism: and Christianity, 54; love mysticism, 56–59, 60, 67; and philosophy, 64–67, 70, 243 (n. 24); and feminism, 96–99, 225; and hermeneutic of subversion, 113–20; and sexuality, 189; and gender justice, 226

Nafs (soul), 37, 39, 143; *nafs al-ammāra* (commanding soul), 37–38, 39–40, 42, 54–56, 60, 80, 207, 208, 227; *jihād al-nafs*, 52, 60; *nafsin wāḥidatin*, 184 *Nafs al-lawwāma* (blaming soul), 38, 40
Nafs al-muṭmaʾinna (soul at peace), 38, 40
Naqāwa (choicest part), 153, 158, 161, 179, 193

Naqsh al fuṣūṣ (Ibn ʿArabī), 170
Naqshbandiyya Sufi order, 21
Nasr, Seyyed Hossein, 14–15, 203–9, 216–17, 248 (nn. 26, 48), 252 (n. 1), 252–53 (n. 9), 254 (n. 35)
Nature, 128–31, 153, 178
Negligence, spiritual, 38, 78, 206–7
Nigeria, 253 (n. 32)
Nikāḥ (sexual intercourse), 122, 123, 181, 196
Al-Nisāʿ bint Rustam, Fakhr, 103
Niswān, 52
Niẓām bint Makīn al-Dīn: Ibn ʿArabī's relationship with, 14, 61–62, 63, 66, 96, 104–5, 194, 242 (n. 9); as inspiration for Ibn ʿArabī's poetry, 59, 102, 103; charismatic presence of, 104
North Africa: and Ibn ʿArabī, 14
Nūna Fāṭima, 123

Ontology: and religious anthropology, 7; and spiritual completeness, 9; and gender, 9, 10, 11, 175, 212, 216, 225; and Sufism, 10, 11, 119, 226; and Islamic feminisms, 23; and Ibn ʿArabī, 32, 71, 73, 79, 82, 85–87, 89, 116, 120, 121, 150–52, 157, 159–60, 162, 164, 165, 166, 169, 170, 171–72, 175, 184–87, 200–201, 226; and gender equality, 82, 85, 86, 87, 89, 120; and creation narratives, 143, 146; and triplicity, 171–72; and gender relations, 184–87, 194–95, 200, 204, 205, 219, 220; and *Sharīʿa*, 224
Ottoman rulers, 18

Parent, 58, 107, 130, 198, 214
Pashazade, Kemal, 18
Patriarchal epistemologies, 11, 97
Patriarchal social context: of Sufism, 12, 47, 53, 56; and Islamic feminisms, 23, 222–23; and textual canon, 26; and gender power imbalances, 78, 81–87, 89–90, 92, 94; and Ibn ʿArabī, 96, 110, 118, 119, 120, 130, 135, 138, 150–51, 158, 179, 184, 189, 203, 206–7, 210–11, 218, 221–22, 227, 250 (n. 25); and God-human relationship, 125–26; devaluing of embodiment, 135-36, 221; and premodern scholars, 145, 150; and sexuality, 189; and Qushayrī, 190–91; and Nasr, 205, 217; and Murata, 209, 210, 212–13, 214, 215, 217; feminist critiques of, 222
Patriarchal theologies: and women's imamate, 17; Islamic legacy of, 23, 24, 213; and Ibn ʿArabī, 219
Perennialist, 111. *See also* Traditionalist/traditionalism
Personality: and Sufism, 36–38
Philanthropy: and Sufi women, 48
Philosophy: and Sufism, 63–68; and mysticism, 64–67, 70, 243 (n. 24); and *coincidenta oppositorum*, 70; and gender, 209
Pious predecessors (*al-salaf al-ṣāliḥ*), 19
Pir Press, 21
Plato, 62, 67, 242 (n. 6)
Plotinian first intellect, 73
Poetics: of creation, 128; of abundance, 162; of subversion, 162
Poetry, 15, 42, 61, 102–3, 109, 116, 125, 135–36, 137–38, 162, 229–31, 254
Porete, Marguerite, 247 (n. 4)
Postmodernism: and feminism, 22
Pregnancy, 4, 30, 125, 126, 131, 159, 178, 180, 219, 221, 252 (n. 19)
Premodern exegesis: and Qurʾānic creation narrative, 145–47; and gender power relations, 148–49
Prophetic tales (*Qiṣaṣ al-anbiyāʾ*), 145
Psychology: and Sufism, 36, 39, 40, 60; Lacanian psychoanalysis, 126; definition of, 238 (n. 3)

Al-Qalʾiyya, Zaynab, 101
Al-Qawī (The Strong), 182–83, 218
Qudra (power), 174–75, 196
Al-Qūnawī, Ṣadr al-Dīn, 108

Qur'ān: interpretation of, 5, 10; Ibn ʿArabī on, 15, 17, 68, 82, 93, 118, 152, 155, 157, 160, 200; and patriarchal interpretations, 23; and divine attributes, 29–30, 77, 79; and Abrahamic creation narratives, 32; and relationship between soul, heart, and spirit, 37–38; and marriage, 58, 241 (n. 97); and mysticism, 68; God as inward (*bāṭin*), 69; and sainthood, 82; and women's legal testimony, 87–88, 245 (n. 83); and women's spiritual capacity, 88, 245 (n. 89); and creation narratives, 141, 142–50, 152, 196, 197, 200, 221, 249 (nn. 3, 4), 250 (n. 11); androcentric narratives on primordial couple, 143–44; and Adam as prophet, 143–44, 249 (n. 8); gender relations, 147; and divorce, 148; and male degree over women, 148–49, 152–58, 160, 171, 175–76, 195, 201, 250 (n. 20); and androgynous Adam, 171; and moral agency, 215; and Islamic feminisms, 222
Qūrī, 16
Al-Qushayrī, Abu'l Qāsim, 190–91
Quṭb (axial saint), 84–87, 175, 188, 189, 214

Rābiʿa al-ʿAdawiyya: and asceticism, 48; as teacher, 51; and masculine language, 52–53; and counternarratives on gender, 54, 55, 56, 241 (n. 83); and love mysticism, 58; and celibacy, 194
Rābiʿa bint Ismāʿīl, 49
Rauf, Bulent, 21
Rāzī, Fakhr al-Dīn, 148
Receptive/receptivity. *See* Active/activity
Reed, Edward S., 238 (n. 3)
Religious anthropology: meaning of being human in Muslim tradition, 6; and gender, 6, 8–9, 10, 11, 12, 36, 53; and moral capacity, 6–7, 9; and Ibn ʿArabī, 31, 63, 68, 71, 75–81, 83, 92–93, 135, 136, 137, 158, 221–22; and creation narratives, 141
Remembrance (*dhikr*), 68
Representation: and Western feminism, 22, 236 (n. 65)
Ricoeur, Paul, 117
Rijāl/rujūliyya (man/manliness), 51, 82, 218
Risāla al-khalwa (A Treatise on Spiritual Retreat) (Ibn ʿArabī), 15
Roded, Ruth, 239 (n. 44)
Roman Empire, 13
Ruether, Rosemary Radford, 234 (n. 14)
Rūḥ (spirit), 37–38, 39; *al-rūḥ al-muḥammadī*, 73
Rūḥ al-quds (Ibn ʿArabī), 100, 101
Rūmī, Jalāl al-Dīn, 21, 58, 115, 116

Al-Saʾī, Ibrāhīm Zakī, 249 (n. 10)
Salafi movements: and Sufism, 19–20
Saleh, Soad, 3
Saudi Arabia, 19, 20, 247 (n. 25)
Schimmel, Annemarie, 50, 238 (n. 4)
Self: refinement of, 35, 39, 44, 52, 76, 77, 78, 81–82, 89, 93, 94, 97–99, 104, 110, 121, 129, 165, 194, 207–8, 226–27, 231; purification, 36–38, 40, 60, 78, 85, 207–8; ideal ethical self, 72, 226, 227; transformation into *al-Insān al-Kāmil* (The Complete Human), 80, 208; and mystical experiences, 97–98; and authenticity, 191; conceptions of, 225; psychology as study of, 238 (n. 3)
Selim I (Sultan), 18
Sells, Michael, 30, 114, 244 (n. 48), 247 (nn. 4, 8)
September 11 terrorist attacks, 21
Servanthood, 73–74, 78, 188, 189, 206, 207, 219
Sexual desire: and women's ritual leadership, 7–9; and culture of empire, 43; and asceticism, 57; connected to

love of God, 60; and Ibn ʿArabī, 141, 163, 166–67, 180, 181, 182–83, 185, 186, 188–89
Sexual intercourse. See *Nikāḥ*
Sexuality: conception of, 11; and Sufism, 24, 35–36, 39–41, 59, 187–88; and Ibn ʿArabī, 32, 116, 122–39, 141, 157, 173, 184–92, 194, 220; and culture of empire, 41–42; and asceticism, 42; and Sufi women, 50; as distraction from spiritual path, 57; and love mysticism, 57; and spirituality, 57; utilitarian, 57; and dressing and modesty, 90–91; and *coincidenta oppositorium*, 189–90; theophanic nature of, 189–90, 220; alternative sexualities, 191–92; and premodern Muslim thinkers, 252 (n. 19)
Sexual union: between humans, 40, 184–85, 187–89, 193; as metaphor for divine creative process, 116, 122–24, 128, 130; as annihilation, 185–87; as greatest self-disclosure of God, 188–89
Shāhid (witness to divine beauty), 59
Shams. *See* al-Fuqarāʾ, Yasmīna Umm
Sharīʿa: and marriage, 40; and mysticism, 68, 243 (n. 30); and Murata, 212, 213–14, 215; androcentric interpretations of, 213–14; and gender justice, 213–14, 224; applications of, 213–14, 253 (n. 20); socially contingent determinants of rulings, 214; and Islamic feminisms, 214, 222–23; in Nigeria, 253 (n. 32). See also *Fiqh*
Sharīʿa Sufism, 16, 20, 224–25
Shaykh Al-Akbar (The Greatest Master), 16, 18, 214
Shiʿī theology, 64
Silsila (chain of spiritual transmission), 102
Silvers, Laury, 216–17, 237 (n. 72), 239 (n. 43), 240 (n. 44)
Similarity (*tashbīḥ*), 76–77
Singularity (*farḍiyya*), 75, 77, 164–65, 172, 220
Slave, 37, 42, 62, 101, 191, 241 (n. 73)
Small universe (*al-ʿālam al-ṣaghīr*), 72
Smith, Jane, 249 (nn. 4, 10), 250 (n. 11)
Socrates, 242 (n. 6)
Sonbol, Amira El-Azhary, 239 (n. 44)
Soul (*nafs*), 37–38, 39, 40, 52, 54, 143
South Africa: and women's ritual leadership, 3–4, 233 (nn. 8, 9); Sufism in, 20
Spirit. See *Rūḥ*
Spiritual capacity: and gender, 82–90, 92, 93, 110, 120, 149, 152, 154, 175, 209, 212–15, 245 (n. 89)
Spiritual completeness: and ontology, 9. See also *Al-Insān al-Kāmil* (The Complete Human)
Spirituality: and sexuality, 57; embodiment integrated with, 105, 131–39, 189, 219, 221, 246–47 (n. 25); social praxis linked with, 214; and gender power relations, 216
Spiritual retreats (*khalwa*), 68
Spivak, Gayatri, 27
Stages (*maqāmāt*), 35
States (*aḥwāl*), 35
Streng, Frederick, 112
Subjectivities: Islam and female subjectivity, 25, 237 (n. 73); Sufism and male subjectivity, 26, 39–40, 44; and mysticism, 96–99; and feminisms, 96–99, 119; gendered nature of, 177–78, 185, 189; and patriarchal social structure, 191
Sufism: and ontology, 10, 11, 119, 226; and Ibn ʿArabī, 10, 16–18; and God-human relationship, 10, 29, 35, 36, 39, 224; and gender, 10–13, 24, 31, 35, 36, 38–41, 43, 53–54, 59, 60, 209, 226, 241 (n. 84); and religious anthropology, 11, 12; and sexism, 12; spiritual hierarchy of, 13, 234 (n. 26); *Sharīʿa* Sufism, 16, 20, 224–25;

contested nature of, 18–21; and male subjectivities, 26, 39–40, 44; and God's oneness (*tawḥīd*), 35, 64, 112; and marriage, 35–36, 40–41, 59–60, 187–88; and *ṭabaqāt* literature, 45–50; and love mysticism, 56–59, 60, 67; and epistemology, 63–68, 97, 242 (n. 13); and layers of meaning, 115; circumventing fixed constructions of God, 127; and socially accrued power, 190–91; cosmology of, 210; Murad on, 253–54 (n. 35)
Sufi women: and gender norms, 12, 47, 48–49, 50, 56, 60, 149; approaches to piety, 12, 47, 239 (n. 43), 239–40 (n. 44); and inner path, 37; and culture of empire, 44–45; and *ṭabaqāt* literature, 45–50; and celibacy, 49, 56, 178, 194, 240 (n. 52); as teachers, 51, 55, 62, 86, 99–101, 103–4, 105; and masculine language, 51–54, 137, 218; and Ibn ʿArabī, 52, 86, 100–101, 105, 106, 123; and counternarratives on gender, 54–56; and love mysticism, 56–59
Suhrawardī, Shihāb al-Dīn, 64, 132, 134
Al-Sulamī, Abū ʿAbd al-Raḥmān, 45–47, 52, 149, 239 (n. 44)
Sunna: Ibn ʿArabī on, 17
Syria: Sufi women of, 48

Ṭabaqāt (biographical) literature, 45–50
Ṭabarī, 92, 146, 147, 148, 250 (n. 20)
Tanzīḥ (divine incomparability), 77
Ṭarīqa. See Inner path (*ṭarīqa*)
Tarjumān al-ashwāq (The Interpreter of Desires) (Ibn ʿArabī), 15, 59, 102, 105, 133, 135
Tashbīḥ (divine similarity), 76
Tawḥīd (divine unity), 35, 64, 112, 215, 216, 227
Textual canon: male-dominated nature of, 24–27
Thaʿlabī, 146
Al-Thawrī, Sufyān, 43, 51, 59
Third World feminism, 22
Traditionalist/traditionalism, 111, 203–4, 209, 215, 216–17, 252 (n. 1)
Truth: interpretations of, 26–27, 64
Turkey: Sufism in, 21
Ṭūsī, Naṣīr al-Dīn, 64
Al-Tustarī, Sahl, 57–58

ʿUbūdiyya. See Servanthood
Umayyad empire, 41–42, 59, 239 (n. 23)
Umm Talq, 37
Union with the divine (*ittiḥād*), 17
ʿUqlat al-mustawfiz (The Spell of the Obedient Servant) (Ibn ʿArabī), 15, 170–71
Urvoy, Dominique, 242–43 (n. 16)

Virgin/whore binary, 252 (n. 21)
Virtuous excellence (*iḥsān*), 35
Visigoths, 13

Wadud, Amina: ritual prayers lead by, 2–3; Friday sermon at Claremont Main Road Mosque, 4, 233 (n. 9); and Qurʾānic creation narrative, 143, 250 (n. 11); on feminism, 236 (n. 61); and hermeneutics of suspicion and hermeneutics of reconstruction, 237 (n. 78)
Waḥdat al-wujūd (unity of being), 16
Wahhabi movement: and Sufism, 19–20
Walad, Bahāʾ al-Dīn, 58
Walāya (friend of God), 52
Western feminism, 22, 236 (nn. 64, 65)
Western rationalism: and Sufism, 20
Wider, Kathleen, 63, 242 (n. 6)
Winkel, Eric, 91–92, 234 (n. 17), 243 (n. 30)
Womb, 147, 153, 158–59, 179–80, 202
Women: spiritual equality of, 2, 4; as authority, 2, 51, 56, 84–87; access to mosques, 4, 8, 9, 233 (n. 8); silences around, 25, 27; and egalitarian gender

narratives, 27; states of soul equated with, 40; and negative gender stereotypes, 43, 44, 46; legal capacity of, 46, 83–84, 86–88, 92, 95, 110, 149, 209, 214, 245 (n. 83); described as men on spiritual path, 51–53; as teachers of wisdom, 62–63; as *Quṭb*, 84–87, 189; as prophets, 88–90; made lovable to men, 99, 165, 174, 185, 220; and creation narratives, 144, 173–76; witnessing God in women, 173, 176, 177–79, 186; and Ibn ʿArabī, 173–84, 202; have degree above men, 175–76; and divine feminine, 176, 179, 183; as theophany of God, 176–84, 202; and *coincidenta oppositorium*, 177; as distraction to men, 187; as religious leaders, 233 (n. 6); and virgin/whore binary, 252 (n. 21). *See also* Muslim women; Sufi women

Women's imamate: debates on, 6, 7–8, 9, 10; Ibn ʿArabī on, 9–10, 91–92; and patriarchal theologies, 17

Women's ritual leadership: and Ibn Taymiyya, 2, 39; Ibn ʿArabī on, 3, 9–10, 84, 91–92, 214; and South Africa, 3–4, 233 (nn. 8, 9); interpretation of, 5; and sexual desire, 7–9; and Ibn Rushd, 245–46 (n. 97)

Yasmīna of Mashena, 14

Yazīd, Abū, 50

Islamic Civilization and Muslim Networks

Saʿdiyya Shaikh, *Sufi Narratives of Intimacy: Ibn ʿArabī, Gender, and Sexuality* (2012).

Karen G. Ruffle, *Gender, Sainthood, and Everyday Practice in South Asian Shi'ism* (2011).

Jonah Steinberg, *Isma'ili Modern: Globalization and Identity in a Muslim Community* (2011).

Iftikhar Dadi, *Modernism and the Art of Muslim South Asia* (2010).

Gary R. Bunt, *iMuslims: Rewiring the House of Islam* (2009).

Fatemeh Keshavarz, *Jasmine and Stars: Reading More than "Lolita" in Tehran* (2007).

Scott A. Kugle, *Sufis and Saints' Bodies: Mysticism, Corporeality, and Sacred Power in Islam* (2007).

Roxani Eleni Margariti, *Aden and the Indian Ocean Trade: 150 Years in the Life of a Medieval Arabian Port* (2007).

Sufia M. Uddin, *Constructing Bangladesh: Religion, Ethnicity, and Language in an Islamic Nation* (2006).

Omid Safi, *The Politics of Knowledge in Premodern Islam: Negotiating Ideology and Religious Inquiry* (2006).

Ebrahim Moosa, *Ghazālī and the Poetics of Imagination* (2005).

miriam cooke and Bruce B. Lawrence, eds., *Muslim Networks from Hajj to Hip Hop* (2005).

Carl W. Ernst, *Following Muhammad: Rethinking Islam in the Contemporary World* (2003).

www.ingramcontent.com/pod-product-compliance
Lightning Source LLC
Chambersburg PA
CBHW020007241225
37250CB00015B/127
* 9 7 8 1 4 6 9 6 1 8 9 0 6 *